Federal Statements of Work

A Practical Guide

Federal Statements of Work

A Practical Guide

Michael G. Martin, PMP

MANAGEMENTCONCEPTS

MANAGEMENTCONCEPTS
8230 Leesburg Pike, Suite 800
Vienna, VA 22182
(703) 790-9595
Fax: (703) 790-1371
www.managementconcepts.com

Printed in the United States of America

Library of Congress Cataloging-in-Publication Data

Martin, Michael G., 1961-
Federal statements of work : a practical guide / Michael G. Martin.
p. cm.
ISBN 978-1-56726-225-4
1. Proposal writing in public contracting—United States.
2. Public contracts—United States. I. Title.
HD3861.U6M375 2008
658.4'0580973—dc22

2008001846

10 9 8 7 6 5 4 3 2 1

About the Author

Michael G. Martin, PMP, is an internationally recognized consultant, speaker, trainer, and author with extensive experience in portfolio, program, and project management. During his career Mr. Martin has been instrumental in helping organizations in public and private sectors achieve excellence in program and project management worldwide.

As a certified project management professional, Mr. Martin has authored numerous articles and papers on project management, including his debut book, *Delivering Project Excellence with the Statement of Work*. He is the past President and Chair of the Atlanta PMI® Chapter, PMP® exam development committee member, and Founding Chair of the PMI® Government Specific Interest Group.

Mr. Martin holds an MBA from the University of North Florida and a BS in Civil Engineering from West Virginia Tech. He is a frequent speaker at various companies, professional organizations, and universities.

Mr. Martin resides in Braselton, Georgia, with his wife and two sons. To contact him, please send an e-mail to MGM@M2ConsultingGroup.com.

To all of my mentors at the U.S. Army Corps of Engineers—Dr. Bory Steinberg, Doug Lamont, John Rushing, Jim Robinson, Dennis Duke, Eric Shannon, and John Hashtak. As a young engineer, these individuals took me under their wing and taught me not only how to be a good engineer and project manager, but how to do it ethically and with class. I am thankful and blessed to have had these individuals as mentors.

Contents

Preface

F*ederal Statements of Work: A Practical Guide* addresses the project manager (PM) faced with the task of writing a clear statement of work (SOW). The book is a practical guide to thinking about what to write in an SOW, choosing the best type of SOW, and executing that choice efficiently and effectively.

The book is divided into three sections. The first section introduces the basic parts of an SOW, the different types of SOWs, how they are written, and what they are used for. The second section offers sample SOWs from various federal agencies and projects. The third section offers additional resources as appendixes.

Chapter 1 introduces the term *statement of work*, provides a historical perspective on how SOWs became a fundamental part of federal contracting, describes the function of an SOW in the contracting process, identifies who reads SOWs, and outlines the elements of a successful SOW.

Chapter 2 describes the basic SOW six-part outline. Each section of the SOW is discussed in detail, including its form and function.

Chapter 3 explains how to plan an SOW. The chapter lays out a ten-step process that carries the PM as SOW writer from the first formulation of needs to a thoughtful decision about SOW types.

Chapters 4–7 introduce and review the elements of the four types of SOWs: performance SOWs, functional SOWs, design SOWs, and level-of-effort SOWs. These chapters describe how the SOW writer can use each type to express a project's particular needs.

Chapter 8 introduces the statement of objectives (SOO). The chapter describes the format of the SOO and its relationship to the request for proposals (RFP) and the SOW.

Chapter 9 describes the types of evaluation criteria an SOW can include and how to write those criteria.

Chapter 10 presents guidelines for writing a quality SOW. The chapter also addresses legal considerations and rights and responsibilities related to SOWs.

Chapter 11 outlines the purchase request package the program manager must compile for the contracting office.

Chapter 12 describes the process of managing changes to the SOW and to the project. The chapter also suggests effective methods for managing project changes.

The second section of this book offers a sample set of SOWs from various federal agencies that cover a wide range of acquisitions, from procuring janitorial services to the development of an electronic acquisition system. Readers can use these samples to help structure their own SOWs and to help generate ideas and thoughts on the type of language and requirements to include in the document.

The appendixes contain various source documents and other resources, including:

- Appendix I—Department of Defense Handbook for Preparation of Statement of Work (SOW)
- Appendix II—NASA Guidance for Writing Work Statements
- Appendix III—Advertisement, Contract, and Specification for a Heavier-than-Air Flying Machine
- Appendix IV—Excerpt from the Competition in Contracting Act

This comprehensive text provides three key benefits to the reader:

- It acts as a guide to developing a quality SOW.
- It provides guidance on the various types of SOWs and when they should be used.
- It provides guidance on how the SOW should be used during the delivery of the product or service and its role in managing changes to project plans.

The supplemental CD contains numerous contracting resources, including federal regulations, sample statements of work—including those contained in the book—and statements of objectives, performance-based services acquisition resources, sample solicitations, best practices, policies and guidance, e-tools, and education and training information.

The CD's contents represent the latest information on federal contracting rules and guidelines as of March 2008. Readers should visit sites such as www.acquisition.gov, www.gsa.gov, and www.whitehouse.gov/omb to obtain the most current information and updates to these rules and guidelines.

I sincerely hope that each individual and agency applying the concepts and techniques described in this text will increase the probability of their projects being successful and, in turn, make their life a little easier. I wish everyone much success. God bless!

Michael G. Martin, PMP
MGM@M2ConsultingGroup.com

Acknowledgments

A special thanks to Carrie Wise for her outstanding effort and assistance in typing the initial draft, particularly on the sample SOWs. Also, heartfelt thanks to the Management Concepts team, particularly Courtney Chiaparas for doing a great job editing this comprehensive text and making it readable and Myra Strauss for her support and advocacy in pulling this text together.

Last, but not least, to Lori, Taylor, Garrett, and Peanut for their patience with me and the many hours that my writing takes away from our family time. I am truly blessed and thankful to have them in my life.

Chapter 1

Introduction to the Statement of Work

Even the best government plans can be frustrated by unanticipated results and loose ends. Guarding against the law of unintended consequences is always important, but it is particularly critical in federal contracting. Tightly drafted specifications produce efficient, effective results, but loosely drawn specifications can set a program back significantly. Consider the following two examples:

- The Small Business Administration ordered a manual on how to purchase a franchise, but when the final product was submitted, it ignored recent civil rights legislation. In the end, what was designed to encourage entrepreneurship caused an unintended public outcry instead.
- The National Science Foundation purchased 12 all-terrain vehicles to support a research project in sub-Saharan Africa, but failed to specify the need for ongoing maintenance. The research project stalled for lack of spare vehicle parts.

In federal contracting, the government is the requiring agent and is separate from the implementing agent, the contractor. Federal contracting requires project managers to fully anticipate all of the government's needs. The attitude of "we'll cross that bridge when we get to it" cannot be tolerated. The government must conceive the full scope of its needs in advance of contract award or there is no guarantee the contractor will be able to fulfill those needs. Statements of work (SOWs) are used to define this scope.

The description or specifications of the work described in the SOW often later become the heart of the request for proposals (RFPs—also known as *solicitations*), offerors' proposals, and the final contract. A description of the work specifies exactly what is being purchased, including its quality, specifications, requirements, and quantity, as well as a schedule for its delivery. The SOW also defines the relationship between the government and the contractor, describing who will do what and the standards by which the government will later measure the contractor's compliance with the job requirements.

If NASA decides that its astronauts need new space suits and contracts out for their development and manufacturing, NASA will need to write a statement of work. If the Corps of Engineers needs 15 tons of riprap to stabilize a levee in Louisiana, the Corp will need to write a statement of work. The Volunteers in Service to America (VISTA) will need to write an SOW if it needs to hire trainers to conduct seminars for its volunteers on Indian reservations in New Mexico. Whether the government wants to purchase products or services, contract for research and development, or hire a firm to construct facilities, a statement of work will always be necessary.

When written well, an SOW is easily understood and attracts high quality, competitive bids. When poorly written, it causes disputes and protests, and results in bids that do not meet the government's needs.

This chapter introduces the statement of work by providing a historical perspective on how SOWs became a fundamental part of federal contracting, describing the function of SOWs in the contracting process, identifying who reads SOWs, and highlighting the benefits of a successful SOW.

A Historical Perspective on the SOW

Government agencies today must be good stewards of the taxpayers' money and deliver successful projects as efficiently and as cost-effectively as possible. The statement of work is one document that can help ensure project success. The significance of this document makes it important to understand how the SOW originated and what generated the original need for SOWs.

It is often said that necessity is the mother of invention. One of the earliest recorded events, occurring several thousand years ago, necessitated a particular product and service to fulfill certain needs. Specific instructions described a product of such magnitude that it ensured the continued existence of the human race: the ark built by Noah around 4000 BC.[1] The description and specifications issued by God informed Noah of the dimensions of the ark, how to build it, and who it was to house in its confines. The book of Genesis in the Bible, chapter 6, verses 14–21, describes the ark:

> *So make yourself an ark of cypress wood; make rooms in it and coat it with pitch inside and out. This is how you are to build it. The ark is to be 450 feet long, 75 feet wide, and 45 feet high. Make a roof for it and finish the ark to within 18 inches of the top. Put a door in the side of the ark and make lower, middle, and upper decks....Two of every kind of bird, of every kind of animal, and of every kind of creature that moves along the ground will come to you to be kept alive. You are to take every kind of food that is to be eaten and store it away as food for you and for them.*[2]

Although succinct, these specifications provided Noah with enough information to build a vessel of sufficient scale to harbor him, his family, and the creatures of Earth during that time, and ensured the survival of the human and animal kingdoms. Although God didn't call these instructions an SOW, the statement provided—at least at a high level—the type of information contained in the SOWs that we use today.

The earliest use of a formal SOW in modern history occurred in the early 20th century, when it was used primarily in government contracting. In 1908, the United States Signal Corps drafted a general requirements document to identify the required specifications of the Wright Brothers' heavier-than-air flying machine (see Figure 1.1). See Appendix III for a transcribed, more legible version of this document.

The document, which is approximately one page in length, includes requirements like, "[T]he flying machine should be designed

Figure 1.1 Signal Corp Requirements Document for the Wright Brothers' Heavier-than-Air Flying Machine

SIGNAL CORPS SPECIFICATION, NO. 486.

ADVERTISEMENT AND SPECIFICATION FOR A HEAVIER-THAN-AIR FLYING MACHINE.

TO THE PUBLIC:

Sealed proposals, in duplicate, will be received at this office until 12 o'clock noon on February 1, 1908, on behalf of the Board of Ordnance and Fortification for furnishing the Signal Corps with a heavier-than-air flying machine. All proposals received will be turned over to the Board of Ordnance and Fortification at its first meeting after February 1 for its official action.

Persons wishing to submit proposals under this specification can obtain the necessary forms and envelopes by application to the Chief Signal Officer, United States Army, War Department, Washington, D. C. The United States reserves the right to reject any and all proposals.

Unless the bidders are also the manufacturers of the flying machine they must state the name and place of the maker.

Preliminary.—This specification covers the construction of a flying machine supported entirely by the dynamic reaction of the atmosphere and having no gas bag.

Acceptance.—The flying machine will be accepted only after a successful trial flight, during which it will comply with all requirements of this specification. No payments on account will be made until after the trial flight and acceptance.

Inspection.—The Government reserves the right to inspect any and all processes of manufacture.

GENERAL REQUIREMENTS.

The general dimensions of the flying machine will be determined by the manufacturer, subject to the following conditions:

1. Bidders must submit with their proposals the following:
   (*a*) Drawings to scale showing the general dimensions and shape of the flying machine which they propose to build under this specification.
   (*b*) Statement of the speed for which it is designed.
   (*c*) Statement of the total surface area of the supporting planes.
   (*d*) Statement of the total weight.
   (*e*) Description of the engine which will be used for motive power.
   (*f*) The material of which the frame, planes, and propellers will be constructed. Plans received will not be shown to other bidders.

2. It is desirable that the flying machine should be designed so that it may be quickly and easily assembled and taken apart and packed for transportation in army wagons. It should be capable of being assembled and put in operating condition in about one hour.

3. The flying machine must be designed to carry two persons having a combined weight of about 350 pounds, also sufficient fuel for a flight of 125 miles.

4. The flying machine should be designed to have a speed of at least forty miles per hour in still air, but bidders must submit quotations in their proposals for cost depending upon the speed attained during the trial flight, according to the following scale:

   40 miles per hour, 100 per cent.
   39 miles per hour, 90 per cent.
   38 miles per hour, 80 per cent.
   37 miles per hour, 70 per cent.
   36 miles per hour, 60 per cent.
   Less than 36 miles per hour rejected.
   41 miles per hour, 110 per cent.
   42 miles per hour, 120 per cent.
   43 miles per hour, 130 per cent.
   44 miles per hour, 140 per cent.

5. The speed accomplished during the trial flight will be determined by taking an average of the time over a measured course of more than five miles, against and with the wind. The time will be taken by a flying start, passing the starting point at full speed at both ends of the course. This test subject to such additional details as the Chief Signal Officer of the Army may prescribe at the time.

6. Before acceptance a trial endurance flight will be required of at least one hour during which time the flying machine must remain continuously in the air without landing. It shall return to the starting point and land without any damage that would prevent it immediately starting upon another flight. During this trial flight of one hour it must be steered in all directions without difficulty and at all times under perfect control and equilibrium.

7. Three trials will be allowed for speed as provided for in paragraphs 4 and 5. Three trials for endurance as provided for in paragraph 6, and both tests must be completed within a period of thirty days from the date of delivery. The expense of the tests to be borne by the manufacturer. The place of delivery to the Government and trial flights will be at Fort Myer, Virginia.

8. It should be so designed as to ascend in any country which may be encountered in field service. The starting device must be simple and transportable. It should also land in a field without requiring a specially prepared spot and without damaging its structure.

9. It should be provided with some device to permit of a safe descent in case of an accident to the propelling machinery.

10. It should be sufficiently simple in its construction and operation to permit an intelligent man to become proficient in its use within a reasonable length of time.

11. Bidders must furnish evidence that the Government of the United States has the lawful right to use all patented devices or appurtenances which may be a part of the flying machine, and that the manufacturers of the flying machine are authorized to convey the same to the Government. This refers to the unrestricted right to use the flying machine sold to the Government, but does not contemplate the exclusive purchase of patent rights for duplicating the flying machine.

12. Bidders will be required to furnish with their proposal a certified check amounting to ten per cent of the price stated for the 40-mile speed. Upon making the award for this flying machine these certified checks will be returned to the bidders, and the successful bidder will be required to furnish a bond, according to Army Regulations, of the amount equal to the price stated for the 40-mile speed.

13. The price quoted in proposals must be understood to include the instruction of two men in the handling and operation of this flying machine. No extra charge for this service will be allowed.

14. Bidders must state the time which will be required for delivery after receipt of order.

JAMES ALLEN,
Brigadier General, Chief Signal Officer of the Army.

SIGNAL OFFICE,
WASHINGTON, D. C., *December 23, 1907.*

Figure 1.1 Signal Corp Requirements Document for the Wright Brothers' Heavier-than-Air Flying Machine (continued)

Form No. 18.

Signal Corps, United States Army.

These Articles of Agreement entered into this-------tenth--------- day of February---, nineteen hundred and-eight--, between ----Chas. S. Wallace----, Captain-----------------, Signal Corps, United States Army, of the first part, and

Wilbur and Orville Wright, trading as Wright Brothers, of 1127 West Third Street, Dayton,

in the county of--------Montgomery----------, State of------Ohio----------- of the second part, WITNESSETH, that in conformity with copy of the advertisement, specifications, and proposal hereunto attached, and which, in so far as they relate to this contract, form a part of it, the said-------------------Chas. S. Wallace, Captain,---------------- Signal Corps, United States Army, for and in behalf of the United States of America, and the said --------------------------Wright Brothers------------------------ (hereinafter designated as the contractor) do covenant and agree, to and with each other, as follows, viz:

ARTICLE I. That the said contractor shall manufacture for and deliver to the United States of America,

One (1) heavier-than-air flying machine, in accordance with Signal Corps Specification No. 486, dated December 23, 1907.

ART. II. That the deliveries of the supplies and materials herein contracted for shall be made in the manner, numbers, or quantities, and for each number or quantity, on or before the date specified therefor, as follows, viz:

That complete delivery shall be made on or before August 28, 1908.

ART. III. All supplies and materials furnished and work done under this contract shall, before being accepted, be subject to a rigid inspection by an inspector appointed on the part of the Government,

8—1169

and such as do not conform to the specifications set forth in this contract shall be rejected. The decision of the Chief Signal Officer, United States Army, as to quality and quantity shall be final.

ART. IV. That for and in consideration of the faithful performance of the stipulations of this contract, the contractor shall be paid at the office of -----the Chief Signal Officer---- ---------of the Army---------, at-----Washington, D. C.---, for all supplies and materials delivered in conformity with the requirements of this contract, on or before the dates above specified (Article II, *supra*) *and accepted*, the following prices, viz:

One (1) heavier-than-air flying machine at a total cost of twenty-five thousand (25,000) dollars.

to be paid as soon as practicable after the acceptance of the same, in funds furnished by the United States for the purpose, reserving per cent from each payment until final settlement, on completion of the contract or otherwise.

ART. V. It is further agreed that for all supplies and materials which shall not be delivered in conformity with the requirements of this contract on or before the dates prescribed therefor in Article II, above, but which shall be subsequently delivered and accepted, the prices shall be as follows:

8—1169

Figure 1.1 Signal Corp Requirements Document for the Wright Brothers' Heavier-than-Air Flying Machine (continued)

ART. VI. That in case of the v of the said contractor to perf he stipulations of this contract within the time and in the manner specified above, Articles I to III, inclusive, the said party of the first part may, instead of waiting further for deliveries under the provisions of the preceding article, supply the deficiency by purchase in open market or otherwise, at such place as may be selected (the articles so procured to be the kind herein specified, as near as practicable); and the said contractor shall be charged with the increased cost of the supplies and materials so purchased over what they would have cost if delivered by the contractor on the date they were received under such open-market purchase.

ART. VII. It is further agreed by and between the parties hereto that until final inspection and acceptance of, and payment for, all of the supplies and materials and work herein provided for, no prior inspection, payment, or act is to be construed as a waiver of the right of the party of the first part to reject any defective articles or supplies or to require the fulfillment of any of the terms of the contract.

ART. VIII. The contractor further agrees to hold and save the United States harmless from and against all and every demand, or demands, of any nature or kind for, or on account of, the use of any patented invention, article, or process included in the materials hereby agreed to be furnished and work to be done under this contract.

ART. IX. Neither this contract nor any interest herein shall be transferred to any other party or parties, and in case of such transfer the United States may refuse to carry out this contract either with the transferor or the transferee, but all rights of action for any breach of this contract by said contractor are reserved to the United States.

ART. X. No Member of or Delegate to Congress, nor any person belonging to, or employed in, the military service of the United States, is or shall be admitted to any share or part of this contract, or to any benefit which may arise therefrom.*

ART. XI. That it is expressly agreed and understood that this contract shall be noneffective until an appropriation adequate to its fulfillment is made by Congress and is available.

ART. XII. That this contract shall be subject to approval of the Chief Signal Officer, United States Army.

IN WITNESS WHEREOF the parties aforesaid have hereunto placed their hands the date first hereinbefore written.

WITNESSES:

John J Mullaney as to Chas. S. Wallace
Albert Lawrence as to ..., Signal Corps, U. S. Army.
C. E. Taylor as to
H. G. Hoffman as to Wright Brothers by Orville Wright

APPROVED: FEB 28 1908, 190

[signature]
Brigadier General,
Chief Signal Officer of the Army.

*Here add to any contract made with an incorporated company for its general benefit the following words, viz: "But this stipulation, so far as it relates to Members or Delegates to Congress, is not to be construed to extend to this contract." See section 3740, Revised Statutes.

(EXECUTED IN QUINTUPLICATE.)

so that it may be quickly and easily assembled and taken apart and packed for transport in army wagons."[3] Other requirements included the capability to be reassembled for operation in an hour, to carry 350 pounds for 125 miles, and to maintain flying speeds of 40 miles per hour in still air.[4]

Compared to SOWs used in federal contracting today, which can exceed several hundred pages in length, this is a relatively simple document for a very complex product.

The Statement of Work Defined

Today, the government has a much more in-depth description of what federal SOWs are required to look like and the level of detail they must include. The Federal Acquisition Regulation (FAR) is the document recognized by all federal agencies that describes the required format and content of federal SOWs. The foreword of its March 2005 edition describes the FAR as follows:

> *The FAR is the primary regulation for use by all federal executive agencies in their acquisition of supplies and services with appropriated funds. It became effective on April 1, 1984, and is issued within applicable laws under the joint authorities of the Administrator of General Services, the Secretary of Defense, and the Administrator for the National Aeronautics and Space Administration, under the broad policy guidelines of the Administrator, Office of Federal Procurement Policy, Office of Management and Budget.*

> *The FAR precludes agency acquisition regulations that unnecessarily repeat, paraphrase, or otherwise restate the FAR, limits agency acquisition regulations to those necessary to implement FAR policies and procedures within an agency, and provides for coordination, simplicity, and uniformity in the federal acquisition process. It also provides for agency and public participation in developing the FAR and agency acquisition regulations.*[5]

Subsection 8.405-2(b) of the FAR describes statements of work as follows:

> *(b) Statements of Work (SOWs). All statements of work shall include the work to be performed; location of work; period of performance; deliverable schedule; applicable performance standards; and any special requirements (e.g., security clearances, travel, special knowledge). To the maximum extent practicable, agency requirements shall be performance-based statements (see Subpart 37.6).*[6]

Subpart 37.6 goes on to describe requirements for performance-based acquisition methods:

> ***37.601 General.***
>
> *(a) Solicitations may use either a performance work statement or a statement of objectives (see 37.602).*
>
> *b) Performance-based contracts for services shall include:*
>
> > *(1) A performance work statement (PWS);*

(2) Measurable performance standards (e.g., in terms of quality, timeliness, quantity) and the method of assessing contractor performance against performance standards; and

(3) Performance incentives where appropriate. When used, the performance incentives shall correspond to the performance standards set forth in the contract (see 16.402-2).

(c) See 12.102(g) for the use of Part 12 procedures for performance-based acquisitions.

37.602 Performance work statement.

(a) A Performance work statement (PWS) may be prepared by the Government or result from a statement of objectives (SOO) prepared by the Government where the offeror proposes the PWS.

(b) Agencies shall, to the maximum extent practicable:

(1) Describe the work in terms of the required results rather than either "how" the work is to be accomplished or the number of hours to be provided (see 11.002(a)(2) and 11.101);

(2) Enable assessment of work performance against measurable performance standards;

3) Rely on the use of measurable performance standards and financial incentives in a competitive environment to encourage competitors to develop and institute innovative and cost-effective methods of performing the work.

(c) Offerors use the SOO to develop the PWS; however, the SOO does not become part of the contract. The SOO shall, at a minimum, include:

(1) Purpose;

(2) Scope or mission;

(3) Period and place of performance;

(4) Background;

(5) Performance objectives, i.e., required results; and

(6) Any operating constraints.

37.603 Performance standards.

(a) Performance standards establish the performance level required by the Government to meet the contract requirements. The standards shall be measurable and structured to permit an assessment of the contractor's performance.

(b) When offerors propose performance standards in response to an SOO, agencies shall evaluate the proposed standards to determine if they meet agency needs.

37.604 Quality assurance surveillance plans.

Requirements for quality assurance and quality assurance surveillance plans are in Subpart 46.4. The Government may either prepare the quality assurance surveillance plan or require the offerors to submit a proposed quality assurance surveillance plan for the Government's consideration in development of the Government's plan.[7]

The SOW is important in federal contracting because it is the only official description of the work requirement in the request for proposals (RFP).[8] As part of the RFP, the SOW allows contractors competing for an award to quote a price without padding for a lot of unknown requirements, which in turn reduces the number of price contingencies needed to hedge against the risk of unanticipated requirements. A common understanding of the required work helps ensure consistency among the various contractor proposals. This allows reviewers to evaluate each proposal on an equal basis.

SOWs today are more extensive and detailed than the document drafted for the construction of the Wright Brother's plane. The greater level of detail and specificity is necessary to handle the complex projects undertaken in the government and private sectors today.

The SOW has become such a critical element of the federal procurement process that several federal agencies, including the Department of Defense (DoD) and the National Aeronautic and Space Administration (NASA), have enhanced specific FAR guidelines to create detailed internal guidelines for preparing and using SOWs in the procurement process (see Appendixes I and II).

Agency Variations on the Definition of a Statement of Work

In federal contracting, the FAR defines and establishes the standard for SOWs. As noted earlier, the FAR states that all SOWs should include, "the work to be performed; location of work; period of performance; deliverable schedule; applicable performance standards; and any special requirements."[9]

Some agencies, however, have slightly revised and customized FAR guidelines to align with their specific agency standards. For example, the DoD defines an SOW as a document that "should specify in clear, understandable terms the work to be done in developing or producing the goods to be delivered or services to be performed by a contractor." In addition, it should define "either directly or by reference to other documents, all work (non-specification) performance requirements for contractor effort."[10] NASA, on the other hand, defines an SOW as simply "a tasking document that specifies effort to be performed by a contractor."[11] See Appendixes I and II, respectively, for full DoD and NASA guidelines for SOWs in those agencies.

How Are Statements of Work Used?

When a federal agency needs a contractor to provide a product or service, it assigns the task of managing the contract to a project manager. The project manager is responsible for writing the SOW for the agency. For the purposes of this book, "project manager" will be synonymous with "SOW writer."

The project manager's first step is to visit the agency's contracting office, where a contracting officer (CO) or a staff member known as a contracting specialist will be assigned to the project. The contracting staff is responsible for soliciting bids or proposals, drafting the actual contract documents, and making an award to an offeror. To accomplish these tasks, the contracting officer will need a concise, clear statement describing the agency's requirements. As the technical expert who is most aware of the agency's needs, the project manager is responsible for articulating these requirements.

The contracting officer will want answers to four basic questions:

- What does the agency want?
- When does the agency want it?
- Does the project require any specialized personnel (if so, who)?
- Where should the product or service be delivered?

The contracting staff needs an SOW to write an invitation for bid (IFB) or a request for proposal (RFP). IFBs and RFPs draw much of their detail from SOWs. Figure 1.2 shows the standard format for RFPs. The sections highlighted in bold contain information often pulled directly from a project manager's SOW.

Figure 1.2 Standard Format for a Request for Proposal (RFP)

Part I –	Schedule	
	Section A	**Solicitation/Contract Form**
	Section B	Supplies or Services and Prices/Costs
	Section C	**Description/Specifications/Work Statement**
	Section D	Packaging and Marking
	Section E	Inspection and Acceptance
	Section F	**Deliveries or Performance**
	Section G	Contract Administration Data
	Section H	Special Contract Requirements
Part II –	Contract Clauses	
	Section I	Contract Clauses
Part III –	List of Documents, Exhibits, and other Attachments	
	Section J	**List of Attachments**
Part IV –	Representations and Instructions	
	Section K	Representations, Certifications, and Other Statements of Offerors
	Section L	Instructions, Conditions, and Notices to Offerors
	Section M	**Evaluation Factors for Award**

The contracting staff writes the IFB and RFP to include a technical description of the work required by extracting the specifications from the SOW. Potential federal contractors turn to the specifications section of the IFB or RFP to measure their ability to fulfill the job requirements.

SOWs that aren't clear and specific can lead to vague IFBs or RFPs, which contractors may avoid bidding on. The more precisely a contractor knows what the agency expects, the less risk it assumes by taking on the contract. This reduction of risk is often reflected in lower prices. A contractor's worst nightmare is to promise a product or service at a given price, only to find out later that it has misunderstood the agency's needs. The more information is left unknown, the more a contractor will protect itself with unrealistic estimates.

Consequently, it is critical that every SOW be written in detail to match the particular needs of the government agency at that time. The practice of using "boilerplate" SOWs—standardized SOWs with detailed wording—can lead to the delivery of a product or service that, although technically compliant with contractual guidelines, fails to satisfy the agency's needs.

For example, if the Federal Reserve System needed software to model cyclical fluctuations in money supply, the SOW would not only define the requirements' general attributes (e.g., "the program must run on both Microsoft Windows® and Macintosh® operating systems"), but it would also describe the specific functions the software would have to fulfill ("the price of the European Union's euro must be downloaded into all M2 calculations within one half hour of the market's close").

IFBs and RFPs may also include information about how the agency plans to evaluate bids and proposals. These evaluation criteria are often extracted from information contained in SOWs. For example, if the Army needed enough new troop transport vehicles to outfit an entire armored division, the SOW should specify that only contractors able to produce at least 1,000 vehicles during the contract term need submit proposals.

Finally, when a bidding firm is awarded the work, the agency contracting officer uses the description of the work given in the SOW to draw up the final contract document. The final contract document also includes information that should never be included in an SOW: legal provisions, financial arrangements, government cost estimates, agency staffing assignments, and the type of contract. Details not pertaining to the technical work specifications are drafted by the contracting staff. The SOW should only include information specific to the description of the work.

Who Reads Statements of Work?

SOWs are detailed specifications from the government to its bidders and offerors, which are its primary audience. However, SOW language should be appropriate to both lay and technical communities, as other audiences include:

- Contracting staff
- Agency attorneys
- Agency heads
- Elected officials
- Budget officers

Focusing on clear language when writing SOWs saves project managers the time they inevitably spend on calls asking for clarification. Taking the time to express what an agency needs in simple terms is often useful in itself, because it tends to expose faulty logic and oversights. Circulating a draft SOW to the agency staff whom are likely to be involved in the contract's administration is also a good practice because it tests for clarity and guards against ambiguity.

The Purpose of Statements of Work

The first purpose of an SOW is to communicate the government's minimum requirements for a job. For example, a project manager buying motor fuel for the U.S. Geological Service cannot specify a need for 10,000 gallons of motor fuel and simply expect to get high-octane premium gasoline. A bidding fuel distributor is likely to present an estimate based on the cheapest fuel it can provide. If the specification simply states "motor fuel" without specifying what kind of motor fuel, the bidding firm will estimate its ability to meet the order based on the least expensive cost of regular gasoline.

If regular gasoline later prevents the Geological Service from doing its job appropriately, it will be because the SOW requirement did not describe what was minimally acceptable to the government, not because the contractor tried to cut corners. The test of a good SOW is in the quality of the end product or service.

The second purpose of an SOW is to clearly state who is responsible for various elements of a contract. Some contracts are simple. For example, the U.S. Navy needs 100 copies of *The Adventures of*

Huckleberry Finn for its on-board libraries. The project manager submits an SOW calling for 100 new, hardcover copies by the end of the year. The responsibilities are clear: the contractor is responsible for delivering the books as specified and the government will cut the check upon receipt.

Other contracts, however, are more complex, often involving partnerships between the government and the contractor. For example, the Environmental Protection Agency (EPA) needs help putting together a plan to have all federal agencies recycle office paper. Its SOW must be clear about which party—the contractor or the government—is responsible for various components of the contract. Government-wide recycling requires coordination among many federal agencies. In the SOW, the EPA might commit to initiating and holding a conference for all federal administrative officers, but stipulate that the contractor will develop and manage the conference program. Assigning responsibilities is at the heart of a precise SOW.

The third purpose of an SOW is to clearly state to both the contractor and the project manager what constitutes compliance. Compliance occurs when all parties to a contract agree that the contract requirements have been satisfied. Disagreements over compliance can give rise to tensions between the contractor and the government.

The National Weather Service (NWS), for example, needs 25 new satellite dishes for its regional reporting stations. The contractor delivers the dishes to the NWS headquarters in Washington, D.C., only to learn from the NWS that they want each dish delivered to the regional stations. The contractor, which estimated costs based on delivery to Washington, now discovers the government wants it to expand the scope of the contract. To do so reduces the contractor's profit margin. Meanwhile, the project manager is concerned about the contractor's non-compliance, arguing that the dishes are no good to the NWS in Washington, D.C., and must be delivered to the regional stations.

Compliance is often an evident problem in complex service contracts. The Department of Transportation (DOT), for example, routinely contracts out for highway studies. It may call an engineering firm to design an expanded interchange and to brief "appropriate officials." The contractor may engineer the overpass, express-mail the final drawings to Washington, D.C., and brief the DOT officials according to schedule. Officials at the DOT, however, might expect representatives from the firm to be available to brief the local city council and handle media inquiries in the region where the interchange will ultimately be built. In this case, the government's definition of "appropriate officials" differs significantly from the contractor's.

Well-written SOWs define what is minimally acceptable to the government, who is responsible for various project elements, and describes how the government will determine whether project requirements have been satisfied. Clearly articulated SOWs protect the interests of both the government and the contractor.

Benefits of Statements of Work

If you've ever been asked to review a failed or challenged project only to find that the situation could have been avoided by simply having a detailed SOW in place, then you can understand what a frustrating experience it can be. The frustration comes from realizing that millions, and possibly billions, of dollars could have been saved and the project could have been successful simply by taking time at the outset to properly document the work to be performed. In these situations, neither the government nor the contractor wins. The contractor will be losing profit and the government will be dissatisfied because their expectations are not being met.

Dr. David Maister, in his book *Managing the Professional Service Firm*, identified what he called "The First Law of Service," which is expressed as: "satisfaction = perception – expectation."[12] In other words, if the government perceives the contractor's level of service or work effort as less than what they originally expected, they are going to be dissatisfied. However, if the perceived level of service is greater than the government's expectations, they are going to be satisfied.

The SOW will help ensure that expectations are properly established and that the contractor doesn't commit to work they're incapable of fulfilling. By properly establishing expectations, the probability of the project team delivering to, and possibly above, expectations is greatly increased. This in turn will result in a higher client satisfaction rating.

The benefits of having a detailed SOW can be enormous. A detailed SOW provides:

- A baseline to measure change
- A baseline for work completion and payment

- A method of recording, measuring, and analyzing products and services
- A baseline for audits
- Defined roles and responsibilities
- A snapshot of party agreements

A Baseline to Measure Change

One of the most important benefits of the SOW is its use as a baseline for determining and measuring change during the project. This is particularly true once the project moves into the execution or implementation phase. Without having a defined baseline to measure change, a project manager may never notice a change when it occurs, which would make change very difficult to manage. Changes inevitably occur on projects, so it's imperative to manage changes properly. Using the SOW to measure and manage change on projects is an extremely important element of project success, and is covered in more detail in Chapter 12.

A Baseline for Work Completion and Payment

Again, if the SOW has been written correctly, it will identify in detail the work contracted for delivery. The SOW's detailed descriptions, and any approved changes amending the original document during the project, should create a clear understanding between the government and the contractor as to what classifies completed work. The work should be considered complete only after the contractor delivers all products and/or services and the government accepts those deliveries. Upon acceptance of the product or service, the government can then issue payment.

A Method of Recording, Measuring, and Analyzing Products and Services

The SOW provides the project team with a single document they can use to specifically address the products and services that will be provided to the government under contract. The SOW is the primary supporting document to the contract, and it establishes the contractual baseline description of each product and service. Having a single document to reference eliminates the confusion that would result if these elements were captured in multiple documents. The team only has to reference one document to measure and analyze the actual work performed.

A Baseline for Audits

Without an established and agreed-upon baseline document, it becomes impossible to determine whether the work is actually meeting the client's requirements and specifications. It is also impossible to determine when a change occurs on a project. Without a baseline document, any changes made to the project during its lifecycle will not be documented and properly accounted for. Having an SOW in place allows the team to easily audit the project to determine where changes from the agreed-upon baseline have occurred, as well as the corresponding impact of the changes to project scope, cost, schedule, and manpower.

This audit trail of changes provides the government with the true cost, time, and manpower required to deliver the project. This information is also extremely important and beneficial for estimating future projects of similar size and scope.

Defined Roles and Responsibilities

The SOW captures government and contractor roles and responsibilities for the work performed as part of the project. Doing so reduces the probability of future disputes between the parties as to who is responsible for the various elements of work. By clearly defining roles and responsibilities, each party can properly plan and staff the appropriate resources required to perform the work, thus avoiding potential schedule delays and rework.

A Snapshot of Party Agreements

In today's fast-moving, dynamic marketplace, the makeup of project teams is constantly changing. Thus, it's extremely important to have an approved SOW in place that captures the baseline description of the products and services scheduled for delivery at a specific point in time. Having the SOW in place will help avoid potential disputes between the various parties, particularly when the project team personnel that made the original agreements changes. The SOW will legally bind both parties to what was agreed to originally. It also provides a baseline document to the new team members, which they can use to institute changes reflecting the current needs and requirements of their respective parties.

The benefits of having a detailed SOW on a project are significant and far outweigh the costs associated with its development. Project failures can occur in any industry and any organization at any time. The amount of money lost or wasted on challenged and mismanaged projects can easily reach into the billions of dollars. Taking the time upfront to develop a detailed SOW and using it to manage the project throughout its lifecycle will help avoid project failures. Doing so will also help projects to be delivered successfully and achieve a higher return on investment for the organization.

NOTES

1. Werner Keller, *The Bible As History,* Second Revised Edition (New York: William Morrow & Company, Inc., 1980).
2. *Life Application Bible* (Co-publishers Zondervan Publishing House, Wheaton, IL, and Tyndale House Publishers, Grand Rapids, MI, 1991).
3. Department of Defense, *Department of Defense Handbook for Preparation of Statement of Work (SOW),* MIL-HDBK-245D, 3 April 1996. Online at http://www.dla.mil/DSS/dss-a/download/DoD%20SOW%20Handbook.pdf (accessed January 2008).
4. Ibid.
5. General Services Administration, Department of Defense, and National Aeronautics and Space Administration, *Federal Acquisition Regulation,* vol. 1–51, March 2005. This edition includes the consolidation of all Federal Acquisition Circulars through 2001–27. Online at http://www.arnet.gov/far/reissue/FARvol1ForPaperOnly.pdf (accessed January 2008).
6. Ibid., 8.405-2(b).
7. Ibid., Subpart 37.6–Performance-Based Contracting.
8. Peter S. Cole, *How To Write a Statement of Work,* Fifth Edition (Vienna, VA: Management Concepts, 2003).
9. *Federal Acquisition Regulation,* 8.405-2(b).
10. See note 3 above.
11. National Aeronautics and Space Administration, *NASA Guidance for Writing Statements of Work,* NPG 5600.2B, December 1997. Online at http://www.hq.nasa.gov/office/procurement/newreq1.htm (accessed January 2008).
12. David H. Maister, *Managing The Professional Service Firm* (New York: Free Press Paperbacks, 1993), 71.

Chapter 2

Framing the Statement of Work

Organization is the key to clearly defining the government's needs in a statement of work. Disorganized SOWs attract unresponsive or confusing proposals from offerors. Thomas Mann once wrote, "Order and simplification are the first two steps toward mastering a subject—the actual enemy is the unknown."[1] The same is true of mastering the SOW.

Because the needs of government agencies vary enormously, SOWs can take many forms. For service and research and development contracts that only include broad objectives for specifications, a loosely written SOW is appropriate. Prospective offerors can be given considerable latitude in structuring their approach to the project. On the other hand, a highly specific SOW is preferable in cases where requirements for testing or survey services must be described in detail. Likewise, projects that focus on end items (completion-type projects) require a different SOW form than those that emphasize levels of labor or effort (term-type projects).

This chapter presents a six-part format for writing SOWs that is both comprehensive and flexible. The format includes all the information a contractor needs to frame a solid proposal, and is flexible enough to apply to the many different types of federal projects requiring SOWs.

A Generic Format for Statements of Work

The elements of an SOW can vary with the objective, complexity, size, and nature of the work to be performed. There is no single correct way of writing an SOW. Nevertheless, having a formatting guide is a good idea, particularly if you have never written an SOW before. The following generic, six-part SOW format has had long and successful usage and could be applicable within any government agency:

1. Introduction and Scope Statement
2. Requirements
3. References
4. Delivery
5. Progress and Compliance
6. Notes and Other Information

Introduction and Scope Statement

In this first section, include a short summary of why the product or service is necessary and how the need came about. Include any background information a contractor may need to know about the greater project or the agency's mission. Discuss how the project relates to previous, ongoing, and future projects, and identify any known difficulties, assumptions, constraints, and any ineffective techniques or methodologies previously tried. This information will enable bidders to understand how the need for the product or service arose, how it fits into a broader context, and what sort of proposal to write.

Keep the background statement as brief as possible. However, sometimes it is necessary to alert prospective contractors to detailed background materials or make such information available to them. In those cases, list the materials and state where they can be obtained or reviewed in a separate references section of the work statement, or provide the materials in the IFB or RFP as an attachment to the SOW.

The introduction should also include a scope statement for the work. The scope statement is not synonymous with the work statement (SOW): the scope statement is a summary of the SOW, or a summary of the work the contractor will be required to perform. In the scope statement, describe the government's general objectives using broad, non-technical terms. Summarize the actions to be performed and the results or products the government expects. Define the limits of the project, including time frames and special areas of interest.

If the work is planned to occur in phases, sketch out each phase and clearly define the relationship of the work in each phase to specific project objectives. For example: *The research is not expected to determine the long-term effects of mandatory retirement. Rather, it is expected to examine the short-term effects, institutional factors, attitudes, and perceptions of mandatory retirement.*

Another option is to state an overall goal first and then spell out specific objectives falling under that goal. For example:

> *The major goal of this project is to develop an outreach program to promote entrepreneurship among women and assist them in the development of their businesses. Specific objectives include:*
>
> > *(1) Identifying public and private programs that provide technical assistance to women entrepreneurs and the types of services they provide.*
> >
> > *(2) Identifying target groups of women who will benefit from information about the programs providing technical assistance.*
> >
> > *(3) Developing a nationwide campaign to inform the public of assistance available to women entrepreneurships.*

The scope statement is an overview of the work. Include all the information a contractor will need to be brought up to speed on the project and give a general sense of what you want accomplished.

Requirements

The requirements section is the most important part of the SOW because it describes exactly what the government wants, whether it is 25 bolts of cloth or 25 battleships. In general, the requirements section includes what the government wants, including quantities and quality standards, and when delivery is due. Depending on the type of SOW, this section can be extremely lengthy and detailed or quite short. For example, an SOW for the construction of a new naval hospital should include blueprints; an SOW for a Department of Energy media campaign should include only a list of objectives.

For each product or service, include the following information:

- Define and explain the work to be performed. Communicate the requirements clearly and completely. Never assume the prospective contractor will know exactly what you mean.
- Outline the main steps and types of actions that the contractor will need to perform to properly conduct the project.
- Clarify any work sequences. Provide a sufficient level of detail to enable the contractor to plan personnel and other requirements in detail.
- Indicate any work phases and describe the specific tasks to be performed in each phase.
- Describe any broad but definable areas of work that must be performed simultaneously.
- Identify intended results and end products. Contractors can devise and propose various approaches to satisfy those objectives.
- Articulate any specific methodology or approach required.
- Refer to, or provide, any information that might be necessary for the contractor to write an effective, responsive proposal, including known specific phenomena, assumptions, constraints, and operational issues.

- Include all illustrations, drawings, and diagrams that describe the requirements. Make sure they are consistent with what has been written.
- Refer to pre-existing standard specifications or standard paragraphs to define the work the contractor is to perform, or incorporate them by reference when appropriate.
- Specify any data, property, or facilities that the government will provide to the contractor.
- State where work is to be performed and any travel that may be necessary.
- Describe the extent of effort required. Make clear, for example, whether a literature search is required, or whether field research and theoretical analysis, including computer modeling, is required.

The requirements make up the essence of an SOW. Describe exactly what is needed from a contractor and be specific in describing the government's minimum acceptable requirements and standards.

References

The references section cites the standard specifications referenced in the requirements section. The references section does not stand on its own, but rather supports the requirements. For example, if the General Services Administration (GSA) decides to order 22,000 Number 10 cans, the SOW should include a definition of a Number 10 can in the references section. Number 10 is shorthand for a specific capacity measurement, metal weight, and shape.

The Competition in Contracting Act of 1984 requires the government to publish advertisements including or referencing all the information needed to perform a job.[2] Unfettered access to all the information necessary to bid on a job is the foundation of free and open competition.

In addition to standard specifications, documents referenced elsewhere in the SOW should be listed by document number and title in this section. The list may include federal, military, and non-government (e.g., commercial organizations, technical societies) specifications, standards, publications, and other materials needed to clarify or support the work. Where appropriate, reference all mandatory government regulations and codes as well.

When referencing government documents, list them categorically under appropriate headers (e.g., federal, military, departmental) and then list them in alphabetical or numerical order. Each listing should be headed by an explanatory paragraph. Figure 2.1 gives an example of the proper way to organize these materials.

References can contribute to or hinder the clarity of the SOW, depending on how they are used. For example, references that point to other reference materials can frequently lead to misunderstandings about which provisions are applicable to the requirements.* If reference material is brief, consider including it verbatim in the SOW, in addition to giving the reference. If the reference material

* Listing documents in the references section does not automatically establish a contractual obligation to adhere to any related provisions. Any such obligation must be stated outright in the requirements section.

Figure 2.1 Listing Government Documents in a References Section

Government Documents. The following documents support the specifications previously listed. In the event of conflict between the documents listed and the specifications, the specification shall be considered a superseding requirement.

List all government documents in the following order:

- Specifications
  - Federal
  - Military
  - Other Government Agency
- Standards
  - Federal
  - Military
  - Other Government Agency
- Drawings
- Other Publications
  - Maps
  - Manuals
  - Regulations
  - Handbooks
  - Bulletins

When referencing non-government documents, list them in the same order as the government documents that precede them. Also explain where the materials listed in the references section may be obtained, or where and when those materials will be available for review.

is lengthy, carefully review it for relevancy, and look for material that contradicts information contained elsewhere in the SOW.

Delivery

The delivery section restates in more detail when, where, and how a product or service is to be delivered to the government. This is especially important regarding the provision of supplies. When the U.S. Merchant Marine orders sensitive navigational equipment, for example, it should specify the need for protective packaging.

First, specify any products or services that must be delivered for each task, phase, or area of work. Specify the intended use of the deliverable. Deliverables may be tangible, such as magnetic tape, graphics, or equipment. Deliverables may be intangible, such as an analysis or an evaluation, but yield a tangible end product, like a final report. For term-type research and development contracts, the deliverable may be accumulated data. If data is the deliverable, identify and describe the specific kinds of data required, and any standards the data must meet.

Next, specify any instructions for preserving, packaging, and/or shipping the product. Provide a specific delivery recipient (e.g., a person, an office) and an address. For services, specify the location where the service is to be delivered (e.g. office/agency location) and when (i.e., date and time) the service is to be delivered.

Being clear about delivery is important. No matter how good a product or service is, if it is not delivered where, when, and how it is required, the contractor has failed to satisfy the government's minimum needs.

Progress and Compliance

The progress and compliance section describes any interim and final reports due to the government, inspection procedures, and most importantly, how the government and the contractor will know when the project requirements have been satisfied.

Again, the detail in this section will largely depend on the type of SOW. For a Forest Service manager required to clear 16 acres, verification is a relatively simple matter. The project manager can walk out to the clearing site and see if anything is left standing. On the other hand, measuring compliance is more difficult for a Commerce Department official who is required to provide a complete listing of all the firms engaged in the production of steel worldwide. Who decides whether the final list of 600 firms is complete, and how? To avoid compliance conflicts in this situation, the Commerce Department would have to think carefully about how to verify its requirement.

In SOWs written for the delivery of products, compliance is determined according to quality assurance provisions. Ask the contractor to submit a first article for examination and testing before you authorize the contractor to proceed with production. Stipulate that random or scheduled inspections will take place, or that samples will be tested at the manufacturer's plant and upon delivery.

Quality assurance provisions in service contracts are more complex and require the contractor to demonstrate or substantiate that it has fulfilled all obligations spelled out in the SOW. Depending on the nature of the service, a range of compliance options are available to the SOW writer, including periodic progress reports, conferences, attendance at periodic consultations, oral briefings, or visual inspections.

When requiring progress reports, be specific. For example: *The contractor shall submit (a) a detailed work outline for the research project and (b) a plan for phasing the work by reporting period.* Or, *The contractor shall give the contracting officer's technical repre-*

sentative (COTR) brief written reports highlighting progress on the first of each month.

State the specific information the contractor will be required to provide. For example, require a monthly status report including the following information:

- Problems encountered during the preceding month and steps taken to address them
- An updated schedule showing work accomplished to date and work yet to be completed, with appropriate explanations
- A summary of significant work to be completed in the next reporting period
- Money already spent and money projected to be spent
- Open issues
- Submitted and approved change orders
- Other information as appropriate

State when a report is due, describe any format requirements, and specify the delivery recipient (person or office) and address (see Chapter 4 for more information on report formats). If there are points that require government approval, state your turnaround time. In other words, state how long it will take you to review the report and reply to the contractor with any comments or questions.

Notes and Other Information

The notes and other information section includes attachments, notes, or information not given outright in the other sections of the SOW. For example, an Air Force SOW could include technical drawings for a new jet propulsion system, and a National Institutes of Health SOW could include a list of personnel qualifications for a research and development project.

Regardless of whether you choose to employ this generic six-part format or design your own, keep the following points in mind:

- The purpose of the SOW must be clear. Avoid telling the contractor how to do a task unless that task must conform to established agency requirements.
- An SOW that takes control of the work away from a contractor, even temporarily, may result in relieving the contractor of responsibility for the end product.
- The SOW must include status reports and a deliverable.

Figure 2.2 includes a more detailed SOW checklist.

▲ ▲ ▲

Chapter 3 presents a ten-step approach to planning an SOW, as well as the steps an SOW writer should take before choosing an SOW type.

Figure 2.2 Generic SOW Checklist

Checklist Item	YES	NO	If not, provide an explanation
1. Does the scope statement accurately reflect the requirements?			
2. Does the background information explain the rationale for the project?			
3. Will the background information help a potential contractor prepare a sound technical proposal?			
4. Does the objective emphasize what is most important to the agency?			
5. Is the breakdown of objectives accurate and logical?			
6. Will the contractor understand the agency's needs?			
7. Have the facts been checked?			
8. Are the requirements realistic, definite, and nonrestrictive?			
9. Do the requirements satisfy the minimum needs of the agency?			
10. Is each requirement capable of being inspected or verified?			
11. Are the references necessary, available, and timely?			
12. Are the modes of transmittal or delivery realistic?			
13. Will the intended inspections, reports, and tests provide an accurate gauge of quality?			
14. Are all report, inspection, and test procedures clearly defined?			
15. Are the deliverables and their acceptance criteria clearly defined?			
16. Have all service levels been clearly defined and quantified (if applicable)?			

NOTES

1. BrainyMedia.com, *Brainy Quote–Thomas Mann Quotes.* Online at http://www.brainyquote.com/quotes/authors/t/thomas_mann.html (accessed January 2008).
2. Competition in Contracting Act, U.S. Public Law 98-369, July 18, 1984. Implemented in 10 U.S.C. 2305, "Contracts: Planning, Solicitation, Evaluation, and Award Procedures." Online at http://www4.law.cornell.edu/uscode/10/2305.html (accessed January 2008)

Chapter 3

Planning the Statement of Work

Note the golden rule of carpentry: measure twice to cut once. Planning does not guarantee success, but it can tip the odds in your favor. This is true for a complex effort like writing an SOW. Chapter 3 presents a ten-step planning process designed to help you write an SOW. It focuses on being clear about what the government needs before you begin writing.

This ten-step planning process is helpful for several reasons. First, it will help you adapt to the new emphasis on flexibility in federal contracting. Specifying exactly how a contractor should perform a service or build a product is no longer automatically considered the best approach. Every contractor has a story about how it could have done what the government wanted more quickly and efficiently without an overly restrictive SOW. The planning process described in this chapter can help balance flexibility with fulfilling the government's requirements.

Second, the planning process ensures that your SOW is complete. Regardless of the nature of work required, you will likely have to recast the project's scope to meet budget realities—also known as sizing a project. Project costs must be estimated, its delivery defined, and its compliance ensured. This ten-step process can help you cover all project bases.

This planning process can also help you decide which type of SOW to write. The different types of SOWs, and the pros and cons associated with each type, are given as a part of Step 10 at the end of this chapter. Step 10 focuses on how to choose the best type of SOW to fit the government's needs.

In general, SOWs are too complex to improvise, making proper planning an imperative before writing begins. Taking time to fulfill the planning steps given below is the best investment you can make to ensure a quality SOW.

The Ten-Step Planning Process

Step 1:	Brainstorm about project needs
Step 2:	Define the problem
Step 3:	Explore various methods
Step 4:	Narrow the choices
Step 5:	Decompose the work
Step 6:	Identify skills
Step 7:	Estimate resources
Step 8:	Size the project
Step 9:	Assess risks
Step 10:	Make choices

Step 1: Brainstorm about Project Needs

Before you begin to write, take a step back and brainstorm about project needs. It's possible that your proposed method of fulfilling government needs is not the most efficient or effective. Brainstorming is a method that can generate various solution alternatives. It involves freeing your mind so that it can operate at its creative best. Remember that there are no wrong suggestions or solution alternatives while brainstorming. The process of selecting the best alternatives comes later.

A famous midwestern novelist once said that when it came to writing, he liked to think of his head as a bridge. Two trolls lived under that bridge, one on either side of the brook. One troll was a very creative writer, the other a skilled editor. Without both trolls, the writer could not produce even one page of prose. If he did not edit what he created, the writing was undisciplined. And without the creative start, he was just another editor re-writing the work of others. The problem, he said, was that the two trolls did not get along, and when they quarreled, he was unable to write. The lesson for him, he said, was to keep his trolls separate by writing in the morning and editing his previous day's work in the afternoon.

Follow this writer's example: keep your creative and editing functions separate. Creating a quality SOW requires good ideas, but it also requires the discipline to throw out bad ideas. Brainstorming is a way of keeping the editor—the part of us that determines why something will not work—at bay long enough for us to generate creative new ideas about why something could possibly work.

It is important to brainstorm with others. When one person brings up an idea, it can spark ideas in a second person. The objective of brainstorming is to collect as many ideas as possible, regardless of their feasibility or organization.

For example, your workplace has become very cramped and uncomfortable. You decide to call a brainstorming session to discuss the problem and possible solutions. Begin by preparing for the brainstorming session. Ask invitees to do some background research about the problem at your organization and to look into what other organizations have done about the same problem:

- *I looked into our space requirements historically and found that we haven't expanded in 17 years, while our client base has tripled over the same time.*
- *The DoD recently signed a lease on a building in Bethesda and got nine months free rent because of the depressed real estate market.*

When the brainstorming session later begins, open by stating the problem up for discussion and invite the group of individuals that the problem is impacting or a group of subject matter experts (SMEs) to offer their thoughts and suggestions:

- *We don't have enough space. We're all packed in here like sardines. None of us can think with all this noise.*
- *We should rent the building across the street.*
- *We should consolidate all our offices, move to the suburbs, and build a campus-style headquarters.*
- *We should move our public access area elsewhere.*
- *We shouldn't do anything this year. We're being asked to make program cutbacks. This just isn't the right time, and besides, this space is not so bad.*

Focus on coming up with all possible solutions, even improbable ones, and their attributes. Describe how the solution would work:

- *If we moved our public access area elsewhere, it would be a lot quieter. Tyrone and Sandy could have their own offices.*
- *A suburban office would move us closer to our contractors.*

A good brainstorming session should fill up a flip chart with ideas and possibilities. After the session is over, push further by asking others, including potential contractors, for input. The Competition in Contracting Act specifically requires federal agencies to conduct market research before sending out requests for contractors.[1] Invite potential contractors to make suggestions on how they would solve the problem. Contractors are usually more than happy to help with this process because it allows them the opportunity to provide feedback on how they might have solved a similar problem in the past. In turn, their solution may lead to the RFP being written in such a way that it plays to their organizational strengths. The competitive process isn't endangered by these discussions; the discussions simply allow participants to get a sense of what solutions are available—a fair and prudent procedure.

Step 2: Define the Problem

The second step in planning an SOW is to define the government's problem clearly and concisely. What is this contract meant to solve? What are the government's needs? Being clear about the problem at hand makes all the difference in finding a solution. Solutions are answers to problems; asking the right questions will lead you to the right answers. Approaching government needs as problems that can be solved, and not as conditions requiring nothing more than conventionally accepted solutions, can open up new possibilities. In other words, it's important to conceive new, cutting edge solutions instead of reverting back to an old conventional method that may no longer be the most effective or cost-efficient solution.

An important step in defining the problem is to get rid of previous assumptions. A well-worn riddle illustrates this point: A young boy is driving home with his father. They are involved in a terrible traffic accident. The boy is taken to the emergency room and prepared for surgery. The doctor walks into the room, gasps, and says, "I can't operate on that boy, he is my son." If people assume that most doctors are male, they wont understand how this boy can be the doctor's son if the father was also in the accident. Assumptions are fatal to logic: In this particular riddle the doctor is actually the boy's mother.

Using the example about the problematic office space, is the problem a lack of space or too much noise? An unchecked assumption that the problem is only a lack of space will most likely lead to an SOW calling just for an increase in floor area. But if the real problem is that the public access area is in the same space as the professional staff, and no one gets any work done because of noise, providing only more space won't solve the problem. Two years later, after much work and expense, the office will be bigger, but the staff will still be unproductive.

A brainstorming session is one way to disrupt certain assumptions about a problem. Another method is to think about a problem in terms of what specifically needs to change. Agencies engage contractors to *change* something. To uncover the nature of a problem, ask how the agency will be different after the work is finished. Ask yourself, "What is it that I want to accomplish by changing the agency in this way?" Answering this question will bring you one step closer to an accurate definition of the problem.

Step 3: Explore Various Methods

With a clearly stated problem in hand, frame an objective that restates the problem in terms of its solution. For example:

> ***Problem:*** Too much noise and too many disruptions, both caused by the presence of the agency's public access desk at the front of the office.
>
> ***Objective:*** Reduce the noise and distractions caused by the presence of the public access desk at the front of the office.

Next, draw up a list of provisional approaches that will fulfill this objective. Return to the ideas that came out of the brainstorming session. Organize those ideas and generate as many methods as possible. For example:

> ***Method A:*** House the public access office elsewhere in leased space.
>
> ***Method B:*** Partition off the public access office and build a separate entrance.
>
> ***Method C:*** Build a larger facility.

This process forces you to take a step back before actually writing the SOW, and it enables you to see the problem in a new way. To be sure, the problem of too much noise and distraction can be solved by building a new facility, but options that are less costly are available as well.

By exploring alternative methods of fulfilling the objective, you reserve a place at the table for a potentially superior method yet to be discovered. One way to solicit ideas is to draft the SOW to state only the government's objective, inviting the contracting community to submit what they think is the best way to fulfill that objective (and thus, solve the government's problem). Keeping the possibility of another option available invites the contractor's creativity and utilizes its expertise. This is the heart of the functional SOW, which is described at the end of this chapter.

Step 4: Narrow the Choices

Now narrow the possibilities to a manageable number. There are two ways to cut down the number of choices:

- **Separate the wheat from the chaff.** Exercise your professional judgment and cull the good ideas from the wild ones. You might conclude that moving public access personnel to a separate facility would solve the government's problem, but the method should be disqualified because it is fundamentally unfeasible.
- **Consolidate.** Lump similar or related approaches together for the purpose of further exploration. For example, leasing a storefront for the public access office is similar to renting office space. Combine them into one approach: relocate public access office.

Step 5: Decompose the Work

Consider the specific steps a contractor would need to take to use this method to solve the government's problem. Understand and describe the tasks required to make the alternative methods work. For each method, first detail key elements and then break each element into distinct tasks. For example:

Approach A: Separate the public access office
Element 1: Partition off public access office
Task: Draw up plans
Task: Purchase materials
Task: Clear office
Task: Re-wire office
Task: Make adjustments to heating and plumbing system
Task: Construct partition
Element 2: Build separate entrance
Task: Draw up plans
Task: Obtain building permit
Task: Sub-contract with mason to build steps
Task: Sub-contract with carpenter to build doorway

Next, describe each deliverable—any products or services that must be delivered for each task, phase, or area of work—and compliance criteria. Compliance is measured by the criteria that must be met for the deliverable to be accepted. For example:

Task: Re-wire office
Deliverable: Six electrical outlets and four sets of fluorescent lights as specified on electrical plan.
Compliance: County building inspection and on-site test.

The Work Breakdown Structure

A more detailed method of decomposing or breaking work elements into distinct tasks is to build a work breakdown structure (WBS).

The WBS has become the *de facto* standard in both public and private sectors for decomposing projects down to the lowest manageable level possible, and is critical in the development of the SOW because of its level of detail. The more detailed the WBS, the more detailed the SOW. If the WBS is poorly developed, the SOW will be less likely to properly serve as a contractual document.

NASA and the DoD have both recognized the importance of the WBS in creating a high-quality SOW. Both cover the subject in detail within their respective handbooks on SOW preparation. (See Appendixes 1 and 2 for copies of the NASA and DoD SOW handbooks.) As with the SOW, DoD is much more mature in the development and application of the WBS than most private sector firms. They have developed a detailed handbook on the subject that provides a standard approach for all DoD departments and agencies to follow when developing WBSs.[2] One significant benefit of DoD's consistent approach to the WBS has been improved communication throughout the DoD acquisition process.

Every agency should have a consistent process, specific to their environment and projects, for developing a WBS. Having a standard approach will help build consistency in the way both WBSs and SOWs are prepared throughout the organization.

Defining the WBS

The Project Management Institute (PMI) defines a work breakdown structure as:

> *A deliverable-oriented hierarchical decomposition of the work to be executed by the project team to accomplish the project ob-*

jectives and create the required deliverables. [The WBS] organizes and defines the total scope of the project. Each descending level represents an increasingly detailed definition of the project work.[3]

The WBS helps define and decompose the products or services into specific tasks, both managerial and technical, at various levels of detail. The more defined and detailed the decomposition, the greater the probability that all of the major activities and tasks will be identified.

There is no standard, one-size-fits-all WBS structure that is accepted universally. Instead, organizations or individual project managers typically determine the structure and detail of their WBSs. The project may be subdivided into many levels, as long as the lowest level is still within the management authority of the project manager.

For instance, consider a project manager (PM) who is managing the construction of a plane. The PM would be responsible for developing a WBS for the major elements of the plane, including the engine, wings, and fuselage. The PM would not be concerned, however, with the detailed WBS for the construction of those various components, if they are out of his or her area of control, which is likely in this case.

In other words, the PM would not be concerned with the technical minutiae of all the activities and tasks required to construct a jet engine. The PM would instead focus on ensuring that these items are completed on time and within budget, so that they don't negatively impact the completion of the total product, in this case the plane.

If your organization doesn't have an approved structure and guidelines for developing a WBS, you may want to consider using a six-level WBS structure. Figure 3.1 depicts this six-level structure, from the program level at the top, down to the subtask level at the bottom.

The six-level WBS can be displayed graphically as a hierarchy, or it can be shown in outline form with the appropriate coding numbers, as shown in Figures 3.2 and 3.3.

Management levels will vary depending upon whether the engagement is classified as a program or a project. If it's a program, then the program manager will typically only be interested in the detail

Figure 3.1 Six-Level WBS Structure

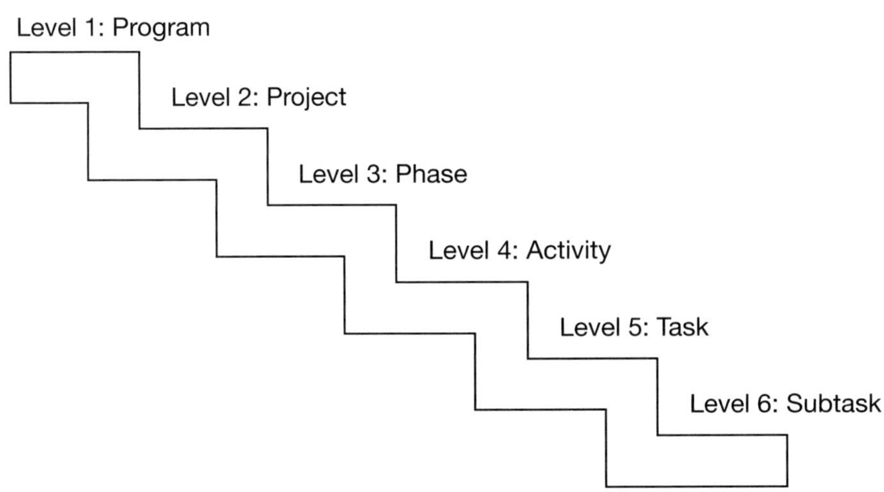

Figure 3.2 WBS—Hierarchical Format

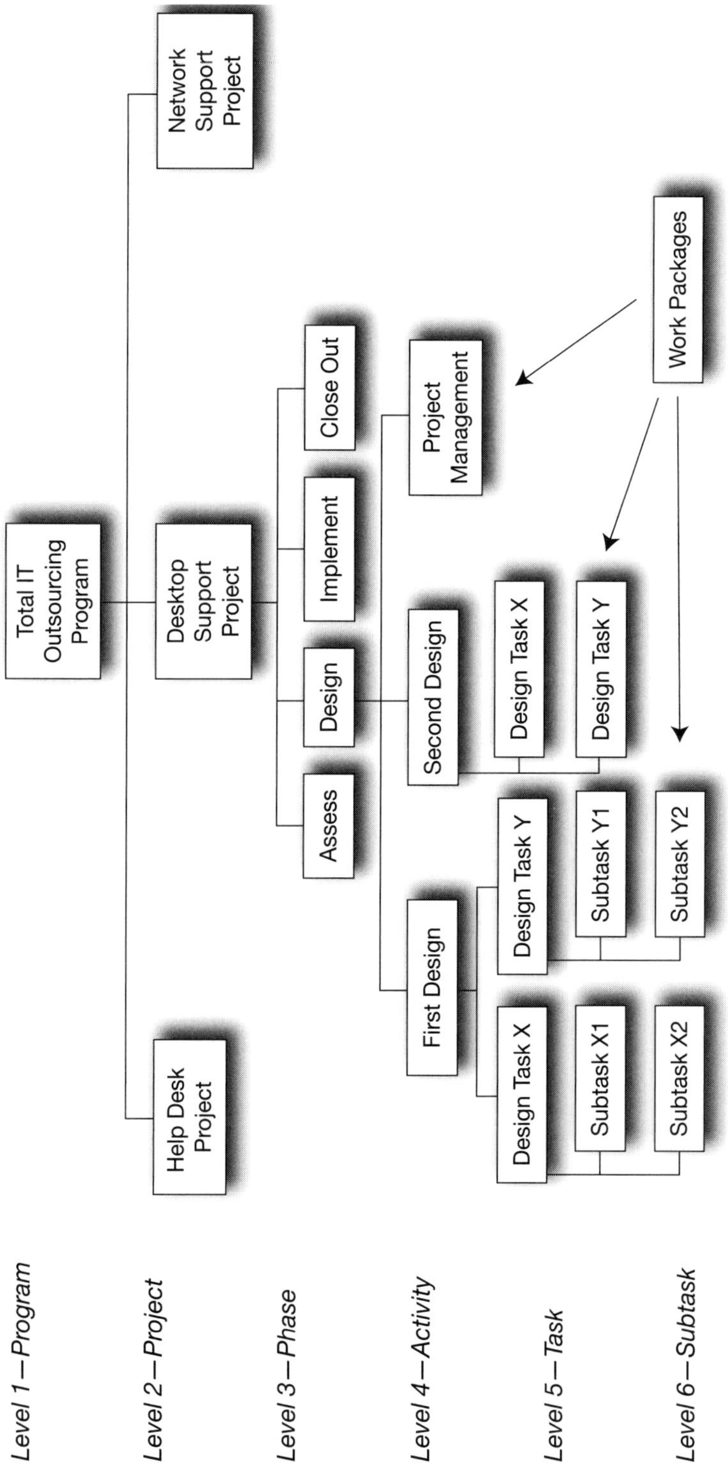

Figure 3.3 WBS—Outline Format

```
1  Total IT Outsourcing Program
   1.1  Help Desk Project
   1.2  Desktop Support Project
        1.2.1  Assess
        1.2.2  Design
               1.2.2.1  First Design
                        1.2.2.1.1  Design Task X
                                   1.2.2.1.1.1  Subtask X1
                                   1.2.2.1.1.2  Subtask X2
                        1.2.2.1.2  Design Task Y
                                   1.2.2.1.2.1  Subtask Y1
                                   1.2.2.1.2.2  Subtask Y2
               1.2.2.2  Second Design
                        1.2.2.2.1  Design Task X
                        1.2.2.2.2  Design Task Y
               1.2.2.3  Project Management
        1.2.3  Implement
        1.2.4  Close Out
   1.3  Network Support Project
```

down to Level 3 (phase level). Project managers typically focus on details down to Level 4 (activity level). Levels 5 and 6—task and subtask levels, respectively—will be specific to technical project elements, and may be assigned to a technical manager or lead to ensure that all the work is captured and performed correctly.

PMI defines a work package as:

A deliverable or project work component at the lowest level of each branch of the work breakdown structure. The work package includes the schedule activities and schedule milestones required to complete the deliverable or project work component.[4]

The benefits of having a good WBS include the following:

- It accounts for all the effort required to achieve an end objective. It encompasses the project's total content by relating the elements of work to each other and to the end objective.
- It displays and defines the total planned work effort in identifiable, measurable, and concise elements that can be easily understood.
- It provides the framework for project planning and control and helps make effective use of contractor support.
- It provides a means for measuring, assessing, and integrating technical, schedule, and cost performance.
- It provides all applicable quality systems and quality assurance requirements, and it defines the type and extent of control necessary to manage subcontracts.[5]

From a project management perspective, the WBS serves as a basis for other critical elements, including:

- Organization breakdown structure (OBS)
- Responsibility assignment matrix (RAM)
- Precedence diagram for the schedule
- Risk analysis
- Cost estimate and budget
- Change control

If the WBS is poorly written, this will ultimately affect the quality of each and every one of these elements and will damage the project or cause it to fail. Perhaps the best description of the WBS is that it's the aggregate which holds the foundations of both the SOW and the project together—just as sand and gravel are aggregates that form concrete when added to a cementing agent.

Developing the WBS

The first step in developing a WBS is to write a clear statement describing the project objective. This may have been done during the initial planning activities, but if not, then it should be done at this stage in Step 5. The next step is to gather a WBS team, preferably a TIGER team—a group of subject matter experts or representatives from each functional unit or division that has some level of responsibility for the product or service—and subdivide the work into activities, tasks, and subtasks according to the six-level WBS structure in Figure 3.1.

One of the most popular methods used to facilitate this process is the Post-it® Notes method. When using the Post-it® Notes method, meet in a project or meeting room that has a large blank wall. Using the six-level WBS structure as a guideline, brainstorm about all the activities, tasks, and subtasks required to deliver the project successfully. Then draft each work element on a Post-it® Note and place it on the wall. Try not to classify the successor and predecessor relationships of these elements at this point because it could inhibit you from identifying of all the required elements.

Continue brainstorming until all elements have been identified. Once it's agreed that all elements have been identified, group the elements into their respective levels. This is where the Post-it® Notes come in handy, because you can easily move the notes around to the appropriate location. Also, if gaps are identified, you can quickly document new elements on a Post-it® Note and place it in the appropriate location.

Once all work elements have been properly grouped, eliminate any duplication or redundancy from the structure. Then you can establish the predecessor and successor relationships between the various elements.

Several software packages currently available in the market can assist you in developing a WBS. One of the best is WBS Chart Pro®, produced by Critical Tools, Inc.[6] This tool provides an electronic version of the Post-it® Note method, only with a lot more functionality. It also seamlessly integrates with Microsoft Project®, which then allows the user to easily develop the project schedule.[7]

The following basic guidelines can assist you in developing a WBS:

- Ensure that the appropriate resources, including subject matter experts, participate in the development of the WBS.
- Develop the WBS structure by decomposing the project into discrete and logical elements of work (e.g. activities, tasks, subtasks).

- Ensure that each lower level of the decomposition represents 100 percent of the work and cost needed to fulfill the level preceding it (the 100 percent rule).[8]
- Ensure that the WBS satisfies all managerial and technical requirements of the project.
- Avoid getting so detailed in the decomposition that it becomes unmanageable.
- Ensure that each work package has a specific deliverable associated with it and can be assigned to one person.
- Avoid duplication and redundancy of work elements.
- Ensure that project management activities are addressed.
- The sequence of the work is not important as long as there is some logic to the structure (sequencing and establishing relationships among the work elements is done later in the process).
- For solicitation purposes, the WBS generally does not have to go lower than the top three to four levels, depending on whether the initiative is treated as a program or project.

Following these simple guidelines can provide a structure for developing the WBS on future projects. If you or your organization is not currently following a consistent approach, this information will hopefully help you take the first step toward establishing consistency, leading to superior WBSs on future projects.

Step 6: Identify Skills

After describing the tasks, corresponding deliverables, and measures of compliance, identify the skills necessary to achieve each task. If too many diverse skills are required to accomplish one task, subdivide the task. For example:

Task:	Re-wire office
	Skills: Electrical, plastering, and painting
Becomes:	
Task:	Tear out and re-plaster office
	Skills: Plastering
Task:	Re-wire office
	Skill: Electrical
Task:	Paint office
	Skill: Painting

Step 7: Estimate Resources

Some methods of accomplishing government objectives will cause a significant strain on agency budgets. A proposed method can be effective and even efficient, but if agency resources aren't available to fulfill it, the method isn't feasible. Before proceeding any further, survey available resources and estimate the project's costs carefully.

Establish two budgets: (1) a time and money budget for conducting the project in-house; (2) a time and money budget for contracting the project out. Generally the first budget will be labor intensive and the second, cash intensive.

After these two budgets are established, estimate how much each method—in-house or contract-out—will cost. Estimate for both the in-house scenario and the contract-out scenario how much labor and money will be required to accomplish each task.

Step 8: Size the Project

Inevitably, some of the methods will require more time or money than the budget allows. When this happens, modify the proposed methods by scaling down their tasks. The time for creativity is over. Think realistically. Invite the "second troll"—the editor—to the table.

First, compare budgeted resources (time and money) with resource estimates for the project. If a method comes up short, take a knife to it, task by task. If the method cannot be pared back to within budgeted amounts, discard it. Even if all methods end up being tossed out for budget reasons, it's always possible that another, undiscovered solution to the government's problem will not break the bank. As discussed in Step 3, it's important to always keep the possibility of another solution open. If each of the methods is too expensive, go back to the drawing board and think of new options, or invite contractors to suggest a way to solve the government's problem within budget. (A functional SOW, discussed below and in Chapter 5, invites contractors to propose the most efficient solution.)

Step 9: Assess Risk

There is often a trade-off between the scope of a project and the risk: a method that could fulfill an objective if fully funded might become less effective if it is downsized to conform to budget realities. Therefore, if it's necessary to reduce a method in scope, think about whether the revised method will still accomplish its objective. In most cases, there is no sure and fast way to estimate the odds. The best you can do is to seek the advice of experienced professionals, both within your agency and within the contracting community. Consulting experienced professionals should enable you to at least disqualify any methods that appear too risky.

Step 10: Make Choices

After paring down the list of possible methods, choose the option most likely to fulfill the government's objective and begin thinking about which type of SOW will best describe that option.

The Competition in Contracting Act states that SOWs may be written in terms of performance, function, or design.[9] Because writing performance SOWs for research and development is significantly different from writing performance SOWs for products and services, this guide additionally describes a fourth type of SOW written in terms of level of effort. Each type of SOW tailors to the basic six-part SOW format, while the content varies to describe different government needs.

Performance SOW

A performance SOW, commonly referred to as a performance work statement (PWS), lists everything the government wants by breaking objectives into tasks and characterizing each in terms of expected performance.

For example, a government project manager responsible for transporting coal from Pennsylvania to Kansas to heat a facility in Topeka needs a fleet of trucks. The performance SOW ordering the trucks would describe the trucks, their payload, required horsepower, and safety features. The SOW would not describe how to build the truck; it would describe how each truck should look and perform. Performance SOWs describe capabilities.

Performance SOWs are best suited for contracts involving products because it's much easier to quantify and measure the performance of a product than the performance of a service. The government uses performance SOWs to control the contractor's methods without having to worry about the details of execution. Assuming that the terms of the contract are satisfactorily executed, the government knows the product will achieve its purpose. This makes measuring compliance a relatively easy task: you simply test to see if the performance criteria have been satisfied.

On the downside, unless you remember to specify minimum quality standards for the product or service, the end deliverable may be inadequate. Maintenance issues can crop up. It can take a significant amount of time to write airtight performance requirements.

Functional SOW

A functional SOW defines what the government wants to do and leaves the contractor free to come up with the most efficient way to fulfill that objective. This kind of SOW expands the variety of subsequent bids considerably. The government might still receive bids offering to provide a fleet of trucks, but it might also receive an offer to ship the coal by rail. The functional SOW focuses on defining the problem and leaves the creation of a solution up to private contractors. It does not include performance attributes or design specifications that describe how to fulfill the objective.

The biggest advantage of using a functional SOW is that it encourages contractor innovation and creativity. It is well suited for service contracts because there are generally many different ways to deliver a service, whereas for a product there are generally very detailed plans and specifications to follow to ensure compliance with government requirements. In turn, delivering a product gives less flexibility than delivering a service.

The functional SOW doesn't require detailed specifications or performance standards, which can save time and effort. However, this makes writing measures of compliance proportionally more difficult. In other words, if the specifications or performance hasn't been quantified, then the measure of compliance can vary according to the interpretation of the measuring party or individual.

Design SOW

The most detailed SOW type is the design SOW, used mainly in construction and manufacturing projects. Here the government might specify not only how many trucks are needed to transport the coal, but also how those trucks should be built. The military uses this type of SOW to satisfy its special needs: the trucks must withstand abnormally heavy use in a variety of conditions. A design SOW enables the military to actually design the truck it needs. Design SOWs often rely heavily on plans or blueprints.

The biggest advantage of a design SOW is that it affords the government the greatest control over its product or service. The downside is that because it is the most detailed of all the SOWs, the design SOW is also the most difficult to write. Unless you are an subject-matter expert in the industry that provides the product or service your requesting, or have access to such experts, designing and describing what you need can be daunting.

Another disadvantage is that designing a product or service doesn't guarantee that it will perform as you expect, and the contractor is in no way responsible for the end performance. The contractor's job is to execute the government's specifications. The government, as the designer, is responsible for its success.

Level-of-Effort SOW

A specialized version of the performance SOW is the level-of-effort SOW, which is used when limited resources preclude guarantees to meet project objectives. Level-of-effort SOWs are most often used on research and development contracts and on contracts where the objective is unlikely to be obtained given limited resources. These contracts require much attention to compliance and delivery issues. The level-of-effort SOW allows the government to require the use of the specified resources to first develop a research strategy, conduct the research, and finally, upon government approval, proceed with the development of a prototype.

For example, the U.S. Postal Service decides it wants to begin funding research to find an alternative to stamps. The agency determines that it will look into and subsequently develop two alternatives, bar codes and magnetized envelopes, and provides $1 million for the project. The level-of-effort SOW cannot ask bidders to guarantee that the research will produce a product superior to the current stamp technology, or that the research will even produce viable alternatives. The government can expect, however, that the research will be undertaken following a logical plan, and development will proceed if appropriate.

In contrast, performance, functional, and design SOWs are limited by technology, products, and services that are already available. Requirements in those SOWs cannot specify something that doesn't exist yet. The level-of-effort SOW allows the government to push the envelope and develop something new.

Choosing the Right SOW

One way to determine which type of SOW to use is to break the decision down into five smaller choices:

1. Conduct in-house or contract out?
2. Choose the best method.
3. Use a functional SOW?
4. Use a performance or design SOW?
5. Use a performance or level-of-effort SOW?

Conduct in-house or contract out? Decide whether to conduct the project in-house or use a contractor on the basis of cost, staff availability, likelihood of success, and capability. Reference the

Office of Management and Budget guidelines contained in OMB Circular A-76 for the federal policy regarding the competition of commercial activities.[10] This will help you determine whether the project can be conducted in-house or if can be contracted out.

If the choice is made to conduct the project in-house, an SOW is not required, but it is recommended. It's still important to define the projects requirements and specifications for the in-house team. An SOW will also measure performance and manage change to the project. If you choose to contract the work out, continue on with the remaining questions to determine which SOW will best suit the government's needs.

Choose the best method. Choose the method that is most likely to accomplish the government's objective. Base your decision on cost, time, risk, and quality, as described in the previous steps.

Use a functional SOW? Compare your best method against the potential value of a yet-to-be-discovered method. If you are concerned that your best method is inadequate, or if you have disqualified all other methods except the undiscovered one, consider the functional SOW. The functional SOW describes the government's objective in detail without specifying a prescribed method. It also allows bidders to come up with their own best methods.

Use a performance or design SOW? If you choose to not use the functional SOW, decide between the performance and design SOWs. If the project must deliver specific performance capabilities and features to the government, it will be necessary to choose between either a performance or design SOW. The performance SOW doesn't include information about how a product should be built or operated, but instead focuses on how it the product should perform. On the other hand, the design SOW provides very detailed requirements and specifications to the contractor about how to construct and deliver a desired product or service.

Use a performance or level-of-effort SOW? If you choose the performance SOW over a design SOW, you still need to choose between its standard form or its level-of-effort form. To do this, determine whether or not the method being pursued has a defined deliverable. If it does, use the standard performance SOW. If the project requires the use of the specified resources only to work *toward* an objective, then the level-of-effort SOW is probably your best choice.

Combining Types

Generally speaking, you should not combine different types of SOWs. If the Census Bureau writes an SOW for an automated payroll processing machine describing what it must do (a performance SOW), and includes technical documents describing how it must be manufactured (a design SOW), it puts potential contractors in a difficult situation. What if the contractor builds the machine the way the Census Bureau requires, but it does not perform the way the SOW says it must? Is the contractor in noncompliance? Any bids the Census Bureau receives in response to this kind of mixed SOW would likely have a considerable price and schedule margin built in to cover the contractor's increased risk.

Sometimes it does make sense to create a "SOW blend." For example, if a project included both the development and service of a product, then it may be necessary to combine elements of a performance SOW and a functional SOW. In such cases, it's important to pay particular attention to a compliance protocol. For instance, the performance SOW will describe the specific capabilities and features of the product, whereas the functional SOW would allow the contractor a degree of flexibility in determining how to service the product.

Drafting an Outline for the SOW

After you choose an SOW type, you can prepare an outline. Depending on the nature of the effort, the technical risk involved, and the requirements of any internal program procedures, consider including the following material in a comprehensive working outline, which you can later distill into the basic six-part SOW format.

1. **Objectives.** Identify desired end objectives of the project and associated technical requirements.
2. **Background.** List contextual information that will help contractors understand the nature and origin of the requirements. Include a brief summary of appropriate agency objectives, statutory program authority, major programs, and goals set by statute, if relevant. Describe the relationship of the effort to major programs and goals.
3. **Scope.** Describe the scope of required contractor efforts in support of project objectives. The clarity of the scope descrip-

tion is essential. Any contractor effort beyond this scope will necessitate changes and require subsequent negotiations of cost, profit or fee, and schedule.

4. **Technical Considerations.** State technical considerations that may influence a contractor's approach or efforts. Specify any known specific phenomena, techniques, methodologies, and the results of any previous related work that may influence a contractor's efforts or approach.
5. **Tasks.** Describe all the tasks the contractor must complete, together with the required sequence of tasks.
6. **Acceptance.** Establish milestones or government management control points in the sequence of tasks where government actions for review, approval, acceptance, or rejection are introduced. Establish relevant and well-defined baselines for contractor performance measurement.
7. **Responsibilities.** Identify all government and contractor participation needed for the project, as well as the nature and extent of all task responsibilities. Specifically state all tasks requiring government support, such as government-furnished equipment, facilities, material, and extra laboratory space, and describe the nature and requirements of that support.
8. **Schedule.** Generate a schedule for the sequence of contractor tasks and a similar schedule for related government responsibilities. This includes establishing successor and predecessor relationships for the tasks and identifying those on the critical path.

9. **Deliverables.** Identify contractor delivery requirements precisely and schedule a delivery date for each. Include details about the type and quantity of all deliverables. State precisely what a contractor is to deliver at specified times as the work progresses and upon final completion of the contracted work.

10. **Date Requirements.** Describe all technical data requirements, including the intended use of the data by the project engineer.

11. **Information Requirements.** Describe all management information requirements that a contractor must satisfy.

12. **Person-Hours.** Estimate the number professional and technical hours, weeks, months, or years the contractor will require to perform the contracted work.

After completing the SOW outline, you can think more critically about how the government's objective will be expressed in the type of SOW you chose. The next four chapters offer more information about each of the SOW types. Read them all, or skip to the chapter devoted to the type of SOW type you chose for a project.

Regardless of the SOW type, the basic six-part SOW format—introduction/scope statement, requirements, references, delivery, progress and compliance, and notes and other information—may be used as a generic format to follow. The next four chapters focus on how the core elements of this format—the requirements, delivery, and progress and compliance sections—differ among different SOW types. To help in the writing process, each chapter starts with a planning section that explains how to transition from the ten-step planning process to the process of actually writing that type of SOW.

NOTES

1. Competition in Contracting Act, U.S. Public Law 98-369, July 18, 1984. Implemented in 10 U.S.C. 2305, "Contracts: Planning, Solicitation, Evaluation, and Award Procedures." Online at http://www4.law.cornell.edu/uscode/10/2305.html (accessed January 2008).
2. Department of Defense, *Department of Defense Handbook for Preparation of Statement of Work (SOW)*, MIL-HDBK-245D, 3 April 1996. Online at http://www.dla.mil/DSS/dss-a/download/DoD%20SOW%20Handbook.pdf (accessed January 2008).
3. Project Management Institute, *A Guide to the Project Management Body of Knowledge*, Third Edition (Newtown Square, PA: Project Management Institute, Inc., 2004), 379.
4. Ibid., 380.
5. National Aeronautics and Space Administration, *NASA Guidance for Writing Statements of Work*, NPG 5600.2B, December 1997. Online at http://www.hq.nasa.gov/office/procurement/newreq1.htm (accessed January 2008).
6. For more information about WBS Chart Pro®, please visit http://www.criticaltools.com/ (accessed December 2007).
7. For more information about Microsoft Project®, please visit http://office.microsoft.com/en-us/project/default.aspx. (accessed December 2007).
8. Gregory T. Haugan, *Project Management Fundamentals: Key Concepts and Methodology* (Vienna, VA: Management Concepts, 2006), 28.
9. See note 1 above.
10. Office of Management and Budget, *Circular A-76: Performance of Commercial Activities*, May 29, 2003. Online at http://www.whitehouse.gov/omb/circulars/a076/a76_rev2003.pdf (accessed December 2007).

Chapter 4
The Performance SOW

It's half time. The home team is behind. The locker room is heavy with the smell of sweat and fear. This is the big game, a must-win. The coach looks around the room at his players. All are quiet.

"Fellas," he says, "this isn't practice. The time for chalkboard analysis is over. The time for drills has passed. This is the real thing. Go out there and do it. Go out there and win!" The locker room explodes and the players flood back out on the field to give it their best.

This is the performance statement of work (SOW) at its most basic. The coach does not spend any time reviewing plays or giving tips to individual players. He lays out the bottom line. Here is what you have to do: win.

The performance SOW does not specify how to build or operate something, only how it must perform. Its specifications all center on the product's capabilities. Compliance is relatively easy to measure: the product or service either performs as expected or not.

Example: The Customs Bureau decides to purchase 65 metal detectors. The SOW describes what the detectors must be capable of doing. The project manager stipulates that each detector must be able to sense all ferrous and non-ferrous metals greater than two ounces in weight and at a distance of at least 12 inches, emit an alarm perceptible only by operating personnel, and require no more than two operators. The contractor chooses how to fill this order. It can put a bid in for handheld detectors or a doorway detector. Compliance with the requirements in a performance SOW is based solely on the ability of a contractor's final product to fulfill government objectives.

Planning

To develop a performance SOW, return to the ten-step planning process described in Chapter 3 and review the list of deliverables. Characterize each of these deliverables for a given project, in terms acceptable to the government, to produce a list of project performance characteristics.

Example: The Department of Health and Human Services (DHHS) decides to improve prenatal care in rural areas. The DHHS project manager's planning worksheet looks like this:

Objective: Improve prenatal healthcare in rural areas.
Method A: Create a prenatal task force
Element 1: Hire staff
Element 2: Provide logistical support
Task: Open 12 regional offices
–Deliverable: 12 regional offices opened, operating, and in compliance with all prenatal healthcare facility codes and regulations.
Task: Purchase 48 all-terrain vehicles
–Deliverable: 48 four-wheel drive, V-8, four-seat vehicles that can go up to speeds of 100 mph and which will last for 15,000 miles with normal maintenance.
–Compliance: Capability verification, dealer receipt, and service contract

List the deliverables for each task in performance terms, restating them where necessary. Take care in expressing those characteristics to ensure that they fully meet—and don't exceed—the government's needs. The performance attributes should be both necessary and sufficient to meet each task.

Requirements

Information found in the requirements section of an SOW defines the government's needs. In the performance SOW, this information is expressed in terms of capabilities. How many acres must be cultivated, the number of bytes a computer system must possess, or how fast a messenger service must deliver parcels.

Example: The Surface Transportation Board (STB) needs new duplication machines. The SOW lists desired attributes: the ability to process up to six reams of paper at one time, reduce and magnify documents, and au-

> tomatically feed multi-page documents. The STB describes how it wants its copiers to perform, not how they ought to be built.

The only rule in writing performance requirements is that all specifications must focus on how a product or service is supposed to perform, and not on how the contractor should achieve that end.

The level of detail expressed in the requirements is a matter of balance. Requirements must be specific enough to get the job done, without needlessly constraining competition. Writing unambiguous and concise requirements will enable potential offerors to make precise estimates of cost and time. Likewise, requirements must be specific enough to ensure that the government's needs are fully satisfied.

On the other hand, being too specific can limit competition needlessly. For example, a good salesman convinces a government project manager that a certain product will achieve agency goals. If the project manager then writes specifications for the product that are so detailed only a few models will qualify, he or she is "wiring" the SOW. Wiring SOWs is illegal, violating the policies and procedures stated in the FAR Part 14.101(a): *Unnecessarily restrictive specifications or requirements that might unduly limit the number of bidders are prohibited.*[1]

More specifically, the specifications should only state the Government's actual minimum needs. The operative phrase *actual minimum needs* means that requirements cannot demand more of a product or service than is needed. In other words, no extras should be included in the specifications. When the DHHS states the need for a four-wheel drive vehicle, it should be prepared to justify that specification on the basis of the technical requirements of the project.

Do not include methodologies, blueprints, travel requirements, or personnel requirements in performance SOWs. Performance SOWs focus specifically on the performance of the product or service, not on how they are to be constructed or operated. Thus, the above items are not critical to the quality of a performance SOW.

Because performance SOWs only describe performance capabilities, the contractor is fully responsible for design. The DHHS would not tell potential bidders how to build four-wheel drive vehicles, only that the final product must perform according to certain criteria. Because of this division of responsibility, specifying how long the product must last and how it will be maintained is critical. If the DHHS ignored these issues, it would very likely receive proposals offering vehicles that perform well in the short term, but are not built to last.

Small construction projects are often well suited for a performance SOW, shifting the burden of design onto the contractor. Instead of including blueprints or detailed designs for the project, describe requirements in terms of their expected performance—what the construction or improvement would do, not how it should look or be built. Performance requirements can include specifications like:

- Use
- Dimensions

- Capacity
- Output (e.g., velocity, power, number of items produced, coverage, rate)
- Weight
- Ability to withstand weather or other forces
- Accuracy
- Color
- Texture or hardness
- Tolerances

Example: The Fish and Wildlife Service decides to build a fish pond at one of its extension stations. In the SOW it specifies that the pond should use existing water supplies, hold 3,000 gallons of water, and allow personnel to feed the fish.

Deliverables

Deliverables are what the government can expect upon the satisfactory completion of a contract. In a performance SOW, the deliverable is the product or service described by its requirements. The deliverables section of the SOW describes how, when, and where the product or service will be delivered. This section also describes any special protocols for accepting the final product.

Example: A Justice Department effort to unravel the connections between crime and homelessness requires a report of specified dimensions as its deliverable. The requirements section of the SOW describes the dimensions of the report. The deliverables section defines the report's schedule for development, due date, and the required number of copies due for submission.

Progress

In all but the smallest of contracts, the government should insist upon progress reports to safeguard its interests. Miscommunication occurs despite clear specifications and uneventful post-award conferences. Establishing a regular means of monitoring projects is not only prudent, it's critical to ensuring that the government's objectives are being accomplished. Progress reports are the means by which the government fine-tunes its needs.

Project managers should also consider including interim approval points as part of their SOWs. Particularly in complex projects, it is important to provide regular opportunities for the government to review work progress.

Example: The Deposit Insurance Fund (DIF) needs to appraise the assets of a failed Massachusetts-chartered savings bank. The SOW requires the contractor to estimate the value of the bank's complete holdings as detailed in an attachment. A report estimating the value of the assets is required by the end of the fiscal year. Monthly progress reports are also required. Three copies of the report are due by the first Monday of every month to the DIF headquarters. The reports must include work

> done to date, work schedule for completion in the next month, and any issues that have arisen. Each report is followed by a face-to-face meeting between the DIF and the contractor.

Figure 4.1 offers a sample outline of progress report specifications.

Figure 4.1 Sample Progress Report Specifications

Outline for Progress Reports:

- Cover Sheet:
  - Title and period covered
  - Contractor name, address, and contract number
  - Agency name
- Executive Summary:
  - Report objective
  - Abstract of progress
  - Contract personnel with qualifications
- Table of Contents
- Body:
  - Progress detailed
  - Progress mapped on master schedule (including milestones)
  - Discussion
  - Conclusion
  - Appendices
- Reporting Schedule
- Number of Reports Required
- Presentations

Compliance

Compliance is the means by which the government ensures that it has received what it ordered. In performance SOWs, compliance is often based on testing. As requirements are framed in terms of capabilities, compliance is a matter of verifying whether or not the product/service performs the way it is supposed to.

Example: Upon delivery of its four-wheel drive vehicles, DHHS drives each vehicle to verify its ability to go 100 mph, inspects its safety features, and measures its cargo carrying capacity to ensure that all performance specifications are met or exceeded.

Testing services for compliance is more difficult.

Example: The DIF's SOW calls for delivery of a final report which includes appraisals of a failed chartered savings bank's assets. Short of double checking each appraisal, testing for complete compliance is impossible; instead, the DIF tests using a random sampling technique.

The key to writing a performance SOW is to remember that although the government specifies what product or service it wants, how the product or service should perform, and what capabilities it ought to have, the government does not specify how it ought to be built or operated. Figure 4.2 includes a short checklist for writers preparing a performance SOW.

Figure 4.2 Performance SOW Checklist

	Y	N	If not, provide explanation
1. Does the SOW require only essentials (actual minimum requirements)?			
2. Has extraneous material been eliminated?			
3. Is background or other introductory information readily distinguishable form the requirements?			
4. Is the SOW sufficiently detailed so contractors can estimate costs and resources accurately for each task or work phase?			
5. Are specific duties and end results detailed so contractors will know exactly what is required and how compliance will be measured by the government?			
6. Does the SOW explain the interrelationship among tasks, the relationships between tasks and required results, and deliverables?			
7. Does the SOW identify constraints and limitations?			
8. Does the SOW contain standards for all parties to measure performance?			
9. Is there a time-phased requirement for each activity and deliverable? Are time limits clearly defined as calendar days or as work days?			
10. Have all requirements for data been specified?			
11. Are proper quantities shown?			
12. Do any standard specifications apply in whole or in part? If so, are they properly cited and referenced?			
13. Are referenced documents properly described and cited?			
14. Are reporting requirements clear? Have timing, content, and level of detail been specified?			

	Y	N	If not, provide explanation
15. If a competitively negotiated procurement is planned, are the tasks descriptors an adequate frame of reference for bidders submitting technical proposals?			

Note: If you are unable to check "yes" in response to all questions, continue working on the SOW until you can do so.

NOTE

1. General Services Administration, Department of Defense, and National Aeronautics and Space Administration, *Federal Acquisition Regulation,* vol. 1-51, March 2005, 14.101(a). This edition includes the consolidation of all Federal Acquisition Circulars through 2001-27. Online at http://www.arnet.gov/far/reissue/FARvol1ForPaperOnly.pdf (accessed January 2008).

Chapter 5

The Functional SOW

In the early 1990s, Washington, D.C., had the highest per capita murder rate of any city in the United States. In one of the city's most crime-ridden neighborhoods, however, stood a defiant example of how inner cities can stage a comeback.

The residents of Kensington Gardens decided that city officials were not doing their job. Police protection in their project was inadequate. The residents thought they could do better. They approached the City Council and asked for permission to buy their building over time, managing it in the interim. The City Council approved the idea, and Kensington Gardens became a national example. The crime rate fell dramatically and the building was clean and regularly maintained. Kensington Garden's secret? The residents had a stake in their future and they guarded it jealously.

Increasingly, whether in business or politics, people are learning that pride and productivity accompany the power to make decisions. Management theory is telling us to loosen our grip on employees. Give them an assignment and set them free with the resources they need. You will be surprised by their ingenuity.

This enthusiasm for the idea of empowering people has spread to federal contracting in the form of the functional statement of work (SOW). The functional SOW treats the contractor as a public sector partner, not as a wage employee incapable of thinking on his or her own. The premise behind the functional SOW is to let potential contractors know the scope of the government challenge and free them to be creative in their solution.

You will be surprised by contractor imagination. Further, once the contract has been awarded, you will be surprised by the contractor's enthusiasm for, and productivity in, executing its idea. The contractor owns the idea and wants to make it work. The functional SOW invites contractors to use their best professional judgment and solve the government's problem in the best way they know how. The results can be exciting.

Example: The Department of Education (DoE) decides it wants to get the word out about the merits of school-based management. It disseminates information about school-based management to local school systems, to look at the underlying problem. Then, instead of dictating a method for the accomplishment of that goal, the DoE issues a challenge to the contracting world: Solve the government's problem in the best, most efficient way you can conceive. This is a functional SOW.

Planning

Before writing a functional SOW, the SOW writer should return to the ten-step process described in Chapter 3 and concentrate on

Step 2, defining the problem. The problem statement is the heart of the functional SOW because it defines the government's challenge contractors must solve. Whereas other SOWs require the writer to sift through and ultimately choose a best method of tackling this problem before writing an SOW, the functional model does not.

The functional SOW must be absolutely clear on the nature of the government's problem, but keep silent on how the contractor should solve the problem. It throws the process open. The SOW writer should expect the contracting community to respond to the SOW with a variety of different approaches to solving the problem.

Example: The President's Council of Economic Advisers decides to ask whether or not the real earning power of families has gone up or down in the last 25 years, discounting the effect of more women in the workplace. This is the Council's objective. As a group of professional economists, the Council wants to design a methodology that produces economic data about the earning power of families. A different approach, however, would be to simply state the objective—the government needs to know more about the average earning power of families—and let bidders propose various methods of obtaining that information.

Example: The U.S. Army Corps of Engineers is seeking ways to prevent flooding in New Orleans during major storm events like Hurricane Katrina. Although the Corps had constructed an elaborate levee system around the city that worked quite effectively for many years, the system was unable to maintain its integrity during a major storm event. Rather than dictating how to fix the problem, the Corps decides to let potential bidders propose various construction methods for protecting the city during a storm event.

Requirements

When writing other SOW types, the requirements section is filled chiefly with various types of specifications. The functional SOW, however, does not include specifications; it focuses almost exclusively on the project's objective. Some examples of functional objectives include:

Objective: To lower the cost of air conditioning in all buildings on Fort Hood, while keeping offices 68 degrees Fahrenheit.
Objective: To increase deluxe lodging capacity in Yellowstone Park by 100 beds.
Objective: To maintain the grounds surrounding the John F. Kennedy Presidential Library in Boston for a period of one year.

The objective, so defined, will then attract a variety of responses once advertised.

Example: The U.S. Marine Corps decides to purchase 2,500 multi-function calculators. Before it writes an SOW, however, it takes a step back and defines its objective—to provide calculating support to various Corps offices. Instead of putting together a performance SOW that describes the various capabilities its 2,500 calculators

> must have, it decides to throw the question open to the contracting world in the form of a functional SOW with requirements limited to a statement of the objective. The result may be surprising. Several firms might offer to provide calculators, but other potential contractors may propose much cheaper software upgrades that would add a calculating function to the Corps' desktop computers.

An objective may be subdivided into sub-objectives as long as they do not describe performance standards or how the job should be done. For example:

Objective:	To provide telephone service for the Department of State **A.** State Department headquarters in Washington, D.C. **B.** 306 embassies, consulates, and missions worldwide **C.** All United States Information Agency facilities

Delivery

Deliverables are what the government expects to receive after a contract has been satisfactorily completed. In a functional SOW, the deliverable is the objective accomplished.

> **Objective:** To redecorate the agency head's suite of offices.
>
> ***Deliverable*:** A redecorated suite of offices.
>
> **Objective:** To provide for the collection and recycling of all office soda cans.
>
> ***Deliverables*:** The collection and recycling of all office soda cans.
>
> **Objective:** To provide safety education to bulldozer operators.
>
> ***Deliverables*:** Bulldozer operators educated for safety.

A project schedule enumerating the completion of all deliverables should be included as part of the SOW.

Progress

Establishing procedures for monitoring a project's progress and compliance are critical to a successful functional SOW. Keeping an eye on a project's progress is difficult when the project manager doesn't know how the contractor intends to fulfill required objectives. Two strategies can help address this problem:

1. Phasing. The project manager can break the objective down so that each element occurs in a distinct period of time or sequence.

***Example*:** The Federal Elections Commission wants to monitor television stations in selected markets for the next three election cycles, for suspected overcharging on Congressional campaigns.

Objective: Monitor television stations for suspected overcharging

1. 2008 elections

2. 2010 elections

3. 2012 elections

Progress: Status report due upon completion of each sub-objective.

By breaking the objective into increments of time and requiring reports at the end of each time period, the government can keep an eye on how its money is spent, without micromanaging the contractor and getting too bogged down in its methodology.

2. Requiring a Schedule. The project manager can simply require a schedule with appropriate government oversight included in the contractor's proposal.

***Example*:** The Justice Department wants to design an annex to its Atlanta offices.

Objective: Design annex for Atlanta offices.

Progress: Include a surveillance proposal as part of bid.

Compliance

Ensuring compliance with a contract using a functional SOW, where the details are largely unknown, is extremely challenging. Essentially, compliance in a functional SOW is based on the use of the product or service after it's delivered. *Use compliance* means that a contractor is judged to be in compliance with the government's requirements if the contractor's product or service solves the government's problem. The government sets the objective; it is the contractor's job to accomplish it. This significantly shifts the burden of compliance and risk away from the government and toward the contractor. The contractor cannot plead that it did what it proposed to do and therefore is in compliance; their proposed product or service has to appropriately address the government's need.

Example: The Drug Enforcement Agency (DEA) needs to protect its personnel from drug dealers. The objective, defined in the functional SOW, is that DEA agents be protected from hostile gunfire in the line of duty. The DEA might expect that firms dealing in various types of body armor would respond. If the contract is awarded to XYZ Bulletproof Vest Company who promises to deliver 500 vests by the end of the year, the company is in compliance so long as the vests protect DEA agents from hostile gunfire in the line of duty.

Chapter 6

The Design SOW

The project manager who catches him- or herself muttering, "If you want it done right, you have to do it yourself," needs to take a look at the design statement of work. The design SOW puts the government squarely in the driver's seat, allowing the SOW writer to specify in as much detail as necessary how a contract should be executed. The design SOW describes what the government wants done and how. The contractor has no latitude in interpreting this type of SOW and must not deviate from any listed specifications.

Example: The Bureau of Land Management wants to construct a new regional headquarters in Boise, Idaho. It chooses to express this need in a design SOW. Not only does it specify exactly how the building will look, but it describes the construction techniques and building materials it wants used as well.

Requirements for a design SOW are often complex and detailed, making compliance easy to measure: either the job is completed according to the requirements or it is not. Since the contractor is not responsible for the end product's capabilities or performance (it is not the contractor's design), extra care must be given in writing design SOW specifications. This type of SOW is also known as the *process model* because of its emphasis on how a project is to be completed.

Planning

A thorough planning effort lays much of the groundwork for a good design SOW. As with performance and functional SOWs, the objective is given as a definition of the problem in a design SOW. Unlike the functional SOW, the design SOW specifies how the objective and individual tasks are to be accomplished. When writing a design SOW, begin with the list of identified project tasks gathered during the planning stage described in Chapter 3, and flesh out each task to describe exactly what is required and the means by which it should be accomplished.

Assessing the likelihood that a method will accomplish its objective is critical in a design SOW (Step 9 in Chapter 3). If the government's approach does not work, the contractor cannot be held liable as long as the work complies with the specifications. An option to seriously consider, particularly with projects that are not complex, is the use of standard designs. Though these "cookie cutter" plans lack originality, they reduce the government's risk and are likely to be much cheaper to use than their more risky, custom-tailored designs.

Example: The Central Intelligence Agency (CIA) decides to build a motor pool garage on the periphery of its Langley campus. It could design the garage from scratch, or it could check its files for any garages it has built in the past, assuming that one garage is not very different from another. If previous garage plans are available, CIA should consider using them. Plans that have produced proven results are always less risky than plans that have not yet been used.

Requirements

As with the other SOW types, the first step in drafting a design SOW is to define an objective as clearly and concisely as possible. Then review the corresponding list of tasks to ensure that they are both necessary and sufficient. Finally, break down the tasks into groups before including them in the SOW. Break down the tasks either by subject or by time:

- **By subject.** The project manager can split projects into several smaller projects by subject area. For example, Element 1 of a construction project might be the headquarters building, while Element 2 is the outbuildings. A training contract might be divided into course development (Element 1) and training the trainers (Element 2).
- **By time.** The project manager can also phase a project over time. Phase 1 of a military jet project might be jet development, while Phase 2 might be jet production.

Develop a detailed work plan for each task, including a timetable, a list of necessary resources, and procedures. From the detailed work plan, draft a master schedule indicating when all work is to occur, with both start and finish dates. Also include how it will relate to other elements of the total project. Finally, attach any plans or blueprints and include any specifications in the reference section.

Specifications, Standards, and Purchase Descriptions

The term *specification is* generally synonymous with a description of the work and includes requirements, references, delivery, and compliance. It can also have a more technical meaning, however, when it refers to a list of pre-calculated product measures.

Example: If the National Passenger Rail Corporation (AMTRAK) wants to buy railway ties, it might refer to a list of railway specifications published by the railway industry. This list may define the standards for manufacturing railway ties (e.g., ties must be 10 feet long by 10 inches wide by 8 inches deep, and made of pressure-treated, creosote-soaked hardwood). The industry specification saves AMTRAK the time of redefining a railway tie every time it wants to purchase more ties.

By referring to specifications, the SOW writer can avoid having to design every nut and bolt from scratch.

Three types of specifications include:

- **Federal.** The General Services Administration (GSA) maintains the *Index of the Federal Specifications, Standards and Commercial Item Descriptions.*[1] Each specification listed is fully coordinated, meaning it has been tested and proven in use and works with other GSA-specified products. Individual agencies also list specifications for particular products they use.

- **Military.** The Department of Defense maintains the *Department of Defense Single Stock Point for Military Specifications, Standards and Related Publications* (DODSSP), which was created to centralize the control, distribution, and access to the extensive collection of military specifications, standards, and related standardization documents that the DoD has either prepared or adopted.[2] The DODSSP also maintains a set of specifications called the *Acquisition Streamlining and Standardization Information System* (ASSIST) management/research database.[3] These specifications and standards may also be used by civilian agencies.
- **Industrial.** Trade associations and other non-governmental groups produce specifications for various industries. These are most common in the construction trades.

The use of most GSA and military specifications are mandatory, with two types of exceptions:

- **Deviations.** Any authorization that doesn't follow specifications or makes a change to specifications *before* work begins is called a deviation. Deviations are tightly restricted.
- **Waivers.** Any authorization that doesn't follow specifications or makes a change to specifications *after* work begins is called a waiver. This form of administrative action is also rare.

Figure 6.1 offers additional resources that can help you develop a list of specifications for your project.

Though they are all closely related, specifications differ from standards and purchase descriptions. *Specifications* define the required technique or design, while *standards* generally describe tolerances or acceptable deviations. For example, specifications for a quarter-inch bolt may include the number of shaft threads, the size of the head, and the type of steel; whereas, a *standard* for potable water may be defined as having not more than .02 percent impurities and

Figure 6.1 Specification Indexes and Resources

- **Acquisition Streamlining and Standardization Information System (ASSIST).** A database system for DoD-wide standardization document information management. The ASSIST database resides at the *Department of Defense Single Stock Point for Military Specifications, Standards and Related Publications* (DODSSP), located at the Document Automation and Production Service (DAPS), in Philadelphia, PA. For more information, visit the DAPS website at http://assist.daps.dla.mil.
- **National Standards Institute (ANSI).** ANSI oversees the creation, promulgation, and use of thousands of norms and guidelines that directly impact businesses and government agencies. The mission of ANSI is "To enhance both the global competitiveness of U.S. business and the U.S. quality of life by promoting and facilitating voluntary consensus standards and conformity assessment systems, and safeguarding their integrity."[4] For more information, visit the ANSI website at www.ansi.org.
- **American Society for Testing and Materials (ASTM).** ASTM International is one of the largest voluntary standards development organizations in the world. It is a trusted source for technical standards for materials, products, systems, and services. For more information, visit the ASTM website at www.astm.org.
- **The Institute of Electrical and Electronic Engineers, Inc. (IEEE).** IEEE, a non-profit organization, is the world's leading professional association for the advancement of technology. IEEE is a leading authority on areas ranging from aerospace systems, computers and telecommunications, to biomedical engineering, electric power, and consumer electronics, among others. For more information, visit the IEEE website at www.ieee.org.

.05 percent chlorine. Another example could be that spark plugs may be required to fire 99.99 percent of the time.

Standards are engineering or technical limits and applications. Two types of standards include:

- **Government.** Many agencies specify lists of products and their government-sanctioned use. They also list agreed-upon tolerances and measurements for certain products. GSA, for example, might list that all hardened steel used by the government must have no more than .05 percent impurities. Instead of requiring the project manager to list this standard every time the government orders a quarter-inch bolt, the project manager can refer to the standard.
- **Professional.** Also called voluntary standards, these measures of acceptability are produced by industry groups.

Intended to ensure uniformity among products, both types of standards are shorthand ways of specifying how goods and services should look and perform. Standards differ from specifications in that standards describe tolerances or acceptable deviation, while specifications detail required technique or design.

Purchase descriptions are undefined descriptions of commonly used products. Purchase descriptions are a form of shorthand. These abbreviated descriptions of products are used where it would not make sense to describe the product in more detail.

Example: The Equal Employment Opportunity Commission (EEOC) decides to run government-wide seminars briefing heads of personnel departments on the provisions of the new Civil Rights Act. In its design SOW, the EEOC might specify the need for 25- to 26-inch display easels. The EEOC shouldn't need to define "display easel" or refer to detailed specifications. Rather, it can simply list a purchase description for the display easel, as a commonly known commodity, and let the contractor decide on the kind of display easel.

Example: The Army decides to build a retirement home for retired Army officers. The SOW calls for each suite of rooms to include a bathroom with a mirror, sink, shower, and toilet, and gives a purchase description of the toilet. The Army could include detailed plans on the optimal toilet design, or it could specify various performance standards (e.g., each flush should have 15 pounds of water pressure). Instead, the project manager chooses to itemize the need for the toilet with a basic purchase description, and leaves the choice of brand and type up to the contractor.

The FAR addresses the use of brand names in multiple locations, including Part 8.405-6, which states, "Brand name specifications shall not be used unless the particular brand name, product, or feature is essential to the Government's requirements, and market research indicates other companies' similar products, or products lacking the particular feature, do not meet, or cannot be modified to meet, the agency's needs."[5] If the minimum needs of the government are met by a variety of toilets, the project manager should just specify toilet generically with a purchase description.

If only one product on the market will meet the government's minimum needs, then the project manager is required to specify those features of the product that the government requires. Also, in specifying the product, the project manager must write the brand name but also add the words *or equal*. This is to ensure that if there is another product on the market which is able to meet the government's minimum needs, it is not excluded from competing with the specific brand name.

Using MasterFormat™ for Construction Projects

When writing a design SOW for construction projects, use the MasterFormat™ established by the Construction Specifications Institute (CSI) to describe key project elements.[6] The federal government and private industries all use the MasterFormat™ as a standard for organizing requirements.

The MasterFormat™ Facility Construction Subgroup contains 13 standard divisions and a specific numbering system to organize requirements. The divisions include:

02 – Existing Conditions

03 – Concrete

04 – Masonry

05 – Metals

06 – Wood, Plastics, and Composites

07 – Thermal and Moisture Protection

08 – Openings

09 – Finishes

10 – Specialties

11 – Equipment

12 – Furnishings

13 – Special Construction

14 – Conveying Equipment

Each section is specified by a six-digit numbering system. For example, if a construction project called for concrete reinforcement, the numbering system referenced would be 03 20 00—"03" represents the concrete division. The first two digits represent the division number, otherwise known as level one. The second pair of numbers represents level two and the third pair represents level three.

Delivery

Deliverables are what the government expects to receive upon completion of the contract. In a design SOW, there should be no ambiguity in this matter because the government designs and specifies what it expects to be delivered. The delivery section also includes a detailed schedule of deadlines and specifies where and when deliveries will take place.

Example: The National Geospatial-Intelligence Agency (NGA) needs a new telecommunications system capable of transmitting maps instantly worldwide to mobile units. Because the system is highly sophisticated, the agency chose to design the system in-house. The SOW lists its objective: a telecommunications firm is to build the system according to the NGA's design. The deliverable is the fully built system, in place and operational.

Progress and Compliance

Compliance occurs when all parties to a contract agree that the contract requirements have been satisfied. For projects using a design SOW, compliance is strict. The contractor is bound to do everything specified in the SOW. As an extra precaution, however, it is a good idea for the SOW writer to build progress reports into the design as checks and balances. Likewise, the project manager should set up protocols for periodic inspections. Third parties—like building inspectors, for example—can be used for this purpose.

Example: The U.S. Government Printing Office (GPO) wants a new warehouse. Its SOW might include blueprints, schedules, and periodic progress meetings. At the progress meetings, the government might indicate that it expects to see local inspection approval for the various phases of the project, including initial site preparation, concrete work, and water, electrical, and gas connections. Monitoring local inspectors' comments can give the government the kind of surveillance and control over the project it requires.

NOTES

1. General Services Administration, *Index of Federal Specifications, Standards and Commercial Item Descriptions*, FMR 102-27. Online at http://apps.fss.gsa.gov/pub/fedspecs/ (accessed December 2007).
2. Department of Defense, *Department of Defense Single Stock Point for Military Specifications, Standards and Related Publications* (DODSSP). Online at http://dodssp.daps.dla.mil/ (accessed December 2007).
3. Department of Defense, *Acquisition Streamlining and Standardization Information System* (ASSIST). Online at http://assist.daps.dla.mil/online/ (accessed December 2007).
4. American National Standards Institute, "About ANSI." Online at http://www.ansi.org/about_ansi/overview/overview.aspx?menuid=1 (accessed November 2007).
5. General Services Administration, Department of Defense, and National Aeronautics and Space Administration, *Federal Acquisition Regulation,* vol. 1–51, March 2005, 8.405-6. This edition includes the consolidation of all Federal Acquisition Circulars through 2001–27. Online at http://www.arnet.gov/far/reissue/FARvol1ForPaperOnly.pdf (accessed January 2008).
6. Construction Specifications Institute (CSI), *MasterFormat™ 2004 Edition*. Online at http://www.csinet.org/masterformat (accessed December 2007).

Chapter 7

The Level-of-Effort SOW

Teddy Roosevelt always attributed his vitality to childhood illness. Stricken by disease at an early age, he spent months confined to bed and grew up as the weakest of his peers. In adolescence he recovered and almost compulsively sought good health. He exercised, ate well, and spent all his free time outdoors in relentless pursuit of the vigor he came to be known by. His story has always touched a national chord, for Americans are people that prize pushing personal limits. The adage, "If you fail, try, try again," the myth of Horatio Alger, and the children's book *The Little Engine That Could* all speak to the way we value tenacity and perseverance.

As a matter of course, the government is often asked to push the limits of what is known to be possible: to cure polio, to develop a nuclear weapon, to put a man on the moon. In each of these cases, neither performance, functional, nor design statements of work would be appropriate. Each is based on the assumption that what needs to be done is possible.

The level-of-effort SOW gives the government the means to push the limits of what is known to be possible, and to surpass what is considered state-of-the-art at the time. It requires contractors to work toward an end product or service—a strategic defense weapon, for example—with a set amount of resources and along a set path. Success is measured by determining whether or not the contractor applied itself in the intended way, not necessarily by whether the effort produced the intended end product or service.

A cure for cancer or AIDS might be just around the corner, or it might be a long time coming. The cure for these diseases will never come, however, unless resources are spent trying to understand and control them. The level-of-effort SOW gives the government the tools it needs to fund contractors in research and development, while keeping the contractors accountable for their work.

Example: The Department of Energy (DoE) decides to fund basic research into solar energy. The objective of the research is the development of a solar power plant capable of producing electricity for 100,000 homes. The DoE caps the budget at $1,000,000 for the first year. The DoE knows that, absent a stunning breakthrough, $1,000,000 will not produce enough information to begin development of a solar power plant. Nonetheless, it wants to spend the $1,000,000 since it is committed to an ongoing investment in basic research.

The level-of-effort SOW ensures that the contractor is both directed and accountable.

Planning

Converting the project plans into a level-of-effort SOW is a matter of setting priorities. Because resources are limited, the government's strategy should be to isolate chunks of activity that can be funded at available levels. To do this, review the list of tasks and determine a cost for each. Second, determine which tasks cannot be undertaken until certain other prerequisite tasks are completed. Finally, frame a project which can be completely funded with available resources. When tasks build on each other sequentially, this is a relatively simple process. Allocate all funding to the first task until it is complete; move on to the second task only when the first task is complete.

When a number of tasks have equal claim on resources, decide whether to allocate all the agency's resources to one task or spread them over several. This is essentially a strategic decision that should be made in consultation with others and using an agency's best professional judgment.

Whether pushing hard on one task or moving steadily forward on a number of fronts, be sure to think clearly about the staff and support that will be necessary to fulfill objectives. The level-of-effort SOW is in essence a specification of allocated resources toward a particular end. Return to the breakdown of each task by skills, and use that information to build a package of job descriptions or areas of expertise, which, if filled, would move the project toward its objective.

Example: The U.S. Department of Agriculture (USDA) needs to know more about grains that were native to the Great Plains 100 years ago. The USDA believes these strains will do less damage to the soils than modern imported hybrid varieties. The agency decides to contract out for research into native grain varieties, with possible subsequent development. The worksheet it produces from the ten-step planning process might look like this:

Objective: Develop a variety of wheat that will not require intense plowing or fertilization.

Element 1: Research grass types native to the Great Plains

- Task: Gather samples from 100 sites
  - *Area of Expertise*: Horticulture
  - *Time*: 800 hours
- Task: Analyze genetic make-up of samples
  - *Area of Expertise*: Plant genetics
  - *Time*: 1,000 hours
- Task: Reproduce samples in controlled environment
  - *Area of Expertise*: Horticulture
  - *Time*: 500 hours
- Task: Test soils for impact
  - *Area of Expertise*: Soils geology
  - *Time*: 200 hours

After pricing each task, the USDA decides to fund all of Element 1. When the project manager sits down to draft a level-of-effort SOW, the first step is to convert each planning estimate of expertise, time, money, and hardware into an estimate of resources:

Task	Resource Estimate
1. Gather samples	One Ph.D. in botany and ten assistants with training in plant identification; one greenhouse
2. Analyze samples	One Ph.D. in plant genetics and five assistants; one laboratory

Task	Resource Estimate
3. Reproduce samples	Two specialists in wild species cultivation; one greenhouse
4. Test soils	Two Ph.D.s in soil geology; one laboratory.

The description of the resource estimate becomes the level-of-effort SOW requirement.

Requirements

Level-of-effort requirements are most often expressed in terms of work and resources directed toward an end. This type of SOW lets the contractor know that the objective—to develop a better hepatitis vaccine, for example—will be difficult or even impossible to achieve, but that the contractor should be prepared to commit a specified amount of resources to work along a prescribed path toward that end.

Requirements in a level-of-effort SOW also describe methodology. The SOW requires the contractor to follow the process wherever it leads, for as long as the resources last.

Example: The U.S. Mint wants to sponsor basic research into long-lasting paper types for possible use in the production of paper currency. In its SOW, the U.S. Mint describes how the research should proceed. Its plan might read as follows:

Objective: Develop long-lasting paper types for possible use in the production of paper currency.
Task: Collect sample papers from other countries
Task: Analyze fiber content
Task: List bonding characteristics of various fibers
Task: Reproduce fiber types synthetically

The contractor is given detailed instructions on how the research should proceed but is left to determine the best way to accomplish each task.

Delivery

A deliverable is normally what the government expects to receive upon completion of a contract. Because the government's ultimate objective might not be realized in a particular contract (e.g., the cure of AIDS), it is doubly important to be specific about government expectations. Specify milestones, reports, and due dates in detail.

Research funded by the government is the property of the government, even though the research is typically conducted by a contractor. Therefore, in addition to requiring a final report and perhaps a detailed recommendation on how the agency should proceed, require the contractor to deliver all gathered and analyzed data. This is particularly important when future contracts are likely to be issued with similar objectives. Instead of asking the second contractor to start over, the government can provide the original data produced under the first contract. See FAR Part 35 for more on this matter.[1]

Progress and Compliance

For level-of-effort SOWs, measuring compliance is difficult. It is frequently unclear how a level-of-effort project will end. Despite this difficulty, it is critical to measure compliance in one form or another. Typically, level-of-effort SOW writers require periodic reports from their contractors. On-site tours or inspections may be required.

Another option is the peer review. This method is widespread outside the contracting world, particularly in the administration of academic grants. Peer reviews in the context of contracting can occur two ways:

- **Government-based.** The project manager (PM) sets up a group of either in-house or specially invited outside experts. The PM then requires in the SOW that the contractor submit periodic reports of its findings to this panel, which may be empowered in various degrees to give the contractor constructive feedback.
- **Contractor-based.** In the second approach, the SOW requires the contractor to set up a peer-based review as part of its proposal. Essentially, the review works the same as the government-based approach, except that the administration of the review is required of the contractor.

The Phased Alternative: Milestones

A second approach to writing level-of-effort SOWs is the phased method. The government defines project phases that allow research to move forward only after the government approves each stage. Instead of specifying requirements, delivery, and compliance, the government defines milestones or phases.

A phased approach allows the government to have significant input into later stages of a project, having first had a chance to review preliminary findings. This makes for a more flexible SOW, one that may change based on the direction the research takes. It also provides the government a failsafe. If the results of an early phase don't meet government expectations, it can opt out of subsequent phases. One approach to writing a phased SOW is to create three phases: information gathering, planning and validation, and development.

Phase I: Information Gathering

The emphasis in the first phase is on information. During this phase, the contractor collects data, conducts background research, and in general, collects information that will be useful in deciding how best to proceed.

Example: The Internal Revenue Service (IRS) wants to develop a software program to run all its collections, and expresses this need in the form of a phased level-of-effort SOW. The first phase instructs the contractor to gather aggregate data such as the total number of IRS collections, the average amount of information stored in each account, and the various demands that agency personnel make on that information—or how frequently IRS personnel will reference or require use of this data. The IRS defines this information-gathering as Phase I; it cannot decide how to proceed intelligently until this data is received.

Phase II: Planning and Validation

In the second phase, data generated in the first phase is used to outline strategies and options. This step can also have an evaluation component. The government may inspect a prototype or do a test sampling to validate proposed methodologies. This phase should also include the development of a schedule for further work.

Example: In this second phase, the IRS settles on an approach to meet its needs and firmly defines the project. The IRS wants to have the contractor define exactly how the new software system will work and be used. This allows the agency to cancel the contract if the product is not what it needs or is too expensive.

Phase III: Development

The third phase of this SOW type is generally the largest and most expensive. In Phase III, the contractor is responsible for implementing the plan approved after Phase II. Monitor this phase closely through a combination of progress reports and schedule updates.

Example: In this third phase, the software development commissioned by the IRS would actually begin.

NOTE

1. General Services Administration, Department of Defense, and National Aeronautics and Space Administration, *Federal Acquisition Regulation*, vol. 1-51, March 2005, Part 35–Research and Development Contracts. This edition includes the consolidation of all Federal Acquisition Circulars through 2001-27. Online at http://www.arnet.gov/far/reissue/FARvol1ForPaperOnly.pdf (accessed January 2008).

Chapter 8

The Statement of Objectives

This guide would not be complete without addressing the statement of objectives (SOO), which is an alternative to the performance work statement (PWS) in performance-based service contracting. Although using an SOO is not a new concept, it has gained new relevance in the past several years, particularly in situations when it's difficult to define performance metrics and measurements. This alternative is used primarily when the government wants to provide potential offerors with maximum flexibility, to propose the most creative and innovative approach possible.

Defining the SOO

Section 5 of the 1996 Department of Defense *Handbook for Preparation of SOWs* defines the SOO as follows:

> *The SOO is a Government prepared document incorporated into the RFP that states the overall solicitation objectives. It can be used in those solicitations where the intent is to provide the maximum flexibility to each offeror to propose an innovative development approach. Offerors use the RFP, product*

> *performance requirements, and SOO as a basis for preparing their proposals including a SOW and CDRL. Note: The SOO is not retained as a contract compliance item.*
>
> *The program SOO should provide the basic, top-level objectives of the acquisition and is provided in the RFP in lieu of a Government-written SOW. This approach provides potential offerors the flexibility to develop cost-effective solutions and the opportunity to propose innovative alternatives meeting the stated objectives. It also presents the Government with an opportunity to assess the offeror's understanding of all aspects of the effort to be performed, by eliminating the 'how-to' instructions to accomplish the required effort normally contained in the SOW the Government provides to prospective offerors.*[1]

In 2001, a group of volunteers from across the federal government joined together to participate in a project known as the *Seven Steps to Performance-Based Acquisition.*[2] This project also addressed the SOO concept and defined it as follows:

> *The alternative process—use of a SOO—is a more recent methodology that turns the acquisition process around and requires competing contractors to develop the performance work statement, performance metrics and measurement plan, and quality assurance plan... all of which should be evaluated before contract award. If the SOO approach is used, FAR 37.602(c) directs us to remove the SOO when the contract or task order is awarded, and replace it with the awardee's winning PWS.*

> *The SOO is a very short document (e.g., under ten pages) that provides the basic, high-level objectives of the acquisition. It is provided in the solicitation in lieu of a government-written statement of work or performance work statement.*
>
> *In this approach, the contractors' proposals contain statements of work and performance metrics and measures (which are based on their proposed solutions and existing commercial practices). Clearly, use of a SOO opens the acquisition up to a wider range of potential solutions.*[3]

The SOO does not replace the SOW. The DoD *Handbook for Preparation of SOWs* also states:

> *The SOO should not address each WBS element, but each WBS element should be traceable to something in the SOO. For example, a SOO may instruct the bidder to address his engineering approach. That is not a particular WBS element, but several WBS elements might be created to break out the engineering tasks. Generally, a broad and sweeping objective statement will trace to more WBS elements than would be the case for a very narrowly focused objective statement.*[4]

Potential offerors use the SOO, along with other information and guidance provided in the RFP, to develop the contract work breakdown structure, SOW, and other documentation supporting their proposals. The SOO should be clear and concise in defining the objectives of the work effort, and it should provide the potential offerors with sufficient information to structure a sound response and satisfy the government's objectives. Once the contract is awarded, the SOO is then replaced by the offeror's proposed SOW.

SOO Format

Although there is no standard format for the SOO, FAR 37.602(c) states that the following elements must be included:[5]

- Purpose
- Scope or mission
- Period and place of performance
- Background
- Performance objectives (required results)
- Operating constraints

Purpose

This section provides a brief description of the problem and how the acquisition fits into the agency's overall program or mission. A sample Veterans Administration (VA) SOO provided on the *Seven Steps* website states the purpose of a task order the following way: "The purpose of this task order is to obtain loan servicing in support of the VA's portfolio that will significantly improve loan guaranty operations and service to its customers."[6] This statement is very simple and straightforward; any potential offeror should know that the VA has a need for loan servicing support services.

Scope or Mission

This section provides a brief description of the magnitude of the work effort, without being detailed or prescriptive. The scope statement from the VA SOO example in the *Seven Steps* website is as follows:

> *The purpose of this delivery order is to provide the full range of loan servicing support. This includes such activities as customer management, paying taxes and insurance, default management, accounting, foreclosure, bankruptcy, etc., as well as future actions associated with loan servicing. This Statement of Objectives reflects current VA policies and practices, allowing offerors to propose and price a solution to known requirements. It is anticipated that specific loan servicing requirements and resulting objectives will change over the life of this order. This will result in the VA modifying this order to incorporate in-scope changes.*[7]

The scope statement may also include language regarding the funding authority for the acquisition. This will allow potential offerors to propose solutions that are as competitive and realistic as possible, within the limits of available funding for the acquisition.

Period and Place of Performance

This section describes where and when the work outlined in the SOO will be performed. The period of performance includes, but is not limited to, information on the work's time frame, the maximum number of labor hours, and planned milestones. The place of performance describes the work's location or delivery site. This includes providing the specific address of the location and any other pertinent information that would assist the potential offerors in understanding where the work must occur. It is important to identify the location of the work, because it could impact how the offerors propose to do the work.

Background

This section describes the background and current environment as it relates to the acquisition. This information will assist the potential offerors in understanding the current state of the environment and provide them with a foundation for conducting their due diligence. The background could include, but is not limited to, elements such as the history of the work completed to date, past problems or issues, mission, history, and structure of the organization, current issues and constraints, and current policies, procedures, methodologies, and processes.

The VA SOO provides the following background information:[8]

- VA loan servicing history
- Current VA portfolio origination/acquisition process
- Overview of the current servicing process

Performance Objectives (Required Results)

This section describes project objectives and performance measurement plans. This includes describing how project quality, cost, and adherence to the schedule will be measured. Success criteria may also be defined, to clearly identify for all potential offerors what objectives must be met for the work to be considered successful.

The VA SOO describes its performance objectives as follows:

> *VA expects to improve its current loan servicing operations through this task order in several ways. Primary among these is to increase the number and value of saleable loans. In addition, VA wants to be assured that all payments for such items as taxes and insurance are always paid on time. As part of these activities, the VA also has an objective to improve Information Technology data exchange, improving VA's access to information on an as-needed basis and improving VA's ability to meet customer needs and to respond to auditors' requirements."*[9]

Operating Constraints

This section describes all constraints that may negatively impact the successful completion of a project. A constraint is defined as any event or situation that may:

- Prevent the service provider from delivering the services or products required
- Limit the availability of alternative solutions
- Inhibit the client from meeting their obligations

In his book *Project Management Terms: A Working Glossary*, J. LeRoy Ward offers a similar, but slightly more detailed definition of constraints:

> *(1) a restriction that affects the scope of the project, usually with regard to availability, assignment, or use of project cost, schedule, or resources; (2) any factor that affects when or how an activity can be scheduled; or (3) any factor that limits the project team's options and can lead to pressure and resulting frustrations among team members.*[10]

Constraints on a project may include the budget, security, facilities, geography, and/or resources. Any constraints identified in the SOO must be considered as a potential risk by offerors, and should be addressed accordingly in their proposals.

The Relationship between the SOO and the RFP

Upon completion, the SOO will be integrated into Sections L and M of the RFP issued for the acquisition. These sections describe the government's intention to evaluate the proposed SOW. According to the DoD *Handbook for Preparation of SOWs*, "Section L includes provisions and other information or instructions to guide bidders/offerors in preparing their offers or bids in a manner that is responsive to the government's RFP. Section M identifies the factors that will be considered in awarding the contract [and it] contains the evaluation criteria listed in order of importance and other factors for award."[11] In addition, the offeror's contract work breakdown structure (CWBS), SOW, and contract data requirements list (CDRL) will be evaluated as critical elements in assessing the offeror's understanding of both required products and/or services, and the work effort required to accomplish them.[12]

Section L

The complete SOO is included in Section L of the RFP. This section includes instructions to the offerors that require the use of the SOO to construct and submit an SOW and CDRL. The DoD *Handbook for Preparation of SOWs* provides the following sample set of instructions:[13]

> *The Statement of Objectives (SOO), included as (cite location of SOO in the RFP), provides the Government's overall objectives for this solicitation. Offerors shall use the SOO, together with other applicable portions of this RFP, as the basis for preparing their proposal, including the CWBS, SOW, and CDRL. The offeror shall ensure all aspects of the SOO are addressed. The SOW should specify in clear, understandable terms the work to be done in developing or producing the goods to be delivered or services to be performed by the contractor.*
>
> *Preparation of an effective SOW requires both an understanding of the goods or services that are needed to satisfy a particular requirement and an ability to define what is required in specific, performance-based, quantitative terms. The offeror's understanding of both required goods/services, and work effort required to accomplish, should be fully demonstrated in the offeror's proposed CWBS, SOW, and CDRL. For complex interrelationships among RFP/contract documents, use of a cross-reference matrix may be helpful (see figure 2 in Section 3 of this handbook).*
>
> *The offeror shall use his proposed SOW to prepare a CDRL including appropriately tailored data item description refer-*

ences. The requirements listed below (if any) are known minimum Government data requirements. The offeror may include additional data requirements. All data requirements shall be traceable to specific tasks defined in the SOW. Each specific data requirement shall be selected from DoD 5010.12-L and specified on DD Form 1423.

(1) (cite minimum data requirements here if any)

(2) . . .

(3) . . .

Section M

Section M of the RFP will describe the evaluation criteria that will be used to determine awardees. According to the DoD *Handbook for Preparation of SOWs*, the evaluation criteria should be sufficient enough to: (1) evaluate the offeror's ability to successfully achieve the SOO objectives, (2) ensure a sound approach is proposed, and (3) verify that all requirements can be met.[14]

An SOO Preparation Guide developed by the U.S. Air Force further states, "When writing Section M evaluation criteria, the program office should include sufficient criteria for evaluating the offerors ability to reflect the objectives of the SOO in the resulting proposal (i.e., SOW, Integrated Master Plan (IMP), CWBS). Since the concept of asking the contractor to propose an SOW without strict guidance is new, the government's intention to evaluate the proposed SOW should be stressed in Sections L and M."[15]

A Sample SOO

Figure 8.1 provides a sample SOO for the NEXRAD Radar Product Generators (RPGs).[16] This sample illustrates one way of formatting an SOO, and offers an example of the type of language an SOO may use.

Figure 8.1 NEXRAD Radar Product Generators (RPGs) SOO Sample

NEXRAD Radar Product Generators (RPGs) SOO

Task Title:	**Work Authorization for Special Project Work under COMMITS Task Order #56CMNW000009 (Title: ORPG Program Completion)**
COMMITS Tracking #:	**SOM00004/S06**
Contracting Officer:	
COTR Name:	
Task Manager:	
Location:	Radar Operations Center, National Weather Service Norman, OK
Performance Period:	Start: January 1, 2001 End: June 30, 2001
Funding Citation for Work:	WE0100 2MFLN62E

STATEMENT OF OBJECTIVES

This requirement supports an upgrade to NEXRAD Radar Product Generators (RPGs) that has been an ongoing design, development, and testing effort. Technical contract support was previously provided through another contract vehicle. The contractor will be required to complete development, testing, system support preparation, and deployment management.

The effort requires the contractor to complete ORPG hardware documentation, system transition plan, hardware DT&E plans and procedures, execute the DT&E test plans and procedures, address anomalous results of testing, produce reports documenting the result of testing, and support ORPG production and deployment. The contractor shall also support the generation of reports documenting project status related to development and production. Development activities are expected to continue up to and including ORPG Functional Configuration Audit (FCA) and ORPG Physical Configuration Audit (PCA). Production activities will proceed until approximately six months following the completion of deployment.

Figure 8.1 NEXRAD Radar Product Generators (RPGs) SOO Sample (continued)

TASK PERFORMANCE EVALUATION CRITERIA (Performance Measures)

General measures of contract performance are:

1. Quality Level of Effort
   a. On-time delivery
   b. Customer satisfaction rating
   c. Innovative approaches to problem solving (e.g., cost avoidance)
2. Schedule Performance
   a. Progress against milestone schedule and creative approaches to achieving schedule
   b. Timely notification of schedule issues, accompanied by recommendations for corrective action.
3. Cost Performance
   a. Timely notification of cost overruns/underruns

MILESTONES, ADMINISTRATION, AND REPORTING

— Test Plans, Procedures, and Reports - 30 days prior to beginning of ORPG System test
— Hardware Documentation - 1/5/2001
— System Transition Plan - 1/15/2001
— Project Status Reports - Weekly
— PPL- 2/1/2001
— IPB -2/1/2001
— Retrofit Management Plan - 2/1/2001

The contractor shall provide all invoices for work that is performed to the COTR for processing.

PLACE OF PERFORMANCE

Work shall be performed at the ROC at 3200 Marshall Avenue in Norman, OK 73072, with frequent visits to the ROC test beds at 1200 Westheimer Avenue in Norman, OK 73069. Telephonic coordination with the NRC and NLSC at 1520 East Bannister Road, Kansas City, MO 64131-3009 may be necessary. If the contractor determines that travel is needed, the contractor shall receive written Government authorization prior to initiating any travel under this SOW. The ROC will provide workspace and computer resources for contractor staff.

PERIOD OF PERFORMANCE

The total contractor staff time for this work assignment shall not exceed 10,500 hours, not including management hours. For significant milestones, see the section: MILESTONES, ADMINISTRATION, AND REPORTING.

Figure 8.1 NEXRAD Radar Product Generators (RPGs) SOO Sample (continued)

DELIVERY FORMAT

Three paper copies of each draft of items 2 through 6 as listed above, along with an electronic copy on 3 two-inch floppy disks or via email, the final decision on electronic media being at the discretion of the Government. For the electronic version of the written deliverables: the text, graphics, and forms portions shall be in Word Perfect 9.0 format; the schedule portion shall be in Microsoft Project 98 format; drawings and diagrams shall be in drawing exchange format (DXF).

Permission to deliver any other electronic format shall be requested in writing and deviation will be allowed only if written Government concurrence is provided in advance of delivery. Hardware drawings and software documentation shall be released in a manner consistent with ROC CM requirements.

NOTES

1. Department of Defense, *Department of Defense Handbook for Preparation of Statement of Work (SOW)*, MIL-HDBK-245D, 3 April 1996, Section 5–Statement of Objectives (SOO) Method. Online at http://www.dla.mil/DSS/dss-a/download/DoD%20SOW%20Handbook.pdf (accessed January 2008).
2. An Interagency-Industry Partnership in Performance: Department of Agriculture, Department of Commerce, Department of Defense, Department of the Treasury, General Services Administration, and Acquisitions Solutions, Inc., *Seven Steps to Performance-Based Acquisition.* Online at http://www.acqnet.gov/comp/seven_steps/home.html (accessed December 2007).
3. Ibid.
4. *Department of Defense Handbook for Preparation of Statement of Work (SOW)*, 28.
5. General Services Administration, Department of Defense, and National Aeronautics and Space Administration, *Federal Acquisition Regulation*, vol. 1–51, March 2005, 37.602. This edtion includes the consolidation of all Federal Acquisition Circulars through 2001-27. Online at http://www.arnet.gov/far/reissue/FARvol1ForPaperOnly.pdf (accessed January 2008).
6. *Seven Steps to Performance-Based Acquisition,* "VBA Loan Servicing SOO," September 8, 2000, 7. Online at http://www.acquisition.gov/comp/seven_steps/library/VBAsoo.pdf (accessed December 2007).
7. Ibid.

8. Ibid.
9. Ibid.
10. J. LeRoy Ward, *Project Management Terms: A Working Glossary* (Arlington, VA: ESI International, 1997), 30.
11. *Department of Defense Handbook for Preparation of Statement of Work (SOW)*, 5.
12. Ibid., 28.
13. Ibid., 27.
14. Ibid., 27–28.
15. *Seven Steps to Performance-Based Acquisition,* "SOO Preparation Guide," 3. Online at http://www.acquisition.gov/comp/seven_steps/library/DOAFsoo-prep.pdf (accessed December 2007).
16. *Seven Steps to Performance-Based Acquisition,* "Commerce NEXRAD SOO," October 21, 2001. Online at http://www.acqnet.gov/comp/seven_steps/library/COMsoo.pdf (accessed January 2008).

Chapter 9

Defining Evaluation Criteria

The FAR permits contracting staff to evaluate bids on a basis other than cost, stating:

This process permits tradeoffs among cost or price and non-cost factors and allows the Government to accept bids other than the lowest priced proposal. The perceived benefits of the higher priced proposal shall merit the additional cost, and the rationale for tradeoffs must be documented in the file in accordance with 15.406.[1]

Example: If the Office of Management and Budget (OMB) decides to upgrade its computers, it might choose a performance statement of work to express its needs. This performance SOW permits the OMB to describe how it wants its computers to perform without having to tell firms how to build the machines. Accordingly, it might specify that the computer should be able to handle the federal budget (capacity) while also being able to run macro-economic analysis (capability). But when describing the desired operation speed, the

> OMB might find that it needs a computer that runs as fast as possible. The performance SOW will not work in this case, because it is limited to expressing specific quantities and is unable to express the need for a computer that exceeds modern standards.

Evaluation criteria can help in situations like this, because they offer special instructions to contracting staff on how to evaluate proposals. Evaluation criteria are special instructions to contracting staff on how to evaluate proposals. Using evaluation criteria, the OMB can direct its contracting staff to give preference to the contractor that offers the fastest machine.

Three reasons to employ evaluation criteria include:

- **Contract considerations.** The competitively bid cost-reimbursement contract almost always requires evaluation criteria. This type of contract, generally used for services or research and development, is open-ended and promises to reimburse a contractor for its efforts upon project completion.

  Cost-reimbursement contracts awarded on the basis of cost alone are likely to generate unrealistically low bids. Because the contractor knows that it will receive both a fee and expense reimbursements, it has no incentive to accurately predict its costs. In fact, if cost were the only criteria, the contracting firm would have an incentive to underestimate costs to win the award, knowing that its estimate would not affect its final payment. In these cases, the government must provide evaluation criteria other than cost to the contracting office.

- **Production considerations.** The manner in which a contractor fills an order is often important to consider. An agency might write an SOW that calls for the purchase of a steady supply of USDA Grade-A veal. Concerns about the calves' treatment might cause the agency to stipulate in the evaluation criteria a preference to contractors that can demonstrate they will not be unnecessarily cruel to animals during production.
- **Design considerations.** Performance SOWs define product sufficiency (e.g., the car accelerates to at least 55 mph and weighs not more than 2 tons). Sometimes sufficiency, however, is not enough. The government often needs the very best—the fastest, the lightest, or the longest lasting. Because performance SOWs cannot express superlatives, the SOW writer must write these provisions into the evaluation criteria.

Criteria Categories

Three categories of evaluation criteria include go/no-go criteria, qualifications criteria, and scored criteria. This chapter describes each category, gives advice to help choose appropriate criteria, and explains how to express the relative weight of each criterion when more than one is required.

Go/No-Go Criteria

If some characteristics are missing from a product, it will prevent the product from doing its job. These characteristics or attributes can be used as a litmus test for potential bidders. If the contractor's proposal includes the attributes, the product can be considered and the proposals are given the "go." If the proposal doesn't include the attributes, the product is automatically disqualified or given a "no-go."

Example: A functional SOW issued by the Federal Emergency Management Agency (FEMA) calls for proposals to put out a wildfire in California. But because FEMA is concerned about extreme drought conditions in the region, it stipulates that any bid that incorporates water in its proposed solution should be ruled out. All water-based solutions fail the litmus test and are given a no-go status.

Qualifications Criteria

Qualifications criteria are a variation of the go/no-go criteria. If the proposal won't minimally satisfy the government's needs unless the contractor's team possesses certain qualifications, these qualifications may be stated as an evaluation criterion.

Example: The United States Agency for International Development (USAID) wants to ship tractors to needy countries, and describes the tractors' performance specifications in the SOW's requirements section. In addition, USAID requires the contractor to have a sufficient plant capacity to handle an order of between 10,000 and 100,000 tractors, and includes that requirement in the notes and information section as a criterion for evaluation.

Scored Criteria

Scored criteria can help when it's necessary to maximize a certain product or service characteristic. Scoring should not be confused with weighting, which gives the relative weights of several different criteria. Instead, scoring ranks each contractor with respect to just one product or service characteristic. For example, if the government needs the best, fastest, or most experienced contractor in a field, it can rate and score all potential bidders, awarding the contract to the bidder with the highest score.

Example: When the Army contracts out for a new ad campaign to promote enlistment, it decides that rather than the cheapest agency, it wants the best, most creative agency it can find. In writes a functional SOW calling for a campaign targeted to 18-year-olds, it establishes a criterion that will help it hire the best in the business. It states that past work, industry awards, and a proven ability to orchestrate large campaigns will be taken into consideration when ranking a field of qualified bidders by merit.

Writing Evaluation Criteria

Establishing evaluation criteria is a balancing act. The SOW writer walks on a tightrope between concerns about hiring a qualified contractor and concerns about preserving a competitive bidding climate. Overly restrictive criteria will unfairly restrict competition. But if the criteria are overly broad, the government could end up with a contractor that is unable to fulfill the job's objectives.

The following four-step process can help SOW writers think about what does and does not constitute fair criteria:

1. Recall the problem.
2. Define the problem's solution acceptance criteria.
3. Compare the worst-case scenario to the solution. (i.e., a worst-case scenario occurs when all of the tasks identified within the requirements section of the SOW are completed as defined but the problem still exists. This comparison may help uncover additional tasks needed to ensure a minimally acceptable solution.)
4. Determine who or what can help.

Recall the Problem

Recall the problem you defined when planning the SOW. The government can only exclude potential contractors from bidding on a contract if they are absolutely unable to meet the government's minimum requirements. The problem defined in the SOW should describe those minimally acceptable requirements.

Example: A Nuclear Regulatory Commission (NRC) project manager is concerned about the squirrels running around in the attic of the Commission's headquarters. They are into everything, chewing up old records and damaging the roof. In this case, squirrels are the problem.

Define the Problem's Solution Acceptance Criteria

Break the problem down into constituent parts. Ask yourself, "How would I know if this problem were solved? What conditions must exist for the government to be free of this problem?" The project manager in the previous example might conclude that only ridding the attic of squirrels completely will solve the government's problem.

Defining the solution to a problem gives you half the information you need. It identifies a standard of acceptability to measure proposed solutions against. There is, however, a critical difference between defining the solution and defining a minimally acceptable solution. To define a minimally acceptable solution, ask yourself, "What would have to happen for me to know I had *not* solved the government's problem?" The NRC project manager might conclude, for example, that the presence of even one squirrel would mean the problem had not been solved. This, in turn, could be the minimally acceptable solution to this problem.

Compare the Worst-Case Scenario to the Solution

Review each of the tasks included in the SOW section on requirements. Cumulatively, they represent the way you intend to solve the problem. Ask yourself, "Is there a case where even if each of the tasks is performed as specified, the minimally defined problem will still persist?" This is the worst-case scenario.

In the NRC example, the project manager might worry that even if the exterminator sprayed the attic (one of the tasks), and the carpenter rebuilt the screens (another task), a hole might be missed that could let one or more squirrels enter (minimally unacceptable). Therefore, these tasks inadequately cover everything that needs to happen to solve the problem. When the tasks are inadequate in this way, it's important to develop evaluation criteria.

Determine Who or What Could Help

To do determine how to resolve any loopholes in the project plan, ask yourself three questions:

1. "Can I design another task that will close the loophole?" If so, add the new task(s). Another specification is better than an unneeded constraint on competition.
2. "Could a professional with particular qualifications ensure that the loophole is closed?" If so, specifying this type of professional is a valid evaluation criterion.
3. Finally, "Could one or more qualities in the product or service, if maximized, close the loophole?" If so, then these qualities are also evaluation criteria.

Our NRC project manager might conclude that specifying qualifications is the best hedge against failure, stipulating that only contractors with extensive experience in rodent control need apply. Alternatively, the project manager might conclude that maximizing a product attribute is the best bet, including an evaluation criterion calling for the longest-acting exterminating spray.

Figure 9.1 offers a list of typical evaluation criteria.

Figure 9.1 Typical Proposal Evaluation Criteria

Not all proposal evaluation criteria are technical; they don't all require a technical response or an evaluation by technical personnel. The following basic criteria represent those frequently used in evaluating research and development procurements. A series of questions follows each criterion, which evaluators can use to assess critical matters.

The proposal demonstrates an understanding of the work's scope and offers a sound approach to accomplish the work.

- Does the offeror clearly indicate an understanding of each task and the problems that could be encountered in its fulfillment?
- Does the offeror represent the manner in which each task can be satisfactorily accomplished?
- Are the proposed solutions logical and reasonable? Will they meet the objectives stated in the RFP?
- Does the offeror propose a unique or novel solution which could result in a marked advance of industry standards?

The proposal is complete and thorough in its compliance with all work statement elements and with other RFP requirements.

- Are the proposal's organization and content in accordance with instructions?
- Are all data presented relevant to specifications in the RFP?
- Does the proposal thoroughly identify, describe, define, and consider each element of the specification?
- Does the offeror recognize and place proper emphasis on the more difficult requirements?
- Is the proposal presented in a clear and precise manner?

The proposal demonstrates a commitment to fulfilling specification requirements within a realistic project schedule.

- Does the proposal contain a schedule for the project that includes the accomplishment of each task given in the work statement?
- Does the proposed performance schedule indicate realistically the satisfactory accomplishment of the task in accordance with the specified timeframe?
- Does the proposal indicate that the offeror is willing to commit its resources to fulfilling the requirements of the work statement?

The proposal indicates the offeror's capability, responsibility, and past performance in similar programs.

- Does the proposal indicate sufficient breadth and depth of management capability for accomplishing proposed tasks?
- Does the offeror have previous experience in performing government contracts in similar programs?

Can the Contractor Do the Job?

Another question to consider is whether the contractor is capable of doing the job. Evaluation criteria concerning a contractor's capability fall into three categories:

- **Performance**—the offeror's plans for performing the contract work
- **Organization**—the characteristics of the offeror as a firm
- **Proposal**—the firm's proposal

Performance

In the performance category, evaluation criteria may include:

- The technical merit and appropriateness of techniques, processes, and tests the offeror plans to use. The greater the degree of such technical merit and appropriateness given in the proposal, the greater the apparent advantage to the government.
- The character of the facilities the offeror plans to devote to the contract work—qualities that are important to successful performance, such as accuracy, capacity, capability, and appropriateness of layout.
- The appropriateness, realism, comprehensiveness, and technical soundness of a contractor's detailed plan and schedule for carrying out the contract work. The completeness of detail, sequence of planned operations, timing and

duration of testing, and time allowed for various phases of the work may significantly bear on the risk of technical failure and delay. Generally, the time of delivery itself is not evaluated, but in some cases the value of early delivery may warrant selecting a more costly proposal.

- The merit of the offeror's plan for managing the project and related contract administration. Among other factors in this regard, it may be pertinent to evaluate the following:
  —The detail and thoroughness of the offeror's project management approach or methodology
  —The degree to which the offeror's management plan has established well-defined lines of authority, responsibility, and communications
  —How swiftly the organization can respond to technical changes and mobilize to resolve problems
  —How well the offeror's management techniques can be expected to identify performance problems at an early stage and help work around subcontractor delays and similar problems

Organization

In the firm category, criteria may include:

- The qualifications of key personnel the offeror plans to employ, including the availability, competency, pertinent education, and related experience of a firm's technical personnel. These factors are generally important in the success of a contract project. For example, are the offeror's project managers certified project management professionals

(PMPs®)? The experience and ability of key administrative personnel are also important.

- In some cases, a firm may be more or less qualified, or particularly well qualified, because of resources organizationally available to the firm (perhaps through affiliates).
- The offeror has a sound and thorough understanding of the problems involved in the work. The offeror's grasp of the difficulties and problems involved in performing a particular job reflects its qualification to perform the job well. The offeror possesses technical qualifications to perform the work (often the offeror's understanding of the work is stated as a separate criterion, although it is essentially an indicator of qualification).
- The extent of the offeror's past experience in carrying out similar work.
- The quality of the offeror's past performance in carrying out similar work, with reference especially to timelines, cost control, and technical success.

Proposal

RFPs sometimes include the completeness and responsiveness of the offeror's proposal as an evaluation criterion, which tells the contracting officer that each task must be covered comprehensively in the proposal. This does not mean, however, that the government is interested in receiving unnecessarily elaborate proposals. In fact, at times the RFP may specifically state that such verboseness is unwanted.

Weighting

When more than one criterion is listed, provide guidance to the contracting office as to the relative weight of each criterion. In other words, not all criteria are considered equal: some are more important to the success of the project than others. In turn, achieving these criteria will be weighted more heavily during the evaluation process. Even when there is only one specified criterion, such as the delivery date, for example, tell the contracting staff how important that criterion is in relation to the need to accept the lowest bidder. The lowest bidder may not be able to deliver the product or service within the desired delivery date. Thus, in order to get the product or service delivered on time, it may be necessary to make an award to a contractor who is not the lowest bidder but can meet the delivery date. Weighing protocols tells the contracting officer how to emphasize various evaluation criteria when awarding the contract.

Three main approaches to weighting include the go/no-go approach, the proportional approach, and the ranking approach.

The Go/No-Go Approach

When criterion is so important that the contract cannot be considered acceptable without its inclusion, it is go/no-go. Its weight is greater than all other criteria combined.

The Proportional Approach

The proportional approach assigns relative weights to criteria in proportion to each other. For example, a weight of 75 percent importance given to price and 25 percent given to quality. The NRC project manager, for example, might weight the evaluation criteria in the following way:

Cost	50 percent
Experience	30 percent
Long-lasting spray	20 percent
Total	**100 percent**

To the potential contractor, this chart means that its proposal will be evaluated primarily on the basis of cost, followed by experience and the kind of spray it chooses to use.

The Ranking Approach

The third approach to weighting is to rank criteria in descending order of importance. The NRC project manager could write, for example:

The NRC will evaluate proposal merit against the following criteria, stated in descending order of importance:

1. Cost
2. Experience
3. Length of spray efficacy

Including evaluation criteria in an SOW is a valuable tool. It allows an agency to tell the contracting office what—other than price—should go into award decisions. In doing so, it further ensures that the winning contractor will be sufficiently qualified to provide what is minimally acceptable to the government.

With this last building block in place, you'll be ready to begin writing an SOW. But before you sit down and commit pen to paper, it's a good idea to read Chapter 10 very closely. Chapter 10 not only provides guidelines on how to write a quality SOW, it also describes how the law interprets SOWs.

NOTE

1. General Services Administration, Department of Defense, and National Aeronautics and Space Administration, *Federal Acquisition Regulation,* vol. 1-51, March 2005, 15.101-1(c). This edition includes the consolidation of all Federal Acquisition Circulars through 2001-27. Online at http://www.arnet.gov/far/reissue/FARvol1ForPaperOnly.pdf (accessed January 2008).

Chapter 10

Writing the SOW

Mark Twain once said, "The difference between the almost-right word and the right word is really a large matter—it's the difference between the lightning bug and lightning." This quote applies to the writing of the SOW. The SOW must be organized and written clearly to avoid any misinterpretation or confusion among the parties who will refer to it throughout the life of the project, and to help the delivery team manage changes that occur during project delivery.

An SOW essentially tells a contractor to do or provide something. The contractor must be able to understand from reading the SOW what to do or provide. The government doesn't casually offer SOWs to the contractor, to be discarded after one reading. SOWs are working documents that shape the invitation for bid (IFB) or request for proposal (RFP), inform the intelligence of proposals, and ultimately determine the quality of the work performed. The contractor must understand what the government has written and what it means. Because misunderstandings often result in contract disputes, SOW writers should concentrate on being concise, clear, and to the point.

Lawyers should always be considered a potential, if unanticipated, third-party audience. Since the SOW is a supporting document to the legal terms and conditions of the contract, it's important that the legal department be involved in the process. Asking the legal department to review the SOW will help prevent redundancy or contradictions in the language of the SOW. Writing the SOW in precise language will help keep you clear of legal complications. This chapter will help you express yourself clearly and precisely.

The Importance of a Well-Written SOW

Writing is a difficult and time-consuming task. Planning, revising, and giving attention to details all serve writers well. Many useful guides to concise writing are available to help you to write well. Two of the most recognized standards are the University of Chicago's *Chicago Manual of Style*[1] and Strunk and White's *Elements of Style*.[2] The first edition of the *Chicago Manual of Style* was published in 1906 and is updated approximately every 10 years; the manual is currently in its 15th edition. *Elements of Style*, at just over 100 pages, is a quick read and well worth the time for general writing advice. Investing in one of these references will pay tremendous dividends on almost any writer's work.

In drafting the SOW, it doesn't matter what the author meant to say, or what was "understood" or spoken about. It only matters how the document actually reads. A written document is a tangible, lasting form of communication: readers can hold it, look at it, contemplate it, reference it, save it, and interpret it. Other forms of communication, such as body language or the spoken word, do not allow the recipient of the communication the same level of analysis that the written word provides.

Although communication is an important objective of writing, it is not the only one. In their book *Thinking on Paper*, V.A. Howard and J.H. Barton propose, "The first goal of writing, like reading, is to understand; only then can one make that understanding available to others in writing."[3] Writing entails first establishing one's thoughts and then *re*-establishing these thoughts in written form to communicate the intent of the message. If thoughts are not articulated well, then the message will not be successfully communicated to the reader.

This thought process applies to writing an SOW. If the document confuses or misleads the reader, then the project is much more likely to be unsuccessful. Thus, it's imperative that the development team clearly understand the importance of style when writing an SOW, because a well-written SOW will clearly articulate what the government products or services it expects the contractor to deliver.

The SOW will be read and used by a diverse group of people who are directly and indirectly involved in the delivery of the project. This includes individuals from varied backgrounds and disciplines, including engineers, attorneys, contract personnel, accountants, technical specialists, and cost estimators. The SOW must be written clearly and concisely so each representative from these various disciplines can easily understand the intent of the text, without requiring interpretation of the product or service to be delivered. All terms of art and acronyms should also be clearly defined.

The Do's and Don'ts of Writing a Quality SOW

The following paragraphs provide guidelines on the do's and don'ts of writing a quality SOW.

Writing Do's

Use simple and direct language for clarity. Write sentences as short and concisely as possible, without sacrificing clarity. Cut out all vague and ambiguous terms, and use language that is easily understandable to all potential stakeholders. Leave nothing open to interpretation.

Words such as *shall* and *will* fit these criteria. The word *shall* indicates that a requirement the SOW identifies is mandatory and binding. For example, "The contractor *shall* deliver the product within 30 days of the contract execution date." The word *will* may indicate a declaration, on the part of either the government or contractor, to perform or deliver something. For example, "The government *will* provide the contractor with a 10' x 30' work space for its staff."

The words *might, may,* and *should* do not convey this same type of directness, which an SOW requires. These words infer a degree of flexibility and a lack of enforcement, and may be misinterpreted by either the government or contractor. They should not be used in the SOW.

Use the active voice. Write the SOW in an active voice, rather than a passive voice. Active voice implies strength, directness, and clarity; the passive voice is weak and can lead to vague statements, which may be open to misinterpretation. The following sentences illustrate this point:

> *Passive Voice* – "A customized software package for the agency is going to be developed by Company Z."

> *Active Voice* – "Company Z is developing a customized software package for the agency."

Use words that convey a form of action or work function, known as *active work words*, to help maintain the conciseness and clarity of the content. Figure 10.1 provides list of active work words.[4]

Figure 10.1 Active Work Words

Work Word	Meaning	Work Word	Meaning
analyze	(solve by analysis)	inspect	(examine carefully or officially)
annotate	(provide with comments)	install	(place; put into position)
ascertain	(find out with certainty)	institute	(set up; establish, begin)
attend	(be present at)	integrate	(to add parts to make whole)
audit	(officially examine)	interpret	(explain the meaning of)
build	(make by putting together)	investigate	(search into; examine closely)
calculate	(find out by computation)	judge	(decide; form an estimate)
compare	(find out likeness or differences)	make	(cause to come into being)
consider	(think about, to decide)	manufacture	(fabricate from raw materials)
construct	(put together; build)	modify	(to change, alter)
control	(direct; regulate)	monitor	(to watch or observe)

Work Word	Meaning	Work Word	Meaning
contribute	(give along with others)	notice	(comment upon, review)
define	(make clear; settle the limits)	observe	(inspect, watch)
design	(perform an original act)	originate	(initiate, to give rise to)
determine	(resolve; settle; decide)	organize	(integrate, arrange in a coherent unit)
develop	(bring into being or activity)	perform	(do, carry out, accomplish)
differentiate	(make a distinction between)	plan	(devise a scheme for doing, making, arranging activities to achieve)
erect	(put together; set upright)	probe	(investigate, thoroughly)
establish	(set up; settle; prove beyond dispute)	produce	(give birth or rise to)
estimate	(approximate an opinion of)	record	(set down in writing or act of electronic reproduction of communication)
evaluate	(find or fix the value of)	resolve	(reduce by analysis, clear up)
evolve	(develop gradually, work out)	review	(inspection, examination or evaluation)
examine	(look at closely; test quality of)	revise	(to correct, improve)
explore	(examine for discovery)	scan	(look through hastily, examine intently)
extract	(take out; deduce, select)	screen	(to separate, present or shield)
fabricate	(build; manufacture, invent)	search	(examine to find something)
form	(give shape to; establish)	seek	(try to discover; make an attempt)
formulate	(to put together, add, express)	solve	(find an answer)
generate	(produce, cause to be)	test	(evaluate, examine)
identify	(to show or to find)	trace	(to copy or find by searching)

Work Word	Meaning	Work Word	Meaning
implement	(to carry out, put into practice)	track	(observe or plot the path of)
inquire	(ask, make a search of)	update	(modernize, make current)

Use positive and specific words and phrases. When writing SOWs, draft the content using positive words, even when an element may be negative. Negative words such as *do not*, *cannot*, and *will not* should be avoided.

> *Negative* – The contractor *will not* deliver help desk services on the weekend.

> *Positive* – The contractor *will* deliver help desk services every weekday.

Negative words and phrases typically have the word "not" in them. A quick review of the SOW can identify where negative words occur, and then it's possible to replace them with positive words and phrases. The following list illustrates how easy it is to transform a negative phrase into a positive phrase by substituting it with a single word.[5]

Negative Phrase	Positive Word
Do not go fast	Slow down
Do not remember	Forget
Not possible	Impossible
Not known	Unknown
Not sure	Unsure

Giving attention to details like this may be difficult and take time, but using positive and specific words will make the content more direct and specific. It will also make it easier for all parties to read and apply the SOW on the project.

Use technical language sparingly. If the SOW is supporting a technical project, it may be necessary to use some technical language throughout the text to convey the intent of the work. However, make every effort to use the technical language sparingly and defer to simple wording in concise sentences as much as possible.

When considering whether to use technical language, consider whether the document's audience will understand its meaning and application. If not everyone will understand the technical language, then you must take special precautions to draft the SOW in layman terms. Everyone reading the document must understand its purpose and intent.

Another option is to reference the technical design or a similar document to readers to review if they want more information about the technical aspects of the project.

Define acronyms and abbreviations. Spell out all acronyms and abbreviations the first time they occur in an SOW, and give the acronym and abbreviations in parenthesis. This suffices to define them for each subsequent occurrence throughout the rest of the SOW. Each acronym and abbreviation should also be defined in the SOW glossary.[6] This provides a single point of reference to readers, so they can confirm the definition or meaning of the words or phrases.

General writing considerations. The SOW should be as easy to read as possible. Consider these general guidelines when writing the SOW:

- Use 8 ½" x 11" paper.
- Allow sufficient margins, preferably a minimum of one inch on every side of the page. This ensures that the lengths of the lines are kept consistent throughout the document.
- Use an easy-to-read font type and size. 12 point Times New Roman works well in most cases.
- For the initial drafts, double-space the text for easier reading and to provide room for reviewers to make comments. Spacing in the final draft can vary, but for maximum readability, it's best to maintain the double spacing for both the initial and final drafts, if possible. Single-spacing may be necessary to reduce the number of pages when the SOW is unusually long.
- For the initial drafts, number each line so reviewers can correlate their comments directly with a line number in the document, rather than a section number, paragraph, and sentence. Line numbers may be removed from the final draft.

Writing Don'ts

Avoid vague or obscure words and phrases with multiple or legal meanings. Ambiguity is one of the leading causes of deficient SOWs. Ambiguity occurs when terms that have two or more possible meanings are used, or when their meaning is vague, indefinite, or uncertain.[7] Common terms that may cause ambiguity include:

- best effort
- adequate
- excessive
- high quality
- reasonably
- similar
- et cetera (etc.)

Legal words and phrases may also lead to ambiguity. Common legal terms that may cause ambiguity include:

- partnership
- alliance
- guaranty
- insure
- ensure
- assure
- warranty
- warrant

Figure 10.2 provides a list of phrases with multiple meanings. Avoid these phrases when drafting an SOW.[8]

If the meaning of the text is unclear to the reader, the likelihood of misinterpretation by the government, contractor, or any other involved party greatly increases. To illustrate how an ambiguous statement can creep into an SOW, consider the following scenario in which a contractor requires workspace within an agency to adequately deliver a specific service. The following sentences give an ambiguous statement and the correct way to document this requirement in the SOW:

> *Ambiguous* – The government will provide *adequate* space to the contractor through the term of this contract.
>
> *Clear and specific* – The government will provide one 50' x 40' (2000 sq. ft) room to the contractor for a period not to exceed six months from the date of contract approval.

In the first, ambiguous sentence above, the word *adequate* can be perceived differently depending on one's perspective. For instance, the contractor may consider *adequate* to mean at least four work areas, each with a minimum of 500 sq. ft. of space. However, the government may interpret *adequate* to mean only one room consisting of 100 sq. ft.

This example shows how easily one word can make this statement ambiguous and open to interpretation. The second, specific sentence shows how to rectify this ambiguity. It clearly defines the amount of workspace the government will provide to the contractor, when it will be available for the contractor's use, and for how long. Strive to achieve this level of detail and specificity when de-

Figure 10.2 Phrases with Multiple Meanings

Phrases with Multiple Meanings
▸ To the satisfaction of the client ▸ As determined by the client ▸ In accordance with client instructions ▸ As directed by the client ▸ In the opinion of the client ▸ In the judgment of the client ▸ Unless otherwise directed by the client ▸ To furnish if requested by the client ▸ All reasonable requests of the client shall be complied with ▸ Photographs shall be taken when and where directed by the client ▸ In strict accordance with ▸ In accordance with best commercial practice ▸ In accordance with best modern standard practice ▸ In accordance with the best engineering practice ▸ Workmanship shall be of the highest quality ▸ Workmanship shall be of the highest grade ▸ Accurate workmanship ▸ Securely mounted ▸ Installed in a neat and workmanlike manner ▸ Skillfully fitted ▸ Properly connected ▸ Properly assembled ▸ Good working order ▸ Good materials ▸ In accordance with applicable published specifications ▸ Products of a recognized reputable manufacturer ▸ Tests will be made unless waived ▸ Materials shall be of the highest grade, free from defects or imperfections, and of grades approved by the client ▸ Kinks and bends may be cause for rejection ▸ Carefully performed ▸ Neatly finished ▸ Metal parts shall be cleaned before painting ▸ Suitably housed ▸ Smooth surfaces ▸ Pleasing lines ▸ Of an approved type ▸ Of standard type

veloping an SOW.

SOW writers and reviewers frequently overlook ambiguities when working on an SOW. Primarily focused on ensuring that all requirements for delivering a product or service are accurately captured within the document, development and review teams are less focused and concerned with the grammatical correctness of the text defining these requirements. It's commonly not until the project is executed that these inconsistencies are found.

Revising the SOW to correct any ambiguities during project execution can become very expensive, very quickly. Sometimes the correction may be handled through a change order process, but in other cases, litigation may be required to resolve the conflict. If litigation results, it won't matter what the SOW writers meant to say, or what was previously understood or spoken; only what is written in the SOW will matter.

To mitigate against potential ambiguities, it's extremely important that SOW writers put themselves in the position of the contractor or delivery team when reviewing the SOW. Reviewing the document from this perspective will help identify the terms or phrases that may be interpreted differently by various professionals and organizations. Writing the SOW with this point of view in mind will make it much easier for reviewers to identify and correct any ambiguities prior to project execution.

Unfortunately, SOWs are sometimes drafted expeditiously and without much forethought and planning. In these situations, the project begins immediately with a high level of risk and with a high probability of failure. An old saying claims *there's never enough time to do something right, but there's always time to do it over.* Do *not* follow this philosophy when developing an SOW. Taking the time to properly plan and draft the SOW will go a long way in avoiding any ambiguous statements in the final document, which will help you avoid problems during the project later.

Don't hedge. *Hedging* is the act of "hiding behind words, refusing to commit oneself or give a direct answer."[9] SOW writers will often *hedge* the text for the following reasons:

- Unclear project requirements and expectations
- Uncertainty about what will be necessary to deliver the project successfully
- The project is unique or has never been done before
- The project is technically complicated or extremely risky
- The agency lacks the skills, resources, or experience in the fields related to the project

Don't confuse hedging with *assumptions* in the document. Assumptions are data elements or factors that are considered true or factual and are used as part of the decision-making process. Whereas, hedging produces vague and non-committal language and doesn't provide a baseline upon which to measure change. Because assumptions are considered true and factual, they provide a reliable baseline to measure change against. Take care to avoid terms and sentence structure that may lead to hedging the SOW.

Avoid terms of art. *Terms of art* are terms that are specific to a particular industry or organization that may not be understood universally. When writing an SOW, use terms widely recognized outside the boundaries of a particular industry or organization. If technical terms are used in the text, they must be clearly defined and understood by all parties. If any misinterpretation were to arise that resulted in legal action, the judge settling the dispute will lean toward the "ordinary and usual" meaning of the word or phrase. An example is the phrase "break-fix," which is commonly used in the information technology (IT) outsourcing sector. If the ordinary and usual meaning of the phrase is to service and support hardware components, the legal decision would be based upon this definition.

Avoid redundancy. Redundancy in the SOW can reduce clarity and increase the probability of ambiguity and contradictions, which in turn may lead to legal claims against the party responsible for drafting the document. Claims may increase costs and lengthen delivery schedules. If it is necessary to state certain requirements in multiple sections of the SOW, state them the same way in each section. Consistency is imperative. Even the slightest change in the description could lead the reader to interpret a new definition for the requirement, which, in turn, may result in ambiguity or outright contradiction. Paraphrasing or using synonyms to describe a requirement will also increase the potential for ambiguity.

If the requirements or specifications are spelled out in an associated document, then they may be incorporated by reference in the SOW. In other words, writers can refer to the requirement by number or some other brief reference in the text of the SOW, as long as an attachment is given elsewhere that includes the full requirement or specification. If the SOW requires revisions or exceptions during project execution, make specific reference to the applicable portions and describe the change through the appropriate change-order process.[10]

Avoid non-specific words and phrases. Avoid words and phrases that imply a choice about what the government or contractor will produce or deliver. A list of these words and phrases, along with the rationale for not using them in the SOW, follows:[11]

Any – The word *any* is ambiguous and can be interpreted to mean an unlimited number of options. It lacks the specificity necessary in an SOW. Writers may use it to denote plurality, but the reader may interpret it to mean a singularity. If *any* is used, the reader will decide how to interpret it, not the SOW writer. If the reader's interpretation is different from that of the writer(s), it could lead to legal claims on the project.

and/or – These words imply a choice and require one of the parties identified in the SOW to choose one thing or another. For example, if the SOW states, "The contractor will deliver product A, B, and/or C." The contractor could infer that product C must be included with products A and B, or that product C may substitute products A and B, or something else. Clearly state what products and services are required.

Assist – The word *assist* is defined as the act of helping and providing aid. However, this definition lacks specific information about the *type* of aid to provide. Take care when using this word to define roles and responsibilities in the SOW; clearly define the roles and responsibilities of each party involved in the project. Don't leave any elements open for interpretation.

As applicable/as necessary – These phrases lack clarity and leave what is applicable to and necessary for the project's success up for interpretation.

As required – This phrase has no defined limitations and is open to interpretation by the reader. As stated, the phrase fails to identify what or who requires something (e.g., as required by the agency, as required by a federal government regulation, as required by an industry or organizational regulation or policy). The SOW must be specific in defining the minimal needs and limitations needed for project success.

As directed – This phrase, like the word *assist*, refers to personnel services. Typically, this phrase would refer to the government's supervision or oversight over the contractor. But unless the relationship is specified, a party can interpret it to mean something else. Clearly state what *directed* means, as well as who will direct and who will follow directions.

Best effort – This common phrase is frequently misused in SOWs. What constitutes a *best effort* is truly in the eyes of the beholder. One person or organization may think a best effort means working 8-hour work days until the originally scheduled project completion date. If the project isn't finished on time, then the client will have to settle for the work that has been accomplished to date or approve a change order for more funding to complete the project.

Another person or organization, however, may think a best effort means doing whatever it takes to get the work done on time, within budget, and of the quality desired by the client. In light of its many interpretations, this phrase should not be used under any circumstances.

Best practice – This phrase is frequently used in SOWs, as well as in organizational descriptions of the best method or process for performing a task or project. However, as with *best effort*, the definition of a best practice is in the eye of the beholder. Even within the same organization, what one may consider a best practice, another may consider antiquated. *Best practice* should not be used in SOWs.

Including but not limited to – This phrase is typically used when the writer is unsure about the requirements or expectations of the project. If used in an SOW, it will create an unspecified requirement, which in turn will create ambiguity. The SOW should not contain any open-ended phrases that are subject to interpretation by the various parties.

Either – This word implies a choice. The SOW should not contain wording that implies a choice.

Etc. – Avoid using *etc.* in the SOW, to prevent unidentified, ambiguous requirements. Only known elements should be listed. Anything beyond this known list should be addressed through the change order process during project execution.

Avoid catch-all and open-ended phrases. Requirements must be specific. Avoid phrases like "use a method/product/approach common in the professional services industry." This phrase is vague and doesn't provide specificities about what "method/product/approach" is common in the professional services industry. Phrases like *as directed* or *as required* may be used, but only when absolutely necessary (see definitions above).

Avoid big words. Writers often think they have to use big or complex words when writing an SOW. This is a common problem on highly complex or technical projects. The focus should be on the right word, not the biggest word. Apply the KISS (Keep It Super Simple) method to all projects, even the most complex or technical. If the document is easier to read and comprehend, then it's less likely to be misinterpreted or misunderstood.

Avoid extraneous material and requirements. Avoid incorporating extraneous material and data requirements that do not add value to the SOW. Only data that is essential to documenting the specific requirements of the project should be included in the document. Extraneous information or data will add unnecessary costs to the SOW without adding any value. In addition, the extraneous information may make the document more vague and confusing.

Avoid bias. If an SOW is part of a competitive bidding process, make sure the requirements don't give bias to the products or capabilities of a particular vendor or contractor. Biased requirements may provide a competitive advantage to certain vendors, or disadvantage others, that are likely to submit a proposal. This could lead to protests, as well as lengthy delays in the procurement process. Part 9.505 of the *Federal Acquisition Regulation* also addresses the importance of preventing bias or an unfair competitive advantage.[12]

Avoid unquantifiable language. Language implying commitments for improvement, cost-reduction sharing, out-of-scope work, increased competitiveness, and satisfied business needs should not be used in an SOW. These statements are difficult, if not impossible, to quantify.

Avoid perfection. Words that imply perfection like *always*, *never*, *minimum*, *maximum,* and *optimum* should not be used in an SOW. There is no way to ensure that something has a 100 percent chance of occurrence on a project; thus, words that imply this type of certainty should be avoided. This type of language is particularly risky for the vendor or contractor, and may reduce the number of proposals.

Avoid superlatives. Words like *all*, *best*, *every*, *greatest*, *least,* and *worst*. These words are difficult, if not impossible, to quantify.

Following these guidelines when writing an SOW will help ensure that the document is grammatically and technically sound, and that it establishes a proper and solid foundation to build the project upon. Failing to follow these guidelines, on the other hand, could ultimately lead to project failure. The benefits of taking the additional time to properly draft the SOW will far outweigh any costs incurred and will pay significant dividends later on in the project.

Legal Considerations

As noted earlier, the SOW is a legally binding agreement supporting the conditions of the contract. As such, it is critically important to pay particular attention to the legal implications of the language within the text.

In particular, SOW writers must understand the rule of parol evidence and the standard nature of contractual language. The rule of parol evidence holds that "if there is evidence in writing (such as a signed contract), the terms of the contract cannot be altered by evidence of oral (parol) agreements purporting to change, explain or contradict the written document."[13] The contract is the final word on the subject. SOW writers need to be especially careful about what they write, because the SOW is the primary document used to measure the performance of both the government and the contractor during project execution.

Most contractual language is a standard boilerplate, and is not often the source of disagreement. Most disagreements on interpretation stem from the specific language used in the SOW. The following basics of contract law will help SOW writers protect against misunderstandings.

Interpreting the SOW

A key principle of contract law is that it makes sense or is reasonable. For instance, the courts and boards of contract appeals presume that the two parties represented in the contract are well-informed and know what they are doing. They assume that the agreement between the two parties is reasonable because the contractor and the government both agreed to it. They support interpretations that flow from that view, and discount interpretations that are illogical, far-fetched, or produce impractical or unjust results.

A second foundation of contractual interpretations regards intent: the law holds that what is written in a contract is what was meant in the agreement; the law disregards other expressions of intent. If the contractor claims it is following SOW instructions and the government complains that the contractor has misinterpreted what was meant, the law is likely to side with the contractor. Although, when the government has accidentally overlooked a detail necessary to the successful operation of a complete system, the court may cite the *principle apparent purpose* of the contract as more important than the letter of the contract and add the needed provision. In other words, without inserting that particular provision, the contractor will be unable to successfully complete the system; thus, the court can cite the *principle apparent purpose* of the contract.

A third principle holds that the contract must be viewed as a whole, and not section to section. The whole contract includes not only specifications, but notes and references as well. Consequently, the SOW writer must not carelessly cite outside sources without first checking to ensure their consistency with the main provisions of the SOW.

The law interprets individual words using their normal definitions. SOW writers should not use jargon that may mean one thing normally and another thing to insiders—including potential contractors. For example, as described earlier, in IT a term known as "break-fix" refers to fixing hardware issues related to an organization's desktop and laptop computers. However, some organizations also use this same term to refer to fixing software application issues. In this case, the law would have to determine which usage was the normal definition for "break-fix."

Finally, the rule of precedence means the law looks on broader or more general requirements as superseding more specific requirements. An SOW writer can avoid this problem by making specifications internally consistent.

Rights and Responsibilities Under the Law

The law is concerned with the rights and responsibilities of both the contractor and the government when they are bound contractually. The law assumes that contract specifications are adequate to do the job. When the government issues a performance SOW, the responsibility to design a product or service and write adequate specifications falls on the contractor.

For other SOWs, if a contractor does what the contract specifies but it doesn't produce the results the government was expecting from the product or service, it is not the contractor's fault. Although the government is required to write adequate specifications, the contractor has a responsibility under the law to ask questions about ambiguous specifications.

The law also states that the government has a right to expect its instructions will be followed. It has a right to expect strict compliance, particularly when it issues a design SOW. The government also has the right to expect quality work. Performance quality is usually measured against the accepted norm in the relevant industry.

Using precise language will help you avoid pitfalls. Writing an SOW with concision and attention to detail will save you time and money, and keep you out of trouble in the courts.

▲ ▲ ▲

Now it is time to write! Clear away the debris on your desk, pull out a fresh pad of paper or pull up a blank page on your computer screen, focus on what you want to write, and do it. If nothing comes, here is one last tip: pretend you are writing a letter to a good friend. Keep it short and just describe your project. By now your creative juices will be flowing and you will be ready to get serious. Good luck!

NOTES

1. The University of Chicago Press, *The Chicago Manual of Style: The Essential Guide for Writers, Editors, and Publishers,* 15th ed. (Chicago, IL: University of Chicago Press, 2003).
2. William Strunk, Jr. and E. B. White, *The Elements of Style,* 4th ed. (Needham Heights, MA: Allyn & Bacon, 1999).

3. V.A. Howard and J.H. Barton, *Thinking on Paper* (New York: William Morrow and Company, Inc., 1986).
4. Adapted from Department of Defense, *Department of Defense Handbook for Preparation of Statement of Work (SOW)*, MIL-HDBK-245D, 3 April 1996, 25. Online at http://www.dla.mil/DSS/dss-a/download/DoD%20 SOW%20Handbook.pdf (accessed January 2008).
5. Rosemary T. Fruehling and N. B. Oldham, *Write to the Point!* (New York: McGraw-Hill, 1988).
6. *Department of Defense Handbook for Preparation of Statement of Work (SOW)*, 12.
7. Merriam-Webster, *Webster's New World Dictionary: Second College Edition* (New York: Prentice Hall Press, 1984), 43.
8. Adapted from *Department of Defense Handbook for Preparation of Statement of Work (SOW)*, 27-28.
9. Merriam-Webster, *Webster's New World Dictionary: Second College Edition* (New York: Prentice Hall Press, 1984), 648.
10. National Aeronautics and Space Administration, *NASA Guidance for Writing Statements of Work*, NPG 5600.2B, December 1997. Online at http://www.hq.nasa.gov/office/procurement/newreq1.htm (accessed January 2008), 23.
11. *Department of Defense Handbook for Preparation of Statement of Work (SOW)*, 20.
12. General Services Administration, Department of Defense, and National Aeronautics and Space Administration, *Federal Acquisition Regulation*, vol. 1-51, March 2005, 9.505. This edition includes the consolidation of all Federal Acquisition Circulars through 2001-27. Online at http://www.arnet .gov/far/reissue/FARvol1ForPaperOnly.pdf (accessed January 2008).
13. Law.com Dictionary, "parol evidence rule." Online at http://dictionary.law.com/dictionary.law.com (accessed on December 2007).

Chapter 11

The Purchase Request Package

After developing the SOW, the project manager must compile a purchase request (PR) for the contracting office. As noted in Chapter 1, the contracting office is responsible for soliciting bids or proposals, drafting the actual contract documents, and making an award to an offeror. To accomplish these tasks, the contracting officer will need a concise, clear statement describing the agency's requirements. One of the requirements included the acquisition plan is the purchase request (PR). Part 7 in the *Federal Acquisition Regulation* recognizes the purchase request as one of the key milestones during the acquisition cycle.[1] The PR package includes the SOW and supporting documents and forms, including a purchase request form, a desired schedule of SOW task accomplishment, and criteria for evaluating proposals.

Figure 11.1 gives a list of items typically included in the PR package. Lists tailored to solicitations specific to certain agencies are available at most contracting offices.

Figure 11.1 Typical Purchase Request Package Contents

- Purchase request form
- Desired schedule for SOW task accomplishment
- The relative weight of price and technical criteria for consideration in award decisions.
- Technical evaluation plan
- Technical evaluation criteria
- Contract data requirements list and supporting data item descriptions
- Technical proposal preparation instructions
- Special approvals or clearances
- Suggested contract type and contracting method
- Suggested special provisions
- Government estimate, together with any information about the availability of sufficient funds
- Specifications identified in the SOW
- Security requirements checklist (when appropriate)
- Justification for restricting full and open competition (when applicable)
- List of qualified potential contractors
- Synopsis of the proposed acquisition for FedBizOpps.gov—a government portal that lists federal procurement opportunities over $25,000.[2]

This chapter focuses on PR documents prepared by program officials, including:

- Special provisions
- Property furnished by the government
- Required reviews and approvals
- Government cost estimates
- Funding information
- Contractor recommendations
- Competition restrictions
- Data regarding future acquisitions
- Contracting officer's technical representative (COTR)
- Technical evaluation plan (TEP)

- Evaluation criteria

Special Provisions

The program official may choose to include suggested contract schedule articles or contract clauses in the PR (e.g., key personnel clauses, government option to extend clauses, dissemination of information clauses, nondisclosure of information clauses). The PR may alert the contracting officer to special circumstances or conditions not mentioned elsewhere, such as mandatory FAR provisions listed in specific sections of the contract. The contracting officer is responsible for the final review and revision of these special provisions.

Property Furnished by the Government

If the government will furnish equipment or supplies to the contractor for use in performing the contract, or if the government is required to acquire property with contract funds, the PR must state: (1) what property will be furnished or acquired, including individual items and quantities; (2) the schedule for furnishing the property; (3) the condition of the property; and (4) suggested provisions for the use and disposition of the property.

Required Reviews and Approvals

The PR package should include copies of the required reviews and approvals. When written documentation of approvals is unavailable, the PR should outline the actions taken to obtain approval and the dates those actions took place.

Government Cost Estimates

FAR Part 15.305(1) states:

> *In limited situations, a cost analysis (see 15.403-1(c)(1)(i)(B)) may be appropriate to establish reasonableness of the otherwise successful offeror's price. When contracting on a cost-reimbursement basis, evaluations shall include a cost realism analysis to determine what the Government should realistically expect to pay for the proposed effort, the offeror's understanding of the work, and the offeror's ability to perform the contract. (See 37.115 for uncompensated overtime evaluation.) The contracting officer shall document the cost or price evaluation.*[3]

The program officer typically estimates this figure, which should be an accurate estimate for the maximum cost of the proposed acquisition. Although this estimate doesn't appear in the RFP and remains confidential until the procurement action is completed, this section of the PR package is an essential government tool for two primary reasons. First, the estimate commits funds to the contract. Committing funds at this stage ensures their availability when the contract is later signed. Second, the estimate is used during contract negotiations as a check against the contractor's proposal, providing a baseline for assessing cost differences between alternative approaches.[4]

The indefinite nature of research efforts makes it difficult to estimate their cost exactly, but the following steps can help you develop a reasonable approximation:

1. Divide the effort into logical phases or individual tasks.
2. Estimate the amount and type of materials required for each phase or task.
3. Estimate the total labor-hours needed to perform each phase. Break down the estimate by each level of effort involved.
4. Identify the tasks or portions of tasks to be subcontracted.
5. Estimate travel and per-diem costs for offsite travel. When you don't know where the winning contractor will be located, base estimates on a contractor that starts in the center of the country and travels to either coast. The contractor can later refine these cost estimates during negotiations.
6. Finally, break down the phases or tasks into three cost elements: direct costs (e.g., personnel, equipment, supplies), indirect costs (overhead, general, and administrative expenses), and profit or fee.

The simplest way to reach a detailed estimate is to identify and compare a similar previous effort for which actual costs are available. Agency personnel should avoid requesting information from non-federal sources, unless it's possible to state the request in general terms that make identifying the specific requirement impossible. A detailed request will alert the organization questioned to a planned acquisition, which gives them a competitive advantage.

Funding Information

The PR must cite the appropriated funds account that will be charged, indicating the amount available for obligation. When complete funding is not available at the outset but will become available, the PR must state that the work will be incrementally funded over more than one fiscal year. Such funding approaches are usually used for high-cost, multi-year acquisitions.

The test for the validity of fiscal year obligations: whether the supplies or services are intended to serve real needs during the fiscal year of the appropriation. Articles or services procured with annual funds are not necessarily required to be delivered or performed in the same fiscal year, as long as the need arose during the fiscal year.

Contractor Recommendations

For competitive acquisitions, program officials should develop a mailing list of potential contractors. Using knowledge of the technical capabilities and performance histories of industry organizations, program officials should provide the names and addresses of qualified groups to the contracting office. If an announcement of the proposed contract in professional journals is likely to increase the field of potential contractors, the program official should also include a list of appropriate journals in the PR. Source mailing lists and contract announcements in professional journals augment the contractor base provided by the FedBizOpps website.[5]

(Note: Program officials should consult with contracting officers about the feasibility of placing contracts with small and disadvantaged business groups. Whenever possible, program officers should facilitate set-aside and SBA 8(a) acquisitions.)

Restricted Competition

When competition in a government acquisition is restricted, the program official must justify that restriction. For example, if a particular product or service is so unique only a couple of contractors in world will have the expertise to meet the requirements or specifications spelled out in the PR package, the competition would be considered restricted. The contracting officer would then be responsible for reviewing the justification for that restriction and including that information in the PR. If the contracting officer is not qualified to review the justification, he or she should forward it to a higher official for review.

Data Regarding Future Acquisitions

If further acquisitions are planned following a proposed contract, the PR should stipulate that specific types and amounts of data are to be recorded during fulfillment of the contract. Allowing other contractors access to recorded data facilitates competition in related future acquisitions.

Contracting Officer's Technical Representative (COTR)

In negotiated procurements, the contracting officer will appoint in writing a technical representative to monitor contractor performance and administer the contract. In the PR, the program official shall recommend an official choice to represent the contracting officer. The program officer should attach any necessary explanation of the choice or choices for the COTR.

Technical Evaluation Plan (TEP)

The TEP is a set of instructions notifying contractors of specific factors that must be addressed in their proposals. Along with the evaluation criteria, the TEP serves to solicit responsive proposals from contractors.

Evaluation Criteria

Government acquisitions that value multiple variables in the contract, rather than just price, must state the criteria for evaluation in the PR. FAR Part 15.204-5(c) tells us to publish evaluation factors in the solicitation along with some indication of their relative importance, although not necessarily their exact weights.[6]

Once the solicitation has been issued, the criteria can only be changed by amending the solicitation. Once the proposals are received, the criteria are final. The criteria are known as the *rules of the game* and must be applied without change in the selection process. This scoring system allows a uniform evaluation of each proposal.

NOTES

1. General Services Administration, Department of Defense, and National Aeronautics and Space Administration, *Federal Acquisition Regulation*, vol. 1-51, March 2005, 7.105(b)(20). This edition includes the consolidation of all Federal Acquisition Circulars through 2001-27. Online at http://www.arnet.gov/far/reissue/FARvol1ForPaperOnly.pdf (accessed January 2008).
2. Government Services Administration, "FedBizOpps—Federal Business Opportunities." Online at http://www.FedBizOpps.gov (accessed December 2007).

3. *Federal Acquisition Regulation*, 15.305(1).
4. *Federal Acquisition Regulation*, 15.306(e).
5. See note 2 above.
6. *Federal Acquisition Regulation*, 15.204-5(c).

Chapter 12

Managing Changes to the SOW

Regardless of how well the SOW is planned, changes almost always occur throughout the lifecycle of a project. To allow for these changes, Part 43.201 of the FAR states:

Generally, Government contracts contain a changes clause that permits the contracting officer to make unilateral changes in designated areas within the general scope of the contract. These are accomplished by issuing written change orders on Standard Form 30, Amendment of Solicitation/Modification of Contract (SF 30), unless otherwise provided (see 43.301).[1]

One of the main responsibilities of the project manager is to maintain a balance between the scope, cost, and schedule of a project. These three variables are typically referred to as the *triple constraints* of a project and are illustrated as an equilateral triangle in Figure 12.1. The SOW establishes the initial parameters for the triangle by defining the baseline scope, cost, and scheduled project completion date. When one side of the triangle increases or decreases, it has a direct impact on the other two.

Figure 12.1 Triple Constraint Triangle

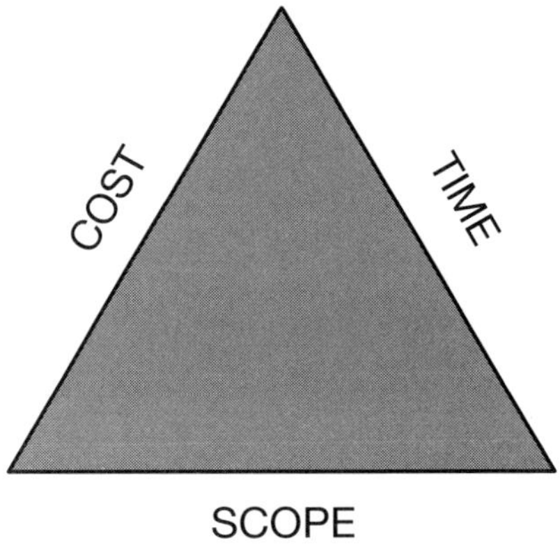

To maintain a balance between these triple constraints, a detailed change management process must be in place. Failing to document and manage changes to any of these constraints properly will force the triangle out of balance very quickly. When this happens, the project is heading for trouble.

Legal Precedents Backing Change Management

Failing to manage project change can lead to a multitude of problems, including scope creep, cost and schedule overruns, poor resource utilization, reduced product quality, and wasted funds. In addition, if either the government or contractor were to seek retribution for any changes that took place without an approved change order, the probability of winning the suit would be very slim.

Several recent court cases have litigated this very issue. In *Miorelli Engineering v. County of Brevard* (1997), Miorelli Engineering sued

Brevard County, Florida, for breach of contract and sought damages for work they had performed outside the scope of the contract. After going through the trial court and the court of appeals, the case was eventually elevated to the Supreme Court of Florida for a decision. The Supreme Court ruled that Miorelli Engineering could not recover the cost of work it had performed outside the scope of the contract with Brevard County because without a written and approved change order, the county was protected by the sovereign immunity doctrine.[2] This doctrine precludes the institution of a suit against the sovereign (government) without its consent.[3]

In the case of *Choate Construction v. Ideal Electrical Contractors* (2000), Ideal Electrical Contractors sued Choate Construction arguing that the theory of quantum meruit allowed them to recover the reasonable value of services performed outside the scope of the contract.[4] In the law of contracts, the theory of quantum meruit is a doctrine by which the law infers a promise to pay a reasonable amount for labor and materials furnished, even in the absence of a specific legally enforceable agreement between the parties.[5] The agreement between Choate and Ideal specified that Choate would pay Ideal the amount set forth in the subcontract, but both agreed that this amount may increase or decrease to accommodate any changes the parties agreed to in writing. The subcontract further specified that Ideal would not be paid for work performed outside the defined scope unless Choate first authorized it in writing before the work was initiated.

Although Ideal won the case in trial court, Choate appealed the decision to the Court of Appeals of Georgia, which, in turn, reversed the decision. In their decision, the appellate court ruled that Ideal had accepted the terms of the subcontract, but they did not follow the change management process for work performed outside the original scope. Since they did not follow the terms of the contract, they were denied payment for the work under the theory of quantum meruit.

The case of *A.H.A General Construction Inc. v. New York City Housing Authority* (1998) provides yet another example of how not following an agreed-upon change management process can negatively impact an organization.[6] In this case, A.H.A General Construction was awarded two contracts with the New York City Housing Authority, one contract for $2.3 million and the other for $2.4 million. Each contract specifically required A.H.A to submit all claims, along with any support documentation, to the Housing Authority in a timely manner. This provision was meant to give the Housing Authority enough time to review the claims, to ensure that any additional work performed outside the original scope was justified and that public funds were being spent wisely.

Upon completing the work for both contracts, A.H.A submitted two claims for additional work that they had performed. The claim on the first contract was for $700,513, and on the second contract, the claim was for $205,125. After reviewing the claims, the Housing Authority only recognized minor adjustments for the additional work and refused to pay the claims in full. A.H.A sued for breach of contract, seeking full payment for the additional work performed.

The trial court and the New York Court of Appeals dismissed A.H.A's claims, ruling that the company had not met the notice of claims and reporting requirements specified under the two contracts. A.H.A lost close to one million dollars in claims on the two contracts, not including legal fees, simply because they didn't follow the change management process agreed to in the contract.

These three cases clearly point to the importance of not only managing project change, but also ensuring that change is managed in accordance with change-management specifications given in the contract or the SOW. The companies in these three cases wasted millions of dollars on mismanaged projects. Extrapolating these figures across all industry sectors, the impact can easily reach well into the billions or trillions of dollars.

Identifying Change

To properly manage project change, one must first identify when a change is proposed or when it occurs. For the purpose of this discussion, *change* is defined as any deviation from the scope agreed to in the SOW, also referred to as a *cardinal change*.[7] Consider the following three factors when determining whether a change is significant enough to be classified as a cardinal change:[8]

- Has the magnitude of the project work been significantly changed, or will it be?
- Is the change requiring the procurement of a totally different product, or is it altering the quality, character, functionality, or type of work defined in the SOW?
- Does the cost of the proposed change greatly exceed the baseline cost established in the SOW?

If the answer to any of these questions is affirmative, one could conclude that the proposed change is a cardinal change. According to the cardinal change doctrine, contract parties are generally restricted to requesting changes within the general scope defined in the SOW. If a proposed change is determined to be a cardinal change, then the contractor will not be required to implement the change unless specific SOW clauses address how to manage changes of this nature.

The cardinal change doctrine also has legal precedent in the case of *Becho, Inc. v. United States* (2000).[9] In January 1997, the U.S. Army Corps of Engineers contracted Becho to deliver two separate piles of riprap to a quarry in Jackson Hole, Wyoming. The contract required Becho to group the riprap in piles containing materials of dissimilar sizes, and in a way that minimized breakage. The Corps would then pay Becho on the total number of cubic yards of acceptable material in each pile.

During the course of the project, the Corps determined that some of the material within both piles was unsatisfactory and did not meet the required specifications. The Corps issued a change order that required Becho to remove the unsatisfactory material from the piles and transport it to another location away from the quarry. The change order, however, did not allow for an adjustment in the contract price of the work. Becho agreed to remove the material from the second pile of riprap, but they refused to do so for the first pile because the Corps had already accepted and paid for the material.

After removing the material from the second pile, Becho removed their equipment and requested payment for the work. The Corps, however, considered Becho to be in breach of contract because they had not also removed the unsatisfactory material from the first pile. Becho refuted this in court by arguing that the Corps had issued a cardinal change, and Becho was therefore under no obligation to perform the work.

The court recognized the cardinal change doctrine in this case and awarded the decision in Becho's favor, noting that a cardinal change did not obligate the contractor to perform work outside the general scope of the contract.[10] This issue could have been avoided if the SOW had contained language or a clause specifying how unsatisfactory material was to be handled, including the cost for removal.

Some SOW development teams will choose to identify out-of-scope elements in the SOW. This is essentially a wasted effort that adds no real value to the SOW or project. Instead, a better approach is to make it clear to all project parties that anything not identified in the SOW is considered out-of-scope. The project manager plays an extremely important role in ensuring that this is clearly communicated to all parties, and that this criterion is adhered to throughout the life of the project. If not, changes on the project can get out of control very quickly.

The Big Dig Project, a federal highway project in Boston, Massachusetts, is a great example of what can happen if change is not managed properly. In April 2000, the Federal Highway Administration released an audit report on the project that identified enormous cost overruns, as well as an overall lack of management control. The report concluded that the estimated total cost to complete the project was approximately $14.8 billion—an increase of $12.2 billion over the original estimate of $2.6 billion.[11] This is for a single project! Clearly, the additional expenditures caused by the unexpected changes on projects across all industry sectors could easily reach into the trillions of dollars.

Managing Project Changes

At first glance, the concept of managing change seems simple. So why do so many organizations have such a hard time with it? The reality is that managing change can be one of the most difficult things to do, particularly if your organization has immature project management processes and procedures. The difficulty is not because the process is technically complex, but rather because of the challenge of getting the project team members to follow the process.

Factors Effecting Change Mismanagement

Some factors that contribute to change mismanagement include:

- Lacking a detailed SOW to establish baseline information to measure future change against
- Lacking a change management section in the SOW that is understood and accepted by all parties involved in the project delivery
- Lacking discipline and rigor among the project team in adhering to and enforcing the change management process
- Poor communications among the project team, causing problems in identifying changes

- Lacking an understanding about what was agreed to in the SOW
- Misinterpreting change(s) as not significant enough to warrant or justify a change order

Each of these factors can easily impede the management of project changes. Thus, it is important to understand what they involve and how they can be avoided on your projects.

Lacking a Detailed SOW

To call a detailed SOW an important factor in managing project change is a tremendous understatement: without a detailed SOW, it's impossible to determine when a change has occurred, and it's impossible to manage the change. It's critical not only to understand when a change occurs, but also to determine how it impacts the projects' scope, schedule, cost, quality, and manpower.

If an SOW is not in place to establish limits on the project's scope, then essentially all changes are in scope. In this scenario, the scope of the project could grow out of control. Without an SOW to establish a baseline to measure change against, there is no way to manage and quantify the true impact of changes to the project. Having a detailed SOW in place will help establish a baseline to determine when a change has occurred and to measure its impact on the project.

Lacking a Change Management Section in the SOW

Even if a project has an SOW guiding it, there is no guarantee that changes will be managed properly. The SOW can describe the scope of the work in great detail, but if it doesn't address how to identify, review, and approve changes, it could easily contribute to the mismanagement of changes to the project. Having the appropriate change management processes and thresholds in place will help avoid cost overruns.

Lacking Adherence to the Change Management Process

Some projects may have a detailed SOW in place that includes a change management process, but the project team simply isn't following the process defined in the document. This situation is often attributed to the lack of discipline and rigor of the organization, the project manager, or the project team responsible for enforcing the process. If a change process is defined in the SOW, then it must be followed. Otherwise, the team will ignore changes that may drastically increase or decrease the scope of the project. Ignoring the changes also means that no adjustments are being made to the cost, scheduled completion date, or manpower.

If you define a change management process and don't follow it, you set a precedent with the team that managing change is not important. The team will ignore the process, leading to scope creep, cost overruns, schedule slips, poor quality, and poor resource utilization. The change process must be enforced with discipline and rigor to ensure project success. The individual leading the project must not only have strong project management skills, but must also be well-respected by the project team.

Applying the change management process must be an objective driven from the executive leadership of the organization down to the individual team members. Visible support from the top will greatly expedite the acceptance of the process at the lower levels of the organization.

Poor Communications

Difficulty in managing change on a project can be amplified if there is poor communication among the project team members. Lacking mechanisms to ensure that changes are identified and communicated will inhibit the project manager's ability to properly manage changes on the project. To avoid miscommunications, the SOW should address the escalation process team members should use to identify or request changes. This process will define who can request a change and how to submit it to the appropriate individuals.

Lacking an Understanding of the SOW

The project team often lacks an understanding about what was agreed to in the SOW because project managers and organization leaders fail to communicate that information. Some organizations may consider certain information to be confidential and not fully disclose it even to their own personnel. Thus, they either neglect or refuse to provide the project team with a full copy of the SOW. When this occurs, the team goes into the project blind, not knowing what has been agreed to or even what deliverables or services the project is meant to provide.

A simple way to avoid this type of miscommunication is to provide a "cleansed" copy of the approved SOW to each team member, with information specific to their area of responsibility. The cleansed version of the SOW simply omits confidential or proprietary sections, and information outside the group's area of responsibility.

When team members are aware of what is meant to be delivered as part of the project, it is much easier for them to determine when a change or proposed change may impact the agreed-upon SOW. This awareness will help ensure that all changes to the project are being captured and properly documented.

Misinterpreting Changes

Sometimes a proposed change may seem so small or insignificant that it seems like it doesn't justify going through the complete change management process. Teams will try to justify the these changes by stating that it will cost more to go through the process than it will to simply document the change. Although this may be true for individual changes, the justification does not hold up against the impact of aggregate changes over time.

A change may seem small or insignificant when proposed, but it may have a cascading impact on other parts of the project later on. The resulting impact could lead to rework and schedule and cost overruns. The cumulative effect of changes could even lead to project failure. Thus, it is imperative that all changes be documented and managed according to the agreed-upon change management process, regardless of their size.

Change Management Tools

To manage change properly, standard processes and tools must be in place to document and track project changes. For the purpose of this discussion, a tool is defined as a customized template or form used by the project manager to manage change. In addition to the

SOW, two primary tools should be used to managing project change: the change order form and the SOW change order tracker.

The Change Order Form

The change order form is typically customized to meet an organization's specific change management requirements. The federal government uses the Standard Form 30, which appears in Figure 12.2.[12]

The FAR Part 43.301 provides the following guidance on the use of the Standard Form 30:[13]

> *(a)(1) The Standard Form 30 (SF 30), Amendment of Solicitation/Modification of Contract, shall (except for the options stated in 43.301(a)(2) or actions processed under Part 15) be used for:*
>
> > *(i) Any amendment to a solicitation;*
> >
> > *(ii) Change orders issued under the Changes clause of the contract;*
> >
> > *(iii) Any other unilateral contract modification issued under a contract clause authorizing such modification without the consent of the contractor;*
> >
> > *(iv) Administrative changes such as the correction of typographical mistakes, changes in the paying office, and changes in accounting and appropriation data;*
> >
> > *(v) Supplemental agreements (see 43.103); and*

Figure 12.2 Standard Form 30

AMENDMENT OF SOLICITATION/MODIFICATION OF CONTRACT

1. CONTRACT ID CODE | PAGE OF PAGES

2. AMENDMENT/MODIFICAITON NO. | 3. EFFECTIVE DATE | 4. REQUISITION/PURCHASE REQ. NO. | 5. PROJECT NO. *(If applicble)*

6. ISSUED BY CODE | 7. ADMINISTERED BY *(If other than Item 6)* CODE

8. NAME AND ADDRESS OF CONTRACTOR *(No., street, county, State and ZIP Code)*

(X) 9A. AMENDMENT OF SOLICIATION NO.

☐ 9B. DATED *(SEE ITEM 11)*

10A. MODIFICATION OF CONTRACT/ORDER NO.

☐ 10B. DATED *(SEE ITEM 13)*

CODE | FACILITY CODE

11. THIS ITEM ONLY APPLIES TO AMENDMENTS OF SOLICITATIONS

☐ The above numbered solicitation is amended as set forth in Item 14. The hour and date specified for receipt of Offers ☐ is extended, ☐ is not extended.

Offers must acknowledge receipt of this amendment prior to the hour and date specified in the solicitation or as amended, by one of the following methods:
(a)By completing items 8 and 15, and returning ______ copies of the amendment; (b) By acknowledging receipt of this amendment on each copy of the offer submitted; or (c) By separate letter or telegram which includes a reference to the solicitation and amendment numbers. FAILURE OF YOUR ACKNOWLEDGMENT TO BE RECEIVED AT THE PLACE DESIGNATED FOR THE RECEIPT OF OFFERS PRIOR TO THE HOUR AND DATE SPECIFIED MAY RESULT IN REJECTION OF YOUR OFFER. If by virtue of this amendment your desire to change an offer already submitted, such change may be made by telegram or letter, provided each telegram or letter makes reference to the solicitation and this amendment, and is received prior to the opening hour and date specified.

12. ACCOUNTING AND APPROPIRATION DATA *(If required)*

13. THIS ITEM ONLY APPLIES TO MODIFICATION OF CONTRACTS/ORDERS.
IT MODIFIES THE CONTRACT/ORDER NO. AS DESCRIBED IN ITEM 14.

CHECK ONE	
☐	A. THIS CHANGE ORDER IS ISSUED PURSUANT TO: *(Specify authority)* THE CHANGES SET FORTH IN ITEM 14 ARE MADE IN THE CONTRACT ORDER NO. IN ITEM 10A.
☐	B. THE ABOVE NUMBERED CONTRACT/ORDER IS MODIFIED TO REFLECT THE ADMINISTRATIVE CHANGES *(such as changes in paying office, appropriation date, etc.*) SET FORTH IN ITEM 14, PURSUANT TO THE AUTHORITY OF FAR 43.103(b).
☐	C. THIS SUPPLEMENTAL AGREEMENT IS ENTERED INTO PURSUANT TO AUTHORITY OF:
☐	D. OTHER *(Specify type of modification and authority)*

E. IMPORTANT: Contractor ☐ is not, ☐ is required to sign this document and return ______ copies to the issuing office.

14. DESCRIPTION OF AMENDMENT/MODIFICATION (*Organized by UCF section headings, including solicitation/contract subject matter where feasible.)*

Except as provided herein, all terms and conditions of the document referenced in Item 9A or 10A, as heretofore changed, remains unchanged and in full force and effect.

15A. NAME AND TITLE OF SIGNER *(Type or print)* | 16A. NAME AND TITLE OF CONTRACTING OFFICER *(Type or print)*

15B. CONTRACTOR/OFFEROR *(Signature of person authorized to sign)* | 15C. DATE SIGNED | 16B. UNITED STATES OF AMERICA *(Signature of Contracting Officer)* | 16C. DATE SIGNED

NSN 7540-01-152-8070
Previous edition unusable

STANDARD FORM 30 (REV. 10-83)
Prescribed by GSA FAR (48 CFR) 53.243

Figure 12.2 Standard Form 30 (continued)

INSTRUCTIONS

Instructions for items other than those that are self-explanatory, are as follows:

(a) Item 1 (Contract ID Code). Insert the contract type identification code that appears in the title block of the contract being modified.

(b) Item 3 (Effective date).

(1) For a solicitation amendment, change order, or administrative change, the effective date shall be the issue date of the amendment, change order, or administrative change.

(2) For a supplemental agreement, the effective date shall be the date agreed to by the contracting parties.

(3) For a modification issued as an initial or confirming notice of termination for the convenience of the Government, the effective date and the modification number of the confirming notice shall be the same as the effective date and modification number of the initial notice.

(4) For a modification converting a termination for default to a termination for the convenience of the Government, the effective date shall be the same as the effective date of the termination for default.

(5) For a modification confirming the contacting officer's determination of the amount due in settlement of a contract termination, the effective date shall be the same as the effective date of the initial decision.

(c) Item 6 (Issued By). Insert the name and address of the issuing office. If applicable, insert the appropriate issuing office code in the code block.

(d) Item 8 (Name and Address of Contractor). For modifications to a contract or order, enter the contractor's name, address, and code as shown in the original contract or order, unless changed by this or a previous modification.

(e) Item 9, (Amendment of Solicitation No. - Dated), and 10, (Modification of Contract/Order No. - Dated). Check the appropriate box and in the corresponding blanks insert the number and date of the original solicitation, contract, or order.

(f) Item 12 (Accounting and Appropriation Data). When appropriate, indicate the impact of the modification on each affected accounting classification by inserting one of the following entries.

(1) Accounting classification
Net increase $ ____________

(2) Accounting classification
Net decrease $ ____________

NOTE: If there are changes to multiple accounting classifications that cannot be placed in block 12, insert an asterisk and the words "See continuation sheet".

(g) Item 13. Check the appropriate box to indicate the type of modification. Insert in the corresponding blank the authority under which the modification is issued. Check whether or not contractor must sign this document. (See FAR 43.103.)

(h) Item 14 (Description of Amendment/Modification).

(1) Organize amendments or modifications under the appropriate Uniform Contract Format (UCF) section headings from the applicable solicitation or contract. The UCF table of contents, however, shall not be set forth in this document

(2) Indicate the impact of the modification on the overall total contract price by inserting one of the following entries:

(i) Total contract price increased by $ ____________

(ii) Total contract price decreased by $ ____________

(iii) Total contract price unchanged.

(3) State reason for modification.

(4) When removing, reinstating, or adding funds, identify the contract items and accounting classifications.

(5) When the SF 30 is used to reflect a determination by the contracting officer of the amount due in settlement of a contract terminated for the convenience of the Government, the entry in Item 14 of the modification may be limited to --

(i) A reference to the letter determination; and

(ii) A statement of the net amount determined to be due in settlement of the contract.

(6) Include subject matter or short title of solicitation/contract where feasible.

(i) Item 16B. The contracting officer's signature is not required on solicitation amendments. The contracting offier's signature is normally affixed last on supplemental agreements.

STANDARD FORM 30 (REV. 10-83) **BACK**

(vi) Removal, reinstatement, or addition of funds to a contract.

(2) The SF 30 may be used for:

(i) Modifications that change the price of contracts for the acquisition of petroleum as a result of economic price adjustment;

(ii) Termination notices; and

(iii) Purchase order modifications as specified in 13.302-3.

(3) If it is anticipated that a change will result in a price change, the estimated amount of the price change shall not be shown on copies of SF 30 furnished to the contractor.

(b) The Optional Form 336 (OF 336), Continuation Sheet, or a blank sheet of paper, may be used as a continuation sheet for a contract modification.

SOW Change Order Tracker

How does a project get to be a year behind schedule? One day at a time!

—Anonymous

This quote speaks volumes on the importance of tracking change on projects. From the perspective of the project manager, it's easy to get wrapped up in day-to-day management activities and only concentrate on the day's most urgent issue. But keeping only a day-to-day perspective can cause problems for the project over the long run.

Along with the Standard Form 30, the SOW change order tracker also plays an important role in managing project change. This tool assists in tracking all approved and unapproved changes to the project by capturing them in one comprehensive document. Having this information in one place provides a powerful perspective to anyone reviewing the evolution of a project's scope, cost, schedule, and manpower from its original baseline estimates to its completion.

The change order tracker provides several benefits to both the government and the contractor. First, having all of the information in one location allows anyone to quickly audit the project to ensure that the final cost is equal to the baseline estimate plus all cost increases attributed to approved change orders. This will confirm that all additional costs were approved by both the government and the contractor, and that no costs were arbitrarily added to the project without prior approval.

Also, if any disputes about increased costs or schedule slips arise between the government and contractor, the change order tracker can be referenced to quickly identify specifically when the change occurred and its impact on the project.

Another benefit of the change order tracker is that the government and the contractor can build a detailed knowledge base simply by analyzing and comparing the types of changes that arose on similar projects. The respective parties can then use this information to develop future estimates or proposals for similar work. Applying this information on future projects will make project teams more likely to address these issues during the planning phase, which should lead to fewer change orders later, during the delivery of the project.

The SOW change order tracker can take on many different forms, depending on the needs or desires of the organization responsible for managing changes to the project. Figure 12.3 provides a sample SOW change order tracker. This tracker captures basically the same information as the change order form. The difference is that it also shows the cumulative impact of all approved change orders on project cost, schedule, and manpower in a single document.

A change order tracker typically includes the following information:

- Project name
- Baseline project cost from the approved SOW
- Baseline scheduled completion date from the approved SOW
- Baseline manpower (number of resources) from the approved SOW
- Change order (CO) number
- Section of the SOW impacted by the change
- Impact of the change on the language contained in the approved SOW
- Impact of the change on the project cost, scheduled completion date, and manpower

Because this information is obtained directly from either the SOW itself or an approved change order for the project, the project team won't need to generate any additional information. Regardless of the particular structure or format of the tracker, it should always

Figure 12.3 Sample SOW Change Order Tracker

Project Name:									
Baseline Cost ($):									
Baseline Scheduled Completion Date:									
Baseline Manpower (# of Resources):									
				Impact (if applicable)					
		Change SOW Language		Cost		Scheduled Completion Date		Manpower	
CO#	Section in SOW	From	To	From	To	From	To	From	To
1									
2									
3									
4									
5									
6									
7									
8									
9									
10									
11									

capture the data elements that correspond to the triple constraints of scope, time, and cost.

The process of managing and tracking changes on a project requires a great deal of discipline and rigor on the part of everyone associated with the project. For organizations with immature project management processes and methodologies, implementing a change management process can be difficult. It's easier to accept new processes and tools, however, if they easily transfer data from one form and process to another without requiring additional effort by the team.

Simply having the processes and tools in place to manage project change is a step in the right direction, but if no one uses them or if they are applied incorrectly, the effort it takes to get to this point will be wasted. When introducing or implementing a detailed change process, it's important to consider the organizational transition to and acceptance of the process. Achieving acceptance at both the organizational and individual level is a major factor in ensuring project changes are managed appropriately. And when this happens, projects will benefit tremendously.

▲ ▲ ▲

The next section offers a sample set of SOWs from various federal agencies that cover a wide range of acquisitions, from procuring janitorial services to the development of an electronic acquisition system. Readers can use these samples to help structure their own SOWs and to help generate ideas and thoughts on the type of language and requirements to include in the document.

NOTES

1. General Services Administration, Department of Defense, and National Aeronautics and Space Administration, *Federal Acquisition Regulation*, vol. 1–51, March 2005, 43.201. This edition includes the consolidation of all Federal Acquisition Circulars through 2001–27. Online at http://www.arnet.gov/far/reissue/FARvol1ForPaperOnly.pdf (accessed January 2008).
2. "Lack of Change Order Sinks Damage Claim," *Civil Engineering* 68, no. 8 (August 1998): 32.
3. 'Lectric Law Library, "The 'Lectric Law Library's Lexicon On Sovereign Immunity." Online at http://www.lectlaw.com (accessed December 2007).
4. "Subcontractor Cannot Recover Payment For Work Performed Outside of Contract," *Civil Engineering* (July 2001): 78.
5. Answers.com™ Business and Finance, Law Encyclopedia, "Quantum Meruit." Online at http://www.answers.com (accessed December 2007).
6. "Recovery for Unclaimed Work Denied," *Civil Engineering* (March 1999): 75.
7. Michael C. Loulakis and Simon J. Santiago, "Cardinal Change Doctrine Excuses Performance," *Civil Engineering* (September 2001): 96.
8. Ibid.
9. Ibid.
10. Ibid.
11. *USA Today*, "Boston must dig deeper to pay for 'Big Dig.'" April 6, 2000, 11A.
12. General Services Administration, *Standard Form 30—Amendment of Solicitation/Modification of Contract*, Rev. 10-83, as prescribed by *Federal Acquisition Report*, 43.301. Online at http://contacts.gsa.gov/webforms.nsf (accessed December 2007).
13. *Federal Acquisition Regulation*, 43.301.

Sample Statements of Work

The following section contains 18 sample SOWs, including performance, functional, design, and level-of-effort SOWs. Readers should pay particular attention to the structure of the SOWs and the type of language used within the documents. These samples, along with the information provided in Chapters 1–12, can be used jointly as a guide when drafting an SOW for your own project.

Sample 1

Operate Mail Service

Type of Work: General Support Services

Objective: To procure the operation of mail services for the Department of Education. Mail services include: picking up and sorting incoming mail, delivering mail to specified mail stations and by mailbag, distributing special, mass-produced materials, controlling accountable mail, reading a routing of misaddressed mail, loading and unloading automated Mailmobiles, and related support activities.

SOW Type: Functional

Comments:

- Good, clear, functional specifications.
- Specifies the minimally acceptable regulations.
- References standard regulations.
- General responsibilities of the contractor are somewhat limited and should be better defined.
- Task specifications are well defined.
- Reporting requirements are clearly defined.

STATEMENT OF WORK
OPERATE DEPARTMENT OF EDUCATION MAIL SERVICE

I. Introduction

The Mail Section, Office Services Branch, Support Services Division, ARMS, serves as a central mail facility for all ED occupied buildings in the metropolitan Washington area. The Mail Section delivers incoming outgoing mail to appropriate destinations, and keeps statistics for annual billing purposes by the U.S. Postal Service.

The Mail Section services the four buildings at ED headquarters in Southwest Washington, DC – FB-6, ROB-3, Reporters and the Switzer Buildings. Fourteen floors collectively in these buildings have a total of 143 mail stations serviced by carriers, who achieve a total of up to four pick-up/deliveries to each station daily. Bulk (i.e., in mailbag) distribution is made for two other buildings outside headquarters, but in metropolitan Washington, two items daily. Special distribution of mass printed material is made to as many as 3196 employees at headquarters and 570 employees in the outlying buildings. Automated Mailmobiles serviced by a carrier from the Mail Section, make four runs daily on the second and third floors of the FOB-6 Building. The Mail Section serves as a focal point for liaison with the Washington Post Office and the U.S. Postal Service.

II. Nature of the Project

It is desired to procure services as specified below. This will be a Government-owned – contractor-operated facility. Services to be performed include: pick-up and sorting of incoming mail, delivery of mail to specified mail stations and by mailbag, special distribution of mass-produced materials, control of accountable mail, reading a routing of misaddressed mail, loading and unloading of automated Mailmobiles, and related support activities.

III. Statement of Work

A. General

As a minimum, all ED and U.S. Postal Regulations referenced in this contract are to be used by the Contractor as guidance in performance of the services required. Government regulations and directives, and portions thereof which require specific compliance are clearly identified in the applicable sections below.

B. Contractor Regulations

Where the Contractor is permitted to use ED and other Government directives as guidance rather than for mandatory compliance in performance of this contract, the contractor shall be governed by the intended effect or product contemplated by the regulations or directives referenced. The Contractor will initiate and keep current a manual of contractor regulations which specifically delineate the Contractor's responsibility and actions where ED and other Government directives are used as guides. Such Contractor regulations and the terms and conditions of this contract will be the basis for the inspection and surveillance of the contract performance. The terms and conditions of this contract shall take precedence in the event of conflict. All the above Contractor regulations shall be submitted for approval to the Government Project manager. Applicable ED or other Government directives shall be the basis for inspection and surveillance of areas where Contractor regulations have not been issued and approved. The Government will have full and unlimited rights in the Contractor regulations.

C. Contractor Responsibilities

The Contractor shall exercise management and operational control and retain full responsibility for performance of assigned work as set forth in this Statement of Work. The Government shall not exercise any supervision or control over Contractor employees performing services under this contract; such employees shall be accountable not to the Government, but solely to the Contractor, who, in turn, is responsible to the Government. All Contractor employees must have some mode of identification, either by wearing a uniform or an I.D. Card attached to their clothing. This I.D. must be displayed so the employee can be easily identified.

D. Subject

The purpose of this contract is to provide goods and services in effectively, efficiently, and economically running a mail operation encompassing the ED occupied buildings in the metropolitan Washington area.

E. Task Specifications

The Contractor shall:

- Perform all work as described in the USPS Domestic Mail Manual, FPMR 101-11-3, Managing the Mail, and the ED Mail Management Directive unless specific authorization in writing is given by the Government Project manager for any changes or deviations from established procedures. The contractor will work on site from the mailroom in the Building, using Government facilities and Government-furnished property as specified herein.
- Be responsible for the work area (i.e., the mailroom) and all the furniture, equipment and supplies pertaining thereto, including the Mailmobiles. If through negligence or carelessness any of this furniture, equipment or supplies is lost or damaged, the Contractor will be held liable.
- Maintain up-to-date records of mail processed (estimate: 1,300,000 pieces in FY 1984) and costs for the purpose of preparing the annual report of same to the U.S. Postal Service.
- Administer, manage, supervise and operate the FOB-6 Mailroom, 400 Maryland Ave., SW, Washington, D.C. 20201.
- Pick up the mail delivered by and from offices within the headquarters complex and sort it by name, title, organization and destination.
- Deposit sorted mail into flats, letter case or mailbag.
- Be present for sorting duty from 6:30 AM – 3:00 PM.
- Sign for accountable incoming mail.
- Place sorted mail in appropriate mail carts within 30 minutes after sorting is completed.
- Make assigned floor route pick-up/delivery trips within 30 minutes. Four trips/day to 143 mail stations on 14 floors required.

- Obtain signatures for accountable mail.
- Dispatch outgoing mail according to service and class.
- Wrap packages as required and prepare them for pick-up by USPS.
- Request changes of address, when appropriate.
- Cross-train carriers in the knowledge of carrier routes.
- Keep abreast of Departmental organizational responsibilities and knowledge of how to acquire required mailing information.
- Ensure security of mail carts and other equipment at all times.
- Control accountable mail by:
    a. Reconciling receipt of accountable mail.
    b. Preparing accountable mail records.
    c. Preparing domestic common carrier forms for parcels.
    d. Reconciling common carrier invoices.
    e. Maintaining records of postage due, address corrections, business replies and other postage accounts.
- Keep informed on organizational responsibilities and changes so as to be able to correctly route reader mail.
- Ensure that records of White House mail, checks and cash received are kept on a daily basis.
- Provide cross-training at other position, including supervisory ones.
- Respond to phone calls relating to mail and other related matters.
- Maintain priorities on incoming mail so that incorrectly addressed mail of high importance can be routed expeditiously and correctly.
- Load, unload, charge the battery and inform Government project manager of need for service on the automated Mailmobiles in order to permit them to make four complete runs daily.

- Make special distribution of mass-produced material to as many mail stations as required in the Washington metropolitan area.
- Make at least two deliveries of bulk mail daily to the buildings outside the headquarters complex (more frequently, as the situation demands).
- Have carriers available for duty from 9:00 AM–5:30 PM daily.

F. Facilities

The Government shall furnish building facilities to the Contractor. Normal building maintenance services will be provided. All equipment furnished by the Government can be utilized by the Contractor for the life of said equipment. The Contractor will be responsible for any replacement or additional delivery type equipment.

G. Hours of Operation

The mail operation shall be staffed appropriately by the Contractor from 6:30 AM (when the Post Office makes its first pick-up/delivery) until 5:30 PM, following the final USPS pick-up/delivery of the day.

H. Fee

The Contractor shall not charge fees beyond those authorized by the U.S. Postal Service or required by private carriers.

I. Training

The Contractor shall train all contractor personnel in the operation of the mail service and proper USPS procedures.

J. Surveillance Plan and Other Technical Requirements

The determination of the quality of the Contractor's performance shall be made on the basis of the Surveillance Plan (SP) given below. The SP shall consist of a combination of questions to be answered by the Government Project Officer and a checklist of items considered to be indicative of quality in mail service. Surveillance will be performed quarterly on a sampling basis.

It is understood that the Contractor staff performing this work will not be under Federal supervision; however, they must work closely with Federal employees, and in many instances, receive approval from the Government Project Officer before action is taken. The contract will also be monitored by monthly statistical and narrative reports prepared and submitted by the Contractor. Spot checks will be made by the Government Project Officer to ensure that work is performed efficiently and effectively. Discussions will be held between the Government Project Officer and contract staff to correct any procedural errors and resolve any differences. Contractor will be responsible for making any corrections required.

IV. Surveillance Plan and Checklist

During performance of this contract, the Contractor shall be monitored by the Government Project Officer, using at a minimum the following questions:

a. Is the Contractor complying with the documents cited as authorities in this Statement of Work?

b. Does the Contractor have a written operating manual within 60 days (draft) and 90 days (completed) following ED directives and other appropriate guidelines, and is it being followed?

c. Is the mailroom facility neat and orderly in appearance?

d. Is the staff of the mail facility courteous and helpful to users?

e. Does the mail facility staff understand the needs of its users and are its services responsive to them?

f. Does the mail facility staff understand the organization it services and know how to route the mail correctly and/or locate addresses?

Checklist Item

a. Workload

1. Delivery (same day service)
2. Collection (four complete trips daily)

3. Bulk delivery (at least twice daily)
4. Desk-to-desk service (timely and accurate)

b. Accuracy of sorting and delivery (less than 5% error rate)

c. Timeliness of reports.

1. Monthly (by 10th of following month)
2. Annual reports to USPS (within 10 working days of notification of requirements)

d. User satisfaction (fewer than five complaints per month)

V. Reporting Requirements

The Contractor shall submit a written monthly financial, statistical and narrative report to the Government Project Officer. This report will include the following information:

1. No. pieces incoming White House mail ____________
2. No. pieces look up addressee mail ____________
3. No. pieces all other mail ____________
4. No. pieces outgoing mail ____________
5. Postage cost outgoing mail ____________
6. No. complaints ____________
7. No. complaints handled satisfactorily ____________
8. No. pieces outgoing Express Mail ____________
9. Cost outgoing Express Mail ____________
10. No. pieces Registered Mail ____________

    Incoming ____________

    Outgoing ____________
11. No. pieces certified mail ____________

    Incoming ____________

    Outgoing ____________

12. No. pieces special (over $100 postage) registered mail________

    Incoming ____

    Outgoing ____

13. Cost total outgoing special registered mail _________________

14. No. invoice reconciliations domestic small parcel common carriers____

15. No. business reply ____________________________________

16. No. postage due ______________________________________

17. Cost postage due _____________________________________

18. No. address corrections _______________________________

19. No. postal manifests reconciled _________________________

Sample 2

Janitorial Services

Type of Work: General Support Services

Objective: To provide janitorial and trash removal services, including management, supervision, labor, materials, supplies, and equipment to perform such services.

SOW Type: Performance

Comments:

- Detailed performance specifications; contract could be awarded firm fixed price by sealed bid.
- Good description of when work is to be performed.
- Detailed description of government- and contractor-furnished supplies, materials, equipment, and utilities.

Contract No. 14-08-0001-23275

Option Year 4: August 1, 1991 – July 31, 1992

Contract Line Item Number (CLIN)	Description	Qty.	Unit	Unit Price	Total
005	Janitorial services & trash removal in accordance with specifications contained herein.	12	month	$82,775.25	$993,303.09

Section C – Description/Specification/Work Statement

C.1 Scope of Work

The contractor shall provide all management, supervision, labor, materials, supplies, and equipment (except as otherwise provided in Section C.5), and shall plan, schedule, coordinate and assure effective performance of all janitorial and trash removal services described herein at the fixed prices set forth in Section B. The contractor will be required to provide janitorial and trash removal services in accordance with the requirements of this solicitation at the John W. Powell and Solid State Physics Laboratory, 12201 Sunrise Valley Drive, Reston, Virginia 22092. Additionally, trash removal services only shall be provided at the E-1 Building, Isaac Newton Square, Reston, Virginia.

C.2 Contract Effort Required

(a) General: The Contractor is cautioned that the daily productive man-hour guidelines set forth below may be less than that which they will require to perform all of the daily and periodic work requirements. The determination of the total daily productive man-hour requirements for the performance of all services herein specified is the sole responsibility of the contractor.

(b) Daily Productive Man-hour Guidelines:

(1) The Government estimates that approximately 356 daily man-hours of productive labor, exclusive of supervisory work, will be required to satisfactorily accomplish the work called for in this contract. This base guideline fig-

ure of 356 daily hours of productive labor is included as a guideline only to assist the Contractor in planning and executing the work. It is of the utmost importance that the Contractor utilizes skilled and productive manpower in order to satisfactorily furnish the required level of services. Failure on the part of the Contractor to utilize skilled and productive manpower may produce unsatisfactory results which may cause the Government to make deductions from the Contractor's monthly invoices for unsatisfactory work or work not accomplished.

(2) The guideline productive man-hours specified in paragraph C.2 (b) above, do not include productive man-hours for utility work.

*Rate(s) subject to increase/decrease in the event the applicable collective bargaining agreement, the applicable DOL wage determinations, or the County of Fairfax rate for disposal of refuse is revised. Labor rates ad other benefits specifically set forth in the DOL wage determination or the applicable collective bargaining agreement, along with subcontracting costs for trash removal services, shall be the only cost elements subject to change.

(c) Utility Man-hours:

A minimum of 8 man-hours per day must be provided between the hours of 6:30 AM and 3:00 PM, Monday through Friday, except Federal holidays, for utility services as outlined in Exhibit 1, item 22. Hours not provided on one day may not be made up on a subsequent day. The utility man shall be furnished with a pager which shall be worn at all times for the purpose of answering emergency service calls.

C.3 Services Required

(a) The Contractor shall provide the janitorial services outlined at the frequencies specified in the Cleaning Work and Quality Requirements, Exhibit 1. Trash removal services are described in Exhibit 4 and Insect and Rodent Control requirements are set forth in Exhibit 5.

(b) The building areas to be serviced are described in Exhibit 2. The figures contained in Exhibit 2 are approximate and are estimates of the building statistical data. The Contractor is responsible for verifying dimensions and quantities.

(c) All work shall be performed between the hours of 6:30 AM and 9:00 PM within the normal 5-day week observed by the building occupants, Federal holidays excluded (New Year's Day, Martin Luther King's Birthday, Washington's Birthday, Memorial Day, Independence Day, Labor Day, Columbus Day, Veteran's Day, Thanksgiving Day, and Christmas Day). No work shall be performed on weekends when the Government has no force on duty available for the inspection of the Contractor's work unless prior written approval of the Contracting Officer's Representative is obtained. Toilet room cleaning shall be accomplished after the normal working hours (6:30 AM–6:00 PM) of the building occupants.

C.4 Supervision

(a) General:

The Contractor shall arrange for satisfactory supervision of the contract work. The Contractor or his supervisors shall be available at all times, when the contract work is in progress, to receive notices, reports, or requests from the Contracting Officer or his Representative. It is policy of the Government that Government direction or supervision of Contractor's employees, directly or indirectly, shall not be exercised.

(b) On-site supervisors:

The Contractor shall provide in writing to the Contracting Officer at least two (2) work days prior to the contract starting date the names, telephone numbers and addresses of on-site supervisors. The term "on-site supervisor" means a person designated in writing by the Contractor who has authority to act for the Contractor on a day-to-day basis at the work-site, and to accept and sign for notices of deductions, inspection reports, and all correspondence on behalf of the Contractor when a contract manager is not specified.

C.5 Government-Furnished Supplies, Materials, Equipment and Utilities

(a) Electrical power at existing outlets for the Contractor to operate such equipment as is necessary in the conduct of his work.

(b) Hot and cold water as necessary. The Contractor shall maintain clean wash basins/sinks at all times.

(c) Space within the building commensurate with the Contractor's personnel complement and operational requirements including clothes locker rooms, if available. Any existing equipment within USGS custodial space such as clothes lockers, tables, benches, chairs, etc., placed within the building by the Government may be used by the Contractor during the term of the contract provided authorization is received from the Contracting Officer's Representative. This space and equipment must be kept neat and clean and returned to the Government at the expiration of the contract in reasonably the same condition as at the time entering into the contract.

(d) Space in the building for the storage of an inventory of supplies and equipment which will be used in the performance of work under the contract. The Contractor shall maintain this space in a neat and orderly condition. The Government will not be responsible in any way for damage or loss to the Contractor's stored supplies, materials, replacement parts, or equipment.

(e) Janitor's closets, where available, at various points throughout the building, for storing equipment including mops, brooms, dust cloths, and other items. These closets and the stored equipment shall be kept clean and in an orderly manner by the Contractor.

(f) Space in the building and furniture and furnishings (to include telephone for restricted use) for a supervisor's office to be used for official business only in the performance of this contract. Telephones supplied by the Government are to be used for communication within the building only. Government property will not be used in any manner for any personal advantage, business gain, or other personal endeavor by the Contractor or the Contractor's employees.

(g) Heating and air conditioning of space to be cleaned during normal working hours of the building occupants.

C.6 Contractor Furnished Supplies, Materials, and Equipment

(a) The Contractor shall furnish all supplies, materials and equipment necessary for the performance of the work of this contract unless otherwise specified herein. These supplies and material shall be of a quality to conform with applicable Federal Specifications listed in Exhibit 3. Upon request of the COR, the Contractor shall submit a list giving the name of the manufacturer, the brand name and intended use of each of the materials that he proposes to use in the performance of the work and he shall not use any material which the COR determines would be unsuitable for the purpose or harmful to the surfaces to which applied.

(b) Any material which the COR suspects of not meeting Federal specifications shall be tested by a recognized testing laboratory at Contractor's expense. If however, the material tested meets the Federal specifications, the Government shall be responsible for the testing expense. A copy of the laboratory report giving the results of the test and a sample of each product, if requested, shall be submitted to the COR. These products shall meet the requirements established by applicable Federal specifications (see Exhibit 3) or be considered unacceptable for use.

(c) All necessary cleaning equipment including power driven floor scrubbing machines, waxing, and polishing machines, industrial type vacuum cleaners, wet pick-ups and all necessary motor trucks, etc., needed for the performance of the work of this contract shall be furnished by the Contractor. Such equipment shall be of the size and type customarily used in work of this kind and shall meet the approval of the COR. Defective equipment shall be repaired or replaced within 72 hours.

(d) The Contractor shall require all employees, including supervisors, to wear distinctive uniform clothing for ready identification, and assure that every employee is in uniform no later than 10 working days form the date an employee first enters on duty. Employees shall wear uniforms consisting of skirts and blouses, slacks or smocks, as appropriate. The uniform shall have the Contractor's name, easily identifiable, affixed thereon in a permanent or semi-permanent manner such as a badge or monogram. Any color or color combination, as appropriate, may be used for uniforms, except green. Employees shall be required to dress neatly, commensurate with the tasks being performed.

(e) The Contractor shall arrange with the telephone company for the installation, at his expense, of private outside business phones for his use in making calls outside the building.

C.7 Qualifications of Personnel

(a) Qualifications of Supervisory Employees

(1) All supervisory personnel engaged in directing the work to be accomplished under this contract shall possess at least 2 years of recent (within the past 5 years) experience in directing cleaning type operations in a supervisory capacity for buildings of the approximate size of the building(s) to be cleaned under this contract.

(2) A detailed resume containing the information specified below must be submitted to the Contracting Officer for approval prior to the assignment of any supervisors to the contract. Both new and replacement supervisors must meet these qualification standards.

(1) The full name of the proposed supervisor.

(2) A detailed description of the previous 5 years employment history of the proposed supervisor.

(3) The name(s) and address(es) of the companies for whom the proposed supervisor worked for the past 5 years, along with the name(s) and the telephone number(s) of his or her immediate supervisor

(3) Part III, Section J, Attachment A contains a format for submitting key personnel resumes.

(b) Qualification of Other Contractor Personnel

(1) General

The personnel employed by the contractor shall be capable employees, trained and qualified in custodial type work. The building shall be fully staffed beginning the first day of work under the contract, and initially not less than 50 percent of the staff shall be trained and experienced cleaning personnel who will exhibit the capability of operating with a minimum of supervision. The remainder of the staff shall be fully trained and qualified within 30 days after the initial starting date. All personnel will receive close and continuing first-line supervision by the Contractor.

C.8 Scheduling Work and Reporting Accomplishments

(a) Five work days after the contract starting date, and annually thereafter if options are exercised by the Government, the Contractor shall submit an annual schedule of all daily and periodic cleaning. The daily cleaning schedule shall include specific areas, day of week and time of day work will be provided. Daily cleaning is defined as services performed every 10 days or less frequently. The periodic cleaning schedule shall include specific areas and dates. Periodic cleaning is defined as work required for performance monthly or less frequently.

(b) The Contractor shall submit to the Contracting Officer's Representative a daily work report of the jobs performed for comparison with the scheduled requirements. Exhibit 6, Quality Control Form, shall be used for this purpose. The Contracting Officer's Representative will examine the Contractor's work and work report daily.

C.9 Quality Control Program

The Contractor shall establish and maintain a complete quality control program to assure the requirements of the contract are provided as specified. One copy of the Contractor's Quality Control Plan shall be provided at the time of proposal submission to the Contracting Officer for approval. Additional plans shall be provided by the Contactor as mutually agreed to changes occur. The program shall include, but not be limited to the following:

(a) An inspection system covering all the services stated in the Cleaning Requirements section (Exhibit 1) of this contract. A checklist used in inspecting contract performance during regularly scheduled or unscheduled inspections. The name(s) of the individual(s) who will perform the inspection.

(b) The checklist shall include every area of the operation serviced by the Contractor as well as every task required to be performed.

(c) A system for identifying and correcting deficiencies in the quality of services before the level of performance becomes unacceptable and/or the Government inspectors point out the deficiencies.

(d) A file of all inspections conducted by the contractor and the corrective action taken. This documentation shall be made available to the Government during the term of the contract, and until such time as final payment is made.

C.10 Physical Security

The Contractor shall be responsible for safeguarding all government property provided for contractor use. At the close of each work period, government facilities, equipment and material shall be secured.

(a) Key control: The Contractor shall establish and implement methods of insuring that all keys issued to the Contractor by the Government are not lost or misplaced and are not used by unauthorized persons. No keys issued to the Contractor by the Government shall be duplicated. The Contractor shall develop procedures covering key control that will be included in the quality control plan.

(1) The Government may, at its option, require the Contractor to replace, re-key, or reimburse the Government for replacement of locks or re-keying as a result of the Contractor losing keys.

(2) The Contractor shall immediately report the occurrence of a lost key to the COR.

(3) It is the responsibility of the Contractor to prohibit the use of keys issued by the Government by any persons other than the Contractor's employees. It is also the responsibility of the Contractor to prohibit the opening of locked areas by the Contractor's employees to permit entrance of persons other than Contractor's employees engaged in the performance of assigned work.

Section D – Packaging and Marking

Reserved

Sample 3

Landscape Maintenance

Type of Work: General Support Services

Objective: To provide landscape maintenance services for the John Wesley Powell Federal Building.

SOW Type: Performance

Comments:

- Extremely detailed performance specification. Could serve as a job description.
- Detailed description of the tasks to be accomplished.
- Supplemental instructions are provided for additional clarity.
- Terms and definitions section is included to reduce the misinterpretation.
- The term "etc." is used multiple times throughout the document. The use of this term creates uncertainty about and hedges the requirements.

Table of Contents
For Section C

Section C – Description/Statement of Work

Landscape Maintenance Specifications
For the John Wesley Powell
Federal Building, Reston, VA

I. FERTILIZING: Fertilizer to be used shall be 10-6-4, with 50 percent of the available nitrogen being organic.

A. Ornamentals

i. Trees: Use 2 pounds of fertilizer for each inch of trunk caliper measured 1 foot above the ground. For trunks with a caliper of less than 3 inches, use ½ pound of fertilizer per inch. Using a soil auger, or equivalent, make holes 6 to 12 inches deep and 30 to 36 inches apart in concentric circles around the trunk, with the innermost holes midway between the trunk and dripline (the area beneath the ends of the longest branches), and the outermost holes just beyond the dripline. Distribute the fertilizer equally among the holes and then fill with soil. Time of application shall be between February 1 and March 15.

ii. Shrubs: The area to be fertilized shall have all weeds and leaves removed. Fertilizer shall be uniformly applied to the area immediately below the branches and at least several inches beyond. Care shall be exercised to avoid damaging shrubs being fed. Shrubs shall be fed at the rate of 4 pounds of fertilizer per 100 square feet of area. Time of application shall be between February 1 and March 15.

iii. Ground Cover: Broadcast fertilizer uniformly over all ground cover areas. Ground cover shall be fed at the rate of 10 pounds of fertilizer per 1000 square feet of area. Time of application shall be between February 1 and March 15.

B. Grass: Prior to Spring fertilization only, the entire lawn area shall be core aerated in two directions by physically removing soil cores by means of hollow spoons or tines. After coring is complete, the area shall be dragged to break up cores and to redistribute the soil. Fertilizer shall then be disrupted uniformly over the entire lawn with a minimum of overlapping or skipping. Grass shall be fed 2 times a year at the rate of 10 pounds of fertilizer per 1000 square feet of area. Time of the first application shall be between March 15 and April 15, and the second application between October 15 and November 15.

NOTE: Liquid fertilizer shall be performed after working hours unless otherwise approved by the Contracting Officer's Representative (COR). Liquid fertilization programs for ornamentals and turf, equal to or better than the above, shall be considered for approval.

II. Mulching: Apply evenly 2 inches of mulch one time, using shredded hardwood bark. Mulch material shall be a commercial grade. It shall be free of sticks, stones, clods, or other foreign material. All area to be mulched shall be raked, debris removed and edge reestablished prior to mulch application. Mulch must be furnished in original containers. If bulk mulch is used, samples and certifications of its contents must be submitted to a Government Designated Representative prior to application. All ornamentals, including borders and openings within ground cover beds, shall be mulched. Mulch shall be applied by April 30. All unmulched trees shall be mulched as follows: No trees shall be mulched with an area of less than 30 inches in diameter, at the rate of 6 inches of mulch per 1 inch of trunk caliper measured 1 foot above the ground, whichever is greater.

NOTE: Any excessive mulch buildup shall be removed by the Contractor before new mulch is applied.

III. Pruning: Pruning shall be done during the dormant season.

A. Trees

1. All necessary precautions shall be taken to prevent personal injury or damage to property. Pruning shall include but not be limited to removing sprouts at or near the base of the tree, elimination of narrow V-shaped forks that lack strength, thinning of crowns, maintenance of natural appearance and maintenance of growth within space limitations, removing branches that limit headroom of pedestrians and/or vehicles, and removing or shortening branches that threaten to interfere with overhead wiring in all areas close to buildings once a year. Additional sucker growth, diseased and infested branches, and branches damaged

by storms, etc., shall continually be removed at no additional cost to the Government, as soon as the condition has become apparent. Tools used for removing diseased wood shall be disinfected immediately after such use.

2. Care shall be exercised not to leave stubs and to avoid stripping of bark. All cuts over 1 inch in diameter shall be covered immediately with an approved tree-wound compound.

3. Nature trails shall be cleared of branches and obstructing growth of 8 feet in height and 6 feet in width (see Exhibit 1).

4. Fallen branches shall be removed from the premises at the Contractor's expense.

5. All support stakes, support apparatus, and wrapping shall be removed after one year from date of installation.

6. Trees of up to 3 inch diameter, when uprooted or disturbed, shall be set vertically, centered, staked, mulched, and watered accordingly, at the Contractor's expense.

B. Shrubs. Individual plants shall be pruned by selectively thinning as much as 25 percent of the existing old wood, including branches that are dead, damaged, diseased, or infested. Any significant reshaping of plants shall first be approved by the Government representative.

C. Ground Cover. All ground cover shall be cut back and/or thinned in accordance with proper horticultural procedure. Herbaceous perennials shall have spent flower stalks and dead foliage removed throughout the growing season, at no additional cost to the Government.

IV. Shearing:

A. Shrubs and Trees: Formal shrubs (hedges, etc.) and formal trees shall be sheared/clipped approximately once every 30 days during the growing season. First service shall be performed when new growth reaches 3 inches. All other types of shrubs, including flowering, shall be sheared in accordance with proper horticultural practice.

B. Ground Cover: During the growing season all ground cover shall be trimmed once each month as needed. Once dormant, herbaceous perennials shall be sheared in accordance with proper horticultural practice, at no additional cost to the Government.

V. Weed Control: Weed control shall be performed when weeds are actively growing and includes the killing and complete removal of all weeds from the following areas:

A. Ornamentals: Trees, shrubs, and ground cover shall be weeded during the growing season (Approximately April through September).

B. Turf: Turf areas shall be treated 2 times with each application consisting of both pre-emergent and post-emergent herbicides. Time of each treatment will be approved by the COR. The Contractor may be recalled for additional weed control, as necessary, under the terms and specifications of this contract, at no additional cost to the Government.

C. Non-planted Areas: Parking lots, sidewalks, gravel areas, etc., are to be weeded once each month.

D. Fences: Fences shall be treated 4 times annually (once in April, June, August, October), and maintained with a 6 inch bare strip on both sides.

E. Snow Roads: Shall be mowed two (2) times during the growing season to remove weeds and woody growth. (See Exhibit 1).

VI. Insect and Disease Control: The contractor shall be responsible for the development and adherence to a pest control program for ornamentals and turf, which shall be preventative as well as remedial. The Contractor shall develop a written pest control program and submit it to the COR within 15 calendar days of contractor's receipt of notice of contracted award. All ornamentals shall be sprayed during one operation. The Contractor shall be liable for all phototoxic reactions. Spraying shall be performed after working hours as approved by the COR (overtime compensation is not authorized for this effort). The Contractor may be recalled for additional spraying, as necessary, under the terms and specifications of this contract, at no additional cost to the Government. Appropriate warning signs shall be posted, and hung in a way so as not to cause injury to plant material.

VII. Turf Renovation: Turf shall be renovated between August 15 and September 15 as follows:

A. Locate and mark all underground irrigation heads.

B. Cut grass to a height of 1 inch to 1 ½ inches.

C. Vertically mow (dethatch).

D. Rake and remove all thatch and debris.

E. Fertilize grass as defined under "Fertilizing" (See Section C.I.B).

F. Seed at the rate of 6 pounds of seed per 1000 square feet of area. Apply seed uniformly by means of a power drill or power disc seeder, or equivalent, so that seed is planted and covered with approximately 1/8 to 1/4 inch of soil. The seed mixture shall be 90 percent K-31 tall fescue and 10 percent Kentucky blue grass, shall be certified, and approval by the COR.

G. Immediately after seeding, the entire area shall be watered and then kept moist to assure even germination.

VIII. Preparation for Flower Bed and Planter: Preparation for the existing 11 flower beds and 29 planters shall be performed once in the Spring when annual flowers are planted and once in the Fall at the time bulbs are planted, as follows: (See Exhibit 1A)

A. Clear soil of all surface growth and till until clumps and clods have been broken up. Depth of tilling shall be no less than 6 inches. Prior to Spring planting only, 1 inch of shredded sphagnum peat horticultural grade and 1 inch of clean builder's sand, shall be evenly spread over the planting area and tilled into the soil. Also, prior to Spring planting only, soil is to be fumigated with methyl bromide, or equivalent.

B. Apply and mix into the soil 2 pounds of 5-10-5 fertilizer per 100 square feet of area in the Spring, and 3 pounds of commercial grade cooked bone meal per 100 square feet of area in the Fall.

C. Rake over keeping within existing grade, but with a slight roll towards the center. The flower bed or planter shall be neat in appearance with a well defined edge.

D. All flowers and bulbs will be furnished by the Government, and shall be picked up by the Contractor within 1 working day after being notified. All flowers and bulbs shall be installed within 5 working days after they have been received. Plants (and bulbs) shall be treated with care at all times. They shall not be dropped, thrown, or handled in such a manner as to be damaging to development of growth. Plants or bulbs which are damaged by the Contractor, or his personnel, shall be replaced by the Contractor at no cost to the Government.

E. Spring Planting – All annuals shall be planted no later than May 21st to maintain early growth and visual appearance.

F. Plant in holes large enough to allow for spreading of roots and at depths recommended for each type of plant. Spacing of plants will be prescribed by the COR. The Government will provide the Contractor with a drawing or plan of plants to be planted.

G. The Contractor shall be responsible for watering the plants immediately following planting. Care shall be taken not to disturb plants, or to induce excessive run off.

IX. <u>Maintenance for Existing flower Bed and Planter</u>: To ensure that flowers are kept in a horticulturally acceptable condition at all times, the Contractor shall provide maintenance services, including all required material, but not limited to, the following: (See Exhibit 1A)

A. Weeding and Cultivation: During the growing season, the Contractor shall remove weeds at least once every 2 weeks. After weeding, the Contractor shall cultivate and restore edges where needed.

B. Planter-Watering: The Contractor shall be required to water ornamentals and turf that are in planters on a regularly scheduled basis, with prior approval through the COR. Adequate soil moisture necessary to encourage growth and development must be maintained.

C. Trimming and Pinching (during the growing season): Spent blooms, dead foliage, and unusual sprouts shall be removed every 2 weeks on a regular schedule. Pinching is included as part of this contract.

D. Fertilization: In July, 2 pounds of 5-10-5 fertilizer per 100 square feet of area shall be applied

E. Pest Control: If pests become evident, appropriate pest control shall be provided by the Contractor.

F. Winter Protection: If necessary, in the Fall after bulbs have been planted, the Contractor shall provide and install protective fencing around the perimeter of flower beds and planters to discourage pedestrian traffic.

G. Removal of Plants: After bulbs have flowered in the Spring and annual flowers have expired in the Fall, all plants shall be removed. Flower beds and planters shall then be cleaned and made ready for the next tilling. Care shall be taken not to remove excessive amounts of soil.

NOTE: The number of frequencies as stipulated in Section B.1 of the pricing schedule was derived by the following formula:

40 beds and planters x 2 times per month x 6 months (growing season) = 480

X. Watering: The contractor shall water plants as required, to maintain soil moisture necessary to encourage growth and development of flowers, and shall be required to apply water when testing or visual appearance indicate additional need.

XI. Plant Removal: The Contractor shall remove shrubs and trees, including stumps, which are marked for removal by the Government representative. Where plants are removed, the hole shall be backfilled with topsoil, tamped, raked and shall be covered with either mulch or sod, at no additional cost to the Government. Base of plant measurement shall determine the diameter size.

XII. Edging: Ornamentals shall have a well defined edge established and maintained once every month during the growing season. All metal edging shall be kept in good appearance, including tamping and realignment.

XII. Leaf Removal: Leaves shall be removed from all ornamentals, flowers, turf, fence areas, and paved nature trails with prior approval through the COR.

XIV. Grass Cutting:

A. Grass cutting shall be scheduled so that it does not interfere with vehicle parking. Areas to be cut shall be policed prior to mowing operations to remove and paper, stones, or debris which may have accumulated. Grass cutting equipment shall be operated, so as not to permit discharge from chutes within 10 feet of buildings, vents, mulch beds, etc. Mowing equipment shall be equipped with sharp blades and shall be set to cut grass at a height of no less than 2 inches. During periods of drought, the period between cuttings shall be extended to allow grass to attain a height of 2 ½ inches (minimum) before cutting. Deviation from the schedule shall not be permitted unless directed by the COR. A grass cutting cycle must be completed prior to starting a new cycle within 4 working days, including edging.

B. Edging around curbs, walks, etc., shall be done with a power edger (blade type) each time the grass is cut. A well defined line must be established and maintained.

C. Trimming around monuments, flagpoles, walls, signs, etc., shall be done each time the grass is cut. Trimming height is the same as the grass-cutting height.

D. Lawn areas containing naturalized plantings of flowering plants (daffodils), shall not be mowed until their foliage has turned yellowish-brown and died back to the ground.

XV. Liming:

A. The Contractor shall be required to test soil in all areas under contract. Soil tests shall be conducted by a Government laboratory or recognized commercial laboratory. Certified copies of the soil test shall be submitted to the COR. A complete analysis of the soil is required. If soil tests indicate a need to lime, it shall be applied uniformly at 50 pounds per 1000 square feet, with a minimum of overlapping or skipping. Time of application shall be between January 1 and the last day of

February. Lime shall be pulverized dolomitic limestone (horticultural grade) and contain not less than 85 percent of calcium and magnesium carbonates. Containers shall be labeled to show chemical and mechanical analysis.

B. In addition, if soil tests or plant material indicate a need for trace elements, they shall be applied by the Contractor at no additional cost to the Government.

XVI. Additional Services: As required, the Contractor shall provide the following services, within fifteen (15) calendar days after receipt of written notice from the Contracting Officer.

A. Filling depressions using the following methods:

i. Furnishing Topsoil: Topsoil shall be fertile, friable loam suitable for growth of grass and other plants. It shall be free of subsoil material, sticks, stones, weeds, debris, and other material harmful or toxic to growth. A sample, with analysis, shall be submitted to the COR for approval. Areas shall be cleared of all growth and debris, scarified, filled with topsoil, tamped and raked. Placement of topsoil shall meet existing grade, with allowances for sod in lawn areas.

ii. Sodding: All grass sod shall be a certified mixture of 90 percent K31 tall fescue and 10 percent Kentucky blue grass. Sod shall be 1 inch thick, well established, and free of pests. Sod shall be approved by the COR. Areas to be sodded shall be cleared of all growth and debris and raked smooth. Soil shall be loose and workable, but firm enough to provide proper footing. Sod shall be laid without voids in a brick-work fashion and tamped or rolled in place. Sod laid on extreme slopes shall be staked until firmly rooted. The completed surface shall be uniform and conform to existing grade. Sod shall be thoroughly watered after installation and kept moist until it becomes thoroughly established. If necessary the Contractor shall provide and install protective fencing.

iii. Additional Seeding: Areas to be seeded shall be cleared of all debris and raked smooth. The seed and its application shall be as defined under "Turf Renovation." If necessary the Contractor shall provide and install protective fencing.

iv. Additional Mulching: Mulch and its application shall be as defined under "Mulching."

v. Excavation: Excavation shall consist of the removal and disposal of unsatisfactory soil unsuitable for planting and comprised of hard and compacted materials, such as disintegrated rock, debris, etc. The Contractor shall locate and mark all underground utilities in areas of work. Excavation does not include any drilling or blasting.

vi. Planting Preparation (for new additional established flower beds & planters): Area to be planted shall be eradicated and cleared of all growth, roto-tilled to a depth of 6 inches, raked over, and brought to grade. Completion of this process includes the removal of debris, etc., and the establishment of an edge. The Contractor might be required to amend the existing soil with peat moss and/or sand.

1. Peat moss: Peat moss shall be a natural product of shredded sphagnum peat, horticultural grade, and shall be evenly spread over the planting area and tilled into the soil.

2. Sand: Sand shall be clean builder's sand, free of toxic materials, and shall be evenly spread over the planting area and tilled into the soil.

B. Planting:

i. Plant pits shall be dug 1 ½ times the dimensions of the root ball. All plants shall be set in the pit on a layer of compacted backfill (topsoil or approved soil mixture) vertically and centered accordingly. The most desirable side of the plant shall face toward the prominent view. All air spaces and voids surrounding the root ball shall be backfilled to half the depth of the ball, and then tamped so as to stimulate the plant in a stable and well aligned position. For balled and burlapped plants, excess burlap and typing cord shall be folded back or removed accordingly. All plastic wrapping shall be completely removed before the placement of backfill. Remainder of pit shall then be backfilled conforming to established grades, tamped and watered thoroughly, and all within the same planting day. Care shall be taken during handling, backfilling, tamping, and watering to avoid plant damage, especially cracking or breaking of the root.

ii. All excavated material shall be removed from the planting area and all seals, tags, cord, etc., shall be removed from the plants.

iii. Smaller plants, such as flowers, bulbs, and ground cover shall be planted in holes large enough to allow for spreading of roots and at depths recommended for each type of plant. Ground cover may be planted after the mulch has been applied.

iv. Potted plants shall be removed from containers, including peat pots, before planting.

v. All plants, as needed, shall be pruned, sheared, wrapped, guyed, and staked, and all planting areas shall be edged, cultivated, and mulched in accordance with standard industry practice.

vi. The Contractor shall locate and mark all underground utilities in areas of work.

vii. The Contractor shall be responsible for a period of 1 year after completion of plant installation to maintain and guarantee all ornamentals. Plants that are dead, unsightly, or unhealthy shall be replaced immediately at no additional cost to the government provided that the government can prove the furnished plant(s) was healthy and the contractor was negligent in maintenance performance.

NOTE: Upon delivery, the Contractor shall be responsible for the unloading, placing, and if necessary, the sustaining of all plant material prior to planting.

C. Transplanting: Plants shall be dug with a firm ball, retaining as many fibrous roots as necessary to assure full recovery. The root ball shall be wrapped in burlap and tied, and transported carefully to avoid cracking or breaking. Plants shall not be handled by the trunk or stems and the roots or balls of the plants shall be protected from the sun, drying winds, and frost. Care should be taken to keep the root ball moist. Antidesicant shall be applied on all plant material dug while in foliage. All plants shall be planted, maintained, and guaranteed as defined under "Planting."

XVII. Supplemental Instructions:

A. Although the performance of all work requirements is under the responsibility and management of the Contractor, the Government reserves the right to review and approve all work items before their accomplishment.

B. The Contractor shall discuss with the COR the scheduling of daily work requirements.

C. The Contractor shall require all employees to wear distinctive uniform clothing for ready identification, and shall assure that every employee is in uniform no later than the time specified by the Contracting Officer, or otherwise, no later than ten working days from the date an employee first enters on duty. The uniform shall have the Contractor's name easily identifiable, and attached in a permanent or semi-permanent manner, such as a badge or monogram. Employees shall be required to dress neatly, commensurate with the tasks of being performed.

D. The Contractor shall be certified for pesticide application as required by law. All pesticide applications shall be applied by certified pesticide applicators, or under the direct supervision of a certified applicator.

E. If functional, the Contractor may connect to existing hose bibs, water lines, or other connections which are provided for the purpose of watering, otherwise water shall be provided by the Contractor.

F. The Contractor shall provide the hose, sprays, sprinklers and/or other equipment needed to properly apply the correct amount of moisture. Watering shall be measured on the day of application only. A definite schedule shall be required from the Contractor. The COR, at his/her own discretion, reserves the right to measure the depth of water penetration. The Contractor is required to apply sufficient water to penetrate a minimum of 6 inches. Care shall be exercised when watering excessively dry planters.

G. The Contractor is responsible for the repair, replacement, and proper functioning of all underground irrigation heads, except in cases of vandalism by others.

H. Work shall not be considered completed until the Contractor has removed from the premises all trash, debris, litter, grass-cuttings, trimmings, etc., which accumulate in the performance of work. Containers for handling this material shall be furnished by the Contractor.

I. The Contractor shall restore any damage caused by his operations, including the replacement of plant material damaged as a result of negligence, at no cost to the Government.

J. The Contractor shall furnish the COR with certification that all materials used in the fulfillment of this contract conform to applicable Federal Specifications.

XVIII. Terms and Definitions

A. Ornamentals: Refers to all trees, shrubs, and ground cover (including vines and herbaceous perennials).

B. Dormant Pruning: The pruning of plants while in a state of dormance. The process involves the removal of up to 25 percent of the woody growth on each plant, without materially changing the visual appearance of the plant. This technique is a highly technical process and shall be performed by experienced gardeners only

C. Planter: Any structure made to contain plants, including turf, such as:

   i. Any planting which is not on grade with its contiguous surroundings, with or without a natural bottom.

   ii. Any planting in a court, on a roof, in deck areas, or plazas.

D. Growing Season: Approximately April through September

Sample 4

Nonprofessional Program Support

Type of Work: General Support Service

Objective: To provide program support services in the following areas: proposal processing and related support, document and report preparation, information dissemination, and special analyses, studies, and evaluations.

SOW Type: Level-of-Effort

Comments:

- The task areas are fairly well defined.
- This level-of-effort contract is also a cost plus fixed fee. This type of work statement is more commonly used in a fixed price level-of-effort contract.
- Good description of the onsite support services to be provided by the contractor.
- Succinct description of the basis for award.
- Detailed description of the technical and business proposal evaluation factors.
- The term "etc." is used multiple times throughout the document. The use of this term creates uncertainty about and hedges the requirements.

CPS 01-001

Section C – Description/Specifications/Work Statement

C.1 Introduction/Background

The National Science Foundation (NSF) is an independent Federal Agency whose mission is to promote and advance scientific and engineering progress in the United States. The Foundation does this primarily by supporting scientific and engineering research and education activities. NSF does not itself conduct research, but receives and review proposals, and makes awards to academic and other institutions which actually conduct the research.

NSF is structured according to academic disciplines with grant-making offices and divisions for the various disciplines. Programs within each NSF office and division receive proposals, review them and make grants or other awards for projects based upon multiple reviews by members of the appropriate scientific community. The objective of the proposed contract is to provide the National Science Foundation with program support services in the following areas:

A. Proposal processing and related support;

B. Document and report preparation;

C. Information dissemination; and

D. Special analyses, studies, and evaluations;

Similar services are being provided under an existing NSF contract to Capital Systems Group, Inc. for specific program support. However, these services will be provided to a variety of NSF offices and divisions and will be primarily performed at the Contractor's facilities. Some work will be performed at NSF and at meeting sites as designated. The work likely to be performed at NSF include Task Areas A.4.a, b, c, d, e and f, and A.5.g Appropriate NSF officials and divisions will provide temporary space for Contractor personnel when working at NSF. Approximately 10,000 proposals will be processed at various times during the first year under this contract. (Proposals in future years are likely to increase).

C.2 Areas of Task Activity – Detailed Scope of Work

The Contractor shall provide the following support services to a variety of NSF Offices and Divisions when specifically authorized by the Contracting Officer.

Task Area A: Proposal Proceeding and Related Support

1. Proposal Processing Support

NSF will perform the following initial data entry support services:

(a) Identify appropriate program and assign appropriate identification numbers to the proposals (The average size of a proposal is 35 pages);

(b) Prepare proposal folders ("jackets");

(c) When requested, pull appropriate number of "reading copies" (up to 2) and deliver to appropriate NSF program office or division;

(d) Prepare proposals for pick up by Contractor.

In providing proposal processing and related support services the Contractor shall perform the following:

(a) Arrange for pick up at NSF and delivery of proposals to the Contractor's office(s). (The Contractor shall receive up to 20 copies of each proposal.) (NOTE: The Contractor will not have access to franking privileges of NSF contract express delivery services);

(b) Affix gummed labels provided by NSF to the proper proposal jacket;

(c) Insert jacket products provided by NSF (i.e., NSF Form 1036, Page 1, and Principle Investigator Form) into proper proposal jacket in a manner specified by NSF (Jacket products for each proposal will be provided each day by program the day after the Contractor has performed data entry);

(d) At the request of NSF, deliver labeled proposal jackets containing the original of each proposal to the appropriate NSF program office or division;

(e) Store extra copies of proposals in numerical order in numbered boxes for quick retrieval (Proposals received from NSF will not be in numerical order due to the use of several log sheets. The Contractor will be required to store up to

20 copies of each proposal at its facility. Approximately 250 square feet of space will be needed. The storage facility used by the contractor should be one with a secured area.);

(f) Maintain listing of proposals which shows the number of each proposal and the number of the box containing the proposal;

(g) Amend proposal jackets with documents that may come in after receipt of original proposal (e.g. reference letters) and;

(h) Perform other related proposal processing support services.

2. Data Entry Support

(a) Provide up to five modems and up to five workstations with the ability to communicate via modem and telephone line at 9600 baud, to the IBM Mainframe Database, located at NSF. At night, NSF transfers data to the host Hewlett Packard 3000 System for printing of jacket products. (Costs for phone line access to NSF computer and installation of modems will be paid by the Contractor under the contract. The Contractor will be required to provide 9600 baud modems for Contractor facility equipment only.);

(b) Test the system at least one month prior to due date of proposals and assist in identification and resolution of problems;

(c) Generate necessary proposal documentation;

(d) Enter proposal data into the NSF database and verify accuracy of data entry. The Contractor may be required to create files for new grantees (e.g. principal investigator or institution code files.) (The contractor is not required to have detailed knowledge of the specifics of the NSF database. Attachment A shows screen descriptions and data fields included in the proposal data entry process);

(e) Log-in the proposals, recording detailed data (such as the institution name and address, principal investigator, title, and amount requested, etc.);

(f) Enter any additional or special data as requested by NSF;

(g) Update existing information already in the system (such as corrections and address changes); and

(h) Perform other related proposal data entry support services.

3. Distribution Support

(a) At the request of NSF, pull the required number of copies of each proposal for panel members and/or ad hoc reviewers and provide additional copies when the number of proposals is insufficient;

(b) Package NSF requested proposals, along with any other transmittal or informational documents provided by NSF;

(c) Mail packaged proposals and documentation to the appropriate panel members and/or ad hoc reviewers by a method that ensures receipt by the addressee within the time specified by NSF. (The Contractor shall return bulk mailings to NSF Mail Room for mailing at the government rate); and

(d) Perform other related distribution support services.

4. Review Process Support

(a) When requested, provide appropriate professionals and experts who, under NSF guidance will assist in identifying and selecting appropriate panelists and ad hoc reviewers for each proposal. (Contractor provided professionals or experts may be required to assist NSF staff and panelists by sitting in on panel discussions, and as appropriate responding to questions, providing advice, etc. based on knowledge of program, the review system and procedures ad the subject being discussed. Professionals or experts provided by the contractor will not be a member of chair review panels or sub-panels);

(b) Contact prospective reviewers, describe the program, invite them to participate in the review, and obtain necessary information form those who agree to serve as reviewers;

(c) Update lists of reviewers as appropriate.

(d) Assist in organizing panels or ad hoc review to ensure that proposals are assigned to appropriate disciplinary panels or ad hoc reviewers and that panelists and ad hoc reviewers represent a variety of institutions in terms of size, type, and other characteristics, and are appropriately balanced;

(e) When requested, assist in the conduct of the panel review, including overseeing panels and sub-panels and providing advice to panelists;

(f) Assist in documenting and verifying panel and sub-panel recommendations; as well as, advise NSF on the basis of such panel or reviewer comments (Verifying includes reviewing, checking and confirming original panel notes, summaries, etc. Verbatim transcription of meetings does not generally occur.); and

(g) Perform other related review process support.

5. <u>Panel Support</u>

(a) Provide up to 10 Microsoft® Windows compatible desktop computers with CD-ROM drives, printers and Microsoft Word® software, and deliver and install them at the designated review meeting site (These may be stand-alone desktop computers of choice since they will not have to communicate with the NSF IBM/HP systems.);

(b) Provide up to two working photocopy machines, capable of producing at least 35 copies per minute (finishing, i.e., stapling, not required), and deliver and install them at the designated review meeting site;

(c) Transport supplies (provided by NSF), to be used at the panel meetings, to the meeting site and distribute them to panel meeting rooms;

(d) Collect unused materials at the end of the meetings, box them, and dispose of them as directed by NSF;

(e) Convert handwritten panel notes and summaries to typed form during the meeting using Microsoft® Word on CD;

(f) Provide corrected versions, both hardcopy and CD, within 3-5 working days after the panel meeting as specified by NSF;

(g) Assist in reviewing all panel documentation to ensure consistency, clarity, and adherence to guidelines provided by NSF;

(h) Perform other related panel support services.

6. Documentation, Final Data Entry, and Proposal Disposition Support

(The Contractor must have the ability to prioritize the final processing of certain jackets as specified by NSF.)

(a) Assemble proposal jackets with all necessary documentation, including the proposal, notification letter, related reviews, and other documentation specified by NSF;

(b) At the request of NSF enter reviewer information, review results and necessary final data into the NSF database for all proposals recommended for award, declination or other disposition;

(c) Prepare and mail packages, including notification letters, program and review information, and any other documentation specified by NSF to all proposers;

(d) After completion of panel meetings, Contractor shall pick up proposal jackets from NSF, insert final jacket products (i.e. NSF Form 7 and Reviewer Comments) at its site and deliver proposal jackets back to NSF to appropriate offices or divisions for further processing; and

(e) Perform other related proposal documentation, data entry and proposal disposition support services.

Task Area B: Document and Report Preparation

In providing document and report preparation support the Contractor shall perform the following:

1. Assist in the preparation of annual summary of awards, program announcements, solicitations, brochures, newsletters, mailings, bibliographies, publications reports and other docu-

ments on an as needed basis during the contract. This support shall include preparation of text and graphics displays, editing and formatting award information, random sampling of data for accuracy, creating an award index, production of draft documents for review by staff members, final editing, creating final copy on a commonly used word processing tool such as WordPerfect™ or Microsoft® Word for printing by the NSF Printing Services Branch, and proofing the galleys.

2. Edit abstracts of NSF awards as needed for publications to assure grammatical, spelling, and document consistency of material prepared by NSF Staff (Attachment B). Editing of abstracts may include the removal of extraneous information, combining two or more paragraphs, removal of personal comments and first person sentence structure, and changing from future to past tense when appropriate. The contractor shall convert the file to a final copy in .doc or other format as specified by NSF and include an output (hard) copy for use by the NSF's Printing Services Branch (PSB) and proof read the galleys provided by the PSB Branch.

3. Enter bibliographic citations for each document (see Attachment C) in the NSF Program Documentation Data Base Maintain this as an up-to-date file for access. Information should include title; accession number (when available); author; awardee name and address; NSF grant number; NSF report number; NSF Directorate and Division; report date; subject key words; abstract; NTIS order number; award amount; fiscal year of award and statement regarding potential commercial application of research.

4. Reduce project summary language to standard, brief format in easily understood language. Communicate with awardee to verify accuracy, including bibliographic information, and secure acceptance of editorial changes.

5. Contact awardees to confirm all names associated with award, title and address. Make necessary changes in NSF data base and documents.

6. Ensure that reports meet submissions standards of the information networks to which program determines dissemination appropriate (Attachment D).

7. Assist NSF in submitting substantive technical reports to the National Technical Information Service (NTIS), and/or other appropriate dissemination networks.

8. Provide ad hoc writing, editorial and short document creation and other related services on an as needed basis. Since time is of the essence when working with short documents, material should typically be edited and returned to the NSF program within 48 hours of receipt.

9. At the request of NSF, respond to requests from the public for information by sending available reports, special bibliographies, or information or other material; and alternate source ordering information of NSF publications.

10. Provide other related report and document preparation.

Task Area C: Information Dissemination

In order to achieve NSF goals, offices and divisions must effectively transmit the results of supported research to scientists, engineers and other users in the public. Exhibits, conferences, and workshops are necessary to disseminate and collect information from the public. The Contractor shall provide the following:

1. Manage report resulting from NSF-supported research and disseminate reports and program announcements on an as needed basis. Periodically, the contractor shall be requested to manage and disseminate materials from the various NSF offices and divisions. The contractor shall be given prior notice of any required dissemination activities. All requests from NSF grantees, the general public and NSF staff shall be handled promptly, and if the material is unavailable, other application available information shall be provided.

2. Provide logistical support for NSF exhibit booths at approximately ten conferences throughout the United States yearly, and assist NSF staff in preparing materials to take to exhibits and conferences. Logistical support provided by the contractor may include arranging and paying for exhibit space (10' standard booth), shipping of exhibit booths, producing sufficient copies of forms to order NSF documents for distribution at each conference, repair and maintenance to exhibit booth, lit-

erature racks, and informing NSF staff of selected upcoming meetings that may be of interest to NSF staff. The booths will usually be staffed by NSF personnel, however, the contractor should be prepared to staff each exhibit if necessary using one person. On-site exhibit support services to be arranged and paid for will usually include:

1 – 4' red-draped table (sometimes a 6' or 8' table is needed)

1 standard sized blue carpet

1 side chair and waste basket

1 electrical outlet (if exhibit has electrical panels)

Daily booth cleaning services

Booth set-up and dismantling

Mailing labels

Two to five exhibits may require a hospitality suite including reserving and paying for the suite, setting up tables and chairs, preparing and sending letters of invitation, production of name tags, providing for coffee and light refreshments. The contractor may be required to provide some staff members to welcome guests and assist in operating the hospitality suite. The contractor shall pick up and warehouse NSF publications for shipment to exhibits, workshops, and conferences. The storage facility used by the contractor will not require a security system or personnel of any type. Representatives from NSF may conduct an on-site visit prior to contract award.

The contractor shall maintain an inventory and distribution report for each exhibit which includes the starting inventory and quantity received, shipped, returned, and distributed. The contractor shall prepare, update, and ship a set of "For Display Only" reference binders to each exhibit. These reference binders contain a sample copy of each publication that is typically distributed at an exhibit.

3. The Contractor shall provide workshop support services as required. Each workshop may have from 20 to 50 people in attendance with an average of 35 people per meeting. Ap-

proximately six of the workshops will be held on-site at NSF and six will be held in the Washington metropolitan area. The contractor shall arrange for coffee, break refreshments, and working lunches to be provided at the workshops, as well as any necessary shuttle transportation to and from the workshop location. The contractor shall meet with the NSF project manager to review the details of each workshop. The Contractor shall provide a variety of planning and on-site facilitation, preparation of conference agendas, schedules, and materials, invitations, pre-registration mailings, site selection and logistical coordination, special events, recording of proceedings, report dissemination and follow-up activities. Recorded data will include workshop names, participant full names, titles, home and work addresses, and phone numbers; resume summaries for all paper authors and chairpersons.

Once the format for all workshop reports, manuscripts, transcripts, etc. has been confirmed following each workshop, the Contractor's technical editor shall prepare and submit to NSF a draft version of the specified workshop product(s) in the designated format within 20 days following the workshop. Following review of all draft workshop documents and upon receipt of the Foundation's editing comments and changes, the contractor shall reproduce and distribute copies of the final documents as directed by the Contracting Officer's Technical Representative (COTR). Upon the COTR's request, the contractor shall submit these documents to the NTIS for public distribution.

Task Area D: Special Analysis, Studies and Evaluations

To ensure successful operation of the information processing and dissemination activities described above, the Contractor shall provide the following:

1. Perform statistical and narrative reports and analyses on the proposals received, their various characteristics including proposing institution, projects identified in proposals, as well as the review and disposition of the proposals;
2. Assist in developing and refining dissemination systems and procedures;

3. Perform special analyses of various aspects of dissemination activities;

4. Assist in evaluation and planning of project activities;

5. Perform other analyses, studies, and evaluations related to proposals.

C.3. Personnel Qualifications

Contractor personnel shall be familiar with the computing and operating environment that NSF offices ad divisions operate under. Contractors shall have previous experience in 3-Com+, WordPerfect™ and dBase software, Lotus 1-2-3™, and the Microsoft® Office suite.

C.4. Additional Information

Most desktop computers at NSF use the Windows operating system. NSF currently has two in-house central computer systems – an IBM 3090 and three Hewlett-Packard 3000 minicomputers. The IBM system runs in parallel with the HP 3000's. NSF uses network servers (3-Com+). NSF is currently reevaluating its network environment and choice of network operating systems. The Contractor is not required to provide mainframe support or applications.

Section D – Packaging and Marking

NOT APPLICABLE

Section E – Inspection and Acceptance

E.1 Evaluation and Acceptance

Evaluation and acceptance shall be performed by the Contracting Officer or _______________, or such other person(s) as may be designated in writing by the Contracting Officer. Evaluation and acceptance shall take place at the National Science Foundation, 1800 G Street, N.W., Washington, D.C.

E.2 Clauses Incorporated By Reference (FAR 52.252-2)

This contract incorporates the following clauses by reference, with the same force and effect as if they were given in full text. Upon request, the Contracting Officer will make their full text available.

FEDERAL ACQUISITION REGULATION
(48 CFR CHAPTER 1) CLAUSES

52.246-5 Inspection of Services – Cost Reimbursement (Apr 84)

All other evaluation and acceptance conditions have been incorporated under Section C, Description/Specification/Work Statement.

Section F – Deliveries of Performance

F.1 Term of the Contract

a. The Government will issue orders against this contract commencing on the effective date of the contract through _____________ (24 months). Each order placed prior to the above expiration date shall remain in full force and effect until its completion and final acceptance by the Government.

b. Should the Government elect to exercise Option One under this contract, in accordance with Section B.4, the term of this contract shall be as follows: _______________ (12 months).

c. Should the Government elect to exercise Option Two under this contract, in accordance with Section B.4, the term of this contract shall be ask follows: ______________ (12 months).

d. Should the Government elect to exercise Option Three under this contract, in accordance with Section B.4, the term of this contract shall be as follows: ______________ (12 months).

F.2 Task Order Procedure

Performance of this contract shall be pursuant to and as directed by written tasks orders which shall be consecutively numbered and contain, as a minimum, the following information:

A. Task Order Number.

B. Task Order subject and description of work.

C. Period of performance.

D. Estimated number of labor hours by labor category.

E. Reporting requirements, and other relevant information as applicable.

F. Accounting and appropriation data.

Task orders will be issued unilaterally by the Contracting Officer and each will name a Contracting Officer's Technical Representative (COTR).

Upon Contractor receipt of a written Task Order issued by the Contracting Officer, a detailed Task Plan shall be prepared by the Contractor, outlining all activities to be accomplished by the Contractor. The Task Plan shall contain, as a minimum:

Section M – Evaluation Factors for Award

M.1 Evaluation Factor for Award

1. Overall Basis for Award

The Government will select the offer which provides the greatest value to the Government. Technical, cost, experience and past performance, and applicable other factors will be considered by the Source Selection Official; however, the primary basis for selection will be the technical factors. Section L, Instruction for Preparation of Technical and Cost Proposals, contains important narrative on technical and cost proposal preparation. The Government reserves the right to make an award without discussions and/or negotiation.

2. Competitive Proposal Evaluation and Relative Importance of Factors

Proposals received in accordance with this RFP will be technically reviewed by an evaluation panel. Technical evaluation will be conducted to determine the relative merits of the offerors proposals in accordance with weighted evaluation criteria established by the Government prior to the receipt of proposals. The evaluation Panel will recommend to the Source Selection Official for award that proposal which offers the greatest value to the Government.

3. Evaluation of Priced Options

The Government will evaluate offers for award purposes by adding the total price for the options to the basic requirement. Evaluation of the options will not obligate the Government to exercise the option(s).

M.2 Technical Evaluation Factors

The technical evaluation factors that will be evaluated by the Government are listed below. The technical proposals should fully address each of the evaluation criteria; however, there is no intent to limit the contents of proposals, and the inclusion of additional pertinent information is permitted.

The factors are listed in descending order of importance with factor A being significantly more important than all other factors.

Evaluation Factors

A. Personnel Qualifications –

1. Project Manager
    a. Education, past experience, and training
    b. Work relevant to proposed effort
    c. Listing of recent project/tasks/jobs on which the individual has worked
    d. Managerial positions held and the number and type of employees supervised
    e. Names and telephone numbers of appropriate references
    f. Statement of commitment in terms of time and availability
    g. Ability to deal with personnel at all levels and special clientele primarily made up of academic scientists and engineers.
2. Other Personnel (contractor and subcontractor personnel, consultants, and experts)
    a. Education, past experience, skills and training
    b. Work relevant to proposed effort
    c. Listing of recent project/tasks/jobs on which the individuals have worked
    d. Names and telephone numbers of appropriate references
    e. Statement of commitment in terms of time and availability

f. Ability to deal with personnel at all levels and special clientele primarily made up of academic scientists and engineers.

B. Comprehension of the Project –

1. Understanding the tasks specified and their purposes and objectives.
2. Demonstrated awareness of the type of situations, problems and requirement to be encountered during contract performance.
3. The realism and completeness of the offerors proposed allocation of staff and other resources to the project effort.
4. The appropriateness of the offerors management plans for organizing its project staff and work efforts.

C. Organizational Qualifications –

1. Demonstrated capability and experience in performing the tasks identified.
2. Availability of and types of experienced support personnel to be utilized.
3. Priority organization would give this work relative to other work.

D. Facilities and Equipment –

1. Availability of facilities suitable for conducting the tasks specified in an efficient manner (including storage space) (See Section C, Task Area A.1.h.)
2. Availability of appropriate and current technological equipment required to satisfy the work requirements.
3. Accessibility of Contractor facility and personnel to NSF Headquarters.
4. List of equipment and facilities to be used under the contract.

M.3 Business Proposals Evaluation

The following factors will be analyzed by a business management panel and will not be numerically scored.

Business Factors

(1) COST/PRICE FACTORS will be analyzed to (a) assess the realism of the proposed cost/price and (b) determine the probable cost/price to the Government. COST/PRICE FACTORS will be considered and analyzed by the Government but will not be weighted or scored. The COST/PRICE FACTORS may also be used as an aid to determine the offerors understanding of the TECHNICAL REQUIREMENTS. Evaluation of COST/PRICE FACTORS will include the proposed cost/price for the basic contract period as well as for any priced option.

(2) EXPERIENCE AND PAST PERFORMANCE FACTORS are an important consideration in the Government's evaluation and selection, and require comprehensive treatment in response to the proposal. In the experience and past performance area, the Government will review and evaluate each offerors overall corporate performance, experience, and accomplishments. Evaluation criteria are:

– Performance History

– Cost Management History

– Termination History

Offerors are further advised that in its analysis, the Government will also assess the overall experience and past performance of subcontractor efforts.

(3) OTHER FACTORS Comprises other factors and issues which will be analyzed based upon information provided in the offerors proposal and data obtained from the Government and other sources. While OTHER FACTORS fall into a separate category that is not directly associated to TECHNICAL FACTORS, COST/PRICE FACTORS, or EXPERIENCE AND PAST PERFORMANCE FACTORS, these factors are pertinent to the acquisition process and are an important consideration of the Source Selection Official in making a final selection. In evaluating other factors, the Government will analyze all those factors (i.e., financial condition, labor relations concerns, and the priority placed by the offeror on work proposed, etc.) which may affect the offerors ability to perform the required effort.

[END OF RFP]

Sample 5

Facilities Operation

Type of Work: General Support Services

Objective: To furnish the necessary management, material, equipment, and supplies for facility operation and maintenance.

SOW Type: Performance

Comments:

- This is a cost plus award fee contract.
- Detailed performance specifications rather than functional. The problem with trying to specify everything is that you always leave something out. This leads to unexpected claims.
- Maintenance and operations requirements are very well defined.
- Definitions for facility maintenance are provided, which will help to avoid any misinterpretations.
- Some language used in the document is vague. For example, "The Contractor will maintain adequate control over films." The term "adequate" does not accurately define how much control over the films is appropriate.

- Time constraints and requirements noted throughout the document do not specify the time zone. With 112 buildings affected by the service agreement, there is a good chance that not all of these are in the same time zone.
- The term "etc." is used multiple times throughout the document. The use of this term creates uncertainty about and hedges the requirements.

SECTION M – EVALUATION FACTORS FOR AWARD

Proposals will be evaluated by a committee of technically qualified Bureau of Mines employees assisted by bureau contracting personnel in accordance with the criteria below.

M-1 MISSION SUITABILITY FACTORS

A. Factor 1 – Management

1. Criterion 1 - Key Personnel

   Evaluation of this criterion will be the proposer's team of key personnel as demonstrated by their education and experience in relation to their proposed assignments and the extent of their authority, responsibility, and time commitments to this effort. The availability and firmness of commitments are to also be evaluated.

2. Criterion 2 – Organization

   Evaluation of this criterion will include the delegation of authority and responsibility in the proposed organization as related to the work requirements, the extent of local autonomy, rational for subcontractor decision, including interface provisions and controls, and proposed interface relationships with USDI/WBM and all tenants.

3. Criterion 3 – Management Information Systems

   Evaluation of this criterion will include the proposed means for handling internal and external communications of management, including the types, frequencies, routine handling, special handling, and other forms such as briefings or conferences. Also to be evaluated will be the adequacy of all systems to provide visibility of status and performance to optimize the management approach for a cost-effective facility operations.

B. Factor 2 – Understanding the Requirement

1. Criterion 1 – Overall Staffing Plan

   Evaluation of this criterion will be the overall staffing plan (to accomplish all of the contract work) which indicates: the types and number of personnel proposed; skill level and mix; the proposer's plan for maintaining these skills; their availability, source (including any subcontractors) during normal operations, and provisions for abnormal fluctuations in work force requirements. Innovative and cost effective ideas and approaches ideas and approaches are encouraged for performance for the required scope of work. However, proposals with unsubstantiated estimates of manpower will be considered as indicating a lack of understanding of the requirement.

2. Criterion 2 – Total Compensation Plan

   Evaluation of this criteria will consider the total compensation plan for professional and non-professional employees and the total compensation proposed (including salaries and fringe benefits), to assume that the plan reflects a sound management approach and understanding of the contract requirements. This evaluation will include an assessment of the offerors ability to provide uninterrupted high-quality work. The professional compensation proposed will be considered in terms of its impact upon recruiting and retention, its realism, and its consistency with a total plan for compensation.

   The compensation levels proposed should reflect a clear understanding of work to be performed and should indicate the capability of the proposed compensation structure to obtain and keep suitably qualified personnel to meet mission objectives. The salary rates or ranges must take into account differences in skills, the complexity of various disciplines, and profession job difficulty. Additionally, proposals envisioning compensation levels lower than those of predecessor contractors for the same continuity, uninterrupted high-quality work, and availability of required competent professional service employees. Offerors are cautioned that lowered compensation for essentially the same work may indicate lack of sound management judgment and lack of understanding of the requirement.

   Compensation that is unrealistically low or not in reasonable relationship to the various job categories, since it may impair the Contractor's ability to attract and retain competent service employees, may be viewed as evidence of failure to comprehend the complexity of the contract requirements.

C. Criterion 3 – Processing and Control of Work

Evaluation of this criterion will include an assessment of the proposed system(s) for receiving/originating, planning, processing and controlling specific work assignments as related to the total Statement of Work. Emphasis will be placed on methods and procedures for timely, efficient, cost-effective performance.

NOTE: For evaluation purposes, the relative importance of the Mission Suitability Criteria is as follows:

1. Most Important
   Overall Staffing Plan
2. Very Important
   Process and Control of Work
   Key Personnel
   Total Compensation Plan
3. Important
   Organization
   Management Information Systems

The Most Important category is of a significantly higher value than any single criterion in the Very Important category, but is not of a higher value than the sum of any two of the criterion within the Very Important category. Within the Very Important category, Processing and Control of Work is higher than either Key Personnel or Total Compensation Plan which are of approximately equal value. The Important category is of a significantly lower value than the Very Important category. Within the Important category, Organization is of a slightly higher value than Management Information Systems.

M-2 Cost Factors

Cost factors are those factors which indicate the adequacy and realism of the cost proposal and the probable costs that will be incurred should the Government choose to contract with the proposer. The evaluation of cost factors will include an assessment of the probable cost of doing business with each proposer during the course of the contract. It will also include a comparison with WBM's estimate of the cost. In addition, the total compensation proposed will be evaluated in terms of enhancing recruitment and retention of personnel and its realism and consistency with a total plan for compensation (both salaries and fringe benefits). Although Cost Factors as such are to be analyzed separately from Mission Suitability, the cost proposal will be used extensively in the Government's evaluation and scoring of Mission Suitability to determine the proposer's understanding of the requirements.

Cost factors will not be numerically scored by the TEC; however, they will be reported by the TEC to the Chairman. The importance of cost factors in the selection will depend on such considerations as the magnitude of the cost differentials between the proposer's, and the credibility of such differentials. The TEC will develop, for each proposal within the competitive range, the probable cost to the Government of accepting that proposal. This will include adjustments required to correct deficiencies and the normalization of projected costs of items or elements common to proposals, as appropriate.

Cost shall be the deciding factor when proposals are ranked in the technically acceptable range.

M-3 Experience and Past Performance Factors

Experience and Past Performance Factors include evaluation of overall corporate experience and past performance either related to this procurement or so significant as to be indicative of the proposer's motivations. This includes experience and past performance of subcontractors as opposed to that of individuals proposed. Experience encompasses the accomplishment of work by the proposer which is comparable or related to the effort required under this procurement. Past performance indicated how well the proposer did on the earlier work. These factors are not numerically scored by the TEC, but they will be reported to the Chairman and considered by him in making a selection.

M-4 Other Factors

These factors are those which have not been included in either the Mission Suitability, Cost, or Experience and Past Performance Factors but which will be considered by the Chairman in determination of relative significance and, accordingly, they are not numerically scored by the TEC. One of the specific other factors that will be assessed is the potential for adverse effect upon performance and maintenance of the required number of non-professional and professional employees with requisite skills from and unrealistically low compensation structure. Other elements are:

1. Financial Condition and Capability

   A proposer's financial condition and capability to properly execute and procurement of this type and magnitude.

2. Labor-Management Relations

   The proposer's labor-management relations will be based upon the information contained in the Labor Relations Plan and other data made available to the Board. An assessment of the potential for adverse effect upon performance and maintenance of the required number of professional and non-professional employees with requisite skills resulting from an unrealistically low compensation structure will be made.

3. Proposed Contract

   The extent of proposed deviations from the proposed contract and the rationale for such deviations.

4. Phase-In

   A proposer's understanding and importance of the problem, plans for assumption of total responsibility and reasonableness of the approach.

5. Equal Employment Opportunity (EEO) Compliance

   A proposer's current EEO compliance program including date of last approval, by whom approved, and any changes proposed relative to the performance of the proposed work.

6. Importance of Business to Corporate Management

   The offerors interest in the commitment to supporting the effort will be assessed based on availability, interface and costing of corporate resources for use in support of the effort.

M-5 Evaluation of Offers for Multiple Awards – FAR 52.215-34 (May 1986)

In addition to other factors, offers will be evaluated on the basis of advantages and disadvantages to the Government that might result from making more than one award (multiple awards). It is assumed, for the purpose of evaluating proposals, that $250 would be the administrative cost to the Government for issuing and administering each contract awarded under this solicitation and individual awards shall be for the items or combinations of items that result in the lowest aggregate cost to the Government, including the assumed administrative costs.

M-6 Evaluation of Options – FAR 52.217-5 (Apr 1984)

A. The Government will evaluate offers for award purposes by adding the total price for all options to the total price for the basic requirement. Evaluation of options will not obligate the Government to exercise the options(s).

B. The Government may reject an offer as non-responsive if it is materially unbalanced as to prices for the basic requirement and the option quantities. An offer is unbalanced when it is based on prices significantly less than cost for some work and prices which are significantly overstated for other work.

ATTACHMENT 1a

SCOPE OF WORK – FACILITY OPERATION AND MAINTENANCE (FOM)

Exhibit 1 Statement of Work – FOC

General

A. The Facility Operating Contractor (FOC) shall furnish the necessary management, material, equipment and supplies (except as specified hereinto be furnished by the Government) to provide for services as herein set forth:

1. Plant Maintenance
2. Warehouse
3. Security
4. Graphic Arts
5. Telecommunications
6. Technical Library
7. Mail/Messenger
8. Copy Center

B. The FOC shall include the following tasks for categories of services set forth herein:

1. Plan and Schedule
2. Methods and Standards
3. Work Measurement
4. Material Control
5. Prepare Budget
6. Staffing

C. Standards

Refer to WBM Standards for specific performance.

All work shall be accomplished in a neat and professional manner according to the practice of the trade subject to the approval of the COR (Contracting Officer's Representative).

The contractor shall be responsible to verify all measurements and data for items within the scope of contract and specifications prior to commencement of the work.

I. Scope of Work – Plant Maintenance

I. General

The contractor shall perform plant maintenance services for the Bureau of Mines throughout 112 buildings and structures and grounds located at the Bruceton Research Center.

1. The support services include the primary functions and sub-functions of the following services:

   Maintenance, repair, inspection, testing of all equipment and systems, fire protection system, buildings and grounds, motor vehicles, structural, electrical, heating, ventilating and air conditioning. In addition to these functions, operation and maintenance of the boiler house. All utility equipment and systems including exterior utility equipment and systems to the point of local utility company responsibility.

2. Where required, the contractor shall provide certification stating that all materials conform to all specified requirements prior to incorporation of any materials in the project. Additionally, the contractor shall maintain a materials control file for cost evaluation.

3. The contractor shall provide as-built drawings included initial preparation and updating existing drawings. Any drawings or sketches supplied by the Government are to be considered as a part of the specifications. Any changes from the drawings must be approved by the CO (Contracting Officer).

4. Specialized equipment installed by or for the special use of the building occupants are excluded from the requirements of this contract.

5. The contractor shall provide a formal, centralized system for control of work. The contractor shall establish a work control center on the premises, in which he shall schedule and project the current and first future month's work

plans. The contractor shall provide to the COR a weekly briefing on the status of the work plans for the current and first future month.

II. Operations Requirements

1. Develop and execute detailed operation, inspection, maintenance, preventative maintenance and repair procedures, in accordance with specifications, for all building equipment and systems that will provide the operational efficiency compatible with adequate maintenance and repair costs and be in accordance with Local, State, National, or Federal guidelines and codes.
2. Operate, inspect and control all mechanical, electrical and systems and equipment on a one-shift basis, with the exception of the Boiler House, consisting of 3 multi-fuel boilers that produce approximately 200,000,000 lbs. of steam per year which shall be operated and maintained on a 24-hour basis, seven (7) days per week, with a minimum of 2 men per shift except during the annual shutdown of 4-6 weeks for maintenance.
3. Perform scheduled and unscheduled maintenance and minor repair, as necessary, on a 24-hour-a-day basis, including emergency call-back service consisting of a prompt response within 2 hours to emergency requests by telephone or otherwise.
4. Develop and maintain up-to-date means of receiving, accomplishing and reporting completion or requests for services. The contractor will accept calls and promptly respond to requests for services.
5. Each element shall follow prescribed inspection and preventive maintenance schedule.
6. Running tests or checks of large or high energy use equipment such as chillers, pumps or air-handling units, etc., will be performed during working hours.
7. The contractor is required to maintain effective operating logs as prescribed by the equipment manufacturer and as specified herein.

8. Operation of building equipment and systems may be required at night on Saturdays, Sundays or Holidays at the direction of the COR.

9. Preventative maintenance as per specifications, on approximately 1,924 equipment items, shall be performed a minimum of once per year and shall be accomplished within the first twelve (12) months of the contract. Semiannual or quarterly requirements will be scheduled so that all maintenance will be accomplished within the time limits of this contract.

III. Facility Maintenance Definitions

Whenever in these specifications maintenance responsibilities are not specifically/discretely identified and reference therefore is made to the contractor responsibility to perform as necessary, the following definition of "maintenance" will be applied.

1. Maintenance

"Maintenance" is defined as the preventive and corrective activities required to keep a facility in condition so that it may be utilized and maintained at its assigned or designed capacity efficiency. The maintenance program shall be such as to provide for, consistent with sound industrial practice, (1) disclosure of need for the performance of servable work, (2) disclosure and reporting of the need for capital type rehabilitation (minor construction and construction projects) and (3) recording the work accomplished under the program. All maintenance activities are subdivided into two ways: Preventive Maintenance and Corrective Maintenance/Repair.

a. "Preventive Maintenance"

"Preventive Maintenance" is defined as those items of planned work required on a periodic (i.e., daily, weekly, semimonthly, monthly, quarterly, semiannual and annual) basis to prevent and/or delay failures and equipment. The factors in considering the degree of Preventive Maintenance to be employed are based upon reliability, criticality and economics to the Equipment/Facility System being maintained.

b. "Corrective Maintenance/Repair"

"Corrective Maintenance/Repair" is defined as those items of work incident to maintenance necessary to change parts, accessories, apparatus, bearings, drive belts, chains, pulleys, sheaves, valves, piping apparatus, strainers, filters, dryer elements and the changeout of components such as generators, pumps, starters, motors, radiators and the total overhaul of the basic item of Equipment/Facility System.

Corrective Maintenance/Repair is performed as a result of Equipment/Facility System breakdown or by detection of a malfunction or potential malfunction. It is further divided into two categories for the purpose of establishing contract responsibility:

(1) Normal Corrective Maintenance/Repair is the responsibility of the contractor, and is defined as those activities (labor and material) required to restore a Facility/Equipment System item to an operating condition when the estimated cost of repair does not exceed 25% of the replacement cost up to a maximum of $25,000.

(2) Extraordinary Corrective Maintenance is not the contractor's responsibility, unless otherwise directed by the CO. It may be contracted for separately, and is defined as tasks requiring the restoration of a worn/failed piece of Equipment/Facility System item to its original condition and capability. Accordingly, this may be effected through repairs, replacement, overhaul, or rebuilding of the item. "Severable (Major) Maintenance Repair projects are considered <u>capital type rehabilitation and/or excessive or above normal maintenance</u> if costs or repair, overhaul or rebuilding exceeds $25,000 but does not warrant replacement.

'Funding for Servable (Major) Maintenance will be on an individual basis'.

'Provide a yearly forecast of expenditure of Servable Maintenance tasks; however, a Servable Maintenance task may be required at any time as the result of failure.'"

IV. Equipment and Systems

1. The building mechanical, electrical, and utilities equipment and systems include, but not limited to:
   Potable Water (Domestic Water System from Meters)
   Sanitary Sewage (Building to Sewer - Sewer to Disposal Plant)
   Gas (Natural)
   Chilled Water
   Condenser Water
   Steam and Condensate
   Hot Water
   Normal Solid waste Disposal
   Mechanical Refrigeration
   Boilers
   Air Distribution (Air-handling Units, Ductwork, etc.)
   Electric Transformers and Switchgear
   Electrical Power and Lighting (Illumination)
   Air and Vacuum Compressors and Piping
   Clocks
   Emergency Lights
   Manhole, Electrical
   All Controls and Auxiliary Equipment
   Fire and Protection of Physical Equipment
   Water Treatment for Boilers and Condensate
   Roadways and Parking Lots
   All Buildings
   Fuel Oil Transfer and Storage Systems (including transportation of fuel from tank trucks to storage and from storage to boilers)
   Cooling Towers
   Storm Sewers

V. Building and Grounds

1. Performs work in all weather conditions on all types of terrain. Uses earth-moving equipment to excavate, grade and roll surfaces. Must be able to accomplish work from oral instruction, rough and fine specifications.

2. Maintenance items to be performed on 280,000 square foot of paved parking, 15,000 square feet of unpaved parking lots, 14 miles of roads and sundry walkways include grading, snow removal, salting, and repair. Temporary barricades shall be installed and removed as required. Road and walkway signs shall be painted, installed, repaired, and removed as required. Culverts, drains, and ditches, shall be cleared out and repaired as required. Parking lots shall be swept and lined. Railroad spurs shall be repaired and kept free of obstacles.

3. Approximately 160 acres of ground (lawns) areas shall be cleared, landscaped, seeded, mowed, fertilized, and irrigated as required. Shrubbery shall be trimmed and new greenery planted, as directed by the COR. Fences and gates shall be kept in good condition. Transformer pads shall be kept clean and free from debris and foliage. For example, clear rocks and trees to perform (1) excavation for building foundations, (2) ponds used for research tests, and (3) parking areas. Adjusts equipment while in motion to allow for proper positioning or placement, terrain, and type of soil.

4. Approximately 470,000 gross square feet of facility as identified in Attachment B shall be kept in good repair. Windows, doors, transoms, and ventilators may require framing, installation, replacement, or sealing. Building exterior may require repainting, preparing of masonry, siding, sheathing, or caulking. Building interiors may require repainting, remodeling, paneling (including sheet-rock, plywood and veneers), insulating, replastering or spackling. Floors and sub-floors may require repair or replacement, or refinishing including sanding of surfaces and replacement of vinyl asbestos tile. Roofing, either sheet, roll, or shingle, may require repair or replacement, and proper alignment and overlap must be maintained.

5. Carpentry skills require range from construction of concrete forms, scaffolding, or storage pallets to finish carpentry such as installation of cabinets, shelves, and bookcases. The current annual effort consists of approximately 1,325 tasks annually averaging 7.0 man-hours per-task. Work shall be accomplished to suit drawings, sketches, or verbal instructions. Carpenters may be required to plan and lay out work

select lumber and materials, and apply their own knowledge of construction practice. They may need to install studs, sills, plates, braces, joists, rafters, and interior or exterior trim. Counters, bulletin boards, plywood ductwork, tables, work benches, and related items must be installed level and in proper alignment with other equipment structures. Interior and exterior trim may be installed by nailing, bolting, mortising, doweling, or gluing. Work may require standing, or finishing when appearance of the finished work is important. Work will be roped off, fenced, or other protection shall be provided for passer-by.

6. Dig and grade ditches and trenches with pick and shovel; fill and level holes in damaged roadways, mix material and leveling surface of patch with tamper; set forms, mix and pour concrete; operate power lawn mower, adjusting mechanisms, oiling and cleaning. Operate jack hammer, vibrators, outdoor vacuum cleaner, snow removal power-driven and hand operated equipment.

7. Load and unload trucks, boxcars, and other conveyances; move, pack, unpack, sort, segregate, arrange, stack, pile, or relocate a large variety of supply items.

8. Paint a variety of interior and exterior surfaces where both appearance and surface protection are important (i.e., building, stationary and mobile equipment, signs, exhibits). 8,321 man hours are the current annual level of effort required to prepare surfaces, spackle, plaster and select mixes with application of paint using the tools of the trade, sand floor and lay vinyl asbestos tile, prepare all types of signs, mix colors of all types of paint, are a few of the tasks involved.

VI. Structural

1. This section applies to the maintenance and servicing of floors, stairs, framing, walls, partitions, ceilings, doors, windows and hardware, elevators, roofs, downspouts, and flashing associated with the 112 buildings and structures identified in Attachment B.

2. The Contractor shall provide for inspection, service, lubrication, adjustment and minor repair following prescribed inspection and preventive maintenance for the following:

   a. Preventive maintenance on all overhead power doors in Buildings 04, 144, 156 and 166 shall be performed yearly. All remaining power doors, ramp doors, revolving doors (roll-up) are to be serviced and adjusted as necessary. Interim maintenance shall be on a service call basis.

   b. Main entrance and fire doors, other than power or revolving doors, shall be inspected semiannually. Door closers, stops, hinges, and other hardware are to be checked, serviced and/or adjusted as necessary.

   c. Service on all doors not included in a. or b. above will be on a service call basis. No scheduled inspection or maintenance is required.

3. Inspect all floors and floor coverings twice a year and make necessary repairs.

4. Windows, transoms, Venetian blinds and/or window shades, window screens and sun screens will be inspected twice a year. Needed adjustments and/or repairs will be made by the contractor.

5. Loading platforms and exterior porches will be inspected twice a year.

6. Directory and bulletin boards will be checked for adequate fastening and where applicable, glass, hinges, hasps and fasteners will be checked for serviceability.

7. Exterior walkways, ramps, driveways, columns and all façade mounted items affecting appearance and/or safety will be inspected on a monthly basis by the contractor.

8. Contractor will furnish the COR a monthly report of inspections made as well as a schedule of required future inspection. Reports will be furnished by the 10th day of each month.

9. The contractor shall repair roofs, flashings, downspouts, mouth pieces, strainers and drains as required. Furthermore, a check of the uppermost floor ceiling will be made for evi-

dence of roof leakage. Roofs will be cleaned at least once a year to remove debris from the roof. Downspouts and drain pipes will be cleaned at this time to insure against stoppage.

10. Contractor shall provide facilities support to MSHA at 4800 Forbes Avenue equating to one person, responsible for general labor, shipping/receiving (including some mail functions) and miscellaneous support functions.

VII. Electrical

The electrical maintenance involved installing, maintaining, modifying, repairing, troubleshooting (tracing and locating defects), loading and testing new and existing electrical lines, circuits, systems, equipment, fixtures and controls of the station. The primary high voltage (4160 and 2400 volts) and the secondary voltage of the distribution system are transmitted above, on and below grade with associated equipment. The operating voltages (480, 240, and 208/120 volts) are normally transmitted within this work area as are low voltages for alarm and control purposes. More specifically, the work is as follows:

Above grade – Repair and maintain approximately 70 poles and 98 crossarms, 325 insulators, 79 arrestors, 33 load break, switches, lighting transformers, capacitors and other pole line accessories and fittings. Size and string wires and cables allowing proper sag, using supports and strains, making proper terminations, splices and jumpers, and marinating phase and ground clearances.

On grade – Repair and install rectifiers, transformers determining capacity, primary and secondary voltages, taps and connection arrangements, wire type and amp capacity, grounding grid, and type and size of fuse cutouts and disconnect switches.

Below grade – Repair and install transformers and switches. Pull conductors, limiting tension, make and test high voltage splices with shielded and unshielded conductors. Make proper terminations and potheads as required in pits and vaults below grade.

Buildings – Repair and install fuse switches, transformers, rectifier, busducts, motors, elevators, cranes, ventilating systems, controllers, power and lighting panels, fuses, circuit breakers, luminaries, switches, receptacles, wires, relays, alarms and security components to satisfy all electrical operating needs within buildings and work areas.

Testing – Determine and conduct current, voltage resistance, wattage, reactance, frequency, phasing, balancing, capacitance, inductance, insulation, and grounding to insure low losses and efficient, reliable and safe operation.

Troubleshooting – Investigate and analyze problems of open circuit, phase and ground faults, overloads, and fuse, circuit breaker, controller and arrestor operations to determine cause and to effect and repair by temporary and/or permanent means. Install, connect, operate, and maintain emergency generation units to minimize service outage until permanent service is established.

Safety – All circuits are assumed to be energized until absolutely known to be de-energized. No circuits shall be energized or de-energized until known to be safe and all affected personnel notified. No work shall be performed on energized circuits without taking the necessary safety precautions. The electrician shall open, lock out, tag all circuits and discharge capacitors and solidly ground high voltage lines; measure voltage to ground on all circuits before any personal contact is made.

Perform all assigned tasks according to general instructions. Plan work sequences, selecting tools and materials needed to complete assignments.

Complete installations, modifications and repairs and loads and tests. Determine nature of maintenance, repair or installation needed and is responsible for knowing and judging effects that alterations have on the total system and insuring proper functioning. Work is subject to spot checks during progress and upon completion for compliance with instructions, codes and standards.

VIII. Heating Ventilation and Air Conditioning

1. Heating, ventilation and air conditioning (HVAC) consists of inspection, servicing, troubleshooting and maintaining 521 steam heaters, 6 central boilers, 1 heat pump, 183 central and zone air conditioners, 240 window air conditioners, 62 exhaust fans, 32 terminal reheat units, 61 water heaters and other related equipment. Related equipment includes electri-

cal heating elements used in combined air conditioning and heating units, electronic air cleaning units, drinking fountains, and other such items. The numbers of equipment cited above are subject to change to due to additions or deletions.

All materials, supplies, units, and equipment furnished shall be the same kind, grade, with the applicable standards of the National Board of Fire Underwriters, The American Standards Associations, Underwriters Laboratories, Inc., and the Warm Air-Heating and Air Conditioning Association. Complete units, equipment, or component parts may be placed at the Government's option when they have exceeded their economical life.

2. This work includes electrical, electronic, and mechanical repairs to all parts of air conditioning and refrigeration units. Repair and maintain motorized steam valves and coils on combined air and heating units. Install, service, and maintain cooling waters, both conventional and forced draft, fan, fan motors, blowers, and water pumps. Maintain and service environmental chambers. Delime all water-cooled units. Install, maintain, and repair high and low side controls, temperature controls, thermostatic controls, and magnetic calves. Check air flow, clean pads, check speed of compressors, and regulate compressors. Keep all compressors, fans, pumps, and motors oiled and greased. Check refrigerant and repair broken lines. Check and guide heat flow. Check and set up super heat flow. Check for moisture and install driving agent. Check and replace shaft seals. Check and replace filters. Install, maintain, and repair water valves, both electric and pressure. Check temperature pressure relations. Keep pressure at desired level. Pump down and balance units.

3. Trouble Service Maintenance

The work shall be performed on call. It shall include placing the system in proper operating condition. Calls indicating critical trouble such as, but not limited to, gas leaks, flare backs, furnace knocking on start-up, and no heat in cold weather, corrected as specified for "Emergency Service." Trouble service which is not of a critical nature shall be completed within two working days.

4. Emergency Service

Immediate response shall be made to all emergency service calls. Such work shall be performed when calls are received indicating that occupants are without heating during cold weather or that conditions which may endanger health or property exist. The work shall be completed to the extent necessary to provide heat. All unsafe conditions shall be rendered safe and property shall be protected. If heat cannot be supplied within a reasonable period, the COR shall be notified promptly.

5. Heating

Clean and lubricate blower and motor and adjust belt tension. Clean furnace room (closet) of all dirt, dust and debris. Thoroughly inspect the heating furnace and repair as necessary.

6. Ventilation

The work shall include, but not be limited to, fans, root ventilators for cleaning, checking, lubricating but also include, louvers, ducts, dampers and other accessories.

7. Air Conditioning

a. General

The work shall include, but not be limited to, condenser coils: checking for moisture and refrigerant change; checking for damage and proper insulation; replacement of worn and lubrication of fan motor bearings; cleaning and replacement of filters; and checking motor starter, wiring and contact.

b. Compressor Replacement

Whenever a compressor on an air conditioner fails, the internal refrigerant system shall be cleaned thoroughly. The cleaning may be accomplished by flushing the system with an approved solvent after the expansion valves or capillary tubes are removed of the system may be cleaned by the use of a suction line filter that has been approved by the manufacturer of the compressor of air conditioner. The method used shall be exactly as specified by the manufacturer of the cleaner including acid testing the oil. Prior to installing the final refrigerant charge, the system shall be evacuated to 100 microns of Hg or less as read on an accurate manometer. The vacuum pump shall be attached to the suction line shut-off valve so that the moisture in the system will not be drawn through the compressor. The vacuum gage shall be connected to the gage port of the liquid line shut-off valve so that the moisture in the system will not be drawn through the compressor. At the time of replacement of compressor or any time the refrigerant system is opened to atmosphere a moisture – indicating sight glass, if not previously provided and a new filter-dryer shall be installed. When the outdoor temperature is below 60 degrees F, the refrigerator lines and receiver shall be carefully warmed to vaporize the condensed moisture inside the tubing. When the vacuum reaches 1000 microns of Hg, the refrigerant valves shall be backseat while the vacuum pump is running. The pump shall then be stopped and the system allowed to stand a minimum of two hours under vacuum. If, at the end of the two hours, the system is still under vacuum, the system may be charged. The vacuum shall be broken with oil-pumped, dry nitrogen or a gaseous refrigerant and then the system let stand for one hour to allow any moisture remaining in the system to be absorbed by the gas. The system shall again be evacuated to 1000 microns of Hg and then charged with the correct type of amount of refrigerant. Pressure reading shall be taken to insure the system is operating correctly. After one week of operation, the system shall be checked to see that pressures are satisfactory and the sight-glass indicates no moisture. If moisture is present of a leak has occurred, the system shall be repaired, evacuated and recharged as specified above. Schrader or equal charging valves are acceptable in lieu of refrigerant charging valves.

IX. Mechanical

The contractor shall perform mechanical maintenance on approximately 11,500 linear-feet of steam lines; 16,500 feet of potable water lines; 14,500 feet of fire water lines; 13,000 linear-feet of sanitary sewer lines; 12,500 feet of site drainage lines; 7,000 feet of gas line as well as internal facility systems and associated equipment. Mechanical maintenance consists of performing the full range of tasks associated with the journeyman level pipe fitter and plumber trades as follows:

1. Pipefitting

   a. Installs, repairs, maintains and/or replaces high pressure piping systems and equipment: such as steam heating, steam power, acids, gas and high pressure air line systems; valves, radiators and heaters; storage and condensate tanks; steam tables, laboratory sinks that may contain acid, mercury, and/or other dangerous materials, steam traps; float and flush control valves; fittings, expansion joints, steam pressure units, pumps, etc.

   b. Works with a variety of pipe and pipe fittings including those made of copper, brass, lead, glass, and plastic. Measures, cuts, bends, threads, packs and joins piping to pipe fittings. Makes pressure test of piping systems to assure pressure-tight joints and proper circulation of flow. Covers pipe with insulating materials. Uses the tools of the trade such as stocks and dies, cutters, threaders, reamers, flange pullers, wrenches, hammers, electric hand-drill, star drill, chisels and welding and cutting equipment.

2. Plumbing

   a. Assembles, installs and repairs pipes, fittings and fixtures of heating, water and drainage systems. Installs and repairs various fixtures and facilities such as water mains, sewage lines, hot water tanks, and water closets.

   b. Measures, cuts, reams, threads, bends, fits and assembles pipe and pipe fittings. Joins pipes by use of screws, bolts, fittings, or solder and caulks joints. Uses the tools of the trade such as tapes, rules, hacksaws, packing and caulking guns, soldering irons, pipe wrenches and welding and cutting equipment.

Also, perform general maintenance duties such as installing exhaust fans, blowers, and hoods.

X. Boiler House

Boiler House systems to be operated are 2 each 700 H.P. Cleaver Brooks Boilers (gas/oil fired) and 1 each Keeler Multi-Boiler (gas/oil/coal) along with the following systems:

Coal Handling and Crushing System
The Redler Coal Feeder system
Make-Up Water Feed System
The Chemical Water Treatment System
Boiler Instrumentation System
The Fly Ash Recovery System
Air Quality Control System (Baghouse)

Along with the Auxiliary Power Generation Systems and U.P.S. The operation entails control of the performance and efficiency of these boilers and systems on a multi-fuels basis 24 hours a day, 7 days a week.

XI. Motorized Equipment

1. Operate and/or maintain the Government vehicles provided for contractor use in performance.

2. Operate and/or maintain heavy-duty equipment provided for contractor use in performance. This equipment includes both gasoline and diesel powered cranes, bulldozers, shovel loader, backhoes, tractors, roller, grader, and forklifts; as well as diesel, gasoline and electrically powered compressors and hydraulic systems.

3. Truck operation consists of driving trucks of ½ to 50 ton capacity, with up to six-wheel drive to transport personnel, articles and materials throughout the compound and on public roads and highways, for long and short hauls. Assure that cargo is properly located, distributed, and secured, and that vehicle is not loaded beyond capacity. Operate winch where vehicle is so equipped; complete trip tickets and preventive maintenance records, fill out driver's accident report in case of accident. Perform driver's maintenance in accordance with established rules and regulations. Occasionally drive other type and size vehicles for which qualified and licensed when required by the work load; i.e., shovel-loader, forklifts, and cranes. Drive vehicles for handling and transporting hydro-

gen, oxygen, methane, propane, and other inert gases; explosive and non-explosive cylinders, and must be familiar with PUC/DOT regulations for handling explosive gases, and operate fuel truck when required.

4. Vehicle Maintenance

   a. Vehicle maintenance consists of repairs to the cars and trucks identified above and maintenance equipment such as forklifts, jeeps, tractors, Cushman runabouts, and other miscellaneous small equipment such as lawn mowers. Work includes: reline brakes and repair brake systems; repair or replace transistorized ignitions; reline disc and drum brakes and repair brake systems; tunes vehicles, set timing, replace points and spark plugs, adjust carburetors; occasionally overhaul small engines and rebuild carburetors; repair tires, balance wheels, repair exhaust systems; find and repair short circuits defective wires, faulty grounds; change oil and filters; lubricate vehicles, refuel vehicles; make road calls, and keep necessary records.

   b. Maintaining, and servicing such government-owned equipment (engineering, materials handling and vehicular types) approved for use by the FOC contactors in accordance with appropriate ANSO standards when applicable.

   c. Performing periodic preventive maintenance in accordance with manufacturer's recommendations and Federal Property Management Regulations. Repairs shall be accomplished by the FOC as required to maintain the equipment, vehicles and gear in first-class operating conditions.

   d. Maintaining appearance of the equipment in a presentable condition with paint applied as necessary.

   e. Maintaining vehicle identification and color per latest directive governing application of logo and official-use decals and color requirements. All over-the-road vehicles and equipment will have government license plates affixed front and rear as required by regulations.

   NOTE: All necessary identification decals and government license plates will be furnished by the government.

f. Make minor and, on occasion, major repairs to heavy-duty equipment. Diagnosis trouble through observation and testing; dismantle equipment; use hand and machine tools of the trade; make repairs, including placing and aligning boom; use welding equipment when necessary, and assemble equipment. Utilize mechanical knowledge in completing tasks. Road test all equipment, assuring safe operation.

g. Accumulating vehicle and equipment maintenance and repair and usage data to determine overall condition and replacement factors required for reports.

h. Provide certification, training and testing of both government and contractor operators of heavy duty equipment and vehicles.

5. The contractor shall, prior to lease of commercial vehicles, make application for GSA motor vehicles through the Property Management Officer. All GSA vehicles obtained pursuant to this procedure shall be subjected to safety inspections every six (6) months or 6,000 miles, whichever is first.

6. The contractor may negotiate a contract with GSA for the necessary vehicles required to perform its duties and carry out the conditions of the contract. Minor and/or major maintenance agreements may also be negotiated with GSA.

XII. Engineering Services

1. Engineering will review the problems; prepare a step-by-step description of work to be done for repair including material lists; and any necessary drawings or sketches. For work beyond in-house capability, Engineering shall prepare a scope of work, specifications, cost estimate and drawings to have the project done by outside procurement. Engineering will then monitor the contract through completion, answering any technical questions posed by the contractor.

2. Prepare work documentation for R&A construction work.

3. Develop and maintain any energy management program to review all uses of energy on the facility and develop short- and long-range plans for conserving energy to include electric, gas, water, steam, HVAC system and building structure.

4. Engineering will develop scope of work, specifications, cost estimates, and a blueprints for all contractor yearly renewable subcontracts.

5. Engineering shall develop scope of work, specifications, cost estimates and blueprints for the procurement of materials and performance of services to operate the boiler house. Work will include, but is not limited to, the following:

Coal	Boiler house control calibration
Water treatment chemicals	Redler conveyor flights
Water softener salt	Ash conveyor operation
Air control bags (bag house)	Fly and bottom ash removal contract

6. Engineering shall prepare as-built drawings for all modifications to existing equipment along with updating all utility drawings, to include gas, water, fire water, electric, storm and sanitary sewer lines, air condensate and cooling water.

7. Engineering shall provide subcontract inspection and monitoring capabilities to provide contract monitoring from pre-bid meeting to contract acceptance. The inspector shall have the capability to answer all technical questions and interface with the government, contractor procurement and subcontract personnel. Monitoring shall include:

    Contractor Service Contracts
    R&A Construction Contracts
    PM Inspections and Quality Control
    Energy Review
    Maintenance Work Order Review

8. Engineering shall inspect all floors and floor coverings twice a year to identify problems and provide repair information and cost estimate to Central Work Control.

9. Engineering shall inspect all windows, transoms, Venetian blinds shades, window/sun screens, inside/outside directories and bulletin boards twice a year, identifying discrepancies and provide repair instructions and cost estimate to Central Work Control.

10. Engineering shall inspect all loading platforms and exterior porches, walkways, ramps, driveways, columns and all exte-

rior facades on a monthly basis, identifying discrepancies and provide repair replacement instructions and a cost estimate to Central Work Control.

II. Scope of Work – Operating Services

A. Refuse

Refuse collection and disposal service includes the following:

1. Description of Refuse

The word refuse includes, but is not limited to, waste paper, trash, food waste, dry and wet garbage, rubbish, loose debris, construction waste, plaster, lunch containers, wrappings, cardboard, beverage containers, scraps of wood, and metal.

2. Placement and Location of Containers

a. 64 Government-furnished containers of 82 gallon and 20 cubic yard capacities are located at various places of BRF. The maintenance and repair of these containers is the responsibility of the FOC.

b. Unrepaired containers shall be removed.

B. Security

1. General

a. The guard will secure appropriate doors and gates as applicable or directed by the Security Supervisor.

b. The guard will raise the United States Flag at sunrise and lower the United States Flag at sunset. The United States Flag will be afforded the proper respect and will be properly folded.

c. Traffic control will be as needed or upon request, depending upon the availability of manpower; that is, when the on-duty patrol is not busy responding to an incident. The patrol will monitor traffic and/or direct traffic as appropriate on normal duty days during the period of 4:15 PM and 4:30 PM. The patrol will meet and assist in assuring the safe backing of a delivery truck to the boiler house, Building 62, during the period of its arrival which is daily on normal duty days sometime during the period of 10:00 AM and 11:30 AM.

d. The guard shall monitor the display of parking tags and issue traffic tickets as required.

e. Guards are responsible to maintaining law and order on 219 acres of Federal property while on duty.

   (1) Guards will report all disturbance or emergency conditions in accordance with applicable procedures. Guards will report any safety hazards observed to the Security Supervisor who, in turn, will notify proper authorities.

   (2) The guards are provided a list of emergency telephone number to be used in the event of disturbances, emergencies or emergency conditions and shall contact appropriate personnel. Guards shall immediately call local law enforcement officials if disturbances are of a violent nature and a Government official is not available.

f. Injuries

   Guards shall immediately notify the health official on duty of any reported personnel injuries. Whenever the health unit is closed, the guard may arrange for ambulance service, if necessary, after notifying the duty officer. Any report to the guard of any injuries will be documented in the security log.

g. Other Functions

   Guards perform other protective, safety and security related tasks which include but shall not be limited to:

   (1) Turning off unnecessary lights.

   (2) Unplugging electrical appliances when not in use, including air conditioners and heaters.

   (3) Checking safes, lock-type repositories and cabinets.

   (4) Closing windows.

(5) Securing doors and gates.

(6) Reporting hazardous conditions during duty shifts.

(7) Barricading/blocking areas upon request.

(8) Conducting building check of designated buildings by physically checking the doors and windows. Presently, there are approximately 25 buildings being physically checked and 30 buildings in which a walk-through check is conducted.

(9) Conducting preliminary investigations of incidents, complaints and accidents.

(10) Issuing traffic tickets.

(11) Accomplishing appropriate security reports and forms.

(12) Conducting vehicle inspection of assigned vehicle.

(13) Utilizing traffic radar unit, speed gun, as appropriate.

(14) Controlling vehicular and pedestrian traffic and performing area patrol.

h. Record of Shift

The guards maintain a daily shift record including the following:

(1) A log of visitors.

(2) A chronological record of events occurring during each shift.

i. Reports

Security reports will be forwarded to the COR upon request or as warranted.

j. Additional Hours Due to Emergency Situations

The Security Supervisor may authorize additional hours of guard service due to mission requirements, sick leave, vacation and other situations that may dictate security coverage.

2. Guard Services

a. Gate/Roving Patrol Guard

The roving patrol shall rove the complex for the purpose of deterring crime, preventing vandalism and ensuring visibility of a protective on-duty force. The patrol shall protect government and personal property.

(1) The complex entrance/exit gates shall be manned as follows:

(a) A gatehouse guard will be at the main gate entrance during the hours of 4:15 PM to 7:30 AM each normal duty day and 24 hours a day during holidays and weekends. Deviations of these times may be approved by the Security Supervisor for reasons of availability of manpower.

(b) Wallace Road Gate (Eagle Pass Gate) will be opened at 6:00 AM and secured at 6:00 PM daily. This gate will not be manned while open. The gate will be secured on Saturdays, Sundays and Holidays.

(c) McElheny Gate will be open from 6:00 AM to 9:00 AM; 11:00 AM to 1:00 PM; and 3:00 PM to 6:00 PM daily. This gate will not be manned while open. The gate will be secured on Saturdays, Sundays and Holidays.

b. Gate Duties

(1) All persons attempting to enter the Bruceton grounds without a vehicle parking tag or pass shall be required to show a Government identification card or other authorized/approved pass.

(2) Guards require non-Government persons to identify themselves and state their business on the Government facility. The guard shall issue visitor passes and keep a record by pass number. The record shall include driver's name, passenger's names, entry and exit times and vehicle license number.

(3) Between the hours of 6:30 PM and 5:30 AM, Monday through Friday and all hour for Saturdays, Sundays, and Holidays, identification of all personnel requesting entry to the facility will be required.

(4) Persons requesting entry during non-duty hours will be logged into the log book.

(5) Telephone night line shall be answered by the guard during anytime outside of regular hours except when on patrol. This is subject to change.

(6) Emergency phone calls received from the Pleasant Hills Sewage Authority shall be immediately forwarded to the appropriate local ambulance, fire, and/ or police organization.

c. Roving Patrol Duties

(1) A guard shall be on duty capable of responding to alarm activations, incidents, complaints, accidents and other police-related tasks.

(2) During patrols, the guard will check for unauthorized parking, speed violations, traffic hazards and other incidents and/or violations.

(3) The guard will issue traffic tickets when warranted.

(4) Conduct preliminary investigations of minor incidents.

3. Uniforms and Equipment

All guards shall wear the prescribed uniform while on duty. No employee may enter on duty until he has a complete uniform. All guards performing under this contract shall wear the same color and style of uniform. Appropriately lettered breast badge and cap ornament shall be worn and prominently displayed as part of the uniform. Shoulder patches lettered to indicate identity of the contractor shall be worn on the left shoulder of the uniform coat and shirt. No other identification of the contractor is to be worn or displayed on the uniform. The uniform shall include coordinated shirt, title, trousers, jacket and cap or hat. All uniform parts shall be consistent in color and weight. Variations for summer and winter wear are permissible.

Uniforms and the wearing of same shall, in general, conform to standards and usage prescribed and in effect for Federal Protective Officers. There shall be no visible rips or tears in the material, nor shall there be any broken or missing buttons or zippers. All items of the uniform shall be in a good state of repair.

The following items of uniforms and equipment in quantities shall be furnished to each employee:

Shirt, long sleeve	3
Shirt, short sleeve	3
Trousers, all season	2
Necktie	2
Cap, summer and winter	1 of each
Jacket, winter-type	1
Gloves	1
Key strap (with flap)	1
Flashlight	1
Raincoat	1
Boots	1
Police jacket	1
Name tag (with initials and last name)	1
Key case	1
Belt keepers	3

Sidearms and ammunition – Side arms will not normally be worn by guards while on duty. Sidearms and ammunition will be kept by the Security Supervisor in an acceptable safe for issue when required to meet emergency situations requiring fire arms. Firearms will only be issued at the direction or approval of the CO. If issued, the type will be a .38 caliber service revolver with a minimum barrel length of 4 inches and a maximum length of 5 inches. Sidearms shall be kept clean, oiled and in the optimum operating condition at all times. The ammunition utilized shall be police service-type, caliber .38 ball M41. A maximum of 5 rounds shall be issued to each guard while on duty. All 5 rounds shall be inserted into the weapon cylinder. The cylinder chamber in line with the firing pin and barrel shall not contain a cartridge. All ammunition shall be accounted for.

4. Property

The guards are responsible for ensuring that they do not disturb papers on desks, open desk drawers or cabinets, or use Government telephones, except as authorized. All Government or personal property entrusted to the guard shall be protected and held accountable for.

5. Work Schedule

The guards shall be provided with a work schedule showing names of personnel to be on duty for at least a one-month period and at least one week in advance posting showing the schedule is required.

A guard shall not leave his post until properly relieved. Temporary shift changes due to sick leave, vacation, etc. may be required; therefore, prior notice may not be possible.

The security log shall be used to record the duty time period of each security guard.

6. Guard Instructions

The contactor shall prepare guard instructions outlining guard responsibilities and duties.

7. Training

a. General

Each guard shall be briefed on responsibilities, duties and appearance standards by the Security Supervisor prior to being assigned to duty.

Prior to employment each guard shall be certified in accordance with Pennsylvania State Act 235 as amended.

b. Initial Training Requirements

Initial training requirements will consist of on-the-job training. Subjects covered will be facility orientation, duties and functions of the security guard, facility entry and exit control and public relations. The Security Supervisor will ensure that the training is conducted by evaluating effectiveness of procedures and visiting the guard at the work center or while on duty.

8. Replacement Employees

During the term of the contract, the contractor shall provide the necessary training to each replacement employee.

9. Waivers

Training requirements may be waived for the following circumstances when it is in the best interest of the Government and approved in writing prior to the guard's entrance to duty:

a. When an unusual "short term" shortage of regularly assigned guards exists.

b. When the contract is amended to increase, within fourteen (14) days of notification, the amount of required man-hours.

c. When a guard has not qualified in the use of a firearm, he shall not be armed while on duty.

10. Authority and Jurisdiction

Police Authority and Gun Permits – Except where precluded by local law ordinance, the contractor shall, at no cost to the Government, make and complete all arrangements with the appropriate officials in the city, county or the state in which the building are located to:

a. Have each employee appointed as a Special Policeman or Conservator of Peace with sufficient authority to detain or make arrests for violations of law occurring at the locations specified in the contract. (Applies only when such appointments are obtainable and/or required by local or state law.)

b. Obtain a permit for each employee to carry a gun.

c. Maintain at the work site a current gun permit for each employee, or maintained by the contractor when required by local or state law.

11. <u>Firearms Qualifications</u>

    Each employee will qualify prior to the beginning of the contract period and yearly thereafter in the use of firearms using a certified NRA 25 Yard Course or one with higher requirements. Misuse of weapons shall be cause for immediate dismissal.

12. Health Requirements

    The Contractor shall ensure that all employees assigned are in good general health without physical defects or abnormalities which would interfere with the performance of duties.

13. Security Supervisor

    The Security Supervisor will be responsible for managing the security force by planning and organizing the security force activities. Develop standards, plans, policies, procedures and instructions to implement the security programs. Determine personnel and equipment requirements. Organize personnel and materials to ensure efficient and effective operations. Conduct surveillance and investigations. Interview witnesses and persons suspected of committing violations. Obtain statements. Compile and process security reports. Accomplish written reports of investigations. Process and control traffic tickets. Issue parking tags and picture identification badges. Prepare and maintain files, reports, material requisitions, correspondence and security force information. Review incoming and outgoing correspondence. Attend and conduct meetings and briefings. Prepare schedules. Conduct drivers tests and issue Government licenses as appropriate.

C. <u>Mail/Messenger Services</u>

1. Conditions Affecting Work

    a. The Government will provide a mailroom area, postal sealing machine, metered mail system, scale, and necessary sorting bins and tables required for performing the contract requirement. All Government equipment will be kept in sound and good operating condition. Failure of equipment to perform properly and causing delay of required work within the specified time will not alleviate the demand of meeting the requirements of the contract.

b. Safety Precautions

The employees shall be instructed about accident prevention and safety. All drivers must have attended a defensive driving course. All employees will follow any and all aspects of OSHA, State, County, and Local rules and regulations applicable to performance of services required herein.

2. Details of Work Requirements

a. Mail person reports at 7:45 AM, picks up Government vehicle, and arrives at the Pleasant Hills Post Office at 8:00 AM to deposit mail left over from previous day and to pick up MSHA, Mines, Contractor, mail, etc., for the Bruceton station. A second mail run is made to the Post Office at 11:30 AM. Mail is distributed throughout the day to approximately 45 various organizational mail stops on the Bruceton grounds at least twice at scheduled times. The mail is dropped off at the Pleasant Hills Post Office at 4:45 PM.

b. Special attention mail, such as Federal Express, DHL, Registered, Certified, etc., will be given preferential delivery but will not interfere with regular deliveries.

c. Hours of departure of messengers and mail stop routes are subject to change to meet organizational requirements with the approval of the CO.

d. Written logs will be maintained for certified, registered, etc., mail in accordance with postal and WBM requirements.

e. Contractor is responsible for the preparation of mail reports as required.

f. Contractor may be required to provide mail/messenger service in the Pittsburgh environs as necessary, such as trips to the Federal Building, Government facilities at 4800 Forbes Avenue, etc. Specifically, the Contractor is required to provide mail pickup and delivery service in support of MSHA at 4800 Forbes Avenue twice weekly (Wednesday and Friday).

D. Technical Library

Technical and scientific personnel require approximately 9,000 transactions annually. The WBM, DoE, and MSHA, require as back-up support to current research programs, on-site library services, such as inter-library loans of books and other materials to supplement the library collection, photocopies of journal articles and other non-circulating library publications, translations, manual and computer-generated literature searches. Behind-the-scenes technical services, such as acquiring new material and cataloging and processing for reader use support and make possible the direct services mentioned above.

At present the library collection consists of approximately 160,000 volumes of books and periodicals divided between the main library, located in Building 140 and the branch library (chiefly chemistry and chemical engineering), located in Building 83. In addition, the library has a large collection of Federal and state documents and a smaller collection of foreign documents concerned mainly with coal, research in mining methods, health and safety of miners, environmental factors in mining and land reclamation, and tangential subjects.

The library serves, besides employees, outsiders, such as libraries of colleges and universities, of corporations and other organizations, local students and the general public who come to the library for reference and study. Educational institutions, other WBM stations, and other Federal and State government libraries also use the library.

Direct Services

Such direct services include but are not limited to:

1. Furnishing photocopies of now-circulating library material, such as:
    a. Periodicals – Specific articles scattered through various volumes of the same title and/or various titles
    b. Symposia, congresses, etc. – Specific papers
    c. Reference books – Tables, diagrams, standards, etc.
    d. State and Federal documents
    e. Foreign documents

2. Lending of circulating materials.
3. Borrowing from other libraries to supplement this library's collection. Bibliographic information is verified by appropriate source and location of material is ascertained by mail and phone. Inter-library loans are typed and sent and maintenance of files are kept for copyright laws. In a reciprocal arrangement, the library also lends some types of materials to other libraries. The Library keeps statistics on all of its inter-library loan activities.
4. Furnishing, upon request, short bibliographies or more lengthy searches, both manual and computer-generated.
5. Answering short questions person-to-person or by phone.
6. Obtaining translations of books and journal articles when available and not part of a file of over 5,000 translations.
7. Maintaining records by individual borrower of books bought by and sent to operating departments, which is known as the permanent loan system.
8. Publishing lists of information for readers:
    a. New books and materials received
    b. New translations received
    c. New periodical titles (supplementing current titles, to which we have multiple subscriptions).
9. On-line information retrieval by computer terminal is initiated. Current systems include dialog and OCLC. Data bases are chosen for pertinence and accuracy of search strategy per request.

Indirect Services

1. Requesting new materials for library collections.
2. Cataloging new materials for library collections.
3. Cataloging new materials for operating departments (permanent loans):
    a. Preparing master catalog card for printing duplication.

  b. Preparing unit card sets by adding subjects and added entries to duplicates of master card, tracing on the back of the mast card <u>all</u> added entries, including shelf list card. Then filing <u>all</u> cards in the proper drawers.

4. Preparing periodical subscription renewal lists for bidding and issuing individual requisitions for subscriptions not on bid lists.

5. Requesting NTIS reports and keeping bookkeeping record of status of deposit account, replenishing it when necessary.

6. Obtaining special request documents form Government Printing Office, maintaining bookkeeping record of status of deposit account, replenishing it when necessary.

7. Maintain status of several deposit accounts (Chemical Abstracts Document Delivery Service, Engineering Index, etc.) and replenishing it when necessary.

8. Maintaining status as a partial depository for Federal documents, checking them in and cataloging them.

9. Ordering, checking-in, and cataloging state documents.

10. Cataloging foreign government documents received on exchange.

11. Maintaining a translation file (now over 5,000 translated items) cataloging them, preparing and filing catalog cards, and filing the translations by accession number.

12. Preparing of periodicals and other materials for bindery pick-up.

13. Circulation cards and forms are filled out to maintain an adequate circulation file and overdue notices are sent out when material is not returned on time. Borrowing policies are explained to patrons.

14. Adequate records are kept to justify expenses of invoices incurred by purchases (books, inter-library loan, etc.).

15. Library collection is weeded and inventoried periodically to discard extraneous materials.

16. Using a computer terminal, staff members maintain automated records for library card catalog, permanent loans and other suitable functions.

17. Mail is sorted and routed to appropriate staff members and records are kept for statistical purposes.

18. Reports on library functions are gathered weekly and monthly in a detailed report.

Miscellaneous Typing and Clerical Duties

1. Maintaining library supplies in cupboard so that an adequate store of constantly-used supplies is always on hand.

2. Typing of Library requisitions:

   a. Invoice payments

   b. Deposit account reimbursements

   c. Books and other library materials

   d. Supply orders, external and internal

E. Telecommunications Services

1. General

   The work covered by this section consists of performing all operations, maintenance, and service of the telephone system at the Bruceton Complex. The system services approximately 1200 employees of WBM, DoE, MSHA and onsite contractors.

2. Conditions Affecting Work

   a. Equipment

      Computerized dimension system, attendant lines, conference lines, cable plant, and station user equipment are existing and subject to changes at BRF.

   b. Duties

      Telephone Operators

      Place conference and other complex calls including overseas telephone communication. Place, receive, and log long distance calls. Report defective equipment and assure timely repair of same. Notify proper authorities in emergency situations; for example, fire department, police, ambulance and appropriate Facility Service personnel.

Train regular telephone operator at BRF and all relief telephone operators in the technical phases of communication duties.

Prepare and input alphabetical and organizational indexes and directory for BRF and assure timely and accurate updating.

Act as a receptionist for all visitors. Identify and evaluate subject inquiries, and direct visitor or caller to the appropriate organizational entity within the WBM, DoE, or MSHA. Be thoroughly familiar with organizational charts and functional statements. Maintain subject index in a timely and accurate manner. Draw and reproduce rough maps to assist visitors.

Direct shipment and/or deliveries to the correct locations, including those for construction contractors, throughout the complex.

Maintenance

The contactor shall provide preventive and remedial maintenance, including labor and other necessary expenses, to keep the cable plant and station user equipment, excluding the Dimension 2000 switch, in good working condition through the life of the contract. All telephone equipment shall be maintained in a good state of repair, consistent with the safe and adequate service performance specifications as furnished by the equipment manufacturer. Broken, damaged, or deteriorated parts must be replaced with new or reconditioned parts. Parts will be provided as Government Furnished Equipment (GFE). Electrical faults, such as leakage or poor insulation, noise induction, crosstalk, or poor transmission characteristics must be corrected.

The contractor shall follow a maintenance program to include periodic testing, inspection of facilities, and preventive maintenance according to the recommended practices furnished by the original equipment manufacturer.

Service

The contractor shall provide for the following services related to telephone equipment: New installs, adds, moves, changes, rearrangements and disconnects. The contractor must be able to provide these services for government-owned/provided equipment. All services must be provided by technicians experienced with telephone equipment.

The contractor will install all required wiring, terminal connectors, and telephone cross connect wiring to provide connection between the telephone instrument, the central switching system, and the telephone company point of demarcation when there is no embedded cable or wire available/or it is not free for reuse.

All cable work to be performed in support of contract requirements includes labor, wire closet backboards, terminal blocks, connectors, wire support rings, and all other wire hardware, as necessary to deliver dial tone from the telephone company point of demarcation to the station equipment interface.

The contractor will maintain permanent record of all new installs, moves, changes, relocations and disconnects, that the contractor has completed. These records shall include but are not limited to: wire closet locations, interface location, circuit pack location numbers, jack and pin numbers and room numbers where equipment is located.

c. Effect

Good communications responsive to the needs of the Government have an impact on the work of the agencies and the Government's public image. For this reason, all responses are required to be efficiently and courteously handled.

d. Hours

The telephone switchboard will be attended 24 hours a day. Maintenance and service will be provided during normal working hours. Emergency repairs and service will be provided on non-duty hours when required.

3. Contractor shall also provide a telephone operator in support of MSHA, 4800 Forbes Avenue, during all business hours.

F. Film/Publication Distribution

1. General

The Contractor shall furnish the necessary management to provide for:

a. Film Distribution Services including Video Tapes, hereinafter referred to as Film.

b. Publication Distribution Services

These services shall be provided to the Bureau of Mines, tenant agencies and other field offices of these agencies.

2. Film, Distribution

a. Film Distribution Services

(1) The Contractor will provide complete film distribution services which will include:

(a) Film Booking – including notification to borrower of booking or refusal.

(b) Print Control – including accurate control of all prints.

(c) Clerical – including accurate records, complete reports for sponsors in approved format, etc.

(d) Film Inspection – including receipt and shipment of films, an adequate repair and maintenance program, maintenance of sufficient parts, supplies and materials for successful film program.

(2) Booking

The Contractor will book (schedule) film for showing in response to requests from the general public. Requests are received by mail, phone, and walk-in. Request data is maintained for both WBM and MSHA. Available films and dates are scanned, and if possible request is scheduled, centrac card and order prepared. Borrower is notified of booking, shipping dates and return dates. If film is not available, refusal motive is sent to borrower. The booking procedure requires the highest degree of accuracy, since booking dates are sometimes a year away and programs are built around the film being available. The WBM would suffer great embarrassment should our commitments not be kept.

The Contractor must respond to all requests within 5 days of receipt. The WBM film program is a nationwide program, and must be prepared to respond to requests on a national basis.

1987	Mines	MSHA	Total
Film Bookings	8,291	2,309	10,600
Video Bookings	375	—	375

(3) Control and Related Duties

The Contractor will maintain adequate control over films. This will include methods for accurate inventory, determining location of all prints, whether enroute, at destination, or available for booking. The above are reviewed regularly to determine print location. If print is late, Contractor must establish tracer procedures with the Postal authorities and the borrowers to recover lost prints.

Condition records must be kept on each print; therefore, every print must be inspected after each shipment and accurate condition records maintained, so that charges can be made for damaged films. Recoveries will be returned to the agency (sponsor). In addition, Contractor must be prepared to make charges for all lost films. Recoveries will be returned to the agency (sponsor).

(4) Film Inspection and Repair

Contractor will inspect manually or mechanically each print before it is sent to a new borrower. All repairs will be made to each print, so that the borrower will get the best possible showing. The Contractor must insure that repaired films do not detract, limit, change or destroy the message of the film. Repairs will include timely replacement of parts of the films to insure story line continuity. The Contractor must maintain an adequate inventory of film parts to insure continuous film servicing. This is to be accomplished by regular contact with the sponsor through the WBM.

Receipt and shipment of films must be coordinated so that films are available to respond to existing bookings in a timely fashion and to insure receipt by borrower for his scheduled showings

(5) Clerical Duties

The Contractor will establish and maintain proper reportage of showings, audience, trends and library volume statistics. This reportage will be incorporated into contactor reports to agency and sponsor. Report format and information required will be prescribed by the Agency. Presently, reports consisted of:

(a) Quarterly – compiled for Agency and sponsors. Data consists of circulation, shipments, showings and attendance, bookings, refusals, withdrawals, receipts and television audience. It also includes updates to our distribution centers, print and title addition sheets, print deletion and new distribution centers.

(b) Semi-Annual – compiled for Agency – Bruceton and Washington. Data consists of prints received, prints withdrawn, prints circulated, load refusals, average copies circulated, average showings per copy, six-month showing and attendance totals, and cumulative showings and attendance by subject.

(c) Annual – compiled for Agency – Bruceton and Washington. Data consists of analysis of effectiveness of Distributing Centers with recall of films from Distributing Centers that under-utilize prints available to them. Analysis of print inventory, age of inventory and an evaluation of the condition of the inventory by subject. As a result of this in-depth study, requests for parts and prints are submitted for consideration by the Agency and sponsor.

Present Status of File Library

1987	Mines	MSHA	Total
Total Subjects	12	67	79
Total prints	2,314	1,706	4,020
Total video	945	—	945
Distribution centers (nationwide)	60	—	60
Condition of Film Library	BOM- sponsored	MSHA	
Less than 4 years	339 – 15%	—	
Less than 8 years	694 – 31%	835 – 49%	
Over 8 years	1184 – 54%	871 – 51%	
	Technology Transfer		
Less than 4 years	40 – 21%		
Over 8 years	61 – 31%		
Less than 8 years	93 – 48%		

b. Publication Distribution Services

(1) The Contractor will provide complete publication distribution services which will include:

(a) Receipt of publication

(b) Storage of publications – includes proper and safe storage, regular inventories, culling and disposal

(c) Filling requests received – all requests filled within 5 working days

(d) Clerical – includes maintenance of all records, inventories, stock controls, etc.

(2) Storage Receipt - Shipping

(a) The Contractor will provide safe, clean, dry storage space for approximately 1-2 million copies of Bureau of Mines Publication

Receipt – Contractor will provide necessary precautions to insure safe receipt of all Government Publications. Necessary records will be maintained to document receipt, storage location and quantity on hand, along with regular inventory entries. Publications are received from in-house printing plant, general outside printing, contractor or Government Printing Office.

Storage – Storage provided by Contractor will include safety and cleanliness with necessary safeguards to offer protection from fire, water damage or vandalism. Contractor shall provide for routine handling, moving, loading and unloading publications. Also, periodic culling of publications deemed by the agency to be beyond the limits of continued public interest.

Shipping – Contractor will respond to requests received from representatives of industry and science and the general public for copies of publications. Requests are received in writing, by phone and walk-ins. Contractor must familiarize himself with subject matter to the point that they can assist the requestor when they are uncertain of what they want. Special agency, departmental or Congressional requests must be expedited, and all mailing lists turned over to the Contractor must be filled and shipped in a timely fashion. For the better part, response to requests is made by mailing the publications to the requestor in an envelope. Occasionally, however, there is a need for packaging the publications for mailing or shipping. The Contractor will provide the necessary competence to handle either of these shipment methods.

Clerical – the Contractor will provide the necessary clerical capability to provide for record keeping. The Contractor will provide regular reportage of requests received, publications shipped, new reports received, and as necessary, status of current inventory.

All requests must be handled within 5 days of receipt.

NOTE: Average request received is for 5 publications.

G. Boiler Plant Operations

Boiler plant operations are contained in Attachment II, Performance Specifications on pages OA, OB, and OC.

H. Warehousing

1. General

The work to be performed hereunder consists of providing the necessary personnel and supervision to operate and manage the Warehouse Operation which entails the preparation of material requisitions for purchases against blanket and purchase orders; central receiving/check-in of GSA of FSS and locally procured material; Warehouse counter services; inventory control, inventory management of supplies/equipment, general housekeeping and pickup and delivery service.

a. The Bureau of Mines Warehouse, located in Building 166, stocks approximately 4,500 line items for support of day-to-day operations. Material generally stocked consists of office, housekeeping, plumbing, electrical, hardware and laboratory supplies, Government and miscellaneous forms, etc.

b. Every item of warehouse stock will be assigned a storeroom number and the stock control record data loaded into the automated Inventory Control System.

c. It will be the responsibility of the Contractor to determine stockage objectives and reorder quantities. Final approval or reorder quantities and placement of orders will be the responsibility of the Government.

d. The Contractor will be responsible for the preparation, publication and maintenance of the storeroom catalog.

2. Specifications

The tasks identified in the Scope of Work – Warehouse Operations are to be performed in the following manner:

a. Receiving

The Contractor will establish a due-in for all material on order and maintain an "open order" file (receiving copy of the requisitioning document) by order number sequence. When stock items are received approximately 15,000 line items per year, the material will be in-checked noting all overages/shortages and damages. Damages and shortages will be annotated to the receiving copy and forwarded, promptly, to the designated Government representative for action. Each line item quantity received will be input to the computer which updates the stock record data and adjusts due-in (if full order was received). Material will be placed on the bulk rack for movement to the storage locations.

b. Stocking

All in-checked and processed material for warehouse stock will be promptly removed from the receiving area and placed in the appropriate storage location. Bulk items will be palletized, as necessary, and placed in the bulk storage area. The Contractor shall be responsible for rearranging shelf and bulk stock material. All hand tools will be etched to identify Government ownership prior to combing with existing stocks and prior to issue.

c. Counter Service (Issue of Stock Material)

(1) Contractor personnel operating the issue counter, perform approximately 35,000 issues annually. Upon receiving a material requisition whether by mail or over the counter, the requisition is verified against the authorization cards and account number prior to processing. Invalid signatures or account numbers on material requisitions will not be processed and the requisition returned to the customer.

(2) Material requisitions will be stamped with the current date prior to entering the input data to the computer. Due-out records will be established for out-of stock conditions unless otherwise specified by the customer. Material requisitions received before 12 o'clock will be processed and delivered the following work day.

(3) Counter service will be provided from 8:00 AM until 11:30 AM and 12:30 PM until 3:00 PM. Emergency requirements will be filled during other hours of the official workday, providing that the requisition contains justification for emergency requirements.

(4) Warehouse personnel will be required to account for towels, overalls, and lab coats. Soiled towels shall be counted and checked against the accompanying storeroom requisition. An equal number of clean towels will be issued. Soiled coveralls and lab coats shall be counted and checked against the storeroom requisition by name and quantity. A copy of the requisition will be retained in order to verify and issue the clean coveralls ad lab coats. Soiled towels, coveralls, and lab coats will be placed in their respective receptacles.

d. Supply Management

The Contractor will review material requirements for availability of stock/non-stock material from GSA, Federal Supply Schedule and local vendor sources. The review will also screen for excessive quantities to preclude stockpiling of normal stocked items. The Contractor will conduct normal routine inventory and commodity management functions.

e. Equipment Management

The Property Coordinator will act as the Contractor's representative for equipment charged to the contract. The representative is responsible to coordinate all equipment transactions with the Government and provide necessary documentation to support changes in equipment status, and conduct an inventory of all contractor equipment accounts as determined by the Government.

f. <u>Warehouse Pick-Up and Delivery Service</u>

The Contractor shall provide the necessary personnel and vehicles to provide for the pick-up and delivery of supplies and equipment to Government personnel. The Contractor's responsibility shall commence upon receipt of the material for delivery and continue until delivery is accomplished and a receipted copy of the acquisition document is processed.

g. <u>Inventory</u>

The Contractor shall be required to conduct a physical inventory of all stock items to be completed by September 30th (each year), and/or as dictated by the needs of the Government.

Inventory differences will be reconciled within five (5) work days after inventory and computer records updated. Variances both plus or minus ½ of 1% will be thoroughly investigated and the findings reported, in writing to the Government.

h. Reports

Operating and financial reports will be issued on a monthly basis identifying the following transactions:

(1) Total number of requisitions processed for each agency including WBM, DoE, MSHA, and FOC.

(2) Total number and value of line items issued for each agency including WMB, DoE, MSHA, and FOC.

(3) Total number of line items ordered.

(4) Total number of line items received.

(5) Number of coverall and lab coat exchanges for each agency including WBM, DoE, MSHA, and FOC.

(6) Routine inventory management reports.

3. Requirements

   a. Contractor personnel shall be experienced in the operation of forklift trucks and be familiar with the use of Warehouse equipment; such as, hand trucks, stencil machine, power hacksaw.

   b. The Government reserves the right to alter or change the method of warehouse operations.

III. Scope of Work – Research Support Services

A. General

The contractor will perform the following research support services:

4. Instrument and Machine Shop
5. Welding
6. Drafting
7. Photography
8. Copy Center

B. Instrument/Machine Shop

Performs specialized, highly skilled work for research laboratories: fabricants, modifies and repairs a wide variety of extremely delicate laboratory instrumentation and apparatus requiring almost continuous work to tolerances of .0001 inches; press fits and drive fits, and on occasion to even finer tolerances, and works to a precision of approximately 10 seconds. Annually approximately 415 separate tasks are performed requiring approximately 15 hours. Frequently, must prepare surface finishes down to two micro-inches, obtained by lapping and checking by profilmeter. Usually works to sketches, prints, or verbal instructions which prescribe generally what is required. Planning sequences of operations, selection of working methods, tools, and materials are the responsibility of the employee. Frequently encounters unusually difficult problems, such as drilling and reaming a hole .003 inches in diameter through stainless steel as thick as twenty-times the diameter of the drill. Frequently designs and makes tools, jigs, and/or fixtures, and accomplishes tasks assigned involving reference to Jonanson blocks. Employees must possess knowledge of shop mathematics, usual machines shop charts and tables; heat treating methods, and be completely familiar with properties and working difficulties of many uncommon metal alloys, as well as mild and stainless steels, aluminum, titanium, brass, copper, alloys of these metals, glass, natural and synthetic rubber, plastics, hard and soft woods, and precious metals.

Extremely precise criteria of diameters, centers and flatness and roundness are commonplace and worker must be completely familiar with capacities and limitations of machine shop equipment of all high precision types. Many finished assemblies must withstand high temperatures (5000°C) and pressures (10,000 p.s.i.) where tolerance of fit is so minute that is must be specified in terms of surface finish.

In addition to above functions, the contractor shall provide for the design, construction, modification, assembly, adjustment and repair of highly complex instruments and apparatus used for scientific research, testing and experimental purposes. Employees must be skilled in utilizing and adopting materials, machines, and tools to accomplish project, greater participation in design of intricate instruments and equipment and possess a high degree of ingenuity and resourcefulness in planning and lay-out work.

C. Welding

Welding Maintenance currently consists of approximately 105 work tasks per year at an average of 22 hours per task from detailed drawings, blueprints, and rough sketches, and/or verbal instructions. Work includes lay-out, fabrication and repairs on research and development laboratory and pilot plant equipment such as vacuum and distillation furnaces, reduction bombs, crucibles, cylinders, water and air tanks, and similar equipment used in research. Also involves, in addition to standard welding operations with electric-arc and acetylene equipment and cutting torches, use a heliarc, automatic, and inert atmosphere welding chambers and vacuum tanks, copper and silver soldering and brazing equipment and powder burning torches required to achieve precise engineering characteristics and meet high and low pressure (vacuum and gas pressures up to 5000 p.s.i.) and corrosion resistance requirements. Much of the work performed is highly exacting, requiring in addition to shop mathematics, familiarity with workability of all types of metals; i.e., mild and stainless steels, brass; aluminum, nickel, zirconium, titanium and molybdenum, plastics and material in form of metal sheet ranging 30 gauge to heavy plate steel. Work requires further, complete ability of flame-cutting techniques, the use of metal-cutting shears, saws, punches, drills, and metal-forming machines such as heavy rolls, bending machines, at plate tolerances of 0.01. When nature of equipment or type of metal cannot be fabricated according to request, contractor is expected to devise and suggest proper welds and fabrication procedures and necessary alterations of sketches or blueprints.

All welding classified as a pressure vessel or system must be accomplished by a certified welder.

D. Drafting

1. Drafting is staffed with competent engineering draftsmen capable of the full spectrum of drafting services to meet the requirements of the Bureau's scientific and technical personnel, and they prepare all of the illustrations and graphs for use in technical publications. The unit does not receive a direct allotment, but supports itself through charges for services rendered. Its services are available to all Bureau stations.

2. Drafting Services

   a. The operating contractor will provide complete drafting services which will include:

      (1) Illustrations – includes illustrations for publications, signs, posters, 35 mm slides, transparencies

      (2) Architectural drawings

      (3) Mechanical drawings

      (4) Topographical (mining) drawings

(5) Geological drawings

(6) Diazo copy work

(7) Paste-ups

NOTE: Consultation sketches and preliminary drawings may be done in pencil – all final drawings must be in ink, in accordance with prescribed format.

3. Drawings

The contractor shall provide all necessary drafting competence to consult on, develop and prepare final drawings or other related drafting services as follows:

FY 1987	Jobs	Hours
Illustrations	601	3,745
Architectural	4	25
Mechanical	65	636
Electrical	61	365
Topographical	59	960
Geological	94	1,262
Paste-up Work	93	346
Diazo	78	62
Total	1,055	7,401

a. Illustrations – graphs, poster, various 3-dimensions (mines, machines), signs, 35 mm slides, various subjects, transparencies.

b. Architectural drawings – new buildings, renovations to old buildings.

c. Mechanical – pumps, valves, piping, machine drawings, duct work, A/C, heating, structural.

d. Electrical drawings – schematics, for electric devices, electrical drawings for buildings, electrical for mechanical devices.

e. Topographic – plot plans, mining layouts and drawings, maps for hard coal mine, soft coal, metal and non-metal. Redraw mine maps after disasters for litigation purposes. Contour maps of all types.

f. Geological drawings – geological section and strata drawings

g. Paste-ups – for photographic purposes

h. Diazo – B/W prints, processing auto-positives, intermediates, transparencies.

Since most drawings will be of a permanent nature, or will be used in agency publications, all final drawings will be completed in ink, unless otherwise specifically directed by the agency. Preliminary and developmental drawings, resulting from consultations on site visits can, however, be in pencil.

Finished drawings will be prepared in format approved by the agency, and completed on tracing paper, paper, Bristol board or vellum as directed.

4. Clerical

The contractor will provide suitable filing and storage facilities for all finished official drawings. These facilities will provide safety from dust, dirt, elements, fire and water damage.

The contractor will provide an adequate recording (numbering) system for all official drawings. Contractor will further provide and maintain accurate numbering system; they will provide suitable filing system for easy retrieval of all drawings, establish and maintain drawing reference log, keep files current, make required weekly and monthly reports in a timely fashion and maintain accurate work records to facilitate accurate charge back for services performed.

E. Photographic Services

1. Photography

The contractor will provide qualified photographer to photograph a) variety of subjects, b) under differing unusual conditions, c) using the full range of equipment, film, and processing techniques.

a. Subjects – consist of routine lab set ups (items related to any ongoing project). Photomicrographs of mineral or explosive samples, copy camera work of charts, graphs, maps, etc., research project shots, award and presentation shots.

b. Conditions – run the gamut from ideally controlled lab and studio conditions, to research site conditions outdoors, underground or aerial photography.

c. Equipment – used shall enable the photographers to utilize the most modern techniques and state of the art to achieve the photographic excellence required by the agency. Photographers should bring to the job sufficiently up to date knowledge of equipment on film use to insure the standard of excellence enjoyed by the agency.

2. Processing

The contractor will provide for complete film processing service, including B/W and color film, prints and enlargements, slides and transparencies. All processed work will be of studio qualify, with all required cropping and dodging.

The following presents statistics on photographic volume (est.) for FY 1987.

Photographer	
Studio	95%
Onsite	5%
B&W Negatives	3,446
B&W Slides (35 mm)	4,300
Color	
Orig. Slides	21,410
Dup. Slides	23,719
Prints	
3-1/2 x 5	4,283
4 x 6	5,735

5 x 7	408
8 x 10	1,972
11 x 14	—
16 x 20	10
Rolls Processed	1,205
B&W Enlargements (Assorted)	
From 4 x 5 to 30 x 40	15,664
Roll Film Processed (135 B/W, Ektochrome, UPS, 120 B&W, Color)	65
Metal Plates	30

3. Clerical

The contractor will maintain a file of official negatives. Negatives to be included in this file will be so designated by the agency. Negatives will be stored in files that will afford safety from dust, dirt elements, fire, and water damage.

The contractor will provide the necessary cross indexed filing system to afford easy retrieval of any negative.

F. Copy Center

The contractor shall operate a Copy Center for the users (BOM and MSHA personnel) who require large runs (in excess of 300 copies) of printed materials. The contractor will be responsible for a sufficient level of supplies to insure efficient operation of the center. The contract will maintain an accurate record of Copy Center usage. Copy charges will be furnished to the user for each job; total charges will be billed monthly. Operational costs will be reviewed periodically to determine "cost per copy" for next period. The contractor will operate the Copy Center in accordance with all G.P.O. regulations and will provide all required production reports in a timely fashion. The contractor will provide necessary operators for the following equipment:

1. Xerox 9900

2. Paper Drill

3. Plastic Punch and Binder
4. Jogger
5. Bunn Tying Machine
6. Paper Folder
7. Book Stitcher
8. Perfect Binder
9. Paper Carts
10. Necessary works tables, shelving and cabinets for effective operation.

Attachment B

Building Types and Square Footage

Building #	Type	Square Feet
01	Office and Labs	15,760
02	Labs	1,851
03	Labs	19,620
04	Labs	6,052
05	Labs	256
06	Storage	1,775
07	Mine Observation	1,314
08	Office, Labs	5,054
12	Fan House	595
13	Office, Labs and Diesel Test	8,847
14	Office Labs and Garage	2,488
15	Shop and Garage	922
17	Garage	400
18	Tunnel	475
19	Maintenance Shops and Storage	19,243
19A	Office	1,440
20	Office and Labs	11,716
21, 22, 23	Hydraulic Transport Test Loop	29,680
25	Labs	659
29	Fragment Bombproof	5,776
30	Photo Labs	1,740
35	Labs	200
36	Utility	62
37	Grinding Facility	3,883
38	Office and Lab	10,752
39	Utility	180
40	Machine Shop and Medical	9,089
41	Lab and Office	2,160
44	Lab and Office	5,576
50	Mine Control Office	600
62	Boiler House and Coal Prep.	7,650
63	Pump House	211

69	Steam Loop	180
100	Guard House	80
101	Dust Gallery	1,984
102	Bomb Preparation	649
103	Storage Lab	4,381
104	Lab	831
106	X-Ray	600
107	Test Lab	200
108	Oven Control	2,212
109	Expl. Research Lab	621
111	Dry House	81
113	Service for Gallery 1	600
114	Service for Gallery 1	1,462
115	Gallery 1	1,215
117	Moon Lab	3,150
118	Explosive Test	1,536
119	Record	253
120	Utility	88
121	Gallery 2 Control	818
122	Gallery 2	261
123	Pack House 1	80
124	Bomb Proof	565
126	Bomb Proof Control	650
127	Bomb Proof Control	863
128	Lab	196
129	Bomb Proof Control	1,785
130	Utility and Control	90
131	Utility	90
132	Utility	90
133	Gas Meter House	192
134	Bomb Proof	396
135	Bomb Proof and Control	397
138	Gas Well	42
140	Administration Building	23,000
142	Bomb Proof	989

143	Office and Labs	12,648
144	Wire Rope Test	11,146
145	Office	6,475
146	Bomb Proof	987
147	Compressor	422
148	Publications and Distribution	2,601
149	Publications and Film Office	720
150	Film Inspection and Distribution	2,500
151	Surface Mining	54,000
152	Surface Mining and Office	54,000
153	Mining Equipment	8,100
154	Test Facility	7,200
155	Surface Mining and Office	18,000
156	Methane Control and Office	25,092
157	Oil Shortage	144
159	Storage (Heavy Equipment)	3,200
160	Materials Test	958
161	Materials Test	508
162	Mine Gallery	3,775
163	Materials Test	757
165	Simulated Mine	5,633
166	Warehouse and Office	11,356
167	Lab and Office	8,500
168	Materials Test	893
169	Materials Test	502
170	Storage Building	3,600
171	Office/Storage	3,800
172	Storage	4,000
211	Safety	420
212	Diesel Storage	200
220	Magazine	108
221	Magazine	330
222	Magazine	49
223	Magazine	225
224	Magazine	120

225	Magazine	49
226	Magazine	49
227	Magazine	49
228	Magazine	200
229	Magazine	70
233	Magazine	252
239	Magazine	49
245	Magazine	25
Total Square Feet		480,455

Sample 6

Research Information Processing and Dissemination

Type of Work: Technical Support Services

Objective: To provide the following technical support services for research information processing and dissemination: report preparation and information dissemination, local area network (LAN) administration, data entry and administrative support, systems development and programming support, and special support services.

SOW Type: Functional

Comments:

- This is a cost plus award fee contract.
- Background is particularly good.
- Functional specifications are well defined.
- Clear identification as to which business units are to receive the requested services.
- Some of the terms used should have better definitions (e.g., "accurate," "adequate"). These terms are vague and can be left open to interpretation, particularly when determining compliance.
- Evaluation criterion is well defined.

Section C – Description/Work Statement/Specifications

Support Services for Research Information Processing, Dissemination and Computer Services

I. Introduction

The reporting of results is an integral part of research programs and studies as is the dissemination of information about grants and programs. The process is not complete until the useful results have been documented and made available to the public. The National Science Foundation's Scientific, Technological, and International Affairs Directorate (STIA) shares with research investigators and performing organizations the responsibility for ensuring that the results of supported research and analysis are appropriately recorded and disseminated. Most of STIA's supported research bears directly on major contemporary problems serving to underscore the importance of such dissemination activities.

II. Background

The Directorate for Scientific, Technological, and International Affairs (STIA) is composed of several divisions and offices with diverse missions and functions. Despite these differences, the Directorate's requirements for technical support services are fairly homogenous.

STIA provides support for approximately 850 projects per year. The support is chiefly in the form of grants to academic institutions, and small businesses. Through the Foundation's Small Business Innovation Research Program, STIA receives approximately 1400 proposals per year from all high-technology firms. STIA also receives several hundred technical reports each year from these grantees, many in the form of technical project reports. Over the past several years, a contractor has assisted STIA with the receipt, processing, storage, and dissemination of these proposals and reports. The Directorate also provides support for international cooperative research activities through the Division of International programs. The Experimental Program is Stimulate Competitive Research is designed to improve the scientific and technological capacity of states with less developed research infrastructures.

STIA requires technical support in the following areas:

A. report preparation and information dissemination;

B. Local Area Network (LAN) administration;

C. data entry and administrative support for the SBIR (Small Business Innovation Research) program;

D. systems development and programming support; and

E. special support services

These services are required by the following units within the STIA Directorate: Office of the Assistant Direct (OAD), the Office of Experimental Programs to Stimulate Competitive Research (EPSCoR), the Division of International Programs (INT), and the Division for Industrial Science and Technological Innovation (ISTI) which includes the Small Business Innovation Research Program (SBIR).

As general background, all desktop computers in STIA use Microsoft® Windows with CD-RW/DVD Combo Drive with 80 gigabytes of hard disk storage and 2 gigabytes of memory. The National Science Foundation currently has two in-house central computer systems – an IBM System Z and three Hewlett-Packard 9000 servers.

Company XYZ of Rockville, Maryland is the incumbent contractor. By the expiration data of the contract, November 30, 2008, the total expended by XYZ for similar work for a three year period is estimated to be $620,000.

III. Statement of Work

A. Prepare, Manage, and Disseminate Reports, Publications and Information

1. The contractor shall prepare STIA Directorate brochures, reports and other documents on an as-needed basis during the contract. This support shall include preparation of text and graphics displays, production of draft documents for review by STIA staff members, final editing, creation of final copy on a commonly used word processing software package such as WordPerfect™ or Microsoft® Word for printing by the NSF Printing Services Branches, and proofing the galleys. It is anticipated that the contractor

will be required to complete no more than one document per year. See Exhibit A for an example of a STIA brochure. An example of a STIA report is NSF 88-6 Science and Technology Report Outlook 2005-2008 available form the NSF Forms and Publication Unit (202) 357-7668.

2. The contractor shall edit abstracts of Small Business Innovation Research (SBIR) Phase I awards. Drawing from project summaries provided by the SBIR staff, the contractor shall edit abstracts of approximately 200 Phase I SBIR awards over a one-year period and deliver to ISTI on a compact disc (CD) by May 1st of each year. The following tasks shall be performed as a part of this activity:

    - Reduce project summary language to standard, brief format in easily understood language. Communicate with awardee (small business) to verify accuracy, including bibliographic information, and secure acceptance of editorial changes.
    - Contact awardee to confirm all names associated with award, title and address. Make necessary changes in NSF data base and documents.
    - Index all SBIR Phase I awards, and prepare and deliver a camera-ready hard copy to the SBIR Contact.

3. The contractor shall manage and disseminate STIA reports and program announcements on an as needed basis. Periodically, the contractor shall be requested to manage and disseminate materials from the various STIA Divisions and Offices. The contractor shall be given prior notice of any required dissemination activities. All requests from NSF grantees, the general public and NSF staff shall be handled promptly, and if the material is unavailable, other applicable available information shall be provided.

4. The contractor shall manage SBIR reports resulting from SBIR-supported research. The contractor shall process up to 300 different documents yearly. The following tasks shall be performed as part of this processing activity:

    - Pick up reports from a designated station in ISTI on a bi-weekly basis during specified periods of processing.

- Provide for receiving and story up to five copies each of approximately 300 different reports yearly.
- Hold reports for two years from the award date (per the agreement made by the SBIR Program with their grantees). At the end of the two year waiting period, prepare abstracts, assign index terms and submit the reports to the National Technical Information Service (NTIS) on a timely basis. (See Exhibit B for Document Preparation Guide and NTIS Form 272).
- Enter bibliographic citations for each document (see Exhibit C) in the NSF Program Documentation Data Base (PDDB) maintained on a desktop computer. Maintain this as an up-to-date file for access. Information should include title; accession number (when available); author; awardee name and address; NSF grant number; NSF report number; NSF Directorate and Division; report date; subject key words; abstract; NTIS order number; award amount; fiscal year of award and statement regarding potential commercial application of research.
- Notify principal investigators and NSF program directors in writing when one of their reports becomes available from NTIS.
- This notification will include the title of the report, the NTIS ordering number, and the price.
- Maintain the automated inventory management system to track receipts of every document processed each month. This list will be submitted with the Monthly Processed Report.

As noted above, the contractor shall submit SBIR reports to NTIS to make them available to the public. As part of this task, problem documents – those that will not meet NTIS standards for acceptability due to poor legibility, copyright restrictions, and missing and/or unnumbered sections – shall be handled in the following way:

- The contractor shall spend up to two hours to correct any acceptability problem (as defined by NTIS, see

Exhibit C) of a single document. In cases requiring more than two hours to fix such problems, the contractor shall notify the principal investigator of the problem. This notification will be made using a form letter.

- The contractor shall keep a list of problem reports, letters mailed to principal investigators, and the subsequent resolution of each problem. A follow-up telephone call shall be made to the principal investigator in each case.
- After an acceptable copy of a report has been received by the contractor from the STIA program director or the principal investigator, the contractor shall continue processing it in the usual manner.

5. The contractor shall manage and disseminate (to NSF grantees and NSF staff) INT's Japanese Language and Cultural Preparation materials, which include:

Video Cassettes

Nihongo: Japanese for Busy People (Volumes 1-3)
Foreign Researchers in Japan
The Japanese Businessman
The Japanese Family
The Tradition of Performing Arts in Japan

Book

Nippon: The Land and Its People

The National Science Foundation will provide franked mailing labels, the contractor shall provide boxes for mailing (approximately 12 x 9.5 x 5 inches) and storage space for 32 sets of 7 video cassettes and the book (approximately 1 bookcase).

This activity requires the contractor to:

- Maintain an in-house supply of materials for quick mailing (the reminder of the material will be stored in the NSF warehouse); the contractor shall notify the Contracting Officer's Technical Representative (COTR) when in-house supply requires replenishing.

- Maintain a log that includes the recipient's name and address, details of materials sent, date sent, and date returned; and
- Prepare materials for mailing to individuals (per notification from INT) in boxes with franked return mailing labels enclosed and deliver the prepared packages to the NSF mailroom for mailing.

Approximately 20 requests for the Japanese Language and Culture Preparation materials are received each month.

B. Local Area Network (LAN) Administration

Three of the units within STIA do not have in-house LAN Administrators – OAD/STIA, EPSCoR and INT. These LANs are set-up using 3-COM+ software and have approximately 10, 6 and 55 users, respectively. Due to the recently announced changes within the 3-COM Corporation, the National Science Foundation will be changing to a new network operating system software (which has not been determined at this time) over the next few years. The contractor shall provide support for this conversion.

In addition to providing access to NSF mainframe application, the LANs also provide access to commercial applications such as WordPerfect™, IBM, Lotus, 1-2-3, and the Microsoft® Office Suite.

The contractor shall:

1. Work with COTR or other appropriate STIA staff to develop a list of specific tasks required for LAN administration, (both on an on-going basis and those of a special, one-time nature) and establish a schedule for implementation.
2. Install PC hardware and software associated with the Local Area Networks (including installation of hard disks and boards and troubleshooting), and manage communications with the NSF mainframe and other LANs. The purchase of hardware and software is not a requirement under this contract. Provide in-house support for "Flexiplace Workplace" NSF staff (such as PC Anywhere access to LAN), as necessary. When possible, system upgrades,

maintenance, repair, etc., that will interfere with user access to the LAN should be done during evenings or weekends.

3. Assure system compatibility and integrity, including compatibility of system enhancements with the current system and protocols established by the NSF Office of Information Systems (OIS). In doing so, the contractor may research, recommend and implement such enhancements with prior approval from the COTR or other appropriate STIA staff.
4. Provide analytic support and, as necessary, implement changes and modifications to system configurations and telecommunications structures.
5. Develop and maintain procedures for daily back-ups to tape and, as necessary, periodic backups on tape and hard disk.
6. Develop and maintain system documentation for the LANs, including User and Administrator Manuals, server and workstation configuration reports, a manual of current standards and procedures, and layout diagrams.
7. Provide demonstrations and user assistance for general LAN use as system modifications occur and provide technical assistance and support to STIA staff as needed.
8. Provide on-site support – 1 full-time employee for INT and 1 full-time employee to be shared by EPSCoR and OAD/STIA. Changes in on-site staff requires the prior written approval of the COTR and the Contracting Officer.

C. Data Entry and Administrative Support for the SBIR Program

The National Science Foundation's Small Business Innovation Research program is administered by the Division of Industrial Science and Technological Innovation. The SBIR program issues an annual solicitation for proposals, with the deadline for submission being mid-June. Approximately 1300-1350 proposals are received each year.

The contractor shall provide data entry and administrative support in the following areas:

1. Proposal processing and data entry for logging of SBIR Phase I proposals.

    - Provide on-site support (approximately 2-3 people for 10-15 days) to assist in the initial review of incoming proposals – checking for completeness and adding items as needed.
    - Arrange for pick up at NSF and delivery of proposals to contractor's site. The contractor shall receive the original and seven copies of each proposal and must provide a separate secure (access in controlled by the contractor) area for the period required for processing these proposals.
    - Provide, at contractor's site, a minimum of five persons with keyboard and data input skills for 10-15 days and up to five modems and workstations with the ability to communicate via modem and telephone lines at 9600 baud to the host Hewlett Packard 9000 servers, located at NSF G Street. Costs for phone line access to the NSF G Street computer and installation of modems will be paid by the contractor under the contract. Contractor must guarantee availability on the block of days to be specified by ISTI. ISTI will specify the dates at least a month in advance of the initiation of the activity. This block will consist of consecutive days immediately preceding and immediately after the deadline date for submission of the SBIR Phase I proposals (usually mid-June).
    - Contractor personnel shall take specified data from the cover sheet of each proposal and enter it into the NSF central computer, creating records for new institutions and principal investigators as required and updating existing information as necessary.
    - Contractor personnel shall verify data entered as a result of the previous instruction. No person shall verify his/her own data input.

- Data on minority, women, disclosure, and other agency submittals shall be entered during the same period.
- ISTI personnel shall train the contractor personnel as required – usually 1-2 days.
- Contractor shall prepare proposal folders ("jackets") as directed by ISTI. Contractor personnel shall affix gummed labels provided by NSF to the jacket flap and insert jacket products provided by NSF (i.e., NSF Form 1036 Page 1, NSF Form 7 and Principal Investigator History Form).
- Contractor shall store proposals in numerical order in numbered boxes for quick retrieval and shall maintain listing of proposals which shows the number of each proposal and the number of the box containing the proposal.
- After completion of above items, contractor shall deliver jackets with proposal copies attached, to NSF discipline offices as directed by ISTI.

2. Storage of Files. The contractor shall pick up and store approximately 2,000 proposal jackets and/or other files per year and manage them such that any one of them may be retrieved for data research. The Contractor shall:
    - Store documents at a contractor supplied facility and provide a monthly report to the ISTI Division indicating the status of SBIR reports by title, accession number, current inventory and processing status.
    - Provide for up to an additional 35 boxes of files per year and purge files only as directed by the ISTI Division.
    - Produce cumulative indexes of the document collection as requested by the ISTI Division.
    - Provide one-day response to any request for file retrieval made by an SBIR staff contact.
3. Ad Hoc Data Entry and Proposal Documentation Review Support. The contractor shall provide a group of experi-

ence data entry technicians and proofreaders, familiar with NSF proposal and award documentation, to respond to special data entry and proposal documentation review requirements (off-site). The ISTI Division has a large backlog of data entry work at certain times of the year, and requires flexible, high-quality support, as needed, with rapid turn around time.

D. Systems Development and Programming Support

The Divisions and Offices within STIA require technical assistance that will permit improvements not only to the management of STIA programs but also to the review and evaluation of program reports and statistics. The contractor shall:

1. Provide support for the EPSCoR management information system which serves as a software tool for collecting information form all state participating in the NSF EPSCoR program (Experimental Program to Stimulate Competitive Research). This system has three main goals:

    - Provide Congress with accurate data to continue support for the EPSCoR experiment.
    - Provide NSF with adequate data and accomplishments so as to properly evaluate and modify the experiment over time.
    - Provide the EPSCoR State Project Directors, Steering Committees, and participants with sufficient data to modify, redesign, and evaluate their own accomplishments and achievements.

This EPSCoR management information system is a complete database system setup at two levels. One level is for each of the individual states where they utilize user input screens to input the requested data into their databases and then generated reports based on their data only. The current database from each state is sent via electronic mail to the National Science Foundation which the current contractor then compiles into the second level of the database system. This second level is maintained at NSF by NSF staff and contains data from all participating states and can generate several standard reports as needed to meet the goals stated. Both levels are user friendly automated systems providing input screens and menu selections to input, validity check, backup, and report on the pertinent information to be stored. The system is based in Microsoft® Access and utilizes clipper routines for speed and efficiently.

2. Provide assistance and any necessary training to EPSCoR staff in maintaining this database both at the state level and at the Foundation level. Also required will be any periodic modifications or revisions to the system as well as adding new standardized reports to the system. If requested, it may be necessary to modify this system to meet other project needs such as providing a similar database system for the European market and/or providing expanded uses for one or more states.

3. In addition to the systems development and programming support for the EPSCoR management information system, the contractor shall provide an individual to attend the Annual EPSCoR Conference and provide one day of onsite training to the EPSCoR Administrative Assistants form the participating States. The annual conference for 2008 will be held in Maine.

4. In addition to providing LAN support, as specified in subsection B of this SECTION C page C-5, the contractor shall supply experienced personnel skilled in the desktop computer environment. Personnel should be familiar with microprocessor software and hardware interfacing, setup, maintenance, requirements analysis, software quality assurance and testing, structured design and programming, databases, operating systems, systems design, micro-mainframe connectivity, security, and communications systems.

E. Special Support Services

1. The Division of International Programs provides data and information for an in-house, on-line information service featuring reports on foreign science and technology. This material is often supplied to INT in hard copy and needs to be keyed in Microsoft® Word for further editing and preparation for uploading to the database. The contractor shall type and proofread approximately 100 pages of

text per month. The contract shall provide courier service to INT on an as-needed basis (usually not to exceed twice per week). INT will provide the 5.25 inch diskettes.

2. The Directorate for Scientific, Technological, and International Affairs convenes conferences and workshops on an ad hoc basis. The contractor shall provide logistical and administrative support for these events, as needed. Examples of the support required includes assistance in making travel arrangements for participants, providing refreshments (no meals), and preparing a draft of meeting minutes NSF requires contractor assistance for no more than one meeting per year on site at NSF.

3. In addition to the proposal data entry requirement for the SBIR Program, these or similar services may be required by the Office of Experimental Programs to Stimulate Competitive Research (up to 17 proposals per year) and the Division of International Programs (up to 100 proposals per year). The contractor shall provide periodic short-term support on an ad hoc basis.

IV. Personnel Qualifications

Contractor personnel shall be familiar with the computing and operating environment that the STIA Directorate operates under. It is essential that those Individuals providing on-site LAN and computer support have previous experience in the following areas: 3-COM+ LAN operating systems; IBM, Lotus, 1-2-3, WordPerfect™ and the Microsoft® Office Suite.

V. Additional Information

NS has three HP9000 servers and a new IBM System Z. The new IBM system runs in parallel with the HP9000s. STIA uses Microsoft® Windows compatible equipment. STIA does not operate its own mainframe and isn't interested in mainframe support or applications. It uses network servers (3COM+ at this time).

The storage facility will not require a security system or personnel of any type. There is no need for import-export controls. Representatives from NSF may conduct an on-site visit prior to contract award.

[End of Section]

Section M – Evaluation Factors for Award

I. Evaluation of Priced Options

The Government will evaluate offers for award purposes by adding the total price for the options to the basic requirement. Evaluation of the options will not obligate the Government to exercise the option(s).

II. Evaluation Factors for Award

The Government will select the offer which provides the greatest value to the Government. Although cost and other business factors will be considered, the primary basis for award will be the technical merit of the proposal.

Proposals received in accordance with this RFP will be technically reviewed by an evaluation panel. The Evaluation Panel will recommend to the Source Selection Official for award that proposal which offers the greatest value to the Government. While total cost will be considered in determining which proposal offers the greatest value, the primary basis for selection will be the technical evaluation criteria.

A. Technical Proposal

The technical evaluation criteria are listed in descending order of importance. Cost will not be scored but will be considered in determining the best value to the Government.

1. Personnel Resources

Because of the support nature of this contract, the specific work experience and qualifications of proposed personnel are critical. Elements to be considered for the proposed personnel are listed below:

A. Professional Experience, and its relation to tasks required in the Scope and Work;

B. Current Responsibilities, and their relation to tasks required in the Scope of Work;

C. Education and Training.

If proposed personnel are not presently employed by the offeror, acceptable evidence must be provided of the offerors ability to obtain these personnel for the immediate performance of this contract. The personnel section should clearly not those personnel who are primary and secondary designees for performance of this effort.

2. Technical Approach

   In this section the offeror shall demonstrate an understanding of the support requirements and of the task areas. The Government's assessment of the offeror's proposed approach will be based on:

   A. The demonstrated awareness of the types of problems and requirements to be encountered during contract performance;

   B. The realism and completeness of the offerors proposed allocation of staff and other resources; and

   C. The appropriateness of the offerors plan for organizing the project staff and the work effort.

3. Corporate Technical Experience

   This evaluation will be based on the offerors technical experience and performance on current or prior Government contracts of a similar nature. The offeror should summarize the technical aspects of these contracts and show the similarity to the tasks described in the Statement of Work.

4. Facilities and Equipment

   A. Availability of facilities suitable for conducting the work specified in the RFP in an efficient and effective manner

   B. Availability of current technological equipment required to satisfy the work requirements.

   C. List of equipment and facilities to be used under the contract

B. Business Proposal

   The Business Proposals will be analyzed but will NOT be numerically scored. The three (3) major areas cited below will be taken into consideration by the Government in their overall evaluation process. Cost/Price factors, Experience and Past Performance factors, and Other Factors will be considered in determining which proposal offers the greatest value to the Government; however, the primary basis for selection will be the Technical factors.

1. The Cost section of the Business Proposal will be analyzed by the Government in order to:

    A. Assess the realism of the proposed cost,

    B. Determine the portable cost to the Government, and

    C. Assist in determining the offerors understanding of technical requirements.

    Evaluation of the Cost section will include the proposed cost for the basic one year period and the two (2) priced option periods.

2. The Experience and Past Performance section of the Business proposal is important is important in the Government's evaluation and selection, and requires comprehensive treatment and response to the proposal. Omission or an inaccurate or inadequate response to this evaluation category could have a negative effect on the overall. The factors evaluated in this area are:

    A. Performance History

    B. Cost Management History, and

    C. Termination History

3. The Other Factors section comprises other factors and issues which will be analyzed based upon information provided in the offerors proposal and data obtained from the Government and other sources. While other Factors fall into a separate category that is not directly associated to the Technical Proposal, the Cost section, or the Experience and Past Performance section, these factors are pertinent to the acquisition process and are an important consideration of the Source Selection Official in making a final selection.

[End of Section]

Sample 7

Management Consulting Services

Type of Work: Management Support Services

Objective: To provide the following management support services: 1) refining and developing a concept of regional service centers to support departmental field operations; 2) preparing an implementation plan for such a concept; and 3) reviewing the general organization of the department's central office.

SOW Type: Level-of-Effort

Comments:

- Very good background discussion.
- Statement of needs includes labor and resources to assist VDOT, thus suggesting a level-of-effort contract.
- Detailed description of the minimum areas that should be addressed in the comprehensive analysis and subsequent action plans to implement the regional service centers.
- Evaluation criterion is well defined.
- Good description of how the contract award will be determined.

I PURPOSE: The purpose and intent of this Request for Proposals is to solicit sealed proposals from qualified sources to establish a contract through competitive negotiations for the purchase of the services of a management consultant to assist the Virginia Department of Transportation (hereinafter referred to as VDOT) in (1) refining and developing a concept of regional service centers to support departmental field operations; (2) preparing an implementation plan for such a concept; and (3) reviewing the general organization of VDOT's central office.

The consultant contractor shall work under the general direction of the Commissioner and in cooperation with a departmental study team, and shall function principally as an expert on DOT organizations and in an advisory and staff support capacity. The consultant shall serve as secretary to the study and will be responsible for preparing and coordinating the draft and final reports of this effort.

II: BACKGROUND: VDOT's mission is to provide a safe, efficient and effective ground transportation system for the Commonwealth of Virginia. It fulfills this mission by planning, constructing, maintaining and operating the roads, bridges tunnels and related transportation facilities which make up that system. The approximately 54,000 miles of roadway for which VDOT is responsible represent the nation's third largest system of state-maintained highways.

VDOT also currently provides financial and technical assistance for local public transportation systems, administers certain funding for capital improvements at airports and seaports, and has limited responsibilities with respect to rail transportation. Some aspects of these reporting relationships are proposed to be changed.

The central office has responsibility for the agencywide management function. The senior management group includes the Commissioner as chief executive officer, a chief engineer, and assistant commissioners for administration, operations, finance, planning and programming, and (temporarily) rail and public transportation. The central office also includes twenty-seven administrative, engineering, and operational divisions which report to members of this senior management group. Attachment 1 depicts the most current organizational chart.

The concept of regional service centers was proposed by an internal study group earlier this year during a broad organizational review of

VDOT as an alternative or adaptation of the existing field organization centered around nine "full service" districts. The nine districts historically have been largely organized the same in the sense that each is staffed to include administration, preliminary engineering support, operations, highway system maintenance, construction, and certain special facilities. Over the past five years, VDOT has been engaged in a conscious process of decentralization intended to place increased authority and responsibility in the field.

While the existing field structure has served well for many years, it was established when the Commonwealth was primarily rural, and in the view of many in VDOT and outside, may not adequately reflect the Commonwealth's growing urbanization. Other factors make consideration of the regional service center concept timely.

One of these factors is that the public's transportation needs continue to grow during a period of scarce financial resources, requiring examination of all potential actions to invest available funds wisely.

Another factor is that VDOT's employment level is being reduced sharply. At present, in an authorized strength level of 12,277 employees, there are approximately 900 vacancies as a result of normal attrition and a hiring freeze, because of a budget shortfall. In addition, approximately 980 more employees, many of them in key field managerial positions, took advantage of a one-time early retirement program. Many of those positions will be eliminated. Currently, VDOT staffing is approximately 15 percent below its authorized level.

Another strategic factor affecting VDOT is the public demand for increased efficiency and productivity. Over the last several years, VDOT has conducted, at its own initiative and at the direction of the Governor, several productivity studies and implemented many recommendations. However, due to the climate of economic uncertainty and the perception that, as the largest state agency, VDOT still may not be operating as efficiently as possible, additional directives have been made by the General Assembly for the Department to review its operations and increase efficiency further.

The proposal regarding the potential for the use of regional service centers as part of or in lieu of the present nine "full service" districts is the result of an internal study. This proposal has advanced the hypothesis that "service centers" at fewer than the nine districts (or regionalized service centers located at appropriate districts) may effectively serve the engineering, technical and other support requirements for field maintenance, operations, and construction, even if existing districts and district boundaries are kept intact for the purpose of allocating construction funds and/or other purposes. The concept of regional service centers, covering a wider geographic area than currently exists, represents an alternative VDOT management has determined should be implemented in on form or another to meet the strategic goals of the organization.

III. STATEMENT OF NEEDS: The contractor shall furnish all necessary labor and resources (including but not limited to equipment, materials and supplies) to assist VDOT staff in conducting the study, provide a thorough and comprehensive analysis and subsequent action plan to implement regional service centers, addressing at a minimum the following areas:

A. Optimum number, location and type of regional centers

B. Effect on existing field structure with its district, residency, and area headquarters locations

C. Resulting roles and responsibilities of residencies and area headquarters

D. Technical, operational, and other functions to establish at regional centers. (Extent to which these functions remain in the central office versus decentralized)

E. Effect realignment to regional centers will have on communities if no service center is physically located at an existing district, to include employment, economic and social effect

F. Reporting relationships between regional centers, districts and the central office

G. Staffing requirements of each scenario regarding regional centers

H. Cost of establishing each scenario regarding regional centers

I. Effect of regional centers on VDOT's delivery of public services

J. Political implications, if any, of regional centers, and how to address them

K. Method and time frame to implement regional centers

L. Approach to minimize effect on employee morale an incentive during the date gathering phase, analysis phase and implementation phase of regional centers

M. Approach to address employee relocation without personal economic loss

N. Other human resource issues to be addressed during both the analysis and implementation of regional centers, such as approaches to employee involvement

O. Other structural changes desirable to reflect the commonwealth's growing urbanization

P. Effect on VDOT efficiently and effectiveness as result of your proposed action plan to implement regional centers

Upon completion of the comprehensive analysis, the contractor shall submit a written report to the commissioner in triplicate. The report shall include, but not be limited to, a summary of the analytical process undertaken by the VDOT team and the consultant, and a comprehensive description of actual findings, analysis and recommendations on implementation of regional service centers, in concert with VDOT's mission and responsibilities.

IV. EVALUATION AND AWARD CRITERIA:

A. Evaluation Criteria: Proposals will be evaluated by a VDOT committee using the following criteria

1. Prior relevant experience
2. Favorable Reference
3. Staff/Personnel Assigned
4. Qualifications/Ability to Perform
5. Approach/Methodology
6. Participation of Small, Women-Owned and Minority Businesses
7. Proposed Fee

B. Award of Contract: Selection shall be made of one or more Offerors deemed to be fully qualified and best suited among those submitting proposals on the basis of the evaluation factors identified above. Negotiations shall be conducted with the Offerors so selected. Price shall be considered, but need not be the sole determining factor. After negotiations have been conducted with each Offeror so selected, VDOT shall select the Offeror(s) which in its opinion, has made the best proposal, and shall award this contract to the Offeror. VDOT may cancel this Request for Proposals or reject proposals at any time to an award, and is not required to furnish a statement of the reason why a particular proposal was not deemed to be the most advantageous. (Section 11-65D, Code of Virginia). Should VDOT determine in writing and in its sole discretion that only one Offeror is fully qualified, or that one Offeror is clearly more highly qualified than the others under consideration, a contract may be negotiated and awarded to that Offeror. The award documents will be a contract incorporating by reference all the requirements, terms and conditions of this solicitation and the Contractor's proposal as negotiated.

Sample 8

Program Evaluation Services

Type of Work: Management Support Services

Objective: To perform an evaluation of the organization's Statewide Systemic Initiatives Program.

SOW Type: Functional

Comments:

- This is a cost plus fixed fee contract.
- The background section, although well written, makes a common mistake: it references a document that is not included in the package. Every prospective contractor will insist on a copy before it prepares a proposal.
- Good functional specifications otherwise.
- Although the document notes that the contractor should "provide on a continuing basis, and in accordance with the approved evaluation design, an evaluation of NSF's SSI program," it doesn't describe the approved evaluation design or give any information about where it can be found. The evaluation design should be clearly defined or offered as an attachment.

- Good description of what should be included in the mid-year, annual, and final reports. However, to avoid any misinterpretation by the contractor, a sample of each type of required report and their supporting data fields should be included as an attachment or reference.
- The term "etc." is used multiple times throughout the document. The use of this term creates uncertainty about and hedges the requirements.

Section C

Description/Work Statement/Specifications

C.1 SCOPE

The contractor shall provide the services, facilities, materials and supplies necessary to perform the evaluation of NSF's Statewide Systemic Initiatives (SSI) program, as described in Section C.3, and shall perform such additional studies as may be ordered in accordance with Section C.5. The SSI program is intended to broaden the impact, accelerate the pace, and increase the effectiveness of improvements in science, mathematics, and engineering education in both K-12 and post-secondary levels through a systematic approach. The evaluation to be performed by the contractor shall provide information on the effectiveness of the SSI program in terms of policy, implementation and outcome issues.

C.2 BACKGROUND

In the spring of 1990, the National Science Foundation released a solicitation for proposals from states for "projects intended to broaden the impact, accelerate the pace, and increases the effectiveness of improvements in science, mathematics, and engineering education in both K-12 and post-secondary levels." Interested states were expected to form a planning group comprised of key leaders in the state; to conduct an analysis of needs and develop an outline of a plan for addressing these needs; and to submit both preliminary and final proposals to NSF.

The SSI program is described in detail in the program solicitation issued by NSF for that initiative (Statewide Systemic Initiative in Science, Mathematics, and Engineering Education Program Solicitation, NSF 90-47). Copies may be obtained by writing NSF's Publications Services Section, Room 231. The program is briefly characterized here as well. Under the SSI program The National Science Foundation considers proposals from states that promise substantial systematic change at the state level. To receive an award as part of the SSI program, each SSI program requires the commitment of the Governor of the state. Moreover, each awarded project must be cooperative effort by many organizations and individuals within each state. Each SSI awarded project must develop a statewide vision of excellence for mathematics, science and engineering education including:

a. rigorous curriculum goals and content (the mathematics and science knowledge, skills and applications that experts deem most important) for all children (every student should have an equal opportunity to study and master important science and mathematics content);

b. institutional decision making and organizational structures that promote effective teaching and learning;

c. enhancement of teachers, administrators and other school staff through quality development and preparation programs;

d. development, acquisition, allocation and continuation of resources (personnel and fiscal) to support systemic change;

e. alignment and articulation within all aspects of the educational enterprise, e.g., match of assessment with curriculum, match of teaching with assessment, match of middle school programs with elementary school programs, match of licensing requirements with needed teaching skills, etc.; and

f. accountability systems that will indicate goal attainment and areas in need of more work.

An important consideration in the awarding and continuation of funding for these projects in the SSI program is the degree to which they incorporate the use of state, local, and private resources with funds to be received from NSF and other Federal sources. Substantial fiscal commitments from state and local sources must be the major and continuing means to assure long term improvement in science, mathematics and engineering education. NSF support should be used to leverage funding from other sources.

The SSI program awards may be up to five years in length for a maximum of $10-million during the five year period. Ten awards were made in the first year of the program. It is anticipated that over the next two years approximately twenty additional awards will be made. The amounts awarded vary depending on the particular proposals, on the amount of cost sharing provided by the states and on the availability of funds. Attachment D to Section J of this document provides a brief sketch of each of the ten funded projects and their evaluation plans based on information provided in their original proposals. Although the projects have evolved through site visits, negotiation of the cooperative agreement's, and other interaction with the principal investigators for these projects, these sketches of the individual awarded projects may be useful in formulating evaluation plans for this overall SSI program evaluation.

C.3 STATEMENT OF WORK

In performance of the work required under this contract, the Contractor shall perform the evaluation of NSF's Statewide Systemic Initiatives program by accomplishing the following tasks:

a. Provide on a continuing basis, and in accordance with the approved evaluation design, an evaluation of NSF's SSI program that answers the following questions.

1. Resources

    a. How were the resources provided by NSF's SSI program used?

    b. Which mechanisms used for the development of addition resources across awarded projects were most successful?

    c. How does the distribution of resources compare across awarded projects?

    d. What role did NSF SSI funding play in achieving the outcomes?

2. Activities

    a. What were the common and unique activities and Contexts across the awarded projects?

    b. What mechanisms of accountability exist across the awarded projects?

3. Systems

    a. To what extent is the SSI systematic approach an effective way to foster basic change in public education?

    b. What elements are critical for SSI systemic reform?

    c. What mechanisms among the awarded projects best promote the coherence and articulation necessary for systemic change?

4. Outcomes

   a. What impact has the SSI program had on improving science, mathematics and engineering education to experiences, student outcomes, structural changes and policies?

   b. What effects of the SSI program will continue after NSF funding?

5. Recommendations

   a. What NSF program level changes should be made in future NSF initiatives of this type?

   b. What conclusions, recommendations or hypotheses should be made by policy makers, educators and researchers from this evaluation?

b. Test the model of change encompassed by NSF's SSI initiative as described in Attachment C, "SSI PROGRAM EVALUATION DESIGN CONSIDERATIONS"/Model for Change.

c. Develop and monitor a science and mathematics indicator system for the awarded projects. The contractor shall help to define variables and, if necessary, to set up data collection procedures; receive collected data from awarded projects; aggregate data; track data overtime; and conduct summary and trend analysis. [See Attachment E to Section J, entitled "Proposed Indicator Variables for SSI projects."]

d. Document existing and changing conditions in educational institutions.

e. Determine equity in student outcomes and student opportunity to learn.

f. Conduct comprehensive case studies, carefully selected to complement the intensive quantitative data collection effort. These case studies shall provide strong evidence of what is accomplished, why and to what effect. The case studies shall document the major players and their roles, critical configurations and components for change, the evolution of policy and implementation efforts and the leveraging of resources.

g. Interface with local awarded project evaluators and data collection efforts.

h. Annually assess the adequacy of the originally proposed evaluation plan in meeting the needs of the various audiences for the evaluation.

i. Provide a series of reports, as follows:

(1) Provide mid-year, annual and final reports of all evaluation activities in accordance with Section F.3. The mid-year reports may be informal and should include discussion of key evaluation issues. Reports should include baseline and continuing information and descriptions of the SSI awarded projects from the different rounds of funding as appropriate. The descriptions should address the purpose, design and implementation of each aspect of the awarded projects in order to characterize the SSI program as a whole. The initial reports should highlight formative information that would be of use both to the individual awarded projects and to NSF at the program level. Later reports would include documentation of what influence SSI initiatives have had on practice and outcomes.

(2) Provide special focus area evaluation reports as appropriate, e.g., evaluations of collaboration, implementation efforts, equity issues, policies, etc.

(3) Provide summary reports addressing the systemic nature of the program in terms of policy, implementation and outcome issues at the end of the fifth year.

(4) Provide reports of the case studies conducted.

j. Conduct meetings.

(1) Organize and hold at least annual meetings of the SSI <u>evaluation advisory committee</u> and NSF staff to discuss the progress of the evaluation and provide committee members, SSI staff and the Office of Studies, Evaluation and Dissemination (OSED) staff with annual reports of the evaluation effort before each meeting.

a. <u>Evaluation Advisory Committee</u> – The NSF is responsible for chartering and reporting the activities of the evaluation advisory committee. This committee shall review documents and provide assistance as needed in data collection methods, analysis, and assessment of findings. The contractor shall be required to maintain the committee and convene meetings in accordance with the Federal Advisory Committee Act (FACA), 5. U.S.C., App 2. Violation of the Act may involve the imposition of penalties. The contractor shall assist NSF in complying with FACA by performing specific tasks as well as providing general cost and group member information as needed by NSF. In addition to any other FACA-related tasks described above, the contractor shall perform specific tasks described above, the contractor shall perform specific tasks in order to assist NSF with FACA reporting requirements:

(1) The contractor shall insure that members of the evaluation advisory committee have completed NSF From 1230, "Conflicts of Interest Statement for New Advisory Committee/Review Panel Members." (Copy of form is provided in Section K.)

(2) The contractor shall have all committee members, staff, and visitors attending meetings sign a roster.

(3) The contractor shall insure that a Federal official designated by NSF is present during entire meetings. A Federal official shall call (or approve the call of) the meetings and must adjourn the meetings when it is in the public interest.

(4) The contractor shall take minutes regardless of whether the meeting is opened or closed. The chairperson shall certify that the minutes are accurate. FACA requires that the minutes include:

- the time, date, and place of meeting;
- a list of committee members and agency employees attending the meeting;
- an estimated number of other members of the public present;
- a complete and accurate description of each matter discussed and conclusions research; and

- copies of each report or other document received, considered, or issued by the committee.

The contractor shall provide the minutes to NSF in a timely manner and shall not distribute the minutes in response to non-NSF requests. The NSF shall distribute sanitized copies of the minutes to anyone requesting them under the requirements of FACA.

(2) Organize and hold mid-year meetings with NSF staff to discuss the progress of the evaluation.

k. Disseminate evaluation findings to interested parties in ways that will facilitate the utilization of the information, e.g., the NSF; the US Congress; the SSI awarded projects staffs; the general public; and the participating students, parents, teachers and administrators.

l. Provide NSF with files of all data in formats compatible with Microsoft Windows™ operating system, along with all documents and coding information. Qualitative data shall be provided in data files that are accessible by some scanning or aggregating system, e.g., Ethnograph.

C.4 SAMPLE TASK PROPOSAL

In order to more accurately compare the technical quality of the proposals, all potential contractors shall present a concrete and detailed plan for completion of task c. – "Develop and monitor a science and mathematics indicator system for the awarded projects" using the proposed indicator variables specified in Attachment E, and considering, at a minimum, the issues raised in Attachment C - Model for Change. This 4-5 page detailed plan should be in addition to the 15 page overall evaluation effort proposal. This detailed plan must include information on at least the following items: how the task is to be accomplished; the recommended approach for accomplishing the task; the staff that would be required; the hours to be spent by each staff member; the problems anticipated in completing the task how these problems would be overcome; what milestones would mark steps in the completion of the task; and the amount of time required to accomplish the task.

A complete and detailed separate cost proposal covering this task should also be provided. This is in addition to the cost proposals required under Section L.2.C. of this RFP. The cost proposal should be clearly marked to indicate it as part of the response to Section C.4.

NOTE: Any instruments to be used for the purpose of data collection, e.g., surveys, questionnaires, etc., during performance of this contract must have prior clearance from the Office of Management and Budget (OMB). The contractor must allow approximately 60-90 days for clearance time.

C.5 ADDITIONAL TASK ORDERS

It is anticipated that there may be requirements from time to time for studies or evaluations of particular issues or questions within the general scope of Section C in a more intensive manner and/or within a shorter time frame than is contemplated under the Statement of Work in Section C.3. When this occurs, the Government reserves the right to issue separately priced task orders in accordance with the procedures set forth in Section G.7. The cumulative total of the estimated costs and fee, if any, under these task orders may not exceed $1,000,000. Nothing in this Section C.5 is intended to limit the Government's right to issue change orders in accordance with the Changes clause of this contract.

[End of Section.]

Section M – Evaluation Factors

M.1 Overall Basis for Award

The Government shall award a contract resulting from this Solicitation to the responsible offeror whose offer, conforming to the Solicitation, will be most advantageous to the Government, price and other factors considered.

"Most advantageous" is defined as the response that is evaluated as the most superior technically with a realistic price/cost; however, in the event two or more competing proposals are assessed as substantially equal, the lower or lowest price/cost considered realistic shall be determinative.

The Government reserves the right to determine which proposal demonstrates the required completeness, and which is the most advantageous to the Government.

The findings will be presented to the Source Selection Official. The Government reserves the right to make an award without discussions and/or negotiations. The primary basis for selection will be the TECHNICAL FACTORS, although BUSINESS FACTORS will be considered by the Government in the evaluation process to determine which proposal offers the greatest value to the Government.

M.2 Evaluation Factors

a. Technical Proposals Evaluation

Technical factors will be evaluated by government staff persons having knowledge and expertise in science, mathematics, education, system evaluation, and contracted program evaluations. Proposals will be evaluated to determine the relative merits of the offerors proposal, in accordance with weighted evaluation criteria established and approved prior to receipt of proposals. The Government will assign a numerical score to the results of its evaluation.

Offerors are placed on notice that any proposals which are not minimally responsive to all the technical factors cited herein will be deemed reflective of an inherent lack of technical competence and may be grounds for the rejection of the proposal.

Evaluation Criteria for Proposals

Technical proposals will be evaluated in accordance with the criteria set forth below. The criteria are listed in descending order of importance. The proposal should fully address each of the evaluation criteria.

A. Technical Quality and Completeness of the Evaluation Plan

1. Extent to which the offeror has demonstrated an overall understanding of the project and of the demands and problems likely to be encountered.
2. Extent to which the liaison and coordination with all organizations and persons involved in the SSI program is feasible, reasonable, and likely to generate responsive and timely products.
3. Extent to which the approach of the offeror in handling the project demands and problems is feasible, reasonable, and likely to generate the required results.
4. Extent to which the proper gives evidence of the necessary flexibility and adaptability to respond promptly and effectively to unanticipated demands and problems.

B. Organizational Capability ad Facilities

1. Extent to which there is adequate direct and/or indirect access to qualified professionals with the capabilities and analytical skills likely to provide the required results.
2. Adequacy and sufficiency of the support facilities in terms of the tasks to be accomplished.
3. Adequacy and sufficiency of the support services and personnel in terms of the tasks to be accomplished.

C. Experience in the Area; Prior Work in Conducting this Type Evaluation

1. Extent to which the proposer has demonstrated the competence to organize and manage large scale evaluation efforts.
2. Extent to which the proposer has demonstrated the competence to effectively utilize a wide variety of evaluation techniques.

3. Extent to which the proposer has conducted prior work in related areas.

The proposal should fully address each of the evaluation factors. However, there is no intent to limit the contents of proposals; the inclusion of any additional pertinent information is permitted. Section L.2, "Proposal Preparation Instructions", contains further narrative on each of the factors and subcriteria in terms of how offerors should structure their technical proposals.

b. Business Proposals Evaluation

THE FOLLOWING FACTORS WILL BE ANALYZED BY A BUSINESS MANAGEMENT PANEL AND WILL NOT BE NUMERICALLY SCORED.

(1) COST/PRICE FACTORS will be analyzed to (a) assess the realism of the proposed cost/price and (b) determine the probable cost/price to the Government. COST/PRICE FACTORS will be considered and analyzed by the Government but will not be weighted or scored. The COST/PRICE FACTORS may also be used as an aid to determine the offerors understanding of the TECHNICAL FACTORS requirements. Evaluation of COST/PRICE FACTORS will include the proposed cost/price for the basic contract period as well as for any priced option periods.

(2) EXPERIENCE AND PAST PERFORMANCE FACTORS are an important consideration in the Government's evaluation and selection, and require comprehensive treatment in response to the proposal. In the experience and past performance area, the Government will review and evaluate each offeror's overall corporate performance, experience, and accomplishments. Evaluation criteria are:

– Performance History

– Cost Management History

– Termination History

Offerors are further advised that in its analysis, the government will also assess the overall experience and past performance of subcontractor efforts.

(3) OTHER FACTORS comprises other factors and issues which will be analyzed based upon information provided in the offerors proposal and data obtained from the Government and other sources. While OTHER FACTORS fall into a separate category that is not directly associated to TECHNICAL FACTORS, COST/PRICE FACTORS, or EXPERIENCE AND PAST PERFORMANCE FACTORS, these factors are pertinent to the acquisition process and are an important consideration of the Source Selection Official in making a final selection. In evaluating other factors, the Government will analyze all those factors (i.e., financial condition, labor relations concerns, and the priority placed by offeror on work proposed, etc.) which may affect the offerors ability to perform the required effort.

Sample 9

Financial Advisor Services

Type of Work: Professional Services

Objective: To obtain assistance in analyzing, structuring, and placing an estimated $125 million in financing over a five-year period and to provide advice on other financing and financial management issues.

SOW Type: Functional

Comments:

- Good, clean, functional statement of work.
- Not clear what contract type is expected.
- Detailed description of the evaluation criteria, including the proposal evaluation matrix and the information to be included in the proposal.
- The term "etc." is used in the document. The use of this term creates uncertainty about and hedges the requirements.

FINANCIAL ADVISOR SERVICES

1.0 PURPOSE

The intent of this Request for Proposal and resulting contract is to obtain fixed retainer proposals from qualified financial advisors to assist the County in the analysis, structure and placement of an estimated $125 million in financing over a five year period and to provide advice on other financing and financial management issues. Consultants responding to this Request for Proposal should have extensive experience, a knowledgeable background and qualifications in the following areas:

a. Evaluation of the financial condition and policies of local government with particular emphasis on the financing of capital improvements and the administration of local government debt;

b. Development of sound financial structures and credit ratings;

c. Preparation and evaluation of Official Statements and other offering documents;

d. Marketing of local government debt, including the timing of sales; and

e. Evaluation of proposals for either competitive sales or negotiated placements.

The County is looking for a competent, professional group capable of evaluating and recommending modifications, if appropriate, to County financial policies and the County's plan for financing capital improvements and assisting County staff and bond counsel in structuring, preparing and marketing debt financings from January 1, 2008 through December 31, 2012.

The firm must provide full disclosure of all existing government relationships that currently or prospectively may give rise to conflicts of interest and disqualification as governed by the codes or rules of professional responsibility and conduct. It is the County's desire that is financial advisor be an independent public financial advisor not linked to underwriting and investor obligations; however, the absence of such independence alone will not disqualify any offeror.

2.0 COMPETITION INTENDED

It is the County's intent that this Request for Proposal (RFP) permits competition. It shall be the offeror's responsibility to advise the County in writing if any language, requirements, scope, specifications, etc., or any combinations thereof, inadvertently restricts or limits the requirements stated in this RFP to a single source. Such notification must be received by the County not later than fifteen (15) days prior to the date set for acceptance of proposals

3.0 BACKGROUND INFORMATION

The County is an issuer of general obligation and other type debt. Total outstanding debt (including appropriation – based financings) totaled approximately $91.5 million as of June, 30, 2007 and will total approximately $99.3 million as of December 31, 2007. The County plans to issue over a five year period approximately $125 million of debt for various public improvements.

Attached to this Request for Proposal are two documents that should give adequate background on the County's anticipated financings during the five year period:

- Schedule of Major Financings, Fiscal Years 2008 – 2012 (including potential financings for fiscal years 2013 – 2015).
- Projected Debt Position and Ratios (including current ratings), Fiscal Years 2007 – 2015.

The estimates of financings contained in these documents, which mirror the Country's adopted 2008 – 2012 Capital Improvements Program, are dependent, for the most part, on voter authorization and other political factors.

4.0 SCOPE OF SERVICES

All proposals must be made on the basis of and either meet or exceed the requested financial services contained herein. The consultant shall be responsible for performing or for assisting County staff and/or bond counsel in completing the following tasks:

4.1 Review and Evaluation of Financial Operations

a. Recommending and assisting in the implementation of improvements to the County's overall financial operations.

b. Assisting in the review and evaluation of certain management improvements in such areas as cash management, capital project tracking, banking and deposit services, and other relevant areas.

c. Providing such additional research and advisory assistance in connection with financial management that the County may deem appropriate.

4.2 Review and Evaluation of Financial Condition, Policies and Plans

a. Reviewing the County's overall financial condition, legal requirements and fiscal policies, with particular emphasis on the financing of capital improvements and the issuance and administration of debt. The consultant shall make recommendations, as appropriate, which would enhance the marketability and rating of the proposed debt issues.

b. Developing an affordability analysis to permit matching of existing and proposed debt service requirements with available resources for each capital plan, <u>including preparation/update of an annual debt capacity study in conjunction with each Capital Improvements Program</u> and periodic refunding analysis (immediate and advance) of outstanding debt.

c. Reviewing the County's plans for financing capital improvement in fiscal years 2008-2012 and the providing assistance in developing an efficient plan of finance to implement the Capital Improvements Program. Current plans are to issue to the estimated $125 million in new financings with the amounts and structure of the issues substantially dependent upon anticipated project start-up and cash requirements and anticipated interest costs. The consultant shall evaluate and, if appropriate, recommend modifications in the County's financing plans (including parameters for alternative debt sizes, average net interest cost, anticipated maturity schedule, annual debt service requirements, interim financings, advisability of refunding, and other financing requirements.)

d. Advising the County of pertinent market factors and expected trends in interest rates and yields for different maturity dates during the next 60 months.

e. Reviewing with County staff the advantages, disadvantages and requirements of alternative financing structures for debt issues, including devices such as taxable bonds, where appropriate, zero coupon bonds, etc. The County currently utilizes the present worth method of determining average net interest cost for evaluating proposals for debt issues. Consultant shall use its analytical capability to test the economics of several alternative financing structures deemed particularly appropriate for consideration by the County for future debt issues.

f. Making recommendations on the timing, structure, technical features and amount of the proposed debt issues, including design features and marketing of the debt with particular emphasis on ensuring full disclosure to investors of relevant financial information related to the County.

4.3 Preparation, Marketing and Settlement of Debt Issuance

a. Assisting staff in establishing a list of duties of all parties involved in a financing and develop a time schedule of the debt issues including scheduling and monitoring of the progress of all activities related to debt transactions, giving consideration to cash needs, expected market conditions and availability of financial data.

b. Evaluating the legal structure and debt covenants necessary to provide flexibility for the County and assure positive reception with rating services and investors and to improve market reception of debt offerings.

c. Working with County staff and attorneys, bond counsel and other advisors to prepare reports and documents necessary to support the issuance of debt and recommend appropriate technical financing features designed to enhance marketability, such as denomination and spread of payment terms.

d. Consulting with and assisting staff and bond counsel in the preparation of legal documentation necessary to support the debt issue.

e. Preparing and evaluating the text of Preliminary Official Statements describing the debt, Notices of Sale, and all other disclosure material provided to analysts, investors and the rating agencies in connection with the issuance and marketing of debt obligations. Work with County staff and attorneys, bond counsel and other related parties to prepare Final Official Statements or other offering documents. This includes coordination of printing and distributing document to rating agencies, underwriters and investors. All disclosures shall be in accordance with the Disclosure Guidelines for State and Local Government Securities published by the Government Finance Officers Association.

f. Assisting with the maintenance of rating agency relations, including preparation of materials for rating meetings.

g. Developing marketing materials, including materials for any information meetings that may be held for potential underwriters.

8.0 EVALUATION OF PROPOSALS: SELECTION FACTORS

The General Contract Terms and Conditions set forth certain criteria which will be used in the receipt of proposals and selection of the successful firm. In addition, the criteria set forth below will be considered.

The County Proposal Analysis Group will independently read, review and evaluate each proposal and selection will be made on the basis of the criteria listed below and as depicted on the Proposal Evaluation Matrix contained herein. The firms submitting proposals shall include the following information:

A. Proven record of expertise in financial management especially as related to issuance of local government debt, and to the review of debt structures and offering documents and their presentation to the financial community.

B. Proven knowledge of applicable Virginia laws, including the Virginia Public Finance Act, and property tax structure.

C. Financial management philosophy and potential cost controls and benefits to the County and depicted in the proposal.

D. Personnel qualifications (i.e., resumes' of key personnel who will be responsible for the work).

E. Cost of services; (i.e., price proposal)

F. References (i.e., satisfaction of former governments) along with names and address of parties for whom comparable work has been performed.

G. Overall completeness, clarity and quality of proposal.

Once each member of the Proposal Analysis Group has rated each proposal and completed a proposal evaluation matrix form, a composite rating is developed which indicates the group's collective ranking of the highest rated proposals in a descending order. At this point, the Proposal Analysis Group may conduct interviews with only the top ranked firms, usually the top three depending upon the number of proposals received. The Proposal Analysis Group will conduct all subsequent negotiations and will make a recommendation for the contract award.

FINANCIAL ADVISOR SERVICES
PROPOSAL EVALUATION MATRIX

Maximum Points: 100

FIRM: ______________________________

	MAXIMUM POINTS	SCORE
1. Proven record or expertise in financial management	15	_____
2. Proven knowledge of Virginia laws and property tax structure	15	_____
3. Financial management philosophy and potential cost controls/benefits as depicted in the proposal	15	_____
4. Personnel qualifications	15	_____
5. Cost of service	25	_____
6. References	10	_____
7. Overall completeness, clarity and quality or proposal.	5	_____
TOTAL	100	

What are the three primary reasons you have for recommending this firm?

____

____

____

What are the three primary reasons you have for rejecting this firm?

____

____

____

General Comments/Clarifications/Questions: ______________________________

____

____

Name of Evaluator ______________________________

Date ______________________________

Sample 10

Imagery Engineering and Technical Support Services

Type of Work:	Engineering and Technical Support Services
Objective:	To provide the following engineering and technical support services: assess digital imagery technologies; test, verify, validate, and document government-developed software; translate program code into alternate operating systems and programming languages; write original program code with documentation; and provide user training for operational software.
SOW Type:	Performance
Comments:	▶ This is a cost plus fixed fee contract. ▶ This contract would require good contract administration to control costs. ▶ Performance specifications are quite detailed, but functions are not. ▶ Good description of the documents applicable to this work effort, including DoD and military standards.

- There is a brief discussion on changes to cost, performance, and operations requirements, but it doesn't include information about what determines a change and how changes should be processed.
- Good description of the required reports and the type of information to include in those reports.
- Contractor clearance requirements were noted in the introductory paragraph. These should be moved to a section which specifically defines the contractor's roles and responsibilities.
- The term "etc." is used in the document. The use of this term creates uncertainty about and hedges the requirements.

Statement of Work
For
Imagery Engineering and Technical Support Services

1. Introduction. The Naval Electronic Systems Engineering Activity (NESEA) is tasked to support worldwide electronic imagery transmission and processing between U.S. naval forces afloat and ashore, and with other joint service users. An engineering services contract is required in support of the tasks specified in the following paragraphs. Certain contractor personnel must have active Top Secret clearances with sensitive compartmented information (SCI) access.

2. Applicable Documents. The following documents are applicable to this effort to the extent specified herein. The issue in effect on the date of the contract shall be enforced.

Number	Title
DoD-STD-2167	Defense System Software Development
DoD-STD-2168	Defense System Software Quality Program
MIL-M-15071	Manuals, Technical: Equipments and Systems; Content Requirements for
MIL-M-38784	Manuals, Technical; General Style and Format Requirements
SPAWARINST 4130.1A	Configuration Management of NAVEL EX Systems/Equipments
SPAWAR CRLCMP	Computer Resources Life Cycle Management Plan for FIST

3. Technical Requirements. The contractor shall provide engineering and technical services for the Navy's Fleet Imagery Support Terminal (FIST); to assess digital imagery technologies; test, verify, validate, and document government developed software; translate program code into alternate operating systems and programming languages; write original program code with documentation; and provide user training for operational software. Services shall be performed at the contractor's facility, at the Naval Electronic Systems Engineering Activity (NESEA) St. Inigoes, Maryland, and at other U.S. government facilities as required.

3.1. Technology Assessment. The contractor shall investigate promising new technologies that have the potential to improve digital electronic imagery transmission, receiving and processing systems. Specifically, the contractor shall:

3.1.1. Review test and evaluation plans, reports, and other technical documentation for technical adequacy, reasonableness, and adherence to specification requirements in accordance with MIL-M-38784 and MIL-M-15071.

3.1.2. Attend technical and engineering reviews with the government technical representative during which existing technologies and their potential applications to specified requirements will be considered.

3.1.3. Technically analyze whether the assessed technologies can fulfill government-specified technical, scheduling, and cost requirements.

3.1.4. Technically analyze whether assessed technologies can be employed to provide potential improvements in SCI security, image compression, communication processors, and video interfaces.

3.1.5. Investigate potential solutions to project related problems in technology areas assigned by the government and compare solutions with the technical requirements. Submit a final report in accordance with CDRL A001.

3.1.6. Perform independent analysis and demonstrate the effectiveness of varied application software. Provide analytic support to assess improved methods and state-of-the-art techniques. Submit a final report in accordance with CDRL A001.

3.1.7. Determine potential compatibility and interoperability of government-specified hardware and software systems with other DoD systems or subsystems. Submit a final report in accordance with CDRL A001.

3.1.8. Provide personnel with SCI access for the assessment of certain state-of-the-art technologies.

3.2. Independent Verification and Validation (IV&V) of Government-Specified Software. The contractor shall test, verify, validate, and document government-specified software for digital imagery transmission and processing. Specifically the contractor shall:

3.2.1. Prepare a software design document in accordance with DoD-STD-2167 and CDRL A002 for government-specified software.

3.2.2. Prepare a software test plan in accordance with DoD-STD2167 and CDROL A003 for government-specified software.

3.2.3. Prepare a software test description in accordance with DoD-STD-2168 and CDRL A004 for government-specified software.

3.2.4. Prepare a software test report in accordance with DoD-STD-2168 and CDRL A005 for government-specified software.

3.2.5. Government-specified software shall include, but not be limited to, the Fleet Imagery Support Terminal (FIST) software developed by NESEA, St. Inigoes, MD.

3.2.6. Required deliverables of section 3.2. shall be provided to the Software Support Activity (SSA) manager at NESEA, St. Inigoes, MD. The SPAWAR CRLCMP shall apply for FIST software and other software when specified

3.2.7. The government will provide access to program code documentation, equipment, and other specialized resources specifically required for IV&V. Government provided program source codes and documentation are considered proprietary and all rights remain with the government or licensed company supplying the software material.

3.2.8. Personnel with SCI clearances will be required for access to government SCI facilities.

3.3. Software Translation and Development. The contractor shall translate program code into alternate languages and operating systems, and develop new program source code. All software developed/written by the contractor in conjunction with this effort is considered the property of the U.S. government. Specifically, the contractor shall:

3.3.1. Translate operating system code to include, but not be limited to, Microsoft® Windows operating system.

3.3.2. Write original source code using government-specified languages to meet government-specified requirements for digital image and transmission processing in accordance with DoD-STD-2167 and DoD-STD-2168.

3.3.3. Establish test requirements and validation procedures which measure software reliability of the software and adherence to specifications in the "total system" context.

3.3.4. Provide configuration management for software in accordance with SPAWARINST 4130.1. Provide a life-cycle management plan when required for new software packages. Participate in software configuration control boards.

3.3.5. Identify computer software configuration items (CSIs), computer software components (CSCs), and computer software units (CSUs). Allocate primary functions to the CSCs and CSUs. Provide a software design document in accordance with DoD-STD-2167 and CDRL A002.

3.3.6. Investigate and prepare engineering change proposals. Determine the effect of these changes on cost, performance, and operations requirements. Identify any conflicting characteristics and make recommendations on their implementation.

3.3.7. Evaluate software trouble reports and recommend modifications to alleviate the problems. Develop software changes to correct software errors.

3.3.8. Develop government-approved system enhancements for joint service interface, color imagery, communication processing, compression techniques. Implement government-approved upgrades to include, but not be limited to, state-of-the-art printers, cameras, and local area networks (LANs).

3.3.9. Provide user training for government-specified software to include text, audio/visual aids, computer software packages, and classroom lectures at contractor or government facilities.

3.3.10. Contractor personnel with SCI access will be required for portions of the translation and development effort.

4. Program Reports. The following reports shall be submitted to the COTR in addition to specific reports for a given task.

4.1. Progress Report. Progress reports shall be delivered no later than 10 calendar days after the end of each month in accordance with CDRL A006. The progress report shall include the following:

a. Cover sheet containing the contractor name, title and date of the report, and a statement that the report was prepared for NESEA, St. Inigoes, MD under this contract.

b. Summary of the progress for each task issued.

c. Major milestone summary.

d. Action items.

e. Identification of new problem areas.

f. Schedule projections for upcoming month.

4.2. Cost Report. Cost reports shall be delivered no later than 10 calendar days after the end of the month in accordance with CDRL A007. The cost report shall include the following:

a. Cover sheet containing the contractor name, title and date of the report, and a statement that the report was prepared for NESEA, St. Inigoes, MD under this contract.

b. Number of hours by contract line item number (CLIN), labor categories used, and number of hours charged to each TDL.

c. Dollar amounts expended, including outstanding commitments for each TDL, monthly and cumulative.

d. Travel and material charges, monthly and cumulative.

e. Monthly totals and costs to complete each TDL.

f. Explanation of any discrepancies between the cost report and the contractor's voucher for the respective month.

5. Material. No investment item material may be procured under this contract.

6. Government Furnished Property (GFP) and Facilities. The Government will provide access to government equipment and to government facilities, when required, in order for the contractor to perform specific tasks under the statement of work. The equipment and

facilities are located at NESEA, St. Inigoes, MD and may include equipment located at other U.S. Government SCIF's world-wide.

6.1. In the event that the contractor is restricted form entry to the workplace due to non-controllable emergencies such as weather, power outages, etc., the offeror shall not charge the non-work time as direct labor to the contract.

6.2. Personal telephone service for contractors will not be provided by the Government. Secure telephone data lines may be provided for the transmission/reception of digital imagery testing and program verification.

M31 Evaluation Criteria and the Basis for Award

(1) The contract resulting from this solicitation will be awarded to that responsible offeror whose offer, conforming to the solicitation, is determined most advantageous to the Government, cost and other factors considered. The offerors Proposal shall be in the form prescribed, and shall contain a response to each of the areas identified in Section L entitled "Instruction, Conditions, and Notices to Offerors" which bear on the below-identified evaluation factors for award (See clause entitled "Submission of Proposals" in Section L for additional instructions). The Navy's evaluation of proposals will consider the offerors technical proposal more important than the offerors cost/price proposal.

(2) The technical evaluation factors are listed below, with Technical Approach, Personnel Resources, Management Plan Approach and corporate experience being of equal importance and Facilities being considerably less important.

1. Technical Approach

2. Personnel Resources

Each labor category is equal to a subfactor. The subfactors Computer Systems Analyst III and Senior Computer Scientist are significantly more important than the other subfactors. All other subfactors are of equal importance.

Labor Category	Resumes Required
a. Program Manager	(1 resume)
b. Computer Systems Analyst III	(1 resume)
c. Senior Computer Scientist	(1 resume)
d. Computer Programmer III	(1 resume)
e. Computer Programmer II	(1 resume)
f. Administrative Assistant	(1 resume)

Shared positions will be evaluated as a composite of the individual resumes offered for that position. If the offeror fails to provide the percentage of effort of each individual, it will be assumed that the personnel are being offered on a 100% basis as alternate proposals and the highest rated individual will be used in the Technical Evaluation and the other individual will be excluded from the evaluation and performance in any resultant contract. Resumes are to be neatly typed and the total number of pages for the required resumes should not exceed 30 pages exclusive of cover sheet, introduction and summary. A maximum of five (5) pages each is allowed for each resume.

3. Management Plan Approach
4. Corporate Resources
5. Facilities

(3) Costs will be evaluated on the basis of cost realism. Cost realism pertains to the offeror's ability to project costs which are realistic and reasonable and indicate whether the offeror understands the nature and scope of work to be performed.

Labor will be evaluated on the basis of 100% straight time. Overtime rates will not be used in the evaluation.

Offerors are cautioned that cost proposals that include unrealistic rates, as determined by the Contracting Officer in cost realism analysis, may result in a reduced technical score.

The government has estimated travel and material costs as specified below:

	Base Year	OPT I	OPT II	OPT III	OPT IV	Total
Travel	$22,000	$23,000	$24,000	$25,000	$26,000	$120,000
Material	$18,000	$19,000	$20,000	$21,000	$21,000	$99,000

The Government estimated costs (plus applicable burden) shall be used for the purpose of evaluating the cost proposal for each cost. Therefore, offerors must use these estimates in preparing their price proposal. Application of material handling charges and/or G&A rates, as appropriate, will be allowed only if the contractor maintains separate accounts for such costs.

The offeror's cost proposal shall be based on a basic period of performance for 01 October 2007 through 30 September 2008 with four option periods as follows:

	Period of Performance
Option I	01 Oct 08 – 30 Sep 09
Option II	01 Oct 09 – 30 Sep 10
Option III	01 Oct 10 – 30 Sep 11
Option IV	01 Oct 11 – 30 Sep 12

The realism of personnel compensation rates will be part of the proposal evaluation. Unrealistic rates, as determined by the Contracting Officer, will be considered in the risk assessment and may result in a reduced rating.

(4) Uncompensated overtime and overtime rates will not be considered in the cost evaluation. Labor will be evaluated on the basis of 100% straight time.

M32 Unreasonably Low Hourly Rates on Contracts

The realism of personnel compensation rates will be part of the proposal evaluation. Unrealistic rates, as determined by the Contracting Officer, will be considered in the risk assessment and may result in a reduced score.

Sample 11

E-mail System and Database Management Services

Type of Work: Technical Support Services

Objective: The objective consists of two major work categories: (1) designing, developing, testing, and documenting a computer-based mail list management system; and (2) operating the system to generate system outputs and performing database and system maintenance.

SOW Type: Functional

Comments:

- Detailed background description
- Good succinct description of functional specifications and performance criteria
- Contract option section is somewhat vague, particularly on the ad hoc statistical reports

RFP CPS 92-001

Section C- Description/Specifications/Work Statement

C.1 BACKGROUND

The National Science Foundation (NSF) is an independent federal government agency established in 1950 to promote and advance scientific progress in the United States. NSF does this primarily by sponsoring scientific and engineering research and education through the awarding of grants and other means of assistance. NSF does not conduct any research; instead it invites proposals for support from the research community. Proposals are accepted in a field of science, including, but not necessarily limited to astronomy, atmospheric science, biological and behavioral sciences, chemistry, computer sciences, earth sciences, engineering, information science, materials research, mathematical sciences, oceanography, physics, and social science. Proposals come to NSF mostly from educational institutions, but also from non-profit organizations, small and large businesses, government entities, and individuals.

Opportunities for support are announced to the public by means of issuances such as Program Announcements, Program Solicitations, Requests for Proposals, and other proposal generating mechanisms. NSF also publishes and disseminates a wealth of information on its programs, policies, activities, award information, and other information of interest to its constituency.

NSF currently maintains an address database of over 110,500 records compiled from sources within NSF and from leased commercial lists. There are 266 mail list ID codes used for generating mail lists; each list ID code represents a defined area of interest and is used to target distribution of material to the proper audience. A significant portion of the records are tagged with more than one mail list ID code.

Monthly, data entry tasks average 800 record inputs, 500 deletions, and 350 modifications; label jobs average 50 requests and 130,000 labels generated. Approximately 75% of the jobs are for less than 2500 labels; the largest single job typically does not exceed 30,000 labels, while the smallest might have as few as 50 labels. These jobs typically consist either of 4-up Cheshire or 1-up pressure sensitive labels.

C.2 SCOPE OF THE REQUIREMENT

This requirement consists of two major work categories: (1) designing, developing, testing, and documenting a computer based mail list management system, and (2) operating the system to generate system outputs and performing database and system maintenance.

C.3 CONCEPT OF SYSTEM AND OPERATIONS

The Contractor shall design and develop the mail list management system that meets the minimum functional specifications set forth in the Statement of Work. The system shall reside and operate on contractor-supplied computer at the Contractor's premises. NSF will have 24 hour remote access to the system via modem with full system privileges except during scheduled system backup and maintenance. After final acceptance of the system by NSF, the Contractor shall perform all system maintenance, data entry and output generation tasks as described in the Statement of Work.

The system shall reside on a file server with the Microsoft® Windows XP Service Pack 2 (SP2) operating system or higher. The Contractor shall design and construct the system to permit and facilitate promote access and operation by NSF personnel by means of a 9600 baud modem. The system must have the capability of allowing the user to direct printed output to printers either at the Contractor's site or at the NSF site.

C.4 STATEMENT OF WORK

C.4.1 SYSTEM DESIGN AND DEVELOPMENT

The Contractor shall design, develop, test, and furnish software and documentation as described in this Section.

(a) Functional Specifications. The system must be capable of accomplishing these minimum functions:

(i) Add, modify, and delete individual address records.

(ii) Select and search by key fields

(iii) Create select files by selection of codes

(iv) Output labels in the following formats:

- 1-up gum labels
- 3-up gum labels

- 4-up gum labels
- 4-up Cheshire

(v) Produce personalized letters on 8 ½" by 11" paper by merging address data with NSF-supplied text in Microsoft® Word.

(vi) Print labels with list ID code to identify associated list.

(vii) Produce reports on demand by the manipulation of any combination of data contained in the database without the need for reprogramming efforts.

(viii) Provide full featured remote access and user selectable options for directing printed output to on-site and off-site printers.

(b) Performance Criteria. The Contractor must develop and implement operational controls that will assure a minimum acceptable database accuracy rate of 95% on a continuing basis. All data input and output requests must be completed not later than 5 business days after receipt. Printed label output must conform to CASS standards (see Section (H.1).

(c) System Documentation. The contractor shall provide full and complete documentation for the system in sufficient detail as to provide a basis for independent review and understanding of the system. This documentation must include, but is not limited to, system and program specifications including programming logic descriptions and flow charts, database specifications including data diagrams, all source code listings and flow charts, operations and users manuals, system testing and performance validation plans covering all system functions, and a working copy of the executable program if developed in a compiled format.

All system documentation should conform in general accordance with FIPS PUB 38 guidance for Level 3 documentation. Copies of FIPS PUB 38 may be ordered from the National Institute of Standards and Technology. A copy will also be made available for reading in the RFP issuing office. Reproduction facilities will NOT be furnished.

C.4.2 CONTRACT OPTION – SYSTEM MAINTENANCE

(a) The Contractor shall perform all system maintenance functions. The Contractor shall perform data backup operations frequently enough to avoid catastrophic loss in the event of a calamity. Copies of each backup shall be provided to NSF not later than the next business day. The Contractor shall perform routine maintenance procedures, including but not limited to duplication checks and corrections, necessary to ensure the accuracy and integrity of the database and system.

(b) The Contractor shall perform periodic Zip+4 merge operations on an as needed basis. The Contractor shall also perform merge operations for incorporating data from commercial lists when required.

(c) At NSF's request, the Contractor shall produce ad hoc statistical reports based on the data in the database.

C.4.3 CONTRACT OPTION – SYSTEM OPERATIONS

(a) The Contractor shall perform all tasks for data entry and generating output except as specified herein. NSF will provide the Contractor with its current mail list database, including the 50 commercial lists it leases annually.

(b) NSF will access the system via 9600 baud modem in order to perform system operations as follows.

 (1) NSF will perform data entry tasks when the accumulated weekly total of data entry items total 50 items or less.

 (2) NSF will generate label jobs requiring 2,500 labels or less.

(c) NSF will initiate label job and personalized letter job requests by providing the Contractor with the list ID code, type of sort, supplies as specified under Section H.3, and delivery to the designated delivery point not later than the second business day after receipt of request.

C.4.4 SYSTEM SOFTWARE SUPPORT

The Contractor shall be required to maintain the system software developed and/or modified under the contract in operational status throughout the term of the contract. The Contractor shall correct any and all latent defects which might arise during the term of the contract, amend/modify all affected items of documentation, and deliver the corrected documentation at no cost to NSF.

Section M – Evaluation Factors

M.1 OVERALL BASIS FOR AWARD

The Government will award a contract resulting from this solicitation to the responsible offeror whose offer, conforming to the Solicitation, will be most advantageous to the Government, price and other factors considered.

"Most advantageous" is defined as the response that is evaluated as the most superior technically with a realistic price/cost; however, in the event two or more competing proposals are assessed as substantially equal, the lower or lowest price/cost considered realistic will be determined.

The Government reserves the right to determine which proposal demonstrates the required completeness, and which is the most advantageous to the Government.

The proposals will be evaluated against TECHNICAL FACTORS and BUSINESS FACTORS (cost/price, experience and past performance, and other factors). Offerors are placed on notice that any proposals which are unrealistic in terms of technical commitment or unreasonably low or high in cost or price will be deemed reflective of an inherent lack of technical competence or indicative of failure to comprehend the complexity and risk of the contract requirements and may be grounds for the rejection of the proposal.

The findings will be presented to the Source Selection Official. The Government reserves the right to make an award without discussion and/or negotiations. The primary basis for selection will be the TECHNICAL FACTORS, although BUSINESS FACTORS will be considered by the Government in the evaluation process to determine which proposal offers the greatest value to the Government.

M.2 EVALUATION FACTORS

M.2.1 EVALUATION OF TECHNICAL PROPOSALS

(a) Technical factors will be evaluated to determine the relative merits of the offerors proposal, in accordance with weighted evaluation criteria established and approved prior to receipt of proposals. The Government will assign a numerical score to the results of its evaluation.

(b) Offerors are placed on notice that any proposals which are not minimally responsive to all the technical factors cited herein will be deemed reflective of an inherent lack of technical competence and may be grounds for the rejection of the proposal.

(c) The technical factors will be evaluated in accordance with the criteria set forth below which are listed in descending order of importance. Factor 1 is significantly more important than either Factor 2 or 3. Factor 2 is more important than Factor 3.

Factors

1 Technical Approach and Understanding of the Requirement

2 Organizational Experience and Qualifications

3 Experience and Qualifications of Personnel

Technical Approach and Understanding of the Requirement

Understanding of mail list management as it relates to the requirement

Quality of overall project plan

Availability and suitability of facilities, hardware and software

Quality of management and quality controls

Organizational Experience and Qualifications

Demonstrated experience in mail list management projects of similar nature and scope

Demonstrated experience in developing mail list management software

Experience and Qualifications of Personnel

Quality of experience and qualifications of personnel in developing mail list management systems

Quality of experience and qualifications of personnel in managing mail list management systems

Quality of staffing and commitment

(d) The proposal should fully address each of the evaluation factors. However, there is no intent to limit the contents of proposals; the inclusion of any additional pertinent information is permitted. Section L.4 contains further narrative on each of the factors and sub-criteria in terms of how offerors should structure their technical proposals.

(1) Technical Approach and Understanding of the Requirement – The Government will evaluate the offeror's demonstrated understanding of and approach to the requirement work, and their demonstrated technical knowledge and management approach to accomplish the Statement of Work.

(2) Organizational Experience and Qualifications. Corporate experience, capability and facilities will be evaluated by the Government based on demonstrated evidence of:

— Company experience on similar projects

— The offerors experience and demonstrated competence in fields related to this procurement which would especially qualify the offeror to perform the work set forth in the proposed Statement of Work

— The scope, magnitude and complexity of its prior and ongoing experience, similar in nature to the proposed requirement

— Availability and commitment of any special facilities relative to this requirement, if applicable

— References from governments for whom the offeror has performed services similar in scope and nature to the requirements described in this solicitation.

(3) Qualifications and Experience of Personnel. Qualification of personnel and technical resources will be rated according to their prior experience and demonstrated competence, and how that relates to the work to be performed. Specifically, the Government will evaluate:

— Education, past experience, and training

- Work presently underway relevant to proposed effort
- Listing of recent project/tasks/jobs on which individual has worked
- Appropriate references
- Statement of commitment in terms of time and availability

(b) Business Proposals Evaluation.

THE FOLLOWING FACTORS WILL BE ANALYZED BY A BUSINESS MANAGEMENT PANEL AND WILL NOT BE NUMERICALLY SCORED.

(1)(i) COST/PRICE FACTORS will be analyzed to assess the realism of the proposed cost/price, and to determine the probable cost/price to the Government. COST/PRICE FACTORS will be considered and analyzed by the Government but will not be weighted or scored. The COST/PRICE FACTORS may also be used as an aid to determine the offerors understanding of the TECHNICAL FACTORS requirements. Evaluation of COST/PRICE FACTORS will include the proposed cost/price for the basic contract period as well as for any priced option periods.

(ii) The offered prices will be evaluated in this manner.

(A) The offered firm-fixed unit prices, except the firm-fixed unit price for personalized letters, will be multiplied by the evaluation volume factor listed below. The prices for personalized letters and ad hoc reports will not be evaluated.

(B) The extended firm-fixed unit prices for each option year will be added to the offered firm-fixed price for the work under Section C.4.1 and the annual firm-fixed price for the system maintenance. The sum of these amounts will be the total evaluated price.

(C) For evaluation purposes, the volume to be used for each category of firm-fixed unit price is as follows:

Evaluation Volume Factor	Category
12	System Maintenance
50	Record Inputs
30	Record Deletions
20	Record Modifications
300	Labels (Pressure Sensitive)
900	Labels (Cheshire)

(2) EXPERIENCE AND PAST PERFORMANCE FACTORS are an important consideration in the Government's evaluation and selection, and require comprehensive treatment in response to the proposal.

In the experience and past performance area, the Government will review and evaluate each offeror's overall corporate performance, experience, and accomplishments. Evaluation criteria are:

— Performance History

— Termination History

Offerors are further advised that in its analysis, the Government will also assess the overall experience and past performance of subcontractor efforts.

(3) OTHER FACTORS comprises other factors and issues which will be analyzed based upon information provided in the offerors proposal and data obtained from the Government and other sources. While OTHER FACTORS fall into a separate category that is not directly associated to TECHNICAL FACTORS, COST/PRICE FACTORS, or EXPERIENCE AND PAST PERFORMANCE FACTORS, these factors are pertinent to the acquisition process and are an important consideration of the Source Selection Official in making a final selection. In evaluating other factors, the Government will analyze all those factors (i.e., financial condition, labor relations concerns, and the priority placed by offeror on work proposed, etc.) which may affect the offerors ability to perform the required effort.

M.3 EVALUATION OF OPTIONS – FIP RESOURCES (FIRMR 201-39.5202-4) (OCT 1990)

(a) The Government will evaluate offers for award purposes by adding the total price for the option to the total price for the basic requirement. These prices will be adjusted by the applicable discount factors show in "Not Applicable" of the application. Evaluation of options will not obligate the Government to exercise the options. Offers containing any charges for failure to exercise any option will be rejected.

(b) Selection of an offer will be made on the basis of the most advantageous alternative to the Government provided that the contract prices reasonably represent the value of bona fide requirements for each year. The determination with respect to contract prices will be made after consideration of such factors as commercial or catalog prices for short-term leases, offeror system startup expenses, multi-year price protection, assured system life availability of equipment, software, and vendor support. If a determination is made that an offer does not meet these criteria, that offer cannot be accepted for award.

[End of Provision]

Sample 12

Development of Rotary Seals for Mining Environment

Type of Work:	Research and Development
Objective:	To develop and demonstrate a long-life rotary water seal suitable to the mining environment and compatible with continuous mining machines to control airborne respirable dust and methane ignition potential.
SOW Type:	Performance/Level-of-Effort
Comments:	▸ This is a cost reimbursement or cost plus fixed fee contract. ▸ Good background discussion. ▸ Emphasis on operation and performance gives contractor total flexibility. ▸ Operating (performance) requirements are well defined. ▸ Detailed description of the phases and the information that should be derived in each phase.

STATEMENT OF WORK
ROTARY SEAL DEVELOPMENT FOR CONTINUOUS MINING MACHINES

Article I and II contain the Government's RFP requirement and deliverable items. Your offer shall respond directly to these articles in this exhibit.

ARTICLE I – STATEMENT OF WORK

Background. The Federal Coal Mine Health and Safety Act of 1969 with revisions in 1977 was enacted to insure more healthful and safer working conditions for miners. One aspect of the regulation, the requirement that airborne respirable coal dust not exceed 2 mg per cubic meter, is intended to reduce the incidence of pneumoconiosis or "black lung" in coal miners. The enactment of this legislation with its subsequent monitoring and enforcement by MESA (now MSHA), required that the Bureau of Mines, and others in the mining community associated with this problem, obtain a better understanding of the respirable dust generation and control than was available at that time. Accordingly the Bureau established a research program containing three major tasks defined as: (1) primary control of dust generation during cutting, (2) secondary control of airborne dust, and (3) dust measurement instrumentation.

This contract addresses a problem associated with both Task 1 and Task 2 when water spray techniques are desirable as a control method on continuous miners. Although spray techniques are widely used, the placement is usually not optimum since the nozzles must be mounted on booms or manifolds behind the cutter/coal interface area of the rotary drum head of the machine. This arrangement is used because the large diameter main drive shaft and drum end seals are in closely confined areas. Lack of suitable materials for these confined areas are so far precluding suitable sealing techniques to put the water at nozzles in the rotating drum. To resolve this problem, designers of underground continuous mining equipment must have available long life, large diameter water seals capable of handling 250 pounds per square inch (psi) nominal pressure with a maximum surface speed of 400 feet per minute. A contract, HO232055, was procured in May 1973 to test and evaluate rotary water seals for continuous mining machines. The results did not provide a useful seal design that would resolve the problem. It is hoped that the several years since then have advanced the state-of-the-art sufficiently to provide the practical solution still needed. Large diameter, high pressure seals are common on marine equipment, nuclear submarines for instance, operating at great depths. NASA and the aircraft industry have done a great amount of development on turbo-pump rotating shaft seals for rocket engines in the last several years. The intent of this contract effort is to adapt some of this high technology seal development to the underground environment for use on continuous mining machines.

One of the major design problems, analysis of thermal and hydrostatic effects on seal stability, has been programmed by NASA for computer handling. These programs are available in two publications; "Simplified Computer Program for Analysis of Phase Change in Liquid Face Seals," Birchak, M. and W.F. Hughes, NASA CR-134668, 1977 and "N on axisymmetric Incompressible Hydrostatic Pressure Effects in Radial Face Seals," Etsion, I., NASA TN D-8343, November 1976. Many other recent references are available on advanced seal designs.

Objective. Develop and demonstrate a long-life rotary water seal suitable to the mining environment and compatible with continuous mining machines to control airborne respirable dust and methane ignition potential.

Scope of Work. The work to be performed by the Contractor shall be divided into five (5) phases totaling eighteen (18) months:

Phase I-Seal System Selection (2 months)

Phase II-Seal Assembly Selection and Preliminary Design (4 months)

Phase III-Seal Component Selection and Detail Design (8 months)

Phase IV-Fabrication and Field Simulation Testing (2 months)

Phase V -Final Report (2 months)

The Contractor shall submit monthly technical letter reports organized as follows:

Section 1-Accomplishments. Brief description of work during reporting period and its relationship to project objective.

Section 2-Future plans. Discuss work planned for next period and its relationship to the present period.

Section 3-Problems encountered. Problems plus solution attempted or planned shall be related to section 2, future plans.

Section 4-Funds expended and program schedule.

The Contractor shall have full responsibility for making any and all arrangements for visits to mine equipment manufacturers but the Bureau Technical Project Officer (TPO) shall be kept informed by the Contractor of all Contractor communications with any mine equipment manufacturers.

A. Phase I-Seal System Selection

1. The Contractor shall determine the arrangement of the seal assemblies useful on underground coal mining equipment which will provide for all extremes of operation and minimize the severity of these extremes on the seal(s).

2. The Contractor must assure that the seal system(s) chosen will be compatible with continuous mining machine shaft(s) and/or drum(s) as they exist today or as they may be modified to be seal compatible. This does not require the Contractor to specify a seal design for each machine configuration but does require that the seal system chosen be adaptable by dimensional changes or other suitable variations to a variety of continuous mining equipment.

3. Operating requirements shall include:

   a. Use of water with/without surfactant

   b. Nominal seal pressure of 250 psi

   c. Maximum seal velocity of 400 feet per minute

   d. Minimum 8-inch ID for shaft seals and minimum 20-inch ID for drum seals.

   e. Maximum leakage of 0.5 gpm

   f. Minimum 6-month normal operating life.

4. It should be specifically understood by the Contractor that ring and/or lip seals, while they may be found useful, may not be the final design. It is anticipated that a high performance mechanical seal may be the only type suitable to the severe environment of a mine but any seal types should be considered that appear promising.

5. The Contractor shall plan and present an oral review of Phase I at Twin Cities Research Center in the last week of this phase, or as close thereto as mutually agreed to by the Contractor's Project Manager and the Technical Project Officer. At this meeting the Project Manager shall discuss the results of Phase I and provide detailed plans for Phase II. The Contracting Officer's representative shall approve or disapprove technical merit of Phase I work at the meeting or within five (5) working days which approval shall be confirmed in writing by the Contracting Officer.

B. Phase II-Seal Assembly Selection

1. The Contractor shall consider in this phase all design problems and performance limitations producing in this preliminary design an acceptable compromise between operating conditions and performance of the seal.
2. The Contractor shall develop an analytic heat transfer model of the seal configuration for finite element analysis.
3. Sealing force, face deformation, and frictional heating in the dynamic mode shall be evaluated for leakage rates and time to failure.
4. Preliminary design of the candidate seal(s) will be performed.
5. The Contractor shall plan and present an oral review of Phase II at Twin Cities Research Center in the last week of this phase, or as close thereto as mutually agreed to by the Contractor's Project Manager and the Technical Project Officer. At this meeting the Project Manager shall discuss the results of Phase II and provide detailed plans for Phase III. The Contracting Officer's representative shall approve or disapprove technical merit of Phase II work at the meeting or within five (5) working days which approval shall be confirmed in writing by the Contracting Officer.

C. Phase III-Seal Component Selection

1. The Contractor shall establish a list of design seal material properties which will satisfy the operating conditions determined to be extant by Phase II.

2. The Contractor shall evaluate these candidate materials selected on a suitable wear test machine to determine wear rate and surface damage under sliding contact conditions expected in the actual seal design.

3. Normal run in wear for these materials shall be determined.

4. Final design of the candidate seal(s) shall be performed using the materials selected as most appropriate.

5. The field simulation test bed shall be designed so the equipment necessary may be obtained in a timely manner (sec. D.2).

6. The Contractor shall plan and present an oral review of Phase III at Twin Cities Research Center in the last week of this phase, or as close thereto as mutually agreed to by the Contractor's Project Manager and the Technical Project Officer. At this meeting the Project Manager shall discuss the results of Phase III and provide detailed plans for Phase IV. The Contracting Officer's representative shall approve or disapprove technical merit of Phase III at this meeting or within five (5) working days which approval shall be confirmed in writing by the Contracting Officer.

D. Phase IV-Fabrication and Field Simulation Testing

1. The candidate seal(s) shall be fabricated for life testing.

2. The life test machine shall be fabricated for the simulated field test. It is expected that some type of lathe would be appropriate for the test bed. A no-cost lease of suitable surplus Department of Defense equipment for the test- bed shall be arranged by the Bureau of Mines during Phase III if the Contractor does not already have suitable equipment.

3. Preliminary life testing shall be performed simulating the normal on-off operating cycle during a minimum 40 shifts (320 hours).

4. An acceptable seal design will be that seal which, when disassembled after the 4Q.shift test, shows no wear in any parts beyond that needed for normal run-in as defined in C.3. 5. The Contractor shall incorporate the oral review of Phase IV with the oral presentation of Phase V.

E. Phase V-Final Report

1. All data acquired during the course of the contract including related correspondence, conceptual drawings, functional diagrams, schematics, final design drawings, and any other materials, books, journals, and/or reference materials pertinent to this contract shall be delivered to the Technical Project Officer at Twin Cities Research Center with the copies of the approved final report.

2. A draft of the final report of all work performed and results achieved shall be prepared and delivered to the TPO for Bureau approval within 30 calendar days after start of Phase V. An oral presentation will be made by the Contractor at Twin Cities Research Center on the content of this report when the draft is delivered. The report shall be prefaced by an Executive Summary not to exceed four (4) pages in length. All basic data from the work performed by the Contractor shall be incorporated as appendices to the report.

Sample 13

Development of Tree-Transplanting Attachment

Type of Work: Research and Development

Objective: To develop and produce an attachment for a front-end loader of 7–12 yards or greater capacity that will transplant clumps of trees for surface mine reclamation. This clump transplanting system will be field tested and evaluated in an operating surface mine with an ongoing reclamation program.

SOW Type: Performance/Level-of-Effort

Comments:

- This is a cost reimbursement contract.
- The development of a new transplanting system trends toward research and development, which generally requires a level-of-effort contract.
- Defines functional specifications.
- Good background discussion and justification for the project.
- The scope of work is somewhat weak: the descriptions of what the contractor is to provide are disorganized. Breaking the tasks down into specific phases would be beneficial (e.g., from due diligence to completion of testing).

STATEMENT OF WORK
LOAD HAUL DUMP TREE CLUMP
TRANSPLANTER ATTACHMENT

ARTICLE I-STATEMENT OF WORK

Sec. 1.1 Colorado State University hereinafter referred to as "Contractor" shall perform the project entitled "Development of a Load Haul Dump Tree Clump Transplanter Attachment" in accordance with this scope of work and its proposal dated September 22, 1978, as amended by a technical supplement dated December 11, 1978 both of which are incorporated herein by reference, provided that in case of any conflict between the proposal, as amended, and the other provisions of this contract, the other provisions of the contract shall govern.

Sec. 1.2 Background and Justification. The design and utilization of equipment to reclaim lands disturbed through surface mining has long lagged behind the development of equipment capable of excavating these disturbances. It has long been an accepted fact by the mining industry, that reclamation can be most acceptably accomplished using mining equipment operated by mining employees. Certain pieces of equipment may be more suitable but are not used because some reclamation functions are for a short period of the year and the acquisition costs often do not justify their existence. To be economically acceptable, reclamation equipment must be capable of being utilized in the mining processes once weather conditions terminate the yearly reclamation activities.

One piece of production equipment that has been widely employed in land reclamation is a front-end loader. Due to its versatility, it has been used for transplanting trees and shrubs on the copper mine tailings of Arizona, the phosphates spoils of Idaho and the leveled coal spoils in North Dakota, Montana, Wyoming, and Colorado. Its availability at almost every mining operation and its successful use in transplanting has added to its usefulness as a reclamation tool.

Even though it has been widely used for transplanting, some limitations exist which have affected its adaptability. The conventional loader bucket does not have the proper shape for efficient loading and removal of trees. Productivity could be improved if a transport device was included in the system.

Conventional buckets are designed to load from piles or embankments. Therefore, they are deep and have relatively high banks and the horizontal distance that the bottom extends beyond thc tops is relatively small. If this type of bucket is filled with trees, the configuration disturbs the trees and after transplanting, they have random orientations. A modified bucket would thus improve the system both in terms of productivity and aesthetics.

Sec. 1.3 Objective. To develop and fabricate an attachment for a front-end loader of 7-12 yd. or greater capacity that will transplant clumps of trees for surface mine reclamation. This clump transplanting system will be field tested and evaluated in an operating surface mine with an ongoing reclamation program.

Sec. 1.4 Scope of Work

1.4.1 Transplanted Attachment Development and Testing

The Contractor shall:

1.4.1.1 Select a mining company currently involved in transplanting tree clumps with a 7-12 yd., or larger front- end loader willing to cooperate in the Load Haul Dump Tree Clump Transplanter Attachment System development and submit to the Government for approval.

1.4.1.2 Determine optimal shape of the bucket in terms of width and rear configuration so the tree clumps can be loaded with sufficient soil for efficient and aesthetic transplanting and prepare specifications and preliminary design drawings.

1.4.1.3 Determine suitable operating procedures and select appropriate connection points for attaching the bucket to the loader so the bucket can be moved and/or rotated for efficient operation and prepare specifications and preliminary design drawings.

1.4.1.4 Determine the mechanical functions required to load and unload tree clumps at the transplanting sites. These functions shall be incorporated into the hauler preliminary specifications and design drawings.

1.4.1.5 Make economic and operational comparisons with conventional tree transplanting systems. The Contractor shall make a market survey of the systems potential application in mining reclamation.

1.4.1.6 Make an oral presentation at the cooperator's mine site on the proposed tree transplanting system not later than three (3) months after the effective date of this contract. The Contractor shall receive approval from the Contracting Officer of the date selected for the oral presentation. STATEMENT OF WORK LOAD HAUL DUMP TREE CLUMP TRANSPLANTER ATTACHMENT

1.4.1.7 Update the final design to incorporate recommended changes from input of the oral presentation after consulting the cooperating mining company and receiving approval of the Contracting Officer.

1.4.1.8 Complete fabrication of tree clump transplanting bucket within nine (9) months of the effective date of this contract. The Contractor shall have written approval by the Contracting Officer for all sub-contracts prior to signing.

1.4.1.9 Make structural and operational tests prior to the start of field tests upon completion of fabrication of bucket.

1.4.1.10 Make lease or purchase arrangements for vehicle to transport tree clumps from the pre-mined area to the reclamation area. The vehicle will be used to complete the system by providing the transportation between areas. Results of the field test will indicate necessary specifications for modifications of this vehicle to round out the tree clump transplant system.

1.4.1.11 Develop a field test program plan and submit in letter form to the Government within six (6) months after the effective date of the contract for approval. This will include an economic evaluation in terms of trees moved and their survival rate.

1.4.1.12 Conduct a field test of the tree clump transplant system according to the approved test plan during a full season at the cooperator's mine site. This test shall be approximately seven (7) months in duration.

1.4.1.13 Make a functional evaluation of the load haul dump tree clump transplanting system and establish procedures for efficient operation of the system in user's manual format.

1.4.1.14 Maintain an accurate daily log throughout the demonstration in order to monitor effectiveness of the tree clump transplanting system as well as to identify problem areas and unscheduled downtime.

1.4.1.15 Be responsible for insuring that the field demonstration conforms to all appropriate State and Federal regulations and requirements.

1.4.1.16 Upon completion of all work under this phase submit to the Government a draft final report within twenty (20) months after the effective date of this contract covering in detail all work accomplished under the contract. The draft final report shall include tables, graphs, photos, technical film footage, and diagrams in sufficient detail to comprehensively explain the results achieved under the phase contract.

1.4.1.17 Within twenty (20) days of submittal of the draft final report make an oral presentation of the results accomplished at the Spokane Mining Research Center in Spokane, Washington. Within twenty (20) days after the oral presentation, the Bureau will notify the Contractor of its approval or recommended changes for incorporation into the final report.

Sample 14

Configuration Management Audit

Type of Work: Audit Services

Objective: To assess the adequacy and compliance of the configuration management plans for the Chief Administrative Officer (CAO). These reviews will focus on compliance, adequacy of the configuration management plans, and guidance.

SOW Type: Functional

Comments:

- Background description of the configuration management plans is very limited.
- Good sample set of questions to ask as part of the audit.
- Description of the work space is very succinct and should be expanded upon to include the location, size, and type of work space.
- Detailed description of the deliverables required.

- The period of performance states that work will commence within 5 calendar days after issuance. It would be better to state that work should commence within 5 business days. This would help to avoid any conflicts of the start date falling on a non-working day.

SECTION C -- DESCRIPTIONS AND SPECIFICATIONS

C.1 STATEMENT OF WORK

ASSESSMENT OF THE CHIEF ADMINISTRATIVE OFFICER CONFIGURATION MANAGEMENT PLANS OF THE U.S. HOUSE OF REPRESENTATIVES

I. INTRODUCTION AND INSTRUCTIONS ON SUBMITTING PROPSOSAL

The Office of Inspector General (OIG), U.S. House of Representatives (House) desires to contract with an independent contractor to assess the adequacy and compliance of the configuration management plans for the Chief Administrative Officer (CAO). These reviews will focus on compliance, adequacy of the configuration management plans, and guidance.

The OIG intends to award a time and materials task order to accomplish this objective. The contractor awarded this task order will coordinate with the OIG Information Systems (IS) audit staff while preparing and conducting briefings with House managers and users, reviewing and analyzing data and documents to meet the objective of this task order, and reporting on the results of this review as necessary. The OIG will provide one auditor from the IS Audit staff for this project.

Proposals shall include:

(1) A resume for each engagement staff member

(2) A technical description of how the task will be accomplished, in sufficient detail for the OIG to evaluate its technical merits (merely restating the statement of work will not suffice)

(3) A brief description of the firm's experience in performing similar reviews with a point of contact and phone number for each reference cited

(4) An estimate of the hours by level of personnel, including subcontractor personnel, plus out-of-pocket expenses, such as travel, to accomplish the tasks identified in Section III, Statement of Work.

II. BACKGROUND

CAO Configuration Management Plans

Information technology divisions within the Chief Administrative Office (CAO) are required to develop and maintain configuration management plans for each system designated as a managed item. CAO configuration management plans are developed using CAO developed configuration management guidance and the guidance from the Institute of Electrical and Electronics Engineers, Inc. (IEEE), such as Standard 828-2005 IEEE Standard for Software Configuration Management Plans.

III. STATEMENT OF WORK

A. Objectives

The contractor will assist the OIG in assessing:

- The compliance of OlG selected configuration management plans against CAO and IEEE configuration management guidance
- The overall adequacy of the configuration management plans and CAD configuration management guidance.

For this review, the OIG has selected configuration management plans for the following systems:

- Campus Data Network, the network hardware (routers, switches, wiring, etc.) for the House backbone network
- Enterprise Tape Backup, the tape backup environment for House applications
- HouseNet, the House intranet web environment
- Procurement Desktop, the House vendor payment environment
- ACF, the House's Alternate Computing Facility
- Intrusion Detection Systems, the House Internet facing intrusion detection system environment.

Specific work requirements for the objectives will include, but not be limited to, the following:

Audit Planning and Preparations

1. Gain an understanding of CAD and IEEE configuration management guidance.
2. Become familiar with the configuration management plans for the selected systems.

Audit Work Requirements

1. Evaluate the CAO process for identifying systems included in the list of managed items.
   - Is CAO management aware of the requirement to include systems as managed items?
   - Are there any CAO systems not included in the list that should be?
2. Assess the compliance of OIG selected configuration management plans against CAD and IEEE configuration management guidance. The contractor will propose a team who has prior experience in evaluating configuration management plans for the six systems previously mentioned.

   Examples of the types of questions that should be answered in this audit for each reviewed configuration management plan include, but are not limited to, the following:
   - Is CAO management aware of their responsibilities to provide configuration management plans for their managed items?
   - Does each configuration management plan selected, adequately address the configuration management elements required by CAD configuration management policy and procedure?
   - Perform a configuration management plan audit of selected systems to evaluate the adequacy and currency of each plan.
   - Is there an approved process for proposing changes to baseline information and for evaluating and approving these changes prior to implementation?

- Is CAO management following change procedures with respect to changes that may require notification outside of an individual manager's particular division?
- Is there a documented process for evaluating the management, technical, and assurance impacts of a change to baseline information, and are these impacts considered before a change is approved?
- Are there records and audit trails on the status of proposed changes that are pending or approved for implementation?
- Determine if CAO management is auditing the configuration management plans, if the audit results are tracked, and deficiencies corrected.

3. Assess the overall adequacy of CAO configuration management policies and procedures. Are these items of sufficient detail to provide for an adequate configuration management process for the CAO? Are there improvements that can be made to the policies and procedures to improve the configuration management process at the CAO?

For all areas reviewed:

1. Identify weaknesses and develop recommendations by providing written workpapers with background information, technical results, conclusions, and recommendations. Documentation of reportable findings will include the following support elements; a description of the finding (condition), the criteria that applies to the finding, the root cause of the finding, the effect the finding has on the House, and recommendations to remedy the finding condition.
2. Prepare briefings for the DIG staff and/or auditee(s) as needed.
3. Document the purpose, source, scope, and results of all work performed in professional working papers, using a workpaper format that will be agreed on by the bidder and the OIG. The contractor will be required to use the PWC TeamMate electronic workpaper product to complete workpapers. All workpapers and reports will be completed on site.

4. Provide an audit report using the OIG report format. OIG personnel will be available to answer contractor questions during the report preparation process

For this Task Order, the contractor will be augmenting the efforts of the OIG and must coordinate and work closely with the OIG. To accomplish the above work requirements, the OIG will work with CAO management to obtain pertinent documentation (e.g. business policies and procedures, processes, and system and application-related documentation) to more effectively utilize contractor's time and avoid collecting duplicative documentation. All data gathering and questions of CAO personnel will be coordinated and requested through the OIG staff. Further, unless specified, the designated OIG staff will arrange and attend key meetings with the CAO management. Lastly, OIG staff will review contractor workpapers to ensure that they are in accordance with government auditing standards. The contractor may need to revise workpapers using OIG guidance.

B. Scope

This is a review of CAO configuration management guidance and its implementation in the configuration management plans of six CAO systems.

C. Methodology

The review should use a risk-oriented approach to fully address the review objectives. The approach should ensure that the CAO has mitigated significant configuration management deficiencies. Merely restating the statement of work does not satisfy the requirements of this task order.

The review approach must adhere to established Federal auditing standards and guidelines, which includes the following:

- The General Accounting Office's Government Auditing Standards (Latest Revision);
- The General Accounting Office's Federal Information System Controls Audit Manual (Latest Edition)

D. Criteria

To facilitate, management acceptance of weaknesses, conclusions, and recommendations, the contractor will be required to identify applicable Federal and private industry criteria and best practices. Criteria adopted by CAO managers include:

- CAO Configuration Management policies and procedures
- IEEE Standard 828-2005 IEEE Standard for Software Configuration Management Plans
- U.S. House of Representatives Information Security Policies (HISPols)

Copies of these criteria will be provided to the winning bidder. The contractor may identify additional criteria that supports best practices or strengthens internal controls for the area reviewed.

E. Current and Prior Engagements

The OIG issued a report on the overall CAO configuration management process in the 2003 timeframe. The report and associated workpapers will be available to the contractor.

F. Work Space

The OIG will provide the necessary workspace for performing this review.

G. Travel

This review will not require travel outside the Washington, DC area.

<u>Contractor Personnel Requirements</u>

A. Qualifications of Personnel

The contractor must assign qualified, experienced personnel for key positions, such as partner, manager, senior review, and industry specialist, to perform work under this task order. The review team, including junior members, must possess the relevant auditing experience, education, and professional accomplishments to successfully perform task order requirements identified in Part III, Statement of Work. Resumes for each personnel member assigned to this task order must be included in the contractor's proposal. Resumes should also reflect personnel members' exposure to industry best practices and technology advancements through continuing education requirements.

For such a sensitive and highly visible project, the OIG prefers one primary person to be assigned throughout this project for continuity purposes. Other staff with specific experience will be acceptable, but data continuity must be maintained.

B. Requirements of Personnel

All contractor personnel assigned to perform work on this task order will be required to read and sign a Certification of Independence prior to the start of the engagement. This certification identifies what is required of the contractor personnel with respect to conflict of interest concerns and the penalties associated with noncompliance with those requirements.

All contractor personnel will be granted access to sensitive information and, as such, will be required to safeguard the confidentiality of that information. Each staff member assigned to this project will be required to complete Affirmation of Non-Disclosure, before gaining access to House information.

If contractor personnel are issued House vendor identification badges, these badges must be turned back to the OIG on the contractor's last workday at the House. Failure to return all House issued vendor identification badges as required will result in the OIG withholding final payment on the contract until all badges are received.

All contractor personnel are required to work on site between the OIG office hours of 8:30 AM and 5:30 PM and permitted one hour for one (1) lunch. Exceptions will be considered on a case by case basis and must be cleared with the OIG in advance. No offsite work by any contractor personnel for this project will be permitted or billable without prior OIG approval.

C. Approval to Change or Remove Contractor Personnel

The contractor must obtain written approval from the GIG to change or remove personnel identified in the contractor's proposal to this task order. Additions of personnel not identified in the contractor's proposal to this task order will be required to provide current resumes detailing relevant experience, education, and professional accomplishments to successfully perform task order requirements identified in Part III, Statement of Work. In addition, the OIG has the option of changing or removing contractor personnel at any time during the engagement.

IV. DELIVERABLES

The successful bidder will deliver the products identified below to the OIG at the following address:

Office of Inspector General
U.S. House of Representatives
386 Ford Building
Washington, D.C. 20515-9990

In addition, all written products shall be submitted to the OIG in electronic (i.e., Microsoft Office 2003 or lower version) format. Microsoft PowerPoint may be used for briefing charts and graphs. Although other Microsoft compatible products, such as spreadsheets and diagrams, may be used in the draft reports or other documents, the products do not always convert easily without the need for additional editing or reformatting requirements. Therefore, other products to be used on this review must be approved by the designated OIG representative.

The required products for each review are as follows:

A. Preliminary Plan and Resource Schedule

The contractor shall prepare a preliminary review plan and resource schedule to accomplish the objectives of the task order, and deliver them to the Inspector General within 7 calendar days after issuance of the task order. In addition, the contractor shall identify all computer assisted audit tools to include commercial and propriety software selected for use in completing this task order. The preliminary plan should also include proposals for coordinating work and requesting information through the OIG staff.

B. Meetings and Interviews

All meeting and interview write-ups must be completed and submitted to the OIG for review within 3 business days from the date of the meeting or interview.

C. Briefs and Presentations

Prepare pertinent briefings and presentations for House personnel and OIG staff as required. Briefing charts should be prepared using Microsoft PowerPoint and submitted to OIG for review at least two working days in advance of presentation.

D. Review Plan

The contractor will develop a written plan (or a set of written review plans) within 21 calendar days after issuance of the task order for OIG review and approval. The review plan must set forth in reasonable detail the procedures necessary to accomplish the objectives of the review. Review procedures will be mapped to established review standards and guidelines where appropriate in order to explain and support the procedures applied. Adjustments to review scope and tasks will be updated in the review plan when identified by the OIG.

E. Status Reports

The contractor shall deliver to the OIG a weekly status report summarizing the contractor's work progress. For each phase of the project, and the project as a whole, each report shall include the estimated dates for each phase of the review including deliverables. In addition, the report must include a schedule of the activities to be performed during the subsequent period, as well as identify potential or actual problems and/or issues that surface during the conduct of the project. Status reports should not indicate the completion of specific deliverables, tasks, and review phases until the contractor has reviewed workpapers supporting those deliverables, tasks, and phases for OIG review.

F. Audit Reports

At the close of the engagement, the contractor will write a report detailing the results of the audit. The report will be indexed to the supporting workpapers and fully document the technical engagement results, conclusions, recommendations, and relevant background information. The following guidance shall be used to document and report all findings requiring management actions.

Finding. Describe conditions disclosed by the detailed engagement work performed. Synopsize and detail support for the findings in the supporting workpapers, schedules, and/or exhibits. Do not include information that does not properly relate to one of the five elements in the finding.

i. Condition. The first (topic) sentence(s) of a finding paragraph is the condition. This element should always state the condition disclosed (i.e. what is wrong or right) by the engagement procedures performed.

ii. Criteria. These are the established internal directives or guidelines, good business practices, and laws used to evaluate the audited functions.

iii. Support. This element provides specific details of the condition. Where appropriate, include specific examples or prepare a schedule (suitable for inclusion in the engagement report) that highlights the magnitude of the deficiency. Also, if a positive finding is included in the engagement report, this is the appropriate place to summarize conclusions in the supporting workpapers. See the General Accounting Office's (GAO) Government Auditing Standards for guidance related to evidence.

iv. Cause. This is the root cause (i.e. weak or absent internal controls or reasons for noncompliance with existing internal controls) of the deficient condition and is the finding element that a recommendation addresses.

v. Effect. This element describes the significance of the finding and why it is important for management to address the issue.

vi. Recommendation(s). This paragraph must address correction of the root cause of the deficient condition as well as correct any specific deficiencies identified in the "support" element of the finding paragraph.

G. Workpapers and Confidentiality

Workpapers are the most critical contractor deliverable since they provide the evidentiary foundation for all audit and review work, conclusions, and reports. The House OIG will provide network access to TeamMate for workpaper preparation for the duration of the task. The contractor will prepare workpapers using the templates within TeamMate or as provided by the OIG. The workpapers will be subject to the OIG's review on day-to-day basis. Therefore, the contractor staff must have experience using TeamMate or similar electronic workpaper software for working paper preparation. All workpapers must conform to workpaper standards established in the GAO's Government Auditing Standards (Latest Revision) and Chapter VIII, Section 7, Field Work Standards, of the OIG's Policies and Procedures Manual. In addition, all workpapers must document the purpose, source, scope, and results of all work performed.

After reviewing the workpapers, the OIG may direct the contractor to modify the workpapers or to perform corrective or additional review procedures to ensure that the review is conducted in accordance with GAO's Government Auditing Standards and OIG guidelines. The contractor shall consider such corrective or additional procedures as part of the scope of this task order, not a contract modification or additional work.

All work performed under this task order will be kept confidential and may not be released to outside parties without the express, written permission of the OIG. All workpapers prepared under this task order are the property of the OIG. All documents, data, information, review results, and results produced by contractor proprietary tools are the property of the OIG. The contractor must deliver all documents, data, and information not already contained in the workpapers to the OIG within 3 calendar days after delivery of the contractor's report. This includes any documents obtained from the House or developed by the contractor such as notes, workpapers, electronic files or photocopies. Upon completion of this contract, the contractor must destroy any extra copies or drafts of documents, data, information, workpapers or electronic files obtained or developed under this task or surrender them to the OIG.

V. PERIOD OF PERFORMANCE

This task order is effective on the date of issuance. It is anticipated that preliminary work under this task order will commence within 5 calendar days after issuance. All work must be completed by December 31, 2007.

VI. ADDITIONAL INFORMATION

We estimate between 40 and 50 staff days, not including 30 OIG staff days, will be required to complete tasks identified in the Statement of Work for this review.

Sample 15

Acquisition of Computer Hardware and Software Applications

Type of Work: Systems Acquisition

Objective: To provide services for acquiring desktop computers, applications software, including upgrades and updates to all delivered software, printers, backup storage devices, removable storage devices, user-installable components, and Contractor-provided support services to operate primarily in a networked office environment. Provide desktop computer hardware and software applications.

SOW Type: Functional

Comments:

- Detailed general description.
- Good use of narrative to achieve complex functional results.
- Requirements section is very detailed and specific.
- Detailed description of the award considerations.

- Description of how the cost/price is to be evaluated is very thorough.
- The term "etc." is used multiple times throughout the document. The use of this term creates uncertainty about and hedges the requirements.

Part I – The Schedule, Section C – Description/Specs./Work Statement

C-1 General Description

The Government has a requirement for desktop computers, applications software, including upgrades and updates to all delivered software, printers, backup storage devices, removable storage devices, user-installable components, and Contractor-provided support services to operate primarily in a networked office environment. The Government's current and future networking environment is based upon the Unified Local Area Network Architecture (ULANA: IEEE 802.3 and TCP/IP) and is migrating to the Government Open Systems Interconnection Profile (GOSIP) (See Section/Paragraph J-1, Attachment 1). The offered computers will enter a computing environment consisting of several hundred thousand Zenith, Unisys and AT&T desktop computers running both commercial and Government-developed applications software. The existing computer base uses commercial applications software (see Section/Paragraph J-5, Attachment 5) including such MS-DOS based packages as Windows, Word for Windows, Excel, PowerPoint, MS-Database, WordStar, Enable, Supercalc, PC-Tools, and dBase. Government applications software includes programs developed using standard languages such as Ada, COBOL, Visual Basic and C++ and databases such as MS-Database and dBase III/III+/IV. Most of the current Government-developed desktop computer applications use the MS-DOS environment. However, current and future Government-developed applications will migrate to an open systems environment conforming to the Federal Information Processing Standards (FIPS) for components affecting software portability (e.g., POSIX, Ada, SOL RDMBS, and X-Windows) and interoperability (e.g., GOSIP and TCP/IP) with migration to the National Institute of Standards and Technology's Application Portability Profile (NIST APP). Where standards are evolving, migration to the standards will be accomplished by procuring and environment which functionally conforms to comparable portions of the X/Open Common Applications Environment (CAE) defined by the X/Open Portability Guide, Issue 3 (XPG3).

C-2 Locations

The Contractor-provided systems will be used worldwide in DoD and other Government locations. Approximately 20 percent of these systems will be for locations outside of 50 United States. The primary geographic regions that must be supported are: (1) all 50 of the United States, (2) England, (3) Central Europe (e.g., Belgium, Germany, Spain, Italy, Turkey, and Saudi Arabia), and (4) the Far East (e.g., Japan, Korea, Guam, and the Philippines). See Section/Paragraph J-4, Attachment 4 for a current list of locations within these regions. These locations have differing power requirements (e.g., 110-120 VAC/50-60 Hz and 220-240 VAC 50 Hz), power connections, communications regulations, and other regulatory requirements which shall be satisfied by the Contractor on all offered hardware items except CLIN 0007, Non-Impact Printer, which shall operate with 110-120 VAC, 60Hz. For some locations (i.e., United Kingdom, Germany and Italy) the Contractor shall provide commercial power adapters/cables for connection of all Contractor-provided equipment to foreign power sources.

C-3 Specific Requirements

The systems provided should include all necessary hardware, software and documentation to enter (using a keyboard and pointing device), manipulate, view, store, and print the information created using the Contractor-provided applications. Users should have an expandable system that includes hardware interfaces (e.g., Centronics compliant parallel and RS-232c compliant serial ports) for connection to other Government-owned printers, modems, and computers. All users shall have the capability to continue to use a large base of previously developed or acquired software and data existing on 3 ½" (720KB and 1.44MB format) floppy diskettes and CD-ROM. All users shall have the capability to execute, without change, standard Government MS-DOS based software applications that are used worldwide in binary form except those applications that bypass MS-DOS/BIOS interrupts to address hardware directly or where these applications contain embedded control codes specific to a Government-owned peripheral. Additionally, users should have the capability to share data among the different types of system and applications acquired from this contract and should have the same capability with other DoD Standard Small Computers (see Section/Paragraph J-1 and J-5, Attachments 1 and 5). All users shall have a system that includes Air Force local area network (LAN) environment compatible hardware and software interfaces, drivers and utilities (TEEE 802.3, TCP/IP, RFC 1001/2

NetBIOS, TELNET, SMTP and FTP). These systems should provide the networking platforms to interoperate with the following network operating systems: DCA 10NET (from the Air Force LAN Software Contract, see Section/Paragraph J-1), Banyan Vines, Novell Netware and Microsoft LAN Manager. The Contractor is not responsible for providing LAN operating systems software. All Contractor-provided software and documentation shall be furnished in accordance with CDRL A004 – Computer Software Product End Item.

a. General User Environment. These desktop computer systems will be primarily in a networked office environment by basic, intermediate, and advanced users. Basic users range from computer illiterate to moderately computer literate and should have an easy-to-use system to perform daily tasks. Intermediate users, while not necessarily having more computer knowledge, will have a greater working knowledge of applications software and will develop more complex documents and perform more advanced functions. Advanced users have a detailed understanding of desktop computers and applications. All users should have a system that is easily unpacked, quickly set up and ready for immediate operation with all software preloaded.

(1) System Requirements. All users should have a user-friendly system with accurate, detailed, easy-to-references and easy-to-understand documentation on hardware and software operation. They also should have the capability to execute Government-developed applications requiring up to 512KB of available memory while the system is simultaneously attached to a LAN server and monitoring the LAN for incoming E-mail [using E-mail software form other contracts (e.g., The Network Courier/MS Mail from Air Force LAN Software Contract)]. Users shall have the option to order these systems with or without the Contractor-provided Office Automation (O/A) software and corresponding documentation (see C-3a (2) (b) below).

(a) Basic System (CLIN 0001). This system will be used primarily to prepare correspondence using a word processor. Other frequently performed functions will include E-mail, a simple data base (e.g., address/telephone number, file management or inventory), a due date tracking system, and a stand-alone or network calendaring package. Spreadsheets, graphics, and larger data bases will be used occasionally. Processor and memory provided should be sufficient to provide responsive, concurrent operation of the Contractor-provided user interface and at least one of the Contractor-provided O/A applications while the system is also monitoring a network for E-mail. Disk storage should be sufficient to store a minimum of 40gigabytes of Government data and applications software after loading the Contractor-provided software (e.g., operating system, user interface software, suite of office automation software, system management software, etc.).

(b) Intermediate System (CLIN 0002). In addition to the functions and capabilities for the basic user, intermediate users will build documents incorporating graphics and text from other application packages, build presentations with a graphics package, build moderately large spreadsheets that may involve complex mathematical operations and create/maintain larger and more complex data bases. The intermediate user will use Government-developed software applications that are typically data base intensive. Processor and memory should be sufficient to provide responsive, concurrent operation of the Contractor-provided user interface and at least two of the Contractor-provided O/A applications while simultaneously monitoring a network for E-mail. Disk storage should be adequate to store a minimum of 60 gigabytes of Government data and applications software after loading the Contractor-provided software (e.g., operating system, user interface software, suite of office automation software, system management software, etc.).

(c) Advanced System (CLIN 0003). In addition to the functions and capabilities for the intermediate users, advanced users will use the advanced system for a much broader ranger of functions. Examples include creating and manipulating large data bases, running simulations, recalculating large spreadsheets, creating and manipulating advanced graphics, using statistical packages, and running other applications program. Most of these functions will involve complex mathematical operations and some will involve graphical simulations. Processor and memory should be sufficient to provide responsible, concurrent operation of the Contractor-provided user interface and at least four of the O/A applications while simultaneously monitoring a network for e-mail. Disk storage should be adequate to store a minimum of 200 gigabytes of Government data and applications software after loading the Contractor-provided software (e.g., operating system, user interface software, suite of office automation software, system management software, etc.).

(2) Software Requirements. The general users shall have a consistent suite of software to support typical office automation and system management functions across all systems. The software should combine ease of use with advanced features, provide several levels of assistance, and allow different operational modes for users with differing levels of experience.

The software should allow easy sharing of data between each Contractor-provided application and other DoD Standard Small Computer applications. Other desktop computer users may utilize Government-owned commercial applications software and peripheral equipment; therefore, the software should support a wide range of commercially-available import and export capabilities and peripheral equipment. Additionally, the Government has a large investment in Government-developed MS-DOS applications and in MS-DOS applications software from previous DoD Standard Requirements Contracts (see Section/Paragraph J-5, Attachment 5). The Contractor shall provide General User Environment systems capable of executing Government developed software without modification except those applications that bypass MS-DOS/ BIOS interrupts to address hardware directly or where these applications contain embedded control codes specific to a Government-owned peripheral.

(a) System Management Software. Users shall have capability to manage and maintain their systems and perform diagnostics (board level checks) with a level of maintenance assistance appropriate for each system component. Users also shall have the capability to perform system configuration and tuning tasks, file and disk management [e.g., file recovery (undelete), data security, disk restoral (unformat), disk optimization, etc.] and memory management for optimizing application software execution.

(b) Office Automation (O/A) Software (CLINs 0005AA and 0005AB). Users shall have software that performs a variety of tasks including word processing, spreadsheet development, database development, graphics development, communications, and personal information management (PIM). The word processor will be used to generate many types of documents from single page memos and letters to multi-page complex reports. These documents will contain graphics images, columnar data, spreadsheet figures, and database records. The spreadsheet will be used for such activities as trend analysis, financial analysis and timekeeping. These spreadsheets should contain text, numbers, functions and formulas, and should generate a variety of graphs. The database will be used for such actions as record keeping, inventory, and report generation. Graphics will be used to produce briefing materials with text, free from drawings, and simple business charts as well as slide shows with text and advanced graphics. The offered communications application will be used to connect and transfer data to remote bulletin boards and hosts. The PIM will be used for such activities as time management (e.g., calendar, appointment list, to-do list, due date tracking, etc.), data management (e.g., address list, simple database) and project management (e.g., simple Gantt charts and task management).

b. Open Systems Common Applications Environment (CAE) (CLIN 0004). The Government requires the capability to use, with little or no change, a growing investment of developed software that is targeted for the Open Systems CAE operating in a networked environment. The CAE software environment (POSTIX, Ada, SQL RDBMS, X-Windows, GKS, PHIGS, CGM, NFS, GOSIP and TCP/IP) should provide a high level of source code portability and interoperability to a wide rage of computers in order to reduce life-cycles costs and risks for the Government. These desktop computer systems will be used by two classes of users: (a) the software developer, and (b) the end user of the developed software. Software development users have a detailed understanding of desktop computers and applications. End users, while not necessarily having more computer knowledge than basic users, have a greater working knowledge of applications software.

(1) System Requirements. Processor and memory capability provided with these systems should be sufficient to provide responsible, concurrent operations for the CAE while running several offered CAE programs simultaneously. Disk storage should be adequate to store a minimum of 200 gigabytes of Government data and applications software after loading the Contractor-provided software (e.g., operating system(s), system utilities, O/A software, communication protocol software, graphical user interface, software development capabilities, suite of office automation software, etc.), in runtime and development versions.

(a) CAE Software Development System (CLIN 0004AA). In addition to the functions and capabilities required for the Advanced System, the software developer will develop a full range of applications using the Contractor-provided CAE development software. These applications will typically be database intensive and operate in a networked environment.

(b) CAE Runtime System (CLIN 0004AB). The end user of this system will use the applications software developed using CLIN 0004AA.

(2) Software Requirements. Users shall have an integrated software environment which conforms to standards for POSTIX, Ada, SQL RDBMS, X-Windows, GKS, PHIGS, CGM, GOSIP and TCP/IP with migration to the National Institute of Standards and Technology's Application Portability Profile (NIST APP) for open system environments (see Section/Paragraph J-1, Attachment 1). In cases where theses standards are still evolving, migration to the standards should be accomplished by delivering and environment which functionally conforms to the X/Open CAE defined by the X/Open Portability Guide issue 3 (XPG3) Volumes 1 through 7. This functionality includes: (1) commands and utilities; (2) system interfaces and headers; (3) supplementary definitions; (4) programming languages; (5) data management; (6) window management; and (7) network services. In case of conflicts among FIPS PUBs, NIST APP, and XPG3 functionality (e.g., GOSIP and XPG3 volume 7), the order of precedence is the FIPS PUB followed by NIST APP and then XPG3 functionality. Additionally, the POSIX Operating System software shall be in compliance with DoD 5200.28-STD, DoD Trusted Computer System Evaluation Criteria (TCSEC), for a class C2 rating.

(a) CAE Development Software (provided with CLIN 0004AA). The CAE system software development user shall have the necessary operating system(s), utilities, libraries, communication protocol software (TCP/IP, NFS, and GOSIP), complier(s) and support environment, SQL RDMBS, and X-Windows software to develop POSIX, Ada, SQL RDMBS and X-Windows-based applications for the POSIX environment. Additionally, the Ada compilers and related support tools should provide a means (e.g., with compatible DOS-based Ada complier) to create executable code for the operating system environment(s) provided on CLINs 0001 through 0003. Development efforts will include requirements analysis, design, development, system testing and maintenance of the applications. Through each phase of the software development life cycle, the user will develop documentation using the Contractor-provided O/A applications (CLIN 0005AB). Users shall have the capabilities to execute MS-DOS based software applications while simultaneously executing the POSIX CAE. This does not apply to those applications that bypass MS-DOS/BIOS interrupts to the address hardware directly or where these applications contain embedded control codes specific to a Government-owned peripheral.

(b) CAE Runtime Software (provided with CLIN 0004AB). The CAE end user shall have the runtime environment and communication protocols to execute software applications developed on the CAE development system in addition to simultaneously executing MS-DOS based software applications. This does not apply to those applications that bypass MS-DOS/BIOS interrupts to address hardware directly or where these applications contain embedded control codes specific to a Government-owned peripheral.

(c) Print Requirements (CLINs 0006 and 0007). Users shall have two basic capabilities to convert system generated products, including graphics, to hard copy output. Some users should have the capability to produce near letter quality documents, wide products using up to 14 ½" wide continuous form pin-feed-tab paper, envelopes, multi-part forms, and labels. Other users should have the capability to produce laser quality documents, forms, overhead type transparencies, envelopes, and labels on a shared network printer.

(d) Backup Storage Requirements (CLIN 0008). Some users require a means of performing backups of the storage devices provided with CLINs 0001 through 0004. The Contractor shall provide hardware, software and media to perform these backups. The back-up process should require a minimum of user involvement. Users of the Advanced and the CAE systems shall have a higher capacity backup device and media than users of the Basic and Intermediate systems.

(e) Removable Storage Requirements (CLIN 0009). Some users require the capability to process classified information. As a result, they shall have a removable storage device (e.g., removable hard disks or removable media) with a minimum capacity of 20 GB on which to store classified information. This removable storage device will be removed from the system daily for storage and will primarily be used with the intermediate systems.

(f) User-Installable Components (CLINs 0010-0015). All users shall have the capability to upgrade system configurations and to perform self-maintenance using Contractor-provided user-installable components. Because of deployment and contingency situations, some users any elect to perform self-maintenance during the warranty period. Such user self-maintenance on any equipment by government personnel during the warranty period shall not affect the warranty of the original end item as addressed by Paragraph C-3h.(1). Users shall have the capability to easily obtain user-installable components and receive them in a timely manner to preclude extended hardware downtimes. All user-installable components have a “shelf life” (e.g., batteries) and should have a minimum of one (1) year of usable shelf life when delivered to the user.

(g) Applicable Standards. The Contractor-provided systems and software shall meet the standards listed in Section/Paragraph J-1, Attachment 1. For each standard, the Contractor shall certify compliance and provide supporting documentation. To maintain full conformance with the evolving FIPS and NIST APP [e.g., GOSIP version 2 (FIPS 146-1)], the Government shall have updated releases of the conforming software and documentation within twelve months after official publication of any new or revised RIPS of NIST APP standard. CLINs 0001 through 0004 and 0006 through 0009 shall be certified by a nationally recognized testing lab (e.g., UL, etc.) as defined in 29 Code of Federal Regulations (CFR) Part 1910 and conform to MIL-STD-454, requirement 1. Additionally, CLINs 0001 through 0004 and 0006 through 0009 shall have FCC Class B certification.

(h) Life Cycle Support Requirements.

(1) Warranty. Users should have a highly reliable and maintainable system and set of peripherals to operate in an office environment. These systems should be user-expandable and maintainable without voiding the Contractor-provided warranty or extended warranty, Users shall be provided with timely warranty support on all offered hardware (CLINs 0001-0004 and CLINs 0006-0015. Additionally, users shall also have the option to purchase extended warranty support for system and peripherals (CLINs 0016-0023) located at Government sites throughout the world. For Contractor planning purposes only, Section/Paragraph J-4, Attachment 4 contains a partial list of the current Government sites where systems and peripherals may be delivered and from which warranty service may be required. As a minimum, for each major geographic region [e.g., (1) all 50 of the United States, (2) England, (3) Central Europe (e.g., Belgium, Germany, Spain, Italy, Turkey, and Saudi Arabia), and (4) the Far East (e.g., Japan, Korea, Guam, and the Philippines)] the Contractor shall provide a warranty program (e.g., on-call, mailback, or carry-in, etc.) to locations within the region. This program shall provide for fixing the systems and peripherals in a timely manner and include the means of transport the systems from the warranty repair locations (e.g., on-call service, mailback, common carrier, carry-in, etc.).

(2) Customer Technical Assistance. Users shall receive periodic assistance and information on such items a warrant service, configuration, installation, and operation of the Contractor-provided software and hardware products. Users should have Contractor-provided assistance in the use of the Contractor's diagnostic software to isolate, identify and repair failures. Thus, all users, including overseas users not having access to toll free numbers, shall have the

capability to ask questions and receive answers to support in a timely and effective manner.

(3) Order Processing Support. The user shall have the capability to quickly determine the complete history and current status (e.g., when the order was received, were there any errors in the order, delays in shipment of the order) of a particular delivery order or group of orders at any time (for use by customers worldwide with differing time zone requirements). The Contractor should provide to the Government central ordering facility(s) the capability to reprioritize delivery orders.

(4) Software Updates/Upgrades. Users shall have the current commercially-available versions of the Contractor-provided software and documentation throughout the base year and first two option years of the contract. The Contractor shall provide each user the latest versions of the software and documentation at no additional cost.

(5) Maintenance Training (CLIN 0025). In order to develop a Government computer maintenance course, the Contractor shall provide a one-time computer maintenance course and course materials, with limited data rights (to reproduce and use within the Government the material for lesson plans and handouts for system maintenance training). The maintenance course shall be presented at the Contractor's facility, utilizing Contractor equipment and materials for up to ten (10) students. Upon completion of Contractor-provided maintenance training, the students will be capable of performing system diagnostics, preventative maintenance, board-level replacement and replenish of consumables. (See CRDL A005 – Training Materials.)

(i) Program Management Office Support. To effectively manage and provide accurate statistical data to higher headquarters, the Contractor shall provide the following monthly reports as well as a Program Management Office Liaison representative.

(1) Production and Delivery Report. A Production and Delivery Report shall be provided in accordance with CDRL A001-Technical Report-Study/Services.

(2) Equipment Failure Information Report. The Equipment Failure Information Report for all CLINs/SLINs on the contract shall be provided. CDRL A002 – Equipment Failure Information Report.

(3) Contractor-Liaison. The Contractor shall provide a Program Office Liaison to facilitate Government-Contractor interface and mutual understanding. The primary function of the Liaison will be to act as the technical and managerial interface between the Contractor and the Government Program Management Office which is located at Gunter AFB, Alabama. If requested by the Contractor in writing, 100 square feet of normal office space, a phone line for local calls, and DDN connectivity (through IEEE 802.3 baseband transceiver connection) will be available on Gunter AFB, AL for use by the Contractor liaison. A status report shall be provided in accordance with CDRL A003 – Contractor's Progress, Status and Management Report.

(j) Labeling. All hardware CLINs or SLINs except cables and internal boards should contain a permanently affixed serial number and manufacturer's name (example, metal plate with screws) which shall be externally visible. The labels shall match the B-Table Part Number.

(k) Production and Delivery Capability. The Contractor should have the capability to produce and deliver the quantities of systems to meet fluctuating Government requirements. For informational purposes, a historical ordering trend for DoD requirements is provided at Section/Paragraph J-6.

M-1 201-39.52902-4 Evaluation of Options – FIP Resources (Oct 90 FIRMR)

a. The Government will evaluate offers for award purposes by adding the total price for the basic requirements. These prices will be adjusted by the applicable discount factors shown in

Section L exhibit formulas of the solicitation. Evaluation of options will obligate the Government to exercise the options. Offers contain any charges for failure to exercise any option will be rejected.

b. Selection of an offeror will be made on the basis of the most advantageous alternative to the Government provide that the contract prices reasonably represent the value of bona fide requirements for each fiscal year. This determination with respect to contract price will be made after consideration of such factors and commercial or catalog prices for short-term leases, offeror system start-up expenses, multiyear price protection, assured system life availability or equipment, software, and vendor support. If a determination is made that an offer does not meet these criteria, that offer cannot be accepted for award.

M-2 Award Without Discussion

The Government intends to evaluate proposals and award contract(s) without discussions with Offerors (other than minor clarifications conducted by the Contracting Officer). However, the Government reserves the right to conduct discussions if later determined necessary by the Contracting Officer.

M-3 Basis of Contract Award

a. The following conditions shall be met in order to be eligible for award:

(1) The Offeror must be determined responsible according to the standards in FAR Subpart 9.1.

(2) The Offeror's proposal must comply with the requirements of law, regulation and conditions set forth in the solicitation.

b. The Offeror's management, technical and cost proposals may demonstrate a clear understanding of the nature and scope of work required. Failure to provide a realistic, reasonable and complete management, technical and cost proposals may reflect lack of understanding of the work requirements of the contract and may result in a determination of the Offeror is technically unacceptable.

c. Upon satisfying the above conditions, the Source Selection Authority (SSA) will determine the proposal(s) which provide the best overall value to satisfy the DoD needs. This selection will be based on Section M, Evaluation Factors for Award.

M-4 Evaluation Criteria.

The acquisition is being conducted under ARF 70-15, Formal Source Selection for Major Acquisitions. Evaluation standards will be written against Section M Evaluation Criteria as follows as well as the requirements in Section C. The results of the evaluation will be based no an integrated assessment of each Offeror's proposal. The Offeror's proposals will be evaluated and rated by the Government. This assessment will address the following areas, listed in order of importance:

(1) Management area and Technical area.

(2) Cost/Price

Although Cost/Price is listed last, it will be a significant criterion for award as part of an integrated assessment with the management and technical areas. The Government reserves the right to award a contract(s) at other than the lowest proposed price after consideration of all factors.

M-5 Assessment Criteria.

The following assessment criteria will be applied against specific criteria described in paragraph M-7 below. For Management evaluation purposes, subparagraphs a. and b. below will apply and are equally ranked. For Technical evaluation purposes, only subparagraph b. below will apply. The assessment criteria include:

a. Understanding of the requirement refers to the extent an Offeror's proposal provides evidence the Offeror understands the management and technical complexities of the effort and has a sound approach to meeting the functional requirements set forth in Section C – Description/Specifications/Work Statement, adheres to sound engineering design and management practices, and reflects an understanding of the program's environment.

b. Compliance with requirements refers to the extent to which the Offeror's proposal provides evidence that functional requirements will be met. The Government will review each proposal against the assessment criteria using both internal and Offeror-provided data.

M-6 General Considerations for Award

a. Pre-Award Survey. Government personnel will review information provided by the offerors in their proposals. Offerors who have not been surveyed within twelve months of the proposal receipt date may be subjected to a pre-award survey. A copy of the pre-award survey report will be requested from the surveying office for offerors who identify a survey within twelve months of the proposal receipt date. The following areas may be surveyed during this source selection:

1. TQM/Quality Assurance Capability
2. Technical Capability
3. Financial Capability
4. Accounting System
5. Government Property
6. Transportation
7. Packaging
8. Security
9. Plant safety

M-7 Specific Criteria

The following paragraphs address the specific evaluation criteria for the management and technical and cost areas.

a. Management

The Government will evaluate the Offerors ability to provide and manage a full range of contract management, customer support, production and manufacturing efforts necessary to successfully perform this contract. The evaluation will consider the quality, timeliness and completeness of performance and services offered to the Government. In evaluating this area, the Government will use a variety of information sources including the Offeror's proposal, financial reports, and industry assessments and contacting both past as well as present commercial and Government customers. The Items listed below are ranked in descending order of importance.

(1) ITEM: Warranty Support

The Government will evaluate the Offerors proposed warranty support solution and the degree to which life cycle support is provided to customers in the United States and overseas locations (England, Central Europe and the Far East). Special emphasis will be given to the type (e.g., mailback, on-call, or on-site), length, scope (e.g., same warranty for all CLINs, same warranty for major CLINs, etc.), mean time to restore and return to the customer, and the location of the offered warranty service centers. Additionally, the Government will evaluate the extended warranty support.

(2) ITEM: Production and Delivery Capacity

The Government will evaluate the Offerors capability to produce and deliver the ordered systems and components in a timely manner to locations located throughout the world. Special emphasis will be given to production and delivery capacity, with the capability to meet both commercial deliveries and the offered Government Maximum Order Limit (MOL). Additionally, the Government will evaluate the Offerors capability to accommodate fluctuating ordering trends (e.g., initial contract ordering, beginning and end of fiscal year ordering, priority shipments and contingency situations).

(3) ITEM: Life Cycle Support.

The Government will evaluate the Offeror's proposed life cycle support solution including: order processing, customer technical assistance, software upgrades and updates and the degree to which life cycle support is provided to customers in the United States and over seas locations (England, Central Europe, and the Far East). Special emphasis will be given order processing. Order processing includes length of time to accept and deliver an order, ability to obtain current order status information, ordering aids available and ability to process and deliver priority orders (e.g., priority delivery orders move ahead of all others without requiring modification of other delivery orders, delivery by UPS, Federal Express, etc., priority orders are handled with surge production capacity.). Additionally, the Government will evaluate the proposed customer technical assistance facilities to include the number of days open per week, number of hours open per day, number of calls that can be answered per month, number and qualifications of the technical support staff and the methods provided to obtain assistance.

(4) ITEM: Commerciality

The Government desires a commercial solution and will evaluate the degree to which the proposed system is, first, a "commercial product," as defined in FAR Part 11. Special emphasis will be given to previous sales and existing commercial base of offered products. Additionally, the Government will evaluate the Offeror's intention to make any distinction in their production or manufacturing process between their Government and commercial customers.

(5) ITEM: Performance and Experience

The Government will evaluate the Offeror's past and present performance and experience with programs of similar size and complexity. Included in this evaluation will be a subjective evaluation of customer satisfaction on the full range of services such as on-time delivery, customer support and technical assistance, quality and timeliness of warranty repair and overall commitment to customer satisfaction.

b. Technical Area.

The Government will evaluate the quality, completeness and technical sufficiency of the products offered in response to the RFP. The evaluation will consider the offered products for characteristics which satisfy the Government's stated functional descriptions. The Government may use a variety of information sources including the Offerors proposal, technical reports, magazine articles, and commercial literature, as well as contacts with present and past commercial and Government customers. The Government will conduct a "hands-on" evaluation of a sample of the offered hardware and software components during proposal evaluation. As part of the evaluation, the Government will unpack the hardware and software components and documentation, connect the system unit to the monitor and printer, power on the equipment, and attempt to create and print documents from the office automation software. In the process of using the above components, the Government will survey the user interface, the office automation software suite, system configuration, and the system management software. The Government will also look at the environmental and physical characteristics of the equipment including location of controls, power requirements, and configuration of internal components. The Items and Factors listed below are ranked in descending order of importance.

(1) ITEM: System Performance, Capacities and Environment.

(a) FACTOR: Systems Units.

The Government will evaluate the performance and capacities of the offered system units. Special emphasis will be placed on the microprocessor type, clock speed, wait states, floating capacity, transfer rate and access time. Additionally, the Government will evaluate the resolution, amount of video memory and size of available color palette of the offered video interface; the number and type of offered ports; and the expansion capability (e.g., memory, number and type of available slots, drive bays and number and type of drivers supported) of the offered system units.

(b) FACTOR: Monitors.

The Government will evaluate the performance of the offered monitor for each system configuration. Special emphasis will be placed on availability of color, the size of the display area, and resolutions supported (i.e., horizontal scan frequency and video bandwidth). Additionally, the Government will evaluate the interlacing scheme, dot pitch size, vertical refresh rate (vertical scan frequency), and frequency synchronization ability.

(c) FACTOR: Printers

The Government will evaluate the performance and capacities of the offered printers. Special emphasis will be placed on the quality of the produced product (e.g., resolution and "smearability"), the sustained printer speed and number and types of fonts provided as well as the page per month duty cycle of the printer. Additionally, the Government will evaluate the size of the printer's buffer or memory, the type of emulations provided, type of interfaces (e.g., RS-232, Centronics, SCSI, etc.) provided, the paper multiple page/envelope sizes, paper weight and type, the ability to produce transparencies) and the amount and consumption rate of consumables (e.g., ribbons, toner cartridges, etc.) provided with each printer.

(d) FACTOR: LAN Interface.

The Government will evaluate the performance and capacities of the offered LAN interface hardware and software. Special emphasis will be placed on the transfer rate (e.g., bytes/se), CPU overhead (e.g., inclusion of additional microprocessors to off load network processing from the system CPU) and amount of memory provided by the interface device and required by the protocol drivers. Additionally, the Government will evaluate the data bus interface width (e.g., 9 or 16 bit), number of simultaneous sessions supported with the TCP/IP, NetBIOS, and GOSIP (CLIN 0004 only) software and number and type of connectors (e.g., 10base2, 10base5, etc.) provided and number of drivers provided to support different LAN operating systems.

(e) FACTOR: Environment.

The Government will evaluate the degree to which the offered system units, monitors, printers, and backup devices perform in and impact on the Government's working environment. Special emphasis will be placed on the physical dimensions (length, height, and width) and accessibility of all adjustments and controls. Additionally, the Government will evaluate the ability to operate with differed input power requirements to support worldwide usage (e.g., 115 vac/60 Hz and 220 vac/50 Hz) and the ease of switching between the differing power requirements.

(f) FACTOR: Backup

The Government will evaluate the performance and capacities of the offered back up device(s). Special emphasis will be placed on the capacity of individual storage media as related to the offered hard disk sizes, speed in backing up and restoring to and from the offered storage devices and the type of backup performed (e.g., file versus image backup). Additionally, the Government will evaluate the ability to perform selective backup and restoral, the degree of user involvement required to perform the backup solution (e.g., handling multiple tapes or disks for one backup and automatic or manual back up software) ands inclusion of media necessary to perform an additional full backup for the offered hard disk drivers.

(g) FACTOR: Removable Storage Devices

The Government will evaluate the performance and capacities of the offered Removable Storage Device(s). Special emphasis will be placed on the capacity, transfer rate and access time. Additionally, the Government will evaluate the insertion and removal rate and the ability of the offered removable storage device to be used on all system configurations.

(2) ITEM: Ease of Use and Functionality

(a) FACTOR: User Interface

The Government will evaluate the ease of use and functionality of the user interface for the General

User Environment systems. Special emphasis will be placed on the use of graphics and the consistency of menus and commands across offered user interface. Additionally, the Government will evaluate the capability to run multiple applications (from the offered O/A package) concurrently, printing features (e.g., support for multiple printers and the ability to use these features across all applications offered in the O/A suite of software), the inclusion of user assistance features (e.g., context sensitive help facility and interactive tutorials) and the ability to adapt the user interface to personal work habits.

(b) FACTOR: Office Automation Features and Functionality

The Government will evaluate the ease of use and functionality of the offered Office Automation suite. Special emphasis will be given to the size of products that can be created with each application (e.g., a spreadsheet with 10 million cells and a database with 1 billion records) consistency of the user interface (e.g., graphics, menus and commands) across the proposed applications (between and among offered systems) and the ability to share graphics and data between offered applications and systems without conversion (e.g., cut and paste). Additionally, the Government will evaluate the user assistance features (e.g., context sensitive help facility, sample files, sample formats, sample graphs and interactive tutorials), consistency of applications across user systems (Basic, Intermediate and Advanced) and advanced functions provided in the proposed applications (e.g., grammar-checker, Thesaurus, tables, 3-D spreadsheets, relational capability, query by example, etc.).

1. The Government will evaluate the functionality of the offered personal information management (PIM) application. Special emphasis will be placed on the time management functions (e.g., calendar, appointment list, to-do list and suspense track-

ing), integration of data between functions and the quality of the hard copy output. Additionally, the Government will evaluate the data management functions (e.g., address list and simple database) and simple project management functions (e.g., simple Gantt charts and task management) offered.

2. The Government will evaluate the functionality of the offered graphics application. Special emphasis will be placed on charting features (e.g., text/word charts, graphs and slide shows), free-form drawing capabilities and fonts provided. Additionally, the Government will evaluate the clip art library and templates provided, viewing options (e.g., slide show) and printing options (e.g., slides, notes and handouts).

(c) FACTOR: System Management Software

The Government will evaluate the ease of use and functionality of the offered systems management software. Special emphasis will be placed on the memory management, and disk management (e.g., data compression, disk optimization, disk restoral or unformat) software. Additionally, the Government will evaluate the file management software.

(d) FACTOR: LAN Interface

The Government will evaluate the ease of use and functionality of the LAN interface. Special emphasis will be placed on the setup and configuration procedures and completeness of networking management and system services (e.g., network management service, remote network device check, domain name/directory service, activity/performance statistics, security function) provided. Additionally, the Government will evaluate the completeness of networking platform functions (e.g., file transfer, remote terminal login and mail transport).

(e) FACTOR: Installation and Configuration

The Government will evaluate the ease of installation and configuration of the offered systems and peripherals. Special emphasis will be placed on the ease of installing the offered system and the degree to which the offered systems are delivered loaded with software and configured for immediate operation.

(f) FACTOR: Documentation

The Government will evaluate the ease of use and functionality of the offered documentation. Special emphasis will be the graphics, use of colors, size and numbers of fonts used, inclusion of examples and screen images, and the type of bindings provided) and the type of documentation (e.g., user, administrator, and maintenance manuals; reference cards; and keyboard templates). Additionally, the Government will evaluate the degree to which the documentation is consistent with and conforms to the original manufacturer's commercial documentation.

(g) FACTOR: Open Systems CAE Environment

The Government will evaluate the ease of use and functionality of the offered Open Systems CAE environment. Special emphasis will be placed on the user interface, user interface support tools, programming tools and database support tools. User interface functionality includes the availability of a standard X-Window manager (e.g., Motif, Open Look, etc.) and the ability to customize the environment. User interface support tools include the number and type of X-Window clients provided. Programming tools include compilers for the POSIX environments and the operating system environments provided on CLINs 0001 through 0003 and support tools for debugging, configuration control, documentation management and generation, code generation and screen generation. Database support tools include report writer, screen generator and 4GL capabilities. Additionally, the

Government will evaluate the MS DOS simulator to include the ability to run as an X-Window government and the level of DOS compatibility (e.g., MS-DOS version 3.3) and the ability to run all the software (e.g., POSIX O/A, SQL RDBMS, etc.) as X-Window clients.

(3) ITEM: Compatibility, Consistency and Compliancy

(a) Factor: Hardware

The Government will evaluate the offered hardware for compatibility with existing Government-owned hardware (see Section/Paragraph J-1 and J-5). Special emphasis will be placed on the physical and electrical characteristics of the offered connectors (e.g., 9 and 25 pin D-connectors, RS-232, Centronics, and IEEE 802.3) ad compliance with applicable standards. Additionally, the Government will evaluate the commercial certifications (e.g., Novell certified, Banyan certified, etc) and the availability of user-installable components from multiple sources.

(b) Factor: Software

The Government will evaluate the offered software for compatibility with existing Government-licensed software, consistency with existing government-licensed user interfaces and compliance with the standards (see Section/Paragraph J-1 and J-5,). Special emphasis will be placed on the capability to import and export different data and graphics types and files and the degree to which the offered user interfaces are consistent with existing government-owned software (e.g., Windows 3.0 and XSight). Additionally, the Government will evaluate the offered operating systems for compatibility with existing operating systems and the offered compilers for compatibility with existing Ada compilers (see Section J, Attachment 5), the network protocol and drivers (e.g., TCP/IP and GOSIP) for compatibility with the existing network software (see Section J, Attachment 5) and the offered Open Systems CAE software (see Section J, Attachment 1) and the offered Open Systems CAE software for compliance with Government and commercial standards (e.g., ULANA, FIPS, NIST PCTS, COS Mark, X/Open XVS and X/Open brandmark).

c. Cost/Price Area

All costs derived from the Offerors proposal will be evaluated to determine the most advantageous proposal to the Government in terms of Present Value (PV) and Most Probable Total Contract Cost (MPTCC) over total contract period. Price will be evaluated for realism, reasonableness, completeness, accuracy/trackability, and risk. Subparagraph (1) below describes these factors. The burden of cost credibility rests with the Offeror. This evaluation will be based upon all costs including escalations, terms, and conditions. The Government will not include prompt payment discounts in its evaluation.

(1) COST/PRICE EVALUATION FACTOR

(a) Realism:

The Government will evaluate the realism of each Offeror's proposed prices by comparing them to the Government's Total Contract Cost (GTCC) estimate and to GSA or commercial prices. This will include an evaluation of the extent to which each Offeror's proposed costs indicate a clear understanding of the requirements of the program Prices which represent a probable loss position of the offeror will be judged unrealistic and may be grounds for eliminating a proposal from competition either on the basis that the offeror does not understand the requirement or has made an improvident proposal. If it is determined that an offeror's estimates are unexplainably low, that offeror may be eliminated from the competition (subject to FAR 15.605 and 15.608).

(b) Reasonableness:

The Government will compare offered prices to the GTCC estimate the to GSA or commercial prices to determine if offered prices are extreme or excessive. If it is determined that an offerors estimates are unexplainably high, the offeror may be judged unrealistic (subject to FAR 15.605).

(c) Completeness:

The Government will evaluate the responsiveness of each Offeror in providing prices for all RFP requirements and all items in Section B.

(d) Accuracy/Trackability:

The Government will evaluate the continuity and traceability of costs proposed by the Offeror. Proposed items in Schedule B will be tracked to the Offerors technical proposal. Prices shown in the applicable L-Exhibit shall match those shown on the B-Tables. If not, prices shown on the B-Tables will be used to evaluate the proposal. The hard copy proposal shall match the proposal submitted on CD-ROM. If not, the hard copy submission will be used to evaluate the proposal.

(e) Risk:

The Government will analyze each Offerors prices, terms, and conditions to assess potential impacts including those associated with schedule, technical capability, Contractor support, and potential cost to the Government not included in the MPTCC.

(2) TOTAL CONTRACT COST EVALUATION

The Offeror shall submit all pricing data in the formats indicated in sections B and L. MPTCC evaluation will be based upon the evaluation of day one purchase.

(3) COST EVALUATION MODEL

For the purpose of cost evaluation only, the Government will use the computerized cost model prepared using Microsoft Excel and provided to each Offeror with the RFP. This cost model will calculate MPTCC based on the proposed prices in the B-Tables and the applicable, based on proposed warranty length. The cost model will also calculate PC MPTCC based on application of present value factors from the applicable L Exhibits to the proposed prices from the B-Tables.

(a) Contract life:

The contract life commences with the assumed date of contract award and ends 60 months later. This contract life includes one basic year and two option years for system purchases and an additional two option years for user-installable components and extended warranty. The following assumptions are made for evaluation purposes only.

Contract Award Date: 30 September 2007
Last Day of Contract Life: 29 September 2012

(b) Residual Valve:

The residual value of all equipment will be considered to be zero.

(c) Quantities

For cost evaluation purposes only, the Government will evaluate the purchase of 300,000 systems and associated support items contained in Exhibits L-1 through L-6, as applicable, based on proposed warranty length. Quantities are estimates based on the maximum total quantities the Government may order. The Government may award to one or two Offerors and does not guarantee ordering of more than a minimum contract dollars as specified in Section/Paragraph B-2a.

(d) Assumptions

The following assumption will be used to evaluate the indefinite delivery aspect of the contract. The B-Tables and L-Exhibits of the RFP have been established for cost evaluation purposes only and it is likely the actual contract yearly ordering schedule will vary. The Government may award to one or two Offerors.

(e) Warranty:

For cost evaluation purposes only, the Government will use a combination of warranty and extended warranty to achieve a three year warranty on every system purchased. After the initial three year warranty period, an estimated 30% of the systems will continue to purchase extended warranty coverage (see applicable L-Exhibit). The Government expects warranties to be offered in one year increments. For cost evaluation purposes, any warranty offered in less than one year increments will be evaluated as an extended warranty for that particular year and priced using the Offerors extended warranty price for the succeeding year.

(4) PRESENT VALUE ANALYSIS

(a) The basis of cost evaluation shall be PC MPTCC. An analysis will be made to determine the present value of monies for the expected price of each offered item and for the total contract.

(b) Present value will be determined using the current five year U.S. Government securities interest rate on Treasury Constant Maturities in effect as of 10 June 2007. Federal Reserve Statistical Release H-25, published weekly, is the authoritative source for Treasury Constant Maturities interest rates. All prices will be discounted from the assumed contract award date on an annual basis. For cost evaluation purposes, the Government assumes purchases are spread evenly throughout each year. Therefore, the present value factor utilized for each price will be the mid-year factor for the particular year the price is incurred. Any Offeror identified price for which the Government is contractually obligated, but which is due beyond the termination of the contract, will be assumed to be payable in the last contract year.

Sample 16

Electronic Acquisition System

Type of Work: System Acquisition

Objective: To acquire an electronic acquisition system to support requisitioning, contracting, and small purchase activities.

SOW Type: Functional

Comments:

- Good functional specifications for the design and development phase.
- Detailed description of the contract administration process, including contract modifications.
- Time zone is identified for the time when technical support is to be provided. This eliminates any confusion about when support will be available.
- Good description of the various management plans, including project management requirements.
- The statement, "The Contractor shall manage this contract in a manner consistent with customary software quality assurance principles...." is vague because of the word

"customary," which can be left open to interpretation.

- Gets very specific in the support phase; might have been better to let the contractor propose the types of personnel to be assigned.
- The term "etc." is used multiple times throughout the document. The use of this term creates uncertainty about and hedges the requirements.

Section C
Table of Contents

C385 General Support Requirements

- C385 (A) Delivery, Installation and Implementation
- C385 (B) Technical Support Services
- C385 (C) System Maintenance/Updates
- C385 (D) Training
- C385 (E) Contract Management and Plans
- C385 (F) Contractor Performance Reports and Meetings
- C385 (G) Contractor Support Services Positions

C386 Documentation

C387 Required Options

- C387 (A) Software Copies
- C387 (B) Supplemental Training

C388 Optional Features

- C388 (A) Electronic Signature
- C388 (B) Electronic Archival
- C388 (C) Federal Assistance
- C388 (D) Acquisition Planning

Section C – Description/Specification/Work Statement

C303 General Requirements

Except for those items specifically identified in Section H of this contract as Government furnished property, the Contractor shall furnish all facilities, labor, and materials to provide goods/services in accordance with the terms and conditions contained herein and the specifications set forth below.

C305 Incorporation of Contractor's Technical Proposal

The Contractor's technical proposal entitled [to be completed at time of award] dated [to be completed at the time of award], is hereby incorporated by reference and made part of this contract. In the event of any inconsistency between the provisions of this contract and the Contractor's technical proposal, the contract provisions take precedence.

C380 Summary and Background

C380 (A) Scope and Summary

(1) This procurement is to acquire an Interior Department Electronic Acquisition System (IDEAS) to support requisitioning, contracting, and small purchase activities within the Department of the Interior (DOI). A primary objective of this procurement is to acquire as much functionality as possible through the acquisition of off-the-shelf software. The off-the-shelf software shall include, at a minimum, functional capabilities in requisitioning, contracts and small purchases. The Government recognizes that a system capable of supplying the three application capabilities (i.e., requisitioning, contracts, and small purchases system modules) may be provided in various methods.

NOTE: The Contractor is expected to provide all of the functionality indicated in each of the three application capabilities. Technical Support Services will be used to tailor the system for DOI customization, training, etc.

(2) Additional contract requirements include a perpetual, irrevocable, non-transferable, non-exclusive software license (see Section H) to the DOI to use the electronic acquisition software, documentation, and training materials provided hereunder; all source code in both hard copy and

machine readable formats; and technical support services for implementation, training, software enhancements and modifications, and maintenance support required to implement IDEAS within the DOI.

(3) The period of performance for this contract is 120 months (i.e., base year plus nine (9) twelve (12) month option periods).

(4) The goal of acquiring IDEAS is to:

(a) Eliminate duplicative systems within the DOI while providing improved procurement operations and customer service, achieving significant management and cost efficiencies;

(b) Standardized and automate the acquisition process in order to eliminate redundant data entry by accessing data throughout the system;

(c) Interface with the Interior Procurement Data System (IPDS) in order to improve the timeliness and accuracy of procurement statistics Department-wide for reporting to the Federal Procurement Data System; and

(d) Interface with the Federal Financial System (FFS), the Department-wide financial management system, in order to transmit, receive, and reconcile commitment, obligation and payment data.

(5) The system shall be capable of supporting the procurement workload of eleven DOI Bureaus and Offices (hereinafter, Bureaus) geographically dispersed throughout the United States as well as all other clients of the Washington Administrative Service Center (WASC) (see Section J, Attachment B for listing of clients). Department of the Interior Bureaus are the: Bureau of Land Management (BLM), Minerals Management Service (MMS), Office of Surface Mining Reclamation and Enforcement (OSM), Bureau of Reclamation (BOR), US Geological Survey (USGS), Bureau of Mines (BOM), National Park Service (NPS), US Fish and Wildlife Service (FWS), Bureau of Indian Affairs (BIA), and Office of the Secretary which

includes the Office of Administrative Services (PMO), and the Office of Aircraft Services (OAS).

(6) Software acquired under this contract shall run on MS-DOS compatible hardware and software as defined by the standard PC configuration in Section J, Attachment E.

(7) The DOI has mainframe equipment at the WASC, located at the USGA National Center, Reston, Virginia, utilizing IBM's MVS operating system. The IPDS is resident on the WASC mainframe computer. Additional mainframe equipment is located at the Denver Administrative Service Center (DASC) in Denver, Colorado. The FFS is currently operational at the WASC at the DASC. However, the WASC mainframe computer will be the host computer for the IPDS and for any centralized departmental IDEAS component.

(8) No Bureau currently uses mainframe, desktop, or non-MS-DOS applications for acquisition workload processing. A more detailed description of hardware currently in use is set forth in Section J, Attachment E.

C380 (B) Department of the Interior Background and Organization

(1) The DOI was created by an Act of Congress on March 3, 1849. As the Nation's principle conservation Agency, the DOI has responsibility for most nationally owned public lands and natural resources. This includes fostering the wisest use of land and water resources, protecting fish and wildlife, and preserving the environmental and cultural values of national parks and historic places. The Department assesses mineral resources and strives to assure that potential resource development is in the public's beset interest. The DOI has a trust responsibility for American Indian tribes, Alaska Native groups, individual Indians, and residents of island territories under United States administration.

(2) The jurisdiction of the DOI includes administration of over 522 million acres of Federal land, trust responsibility for approximately 50 million acres of land; conservation and development of mineral and water resources; and

the conservation, development, and utilization of fish and wildlife resources. In addition, the Department coordinates Federal and state recreation programs; preservation and administration of the Nation's scenic and historic areas; reclamation of arid lands in the west through irrigation; and the management of hydroelectric power generation systems.

(3) Departmental responsibilities are met by the operating Bureaus identified in Section C380 (A) (5). The basic missions of each Bureau are briefly described in Section J, Attachment C. The general organization of the DOI and its Bureaus is outline in the charts shown in Section J, Attachment D.

C380 (C) Current Operating Environment

(1) The objective of the DOI procurement program is to develop, award, and monitor acquisitions required to support the missions of the Bureaus. Interior Bureau procurement offices must ensure that procurements are handled in a manner that supports competition, secures quality contractor performance, and ensures award at a fair and reasonable price. The DOI acquisition process encompasses the procurement of supplies and services, construction, alteration and repair, automated data processing equipment and services, teleprocessing, research and development, and Architect-Engineering services.

(2) The acquisition function is governed by the Federal Acquisition Regulation (FAR), Federal Information Resources Management Regulations (FIRMIR), Federal Property Management Regulations (FPMR), Office of Management and Budget (OMB) Circulars and Bulletins, Office of Federal Procurement Policy (OFPP) Letters, Department of the Interior Acquisition Regulation (DIAR), Interior Departmental Manual (DM), and Bureau specific manuals and regulations.

(3) Department of the Interior operations are widely dispersed geographically and programmatically. Acquisition activities are performed at approximately 85 major con-

tracting offices and 1,100 locations with authority limited to small purchases (i.e., the ceiling established in FAR Part 13). Small purchases are performed in every state of the Union, including isolated areas, such as wildlife refuges, National parks, and Indian reservations. Offices with contracting authority (usually valued in excess of the FAR small purchase ceiling) are more centrally located in metropolitan areas. It is not expected that the number of procurement locations will substantially increase.

(4) Bureaus have differing organizational structures for processing procurements. Generally, each Bureau headquarters procurement office is the central point for coordination and policy within the Bureau and with the Department. In addition, these headquarters offices are responsible for awarding and administering contracts and small purchases. Most Bureaus have regional, state, or area procurement offices with delegated authority for processing contracts and small purchase acquisitions; and multiple field offices (including parks, hatcheries, district and agency offices) that only have small purchase authority.

(5) There are over 2,400 warranted Contracting Officers in the Department. Approximately 625 Contract Specialists, Contract Negotiators, and Contract Administrators (Federal vocational series GS/GM-1102) are currently using a variety of IBM-compatible personal computer-based commercial or in-house developed software with DOS operating systems. Over 500 Purchasing Agents and Procurement Assistants (Federal vocational series GS-1105 and GS-1106), and approximately 1500 collateral-duty personnel located in field locations use a variety of similar equipment and software. Many employees in these categories still use typewriters and word processors to process purchase and delivery orders. (See Section J, Attachment K).

(6) Nationally, procurements are currently processed either manually or by using both electronic and manual methods. No DOI Bureau has completely automated acquisition system. Procurement data is manually keyed into the IPDS and FFS systems.

(7) Approximately 15,000 contract transactions (including new contracts and delivery orders and modifications to existing contracts and orders) and over 600,000 small purchase transactions are processed each year valued at approximately $1.5 billion.

(8) Since most of the Bureaus are maintaining their own unique acquisition systems, multiple procurement forms, clauses, special provisions, and procedures have been developed. Some standardization, by the Government, will be required in areas such as the Procurement Instrument Identification Number (PIIN), forms, and procurement terminology. Forms standardization throughout the DIO is anticipated by October 1, 1992; Department-wide standardized clauses, provisions, and procedures are scheduled during Fiscal Year 1993.

(9) In spite of diverse operating conditions, there is commonality in the method and performance of procurement functions throughout the DOI. The functional requirements for requisitioning, contracts, and small purchases (outlined in Sections C381, C382 and C383) are not intended to be all inclusive, but are intended to identify significant acquisition activities that may be subject to automation.

NOTE: These functional requirements were developed based on the Department of the Interior Contracts and Small Purchase Standards and the IDEAS Conceptual Model. These documents were developed as a precursor to this contract requirement. Copies of these documents will be available for review at the USGS National Center. Please contact the Contracting Officer (703/648-7366) for an appointment.

These common functions include:

(a) Requisitioning;

(b) Solicitation;

(c) Evaluation;

(d) Award;

(e) Administration; and

(f) Interface with the IPDS, FFS, and other administrative systems

(10)Personnel performing/supporting the acquisition function are:

(a) Contracting Officers who are authorized to conduct procurement activities and to obligate Government funds to acquire goods and service within the specific limitations of his or her delegated warrant authority. These activities include, but are not limited to, developing Individual Contract Plans (ICP's), issuing solicitations, evaluating bids and proposals, conducting negotiations with potential contractors, awarding contracts and/or small purchases, processing amendments and modifications, and issuing various Determinations and Findings associated with the procurement process, protests, contact claims, appeals, etc.

(b) Contract Specialists, Contract Negotiators, and Contract Administrators who are responsible for various tasks related to processing requisitions and contract administration. Typical tasks may include accepting procurement requests, determining the competitive nature of acquisitions, preparing solicitations, developing and maintaining contract files, preparing correspondence relating to procurement, monitoring contract performance, and developing various procurement documents for signature by the Contracting Officer. Contract Specialists, Contract Negotiators, and Contract Administrators may or may not be a warranted Contracting Officer.

(c) Purchasing Agents (or Buyers) who are responsible for small purchase awards valued less than the FAR 13 ceiling, and for orders issued against Federal Supply Schedule contracts and other Government sources of supply. Tasks may include receiving requisitions, preparing Requests for Quotations (RFQ's), obtaining competition or determining that adequate sole source justification exists, obtaining and evaluating quotes, and making and disserting awards. Purchasing Agents may have limited warrant authority.

(d) Procurement Analysts, Contract Cost/Price Analysts, and Business Utilization and Development Specialists are procurement professionals who provide support to Bureau Contracting Officer, Contract Specialists, Contract Negotiators, Contract Administrators, and Purchasing Agents, as follows:

(i) Procurement Analysts are responsible for implementing Federal and Interior acquisition regulations, policy, and procedures;

(ii) Contract Price/Cost Analysts coordinate contract audits with the Office of Inspector General and/or other Agency offices, develop weighted guidelines to determine appropriate contract profit/fee, and provide price and cost analyses to assist in contract negotiations; and

(iii) Business Utilization and Development Specialists review proposed acquisitions for set-aside to small and small, disadvantaged businesses, suggest sources for prime or subcontract work, monitor award statistics for transmittal by DOI to the Small Business Administration (SBA), etc.

(e) Procurement Assistants and Procurement Clerks who are responsible for supporting Contracting Officers and for all clerical tasks including filing, forms entry, and typing.

(f) Requistioners who are responsible for identifying and documenting their particular requirements.

(g) Additionally, there are personnel throughout Bureau field offices who perform limited procurement functions as collateral duties.

C381 Requisitioning Functional Requirements

C381 (A) Requisitions

Bureau procurement offices review requisitions form program offices geographically dispersed throughout the United States and Trust Territories. Requisitions identify supplies and/or services to be acquired and contain supporting documentation in the form of justifications, statements of work or specifications, attachments and exhibits. After approval at varying levels within each Bureau, the requisition is forwarded to the responsible fund certifying official for commitment of funds. The procurement requisition, including appropriate financial information, is transmitted to the procurement office for assignment to a Contracting Officer. The IDEAS requisition module shall have the capability to:

(1) Generate requisition numbers, which may also be manually assigned, and prevent duplication of requisition numbers within a Bureau;

(2) Perform calculations and extend line item amounts, and subtotals and totals for all line items;

(3) Allow users to create, display, edit, and print the requisition form;

(4) Permit awards against requisitions which:

  (a) Involve multiple fiscal years;

  (b) Indicate a "Not to Exceed" amount;

  (c) Are subject to availability of funds; and/or

  (d) Have no funds indicated.

(5) Permit preparation and distribution of supporting documentation, including statements of work or specifications, attachments and exhibits, and required justifications to multiple locations;

(6) Retrieve and display archived requisitions in order to reuse and edit their electronic content to create a new requisition for a similar requirement;

(7) Route and track requisitions and supporting documentation to multiple locations (in no particular order) for review and Bureau specified review(s) and approval(s);

(8) Transmit commitment data and other information to the FFS; and

(9) Permit cancellation by either individual requisition line item(s) or by entire requisitions, maintain a record of req-

uisition cancellations, and provide cancellation notifications to appropriate offices based on security levels.

(10) Permit reviewers and approving officials to document comments and place conditions upon their approvals. <u>Note: the use of requisitions within the DOI is not limited to the procurement function. However, no other requisition use within the DOI will be subject to the IDEAS.</u>

C382 Contracts Functional Requirements

C382 (A) <u>Pre-Award Process</u>

(1) <u>Solicitation</u>

Generally, the solicitation process begins when a requisition is received and accepted by the Contracting Officer. The process involves establishing Individual Contract Plans (ICP's), publicizing procurement notices in the Commerce Business Daily (CBD), developing and maintaining lists of potential sources, generating associated documentation and issuing solicitations and any necessary solicitation amendments. The IDEAS contracts module shall possess the capabilities to:

(a) Accommodate and process all solicitation methods and types authorized by statute and regulation against one or more requisitions;

(b) Retrieve, display and/or print a list of unassigned requisitions that have been received in the procurement office; provide for on screen review of unassigned requisitions provide manual and automated methods for requisition assignment and reassignment;

(c) Permit the responsible procurement staff member (hereinafter, Contracting Officer) to identify and consolidate contract line items form one or more requisitions into one or more solicitation(s) and award(s);

(d) Track the source of contract line items to one or more requisitions;

(e) Generate unique solicitation numbers and prevent number duplication within a Bureau;

(f) Allow the Contracting Officer to track Government developed pre-award ICP milestones; generate, modify and print a pre-award ICP document;

(g) Generate and print the DI-1886, "Acquisition Screening and Review Form";

(h) Establish, maintain, and provide search and selection capability from vendor tables containing current information and historical vendor data relating to performance under previous procurements. Each Bureau employs one or more vendor tables that are unique to the Bureau, one Bureau site, or even to a work unit within a site. There is no Department-wide vendor table;

(i) Generate a list of vendors to be solicited for individual procurement actions; print source lists and mailing labels;

(j) Permit the Contracting Officer to generate, edit, and transmit synopses to the CBD in accordance with FAR Part 5; record verification of synopsis receipt; retrieve and print copies of the published text;

(k) To assemble the solicitation document, the system shall possess the capabilities to:

   (i) Generate, edit, print and route for approval(s) complete solicitations (e.g., Requests for Proposals (RFP's) and Invitation for Bids (IFB's)), including supporting documentation and necessary forms, and sequentially numbered solicitation amendments;

   (ii) Access and assemble FAR, FIRMR, and DIAR clauses, provisions, and prescriptions; access and assemble Bureau terms and conditions; and

   (iii) Capture applicable data from requisitions, specifications, statements of work, purchase descriptions, etc., merge with text of clauses and provisions, and assemble into a complete document which can be edited.

(l) To cancel the solicitation in its entirety at any time preceding the point of award.

(2) Evaluation

The evaluation process begins when a proposal or bid is received. The process involves technical and price evaluation activities, and preparation and review of supporting documentation leading to contract award. The IDEAS contracts module shall possess the capability to:

a. Access and obtain information regarding vendor responsibility and eligibility (i.e., from the General Services Administration's (GSA's) List of Parties Excluded from Federal Procurement and Non-procurement Programs, Department of the Treasury's List of Approved Sureties, etc.. Information concerning availability of these listing is detailed in Section J, Attachment L.);

b. Enable the Contracting Officer to record and print bid abstracts and cost/price analyses; and

c. Enable the Contracting Officer to document the results of technical and price proposal evaluation, responsibility determinations, and negotiations and Best and Final Offers, as appropriate.

(3) Award

This process includes generating the appropriate contract type, obtaining pre-award clearances, requesting and receiving additional or amend requisitions when necessary, and interfacing with the IPDS and FFS. The IDEAS contracts module shall provide the capabilities to:

(a) Permit issuance of any combination of one or more awards (including different award types) against one or more requisitions and solicitations;

(b) Prevent issuance of awards exceeding the Contracting Officer's delegated warrant authority and control obligations exceeding the commitment amount on the requisition;

(c) Provide up-to-date status of requisitions; maintain a record of contract line items; permit the Contracting Officer to create contract line items which are not specifically identified on requisitions but are nonetheless necessary for the award.

(d) Generate a unique Procurement Instrument Identification Number (PIIN) which identifies the procurement; and

(e) Generate a contract document as follows:

   (i) Access and assemble any necessary changed FAR, FIRMR, and IDAR clauses; access and assemble Bureau terms and conditions; and

   (ii) Incorporate applicable data from the requisition, solicitation and solicitation amendments (if any), specifications or statement of work, and merge with appropriate clauses (by reference or in full text as authorized by FAR) into a complete document (including applicable forms).

(f) Enable the Contracting Officer to generate, edit and print the contract and supporting documentation and route it for required approval(s).

(g) Transmit obligation and de-commitment data to the FFS;

(h) Serve as the data source for the IPDS; the system shall collect reportable award statistics (which may be manually generated and edited) and transmit them to the DOI. Thee IPDS is further defined and described in the IPDS Reporting Manual, IPDS Users' Guide, and IPDS Operations Guide (see Section J, Attachment A); and,

(i) Print a Form DI-1940, "Individual Contract Action Reports", for the official contract file.

C382 (B) <u>Contract Administration Process</u>

The contract administration process consists of post-award activities through contract closeout. Contract administration can be performed by the awarding Contracting Officer or delegated to another Contracting Officer. The IDEAS contracts module shall possess the capabilities to:

(1) Permit reassignment of active contracts by Contracting Officer and by procurement office;

(2) Record the designation of various Government officials assigned contract administration duties;

(3) Permit recording, tracking, and monitoring contractor performance and significant contract events (including providing advance notice of pending required actions).

(4) Contracts may be modified multiple times. The system shall permit the Contracting Officer to:

  (a) Generate, edit, print and route for approval(s) complete modifications and delivery/task order documents, including forms;

  (b) Merge applicable data from the requisition, contract, specification or statement of work into a complete document which can be electronically edited.

  (c) Reference the contract PIN in modifications and delivery/task orders.

  (d) Access and incorporate FAR, FIRMR, and IDAR clauses and provisions, and Bureau terms and conditions;

  (e) Sequentially number modifications on an individual contract basis and prevent duplication of modification numbers on a particular contract;

  (f) Permit the Contracting Officer to modify contracts with or without a requisition; requisitions are required for modifications obligating additional funding;

  (g) Prevent issuance of modifications in excess of the Contracting Officer's delegated warrant authority; and

  (h) Prevent de-obligation of funds without the Contracting Officer's approval.

(5) Collect modification, termination, and closeout data as required by the IPDS and transmit the information to the DOI; print an IPDS Form DI-1940 for the official contract file.

(6) Permit collection and transmittal of funding changes and essential modification and delivery/task order information to the FFS; access and obtain contract financial information from the FFS.

(7) Transmit notice of receipt, inspection and acceptance of deliverables (including partial deliveries) to the FFS authorizing payment.

(8) Generate and print contractor performance evaluation forms, release of claims forms, invention and patents reports, and contract completion statement which may be manually edited.

(9) Track records of contract documents sent to the National Archives and Record Retention Centers.

C383 Small Purchase Functional Requirements

C383 (A) Solicitation and Evaluation

Small purchase and other simplified purchase procedures are designed to meet needs for supplies and services the price of which will not exceed the ceiling limitation set forth in FAR Part 13. Upon receipt of a requisition in the purchasing office, the Contracting Officer determines the appropriate acquisition method which will satisfy competition requirements, be most cost effective, and expeditiously meet the requestor's needs. The IDEAS small purchase module shall provide the capabilities to:

(1) Permit processing of all types of small purchase procedures authorized by a statute and regulation;

(2) Provide up-to-date active requisition status. Maintain a record of requisition contract line items. Permit status queries by individual requisitioners throughout the procurement process;

(3) Enable Contracting Officers to consolidate requisitions, combine similar items, track the acquisition of line items to single/multiple awards and create contract line items not specifically identified on requisitions but nonetheless necessary for the award;

(4) Retrieve and display a list of unassigned requisitions; provide for on-screen review of assigned requisitions; and provide automated and manual methods for requisition assignment/reassignment;

(5) Provide a table of mandatory sources, as defined in FAR Part 8, for acquiring goods and services. The system

shall enable Contracting Officers to document mandatory source research and source selection rationale;

(6) Establish, store, search, retrieve, and maintain Bureau vendor tables (i.e., libraries of current and historical bidder information related to a Bureau site, work unit, or entire organization) for procuring goods and services; generate mailing lists and printed labels from vendor table information;

(7) Enable the Contracting Officer to create, edit and transmit procurement synopses to the CBD in accordance with FAR Part 5; verify synopsis receipt; and retrieve and print a copy of the published text.

(8) Assist the Contracting Officer in the informal and formal process of soliciting quotations. For information purposes, the informal method is predominately used over the more formal Request for Quotation (RFQ) method. The system shall have the capability to accommodate both solicitation methods as set forth below.

(a) In the informal process of verbally soliciting quotations, the small purchase module shall provide:

(i) A method to record verbal solicitations and vendors' verbal quotations;

(ii) A method to record verbal solicitations which result in written quotations form vendors;

(iii) A method to fully document the competitive nature of the procurement.

(b) In the more formal RFQ process of soliciting written vendor quotations, the small purchase module shall have the capability to:

(i) Store, identify, and assemble appropriate FAR, FIRMR and DIAR clauses, and Bureau terms and conditions; allow users to incorporate pertinent clauses and documents into the RFQ;

(ii) Permit editing of the assembled document prior to printing;

(iii) Route the RFQ for review and/or approval(s); and

(iv) Issue sequentially numbered amendments to prevent duplication of numbers associated with a particular RFQ.

(9) Provide a method to record written and verbal quotations and competition. Provide a capability for analyzing vendor's verbal and/or written quotations.

(10) Access and obtain information regarding vendor responsibility and eligibility (i.e., GSA's List of Parties Excluded from Federal Procurement and Non-procurement Programs, Department of the Treasury's List of Approved Sureties, etc.). (See Section J, Attachment L).

C383 (B) Award

The system shall have the capability to process and record various small purchase awards. The system shall prevent awards in excess of the Contracting Officer's warranted authority. The IDEAS small purchase module shall allow only authorized procurement personnel to change/delete award data and release orders. The IDEAS small purchase module shall have the capability to:

(1) Generate and track a unique award number identifying the procurement;

(2) Allow users to create, store, and edit supporting procurement documentation pertaining to the award document;

(3) Permit the Contracting Officer to generate, edit and print purchase/delivery orders resulting from verbal quotations or RFQ's;

(4) Perform calculations and extend line item amounts, and subtotals and totals for all line items on the award document;

(5) Transmit obligation and award data to the FFS;

(6) Collect reportable award statistics (which may be manually edited) and transmit them to the DOI in accordance with the IPDS Reporting Manual (see Section J, Attachment A); and

(7) Print an official file copy of each DI-1940; print quarterly summary SF-281, "FPDS-Summary Contract Action Report ($25,000 or less)", reports, and SF-281 reports at various organizational levels, as needed.

C383 (C) Administration

Administration consists of post-award activities through close-out of the award. The IDEAS small purchase module shall provide the capabilities to:

(1) Permit recording, tracking, and monitoring of due dates for deliverables, and delivery, receipt, inspection and acceptance;

(2) Create, edit, route for Bureau approval (if any), and print necessary purchase/delivery order amendments. Amendments shall be sequentially numbered and shall reference the original award number;

(3) Collect and transmit amendment, termination, and close-out data to the IPDS; and

(4) Transmit to the FFS obligation and de-obligation data resulting from amendments; access and obtain payment information from the FFS.

C384 ADP Systems Requirements

C384 (A) General System Capabilities

(1) The system shall be flexible enough to accommodate promptly changes to the requisitioning, small purchasing and contracting processes required by Federal statutes and regulations, and DOI regulations, policies, and procedures.

(2) The system shall be capable of individually supporting the workload of eleven DOI Bureaus geographically dispersed throughout the United States having unique organizational structures.

(3) The system shall permit concurrent independent acquisition operations by both single and multiple users at a site.

(4) Newly implemented or enhanced common modules shall be able to be readily disseminated to all operational locations, efficiently, easily and rapidly.

(5) The system shall permit data retrieval and inquiry being performed and viewed via all of the following methods:

(a) Interactive retrieval;

(b) Hard copy reports; and

(c) By downloading or uploading files

C384 (B) System Design Requirements

The baseline software shall be "off-the-shelf" (i.e., it is proven and available for immediate use; design, programming, testing, and documentation are complete). [NOTE: baseline software is defined as the software package in existence at time of submission of technical proposal.]

(1) All software acquired under this contract shall conform to specifications contained in the applicable Federal Information Processing Standards Publications (FIPS PUBS) and Federal Communications Standards (FED STDS) as set forth in Section H.

(2) The Contractor shall utilize good design approach strategies, e.g., structured design techniques and modular coding concepts which facilitate making changes and enhancements with speed and ease in addition to being easily adapted to changing user needs.

(3) Each functional subsystem shall be fully integrated with other subsystems, including any optional features offered.

(4) The system shall provide the ability to add, delete and/or change data elements.

(5) The system shall provide the capability to aggregate, define, and retrieve data.

(6) The system shall facilitate user friendly and efficient user navigation throughout all applications.

(7) The system shall generate standard reports printed in hard copy and be viewable on a monitor screen.

(8) The system shall provide efficient and comprehensive interactive context-sensitive "help" facilities.

(9) Because Bureau organizational delegations of procurement authority differ, some procurement offices will require both contract and small purchase modules. The system shall be capable of being implemented in any combination of the following independent module configurations:

(a) Requisitions;

(b) Contracts; and,

(c) Small purchases.

(10) The system shall be flexible enough to preclude and inordinate amount of effort to accommodate:

(a) An upward migration of compatible hardware, operating system or network(s);

(b) Software enhancements and modifications; and,

(c) Bureau unique requirements.

(11) The system shall be designed to ensure that each Bureau's data is segregated in separate files.

(12) The system shall allow the user to vary the sequence of steps in the procurement process and by-pass steps dependent upon the requirements of the procurement action.

C384 (C) Security Requirements

(1) The system shall comply with Government regulations, standards, guidelines, and legislation applicable to ADP security.

(2) The system shall provide controls to ensure the confidentiality of sensitive procurement data (e.g., Government source selection information and Contractor proprietary data as set forth in FAR 3.104-5).

(3) The system shall be secured to prevent unauthorized access and to prevent authorized users from performing unauthorized activities (i.e., users are restricted to specified activities) through the use of multi-layered access. Examples of layers are: hardware, application, function, and document.

(4) The system shall include protective mechanisms to prevent computer virus infections.

C384 (D) Text Processing/Routing Requirements

(1) The system shall have the capability to import and export spread sheet and other data in American Standard Code for Information Interchange (ASCII) format.

(2) The system shall have the capability to transmit and receive correspondence and text.

C384 (E) Data Entry Requirements

(1) The system shall provide for on-line data entry.

(2) The system shall allow concurrent access to common files (i.e., data files shared by more than one program or user).

(3) The system shall generate or accept batch transfers of data, in a readily accessible format, sent to and from field offices or remote locations to a regional/headquarters location for further processing.

C384 (F) Data Edit Requirements

(1) The system shall provide for comprehensive and complete editing and error correction capabilities to ensure the integrity of the data submitted and stored within the system.

(2) The system shall provide clear edit messages for correction/re-entering of previously rejected user data.

(3) The system shall provide for easy adjustment of edits.

C384 (G) System Processing/Data Management Requirements

(1) The system shall provide backup and recovery capabilities.

(2) The system shall provide safeguards and well documented procedures to avoid or prevent corruption of acquisition data.

(3) The system shall provide the capability to permit and control the transfer of data to and from external systems.

(4) The system shall have the capability to provide system audit trails.

(5) The system shall have the capability to generate reports identifying user access privileges.

C384 (H) Hardware/Software Environment

(1) The system shall be compatible with and operate on the existing DOI hardware and software configuration as defined by the standard PC configuration in Section J, Attachment E.

(2) The system shall be compatible with the current DOI communications network(s) described in Section J, Attachment F.

C384 (I) Management Information Requirements

The system shall have the capability of generating Departmental and Bureau standard and ad hoc reports.

C385 General Support Requirements

The Contractor shall deliver the software, all source code in both hard copy and machine readable formats (ASCII), documentation, maintenance, training, and other Contractor support services required to implement, enhance, and maintain all software, hardware and documentation delivered under this contract.

C385 (A) Delivery, Installation, and Implementation

(1) General

(a) The Contractor shall deliver two (2) original copies of all the IDEAS software (including the baseline software and any enhancements, upgrades, modifications and corrections to the baseline software) and associated documentation to the COR at the address set forth in Section F980. [NOTE: Baseline software is defined as the software package in existence at time of submission of technical proposal.]

(b) It is the Contractor's responsibility to ensure installation of the software and delivery of all relevant documentation prior to, and in preparation for, acceptance testing by the Government.

(c) The Contractor shall maintain an established system of quality assurance and system testing during installation of the IDEAS software and any supplementary or corrective software which is required during the acceptance period.

(d) Installation of software shall be in accordance with the terms and conditions of this contract and the Contractor's Government approved Implementation Plan. In the event of any inconsistency between this contract and the Contractor's Implementation Plan, this contract shall take precedence.

(2) Delivery and Installation of Software

(a) Within 20 work days of award, the Contractor shall deliver two (2) original copies of the IDEAS baseline software and associated documentation (and any necessary software and hardware) to the address in Section F980 and install one (1) software package at the USGS in Reston, VA.

(b) At the time of installation, the Contractor shall deliver to the COR, procedures, set up instructions, and other relevant information and documentation and any security facilities (e.g., passwords, time dependencies) embedded within the tool that must be activated to enable the Government to reproduce, install and operate the software properly.

(c) The Contractor shall complete installation of all necessary software for inspection and acceptance testing at the acceptance test site within 10 work days of delivery of the software to the test site.

(d) Upon installation completion at the test site, the Contractor shall certify in writing to the COR that the software installation has been successfully tested and evaluated by the Contractor, and is ready for Government acceptance testing in accordance with Section E.

(e) The Contractor shall then rerun the Contractor's successful pre-award Operational Capabilities Demonstration prior to system acceptance in accordance with Section E.

(3) Implementation of Software

(a) Implementation will be dependent upon the level of existing functionality of the baseline system installed. However, the Government anticipates a scenario similar to the following:

(i) It is anticipated that the first implementation of the IDEAS software will be accomplished through a phased modular approach. The actual sequence of the modules to be implemented will be dependent on the software acquired under this contract and the Contractor's Government approved Implementation Plan (see Section C385 (E) (4)). Additionally, all portions of a particular module may not necessarily be fully functional at time of implementation of the software. Portions of the module may still require further development and/or customization.

(ii) The Contractor shall implement the IDEAS system at the USGS Headquarters Office of Procurement and Contracts in Reston, VA. Enhancements to the baseline software will be acquired through issuance of delivery orders under this contract. As enhancements are made and installed to a particular module, the Government will perform acceptance testing on the enhancements. Once a module is deemed functionally complete, it will then be implemented at one of the two regional USGS procurement offices.

(iii) Upon final implementation of all the software at the USGS, the Contractor will begin implementation at another DOI Bureau.

(b) The Contractor shall provide initial installation support to the Government for the baseline software delivered under this contract.

C385 (B) Technical Support Services

(1) The Contractor shall furnish technical support services in support of the system. These services may be required following acceptance of the acquisition software and will be ordered through the issuance of delivery orders in accordance with Section H1486.

(2) Based on the acquisition modules selected and on available DOI resources, Contractor tasks would include, but are not necessarily limited to:

(a) Module software installation;

(b) Interfacing with existing administrative systems;

(c) Preparing customized reports and/or one time utility programs;

(d) Developing bridges to management support systems;

(e) Converting current and historical data; and

(f) Software enhancements and modifications.

(3) The Government estimates that approximately 250,000 labor hours of technical support services will be required under this contract during the 120-month contract life. The phased yearly hourly usage will be dependent upon date of contract award and the system acquired, but is estimated as approximately 15% for the base year, 25% for option year one, 20% for option year two, 16% for option year three and 4% per year for the remaining option years.

(4) It is anticipated that approximately 20% of the estimated labor hours will be used for managerial labor categories (Project and Implementation Managers and Senior Computer Programmers and Systems Analysts) and approximately 80% of the estimated labor hours will be used for specialist labor categories. It is anticipated that the following labor categories will be needed under this contract:

Project Manager
Implementation Manager
Senior Computer Systems Analyst

Senior Computer Programmer
Contract Specialist
Quality Assurance Specialist
Computer Systems Analyst
Computer Programmer
ADP Technical Specialist
Data Communications Specialist
Instructor/Training Specialist

C385 (C) <u>System Maintenance/Updates</u>

(1) The Contractor shall provide full maintenance and support services for all software installed under this contract on fiscal year basis (October 1, XXXX – September 30, XXXX) for the maximum 120-month system life. If the base and/or last contract period is less than 12 months, maintenance for those periods will be prorated accordingly (see Section F911).

(2) Required maintenance and support services shall include, but not be limited to:

(a) Assistance in resolution of software problems, including abnormal system terminations and software responses that are not consistent with system documentation;

(b) Responses to informational and procedural requests from the COR, who is the single DOI maintenance contact point; and

(c) Providing software updates and upgrades.

(3) The Contractor shall maintain a log of user contacts for maintenance and support services and provide a monthly status report to the COR on open problems.

(4) The Contractor shall respond to COR reported software and documentation problem(s) within one (1) working hour from receipt of COR's report.

(a) The Contractor shall provide required software correction(s) in the form of a new Master Diskette(s) and any required documentation page changes to the Government in accordance with the delivery schedule set forth in Section F981.

(b) Software and documentation corrections shall be delivered to the WASC at no additional cost to the Government.

(c) In the event that the Contractor anticipates difficulty in meeting the required time frame for submitting a correction, the Contractor shall notify the Contracting Officer within 10 working days before the established due date. The Government may, at its option, authorize an alternative correction process. Accordingly, the Contractor shall submit for the Contracting Officer's written approval documentation which sets forth:

(i) An avoidance procedure to be undertaken within 24 working hours; and

(ii) Correction within 10 working days, or

(iii) Demonstration of why no problem exists.

(iv) Nothing in this paragraph C385 (C) (4) (c) shall waive the Government's rights nor the Contractor's responsibility under the requirements of Section H1338, Notice to the Government of Delays.

(d) Costs associated with identifying and correcting software problems and deficiencies attributable to the Contractor shall be borne by the Contractor.

(5) Hot-Line Technical Support

(a) As part of system maintenance, the Contractor shall perform Hot-Line technical support services in response to telephone inquiries concerning the software furnished under this contract. The COR and any designated representative will be the sole Government designated point-of-contact for requesting Hot-Line technical assistance from the Contractor. The Contractor shall respond to a Government Hot-Line call within one (1) working hour.

(b) This technical support shall be furnished via telephone and shall be available from 8:00 AM through 7:00 PM, Eastern Standard Time, Monday through Friday (excluding Federal holidays).

(6) Subscription Services

(a) The Contractor shall provide subscription services which shall include delivering updates to regulatory changes to prescriptions, provisions, and clauses in the FAR, FIRMR, and DIAR databases referred to in the Sections C383(A) (1) (k) (ii), C383 (A) (8) (a), etc.

(b) The Contractor shall deliver updated versions to these databases in the form of new diskette(s) and any required documentation page changes to the COR within 10 work days of the effective date of the changes.

C383 (D) TRAINING

Contractor provided IDEAS training shall assist Departmental and Bureau system users and technical staff in the transition and the use of the IDEAS system. The Contractor shall provide comprehensive and complete IDEAS training and support to enable software implementation to be as smooth and efficient as possible. Contractor support training will be for the purposes of training Government personnel to install the software on the specified equipment and to satisfactorily perform all software functions. Contractor personnel providing training to DOI employees in the operation of the software shall be fully knowledgeable of IDEAS and shall meet the qualification requirement specified in Section C385 (G) (11).

(1) METHOD OF TRAINING

(a) Training shall be conducted in a modular manner (i.e., based on functional area of the system) and be tailored for each audience. Each stage of training shall be customized to the particular "need-to-know" of the audience and shall include examples of DOI and Bureau uses. The training program shall be designed with future expansion and other uses in mind (e.g., refresher training, new employee training, etc.).

(b) Except as specified in paragraph (d) below, all training shall be presented by Contractor instructors through the lecture and workshop method. The COR and the Contractor shall maintain an ongoing evaluation of the effectiveness of the training. Students will evaluate each class. The Government may require the Contractor to make modifications to training where needed if the objectives of the training are not fully met.

(c) The Contractor shall develop and provide a training approach using a variety of media and methods to include both hands-on classroom and self-study (including Contractor developed video training). The Contractor shall submit recommended training media and methods to the COR for approval by the Government. (To be added to Section F981 at later date.)

(d) The Government reserves the right to select DOI and/or Bureau personnel to become instructors to other Bureau personnel to supplement Contractor conducted training. These instructors will possess knowledge of the system through completion of the installation and implementation course provided by the Contractor.

(2) <u>CONTRACTOR DEVELOPED TRAINING PLAN</u>

(a) The Contractor shall deliver, implement and maintain a training plan throughout the life of the contract. The Contractor's technical approach provided in its accepted proposal shall serve as the basis for the final training plan. The Contractor shall deliver the final Training Plan to the COR in accordance with the delivery schedule in Section F981.

(b) The training plan shall include training course designed to provide:

(i) <u>User managers</u> (e.g., supervisory procurement manager and requisitioner(s) with a basic understanding and overview of the system's capabilities and considerations for implementing the acquisition concepts employed by IDEAS;

(ii) <u>User technical support staff</u> (e.g., System Programmers, Analysts, and Administrators, etc.) with an understanding of the concepts, operation and uses of the computer and application software necessary to operate all acquisition concepts and activities performed by IDEAS. In addition, the training shall enable this group to develop, program and impellent any Bureau unique reports, and to access and use interfaces;

(iii) User staff (e.g., Contracting Officers, Contract Specialists, Contract Administrators, Purchasing Agents, Procurement Assistants, Procurement Analysts, Cost/Price Analysts, Procurement Clerks, and requisitioners) with an understanding of the concepts, operation and uses of the computer and application software necessary to operate all acquisition concepts and activities performed by the system; and

(iv) Users of acquisition information with an overview of the system's production and ad hoc reporting capabilities.

(v) Training of DOI instructors to become instructors to other DOI/Bureau personnel (see Sections C385 (D) (1) (d).

(c) Additionally, the following minimum training courses shall be required as a part of the Contractor's training plan:

(i) Acceptance Test Training. The purpose of this training is to provide the acceptance test team with an understanding of the concepts, operation and uses of the computer and application software necessary to test comprehensively all acquisition concepts and activities performed by the system.

(ii) Pilot Installation Training. The purpose of this training is to provide the WASC/PAM implementation team with and understanding of the concepts, operation and uses of both the computer and application software in order to maintain effective control over IDEAS use.

(iii) Formal Implementation Training. The purpose of this training is to provide the DOI and Bureau personnel with an understanding of the system operation, software maintenance, acquisition operation, and management reporting as pertinent to the DOI and Bureaus.

(iv) Management overview of the system for presentation to DOI and Bureau executive management personnel in Washington, DC, and Denver, CO.

(3) <u>TRAINING MATERIALS</u>

(a) The Contractor shall deliver training materials as described herein. Training materials delivered shall include all required course materials plus instructor guides.

(b) All training shall be supported by Contractor developed written materials (i.e., manuals, handbooks, text) designed to provide each trainee adequate materials needed to achieve course objectives and to use the system. In addition, visual training aids (i.e., slides, overhead transparencies, video tapes) shall be developed by the Contractor to enhance and facilitate training.

(c) Training materials and programs developed or acquired for instructional purposes shall be customized to address DOI and Bureau requirements. All training materials and programs shall be designed to support and enhance user acceptance of the system. Technical and user documentation provided with the operational system shall be integrated with training programs.

(d) Copies of training materials shall be submitted to the COR for review and approval in accordance with the schedule in Section F981 prior to the scheduled start of each training stage, (i.e., test, pilot implementation and formal implementation stages).

(e) All training material developed under this contract shall become the property of the Government; therefore, the Government is authorized to make copies for distribution to and use by the DOI (including all

Bureaus and Office and the clients of the WASC and DASC).

(4) SCHEDULE OF TRAINING

(a) Training shall not commence until receipt and approval by the COR of the Contractor developed Training Plan. Training shall proceed in accordance with Section F981.

(b) The schedule of training and number of personnel to be trained may be revised by the Government, provided the Government notifies the Contractor, in writing, of the changes at least 15 work days prior to commencement of the specific training.

(5) LOCATIONS OF TRAINING.

(a) Training will be conducted in Government furnished facilities in the metropolitan areas of Washington DC and Denver CO, and Menlo Park, CA the first year the system is implemented. For the second year of implementation, training will be conducted at Washington DC, Denver and two additional sites, dependent upon the Bureau implementation schedule. Training locations may be added through delivery orders as necessary to accommodate the diverse requisitioning, contracting and small purchasing activities with the DOI.

(b) Acceptance test training will be conducted at the WASC in Reston, Virginia.

(6) TRAINING EQUIPMENT

The Government will provide any reasonable equipment necessary for course presentation (e.g., desktop computers and peripherals, slide, overhead and/or video projector/monitors). The Contractor shall notify the COR of the need for such equipment at least 10 working day prior to course presentation.

C385(E) CONTRACT MANAGEMENT and PLANS

(1) QUALITY ASSURANCE

(a) The Contractor shall manage this contract in a manner consistent with customary software quality assurance principles and the methodology set forth in the Contractor's accepted proposal.

(b) The Contractor shall have a formal system of measurement which shall include metrics related to software attributes of quality, maintainability, testability, and software development productivity (including data collection). The Contractor shall meet all performance requirements related to quality, reliability, maintainability, and productivity developed to support these measures.

(c) The Contractor shall maintain an established system of quality assurance and system testing during installation of the IDEAS software and any supplementary or corrective software which is required during the acceptance period

(d) The Contractor shall develop, deliver, implement and maintain a Quality Assurance Plan throughout the life of this contract. The Contractor's Quality Assurance Plan provided in its accepted proposal shall serve as the basis for the final Quality Assurance Plan. The Contractor shall deliver the final Plan to the COR in accordance with the delivery schedule in Section F981. The Quality Assurance Plan shall consist of a detailed, systematic method of ensuring that material, data, supplies, and services fulfill technical requirements and that the software performs in accordance with the requirements of this contract.

(2) PROJECT MANAGEMENT

(a) The Contractor shall develop, deliver, implement and maintain a Project Management Plan throughout the life of this contract. The Contractor's Project Management Plan provided in its accepted proposal shall serve as the basis for the final Plan. The Contractor shall deliver the final Project Management Plan to the COR in accordance with the delivery schedule in Section F981. The Plan shall consist of the following:

(i) A high level overview of all aspects of the IDEAS project, including a summary of the schedule and work plan, technical approach to the project, and a description of the relationship among the plans specified below;

(ii) A project schedule depicting the work plan (work breakdown structure) of tasks and subtasks using an automated project management tool; and

(iii) A Gantt chart, critical path method analysis and diagram, and work breakdown structure accepted by the Government.

(b) The Contractor shall incorporate its staffing plan as accepted by the Government.

(3) CONFIGURATION MANAGEMENT

(a) Configuration Management is a method for the management of installation and maintenance of all software, data communications, and documentation delivered under this contract. For purposes of this contract, the Configuration Management process is defined as follows:

(i) Identifying and documenting the baseline functional and physical characteristics of a configuration item;

(ii) Controlling changes to those characteristics; and

(iii) Recording and reporting change processing and implementation status.

(b) The Contractor shall develop, deliver, implement and maintain a Configuration Management Plan throughout the life of this contract. The Contractor's Configuration Management Plan provided in its accepted proposal shall serve as the basis for the final Plan. The Contractor shall deliver the final Configuration Management Plan to the COR in accordance with the delivery schedule in Section F981. The Configuration Management Plan shall consist of the following:

ADDITIONAL INFORAMTION WILL BE PROVIDED AT TIME OF RFP RELEASE.

(4) IMPLEMENTATION MANAGEMENT

The Contractor shall develop, deliver, implement and maintain software Implementation Plan throughout the life of this contract. The Contractor's plan provided in its accepted proposal shall serve as the basis for the final Implementation Plan.

(5) TRANSISTION MANAGEMENT

The Contractor shall develop, deliver, implement and maintain a Transitional Plan throughout the life of this contract. The Contractor's Transitional Plan provided in its accepted proposal shall serve as the basis for the final Transition Plan. The Contractor shall deliver the final Transition Plan to the COR in accordance with the delivery schedule in Section F. Plans shall consist of the methodology for migrating from each Bureau's current environment to IDEAS.

C385 (F) CONTRACTOR PERFOMANCE REPORTS AND MEETINGS

(1) Throughout the life of the contract, the Contractor shall deliver, performance/status reports to the COR and participate in performance/status meetings in accordance with the delivery schedule set forth in Section F. The Contractor shall concurrently deliver a copy of the transmittal letter to the Contracting Officer at the address in Section G.

(a) Performance/status reports shall provide the status of actual Contractor performance in relation to anticipated performance/completion specified in the Contractor's proposal. Any and all differences between the Contractor's proposed performance schedule, and actual performance and completion dates shall be fully explained and documented in the report. However, nothing in this paragraph shall be construed to limit the rights of the Government under the excusable delays clause in Section I.

(b) The Contractor shall provide proposed corrective action measure to be taken when the Contractor anticipate a delay. In addition, the Contractor's performance reports shall furnish the status of any changes being made by the Contractor during the acceptance period.

(c) The Contractor shall hold performance/status meetings in accordance with the schedule set forth in Section F981. The purpose of the meetings is to discuss with the Contracting Officer, COR and other Government representative the status of software development, enhancement(s), installation, preparation of documentation, training courses, and acceptance and to discuss any outstanding or anticipated issues or problems.

(i) All meetings shall be held at the USGS National Center in Reston, VA, unless another location is mutually agreed to by all parties.

(ii) The COR will maintain an issue resolution log documenting all issues raised in the meeting. The Contractor shall provide written response(s) to issues, problems, or omissions identified by the COR or his designated representative(s) within ten (10) work days. The Contractor shall provide a copy of all such correspondence concurrently to the Contracting Officer.

C385 (G) <u>CONTRACTOR SUPPORT SERVICES POSITION DESCRIPTIONS</u>

In accordance with Section H, Key Personnel, the Contractor shall designate personnel listed therein for the duration of the contract.

<u>NOTE: Vendor comment is requested on the following representative labor categories and vendor recommended qualifications.</u>

(1) <u>PROJECT MANAGER</u>

The Project Manager shall serve as the contract manager, and shall be the Contractor's authorized point of contact with the Government Contracting Officer and the Contracting Officer's Representative (COR). The designated individual shall be responsible for coordinating all software and documentation, installation, training, and delivery schedules with the Government. The Project Manager shall be responsible for formulating and enforcing work standards, assigning schedules, and reviewing work discrepancies, and communicating policies, purposes, and goals of the organization to subordinates. The Project Mange's sole purpose is to insure effective contract performance; therefore he or she shall not serve in any other capacity under this contract.

(2) IMPLEMENTATION MANGER

The Implementation Manager shall be responsible for managing the installation of the software in preparation for inspection and acceptance testing. Interface with Government representatives is required to insure successful implementation testing, evaluation and certification of software installation. The Implementation Manager shall oversee installation of initial, supplemental and corrective software for all designated sites during the contract performance period.

(3) SENIOR COMPUTER SYSTEMS ANALYST

A Senior Computer Systems Analyst works independently or only under general direction on complex application problems involving all phases of systems analysis, providing solutions to the problems. He or she provides technical and administrative direction for personnel performing software development tasks, including the review of work products for correctness, adherence to the design concept and user standards, and for progress in accordance with schedules. The Senior Computer Systems Analyst coordinates with the Project Manager to ensure that the problems are solved and users are satisfied. He or she makes any necessary recommendations for approval of system installation. The Senior Computer Systems Analyst provides technical direction to lower level system analysts who provide assistance.

(4) SENIOR COMPUTER PROGRAMMER

(a) Under general supervision, the Senior Computer Programmer analyzes systems requirements and design specifications. He or she develops block diagrams and logic flow charts, and translates detailed design into computer programs. He or she tests, debugs, and refines the computer program to produce the required product. The Senior Computer Programmer prepares required documentation including both program and use level documentation. He/she enhances program(s) to reduce operating time or improve efficiency, and provides require technical direction to less experienced programmers to insure that deadlines are met.

(b) This employee should have experience conducting detailed analysis studies of program specifications and developing the appropriate flow charts, possessing the ability to develop programs for automatic data processing within time and resource constraints. Experience in Data Base Management Systems, desktop computers, telecommunications, statistical package, business package, and FORTRAN or other high level language is desirable.

(5) CONTRACT SPECIALIST

(a) This person serves and the Contractor's functional specialist on the Federal procurement process for purposes of software development and implementation. Through communication with programmers and other technical personnel, the Contract Specialist makes certain that the system is developed and implemented in a manner consistent with Federal and DOI procurement regulations, policies and practices. The incumbent DOES NOT serve as the Contractor's contract administrator under this contract.

(b) The employee shall possess extensive knowledge of Federal procurement regulations, policies and procedures including knowledge of the FAR, FRIMR, and OMB Circulars. National Contract Management Association certification is desirable. A bachelor's degree in Business Administration (or related field) is required. Knowledge of computer systems and procurement automation applications in a procurement office setting is highly desirable.

(6) COMPUTER SYSTEMS ANALYST

The Computer Systems Analyst works independently or only under general direction on problems that are moderately complex to analyze, plan, program, and operate. He or she develops plans for ADP systems from project inception to conclusion. Defines a problem, and develops system requirements and program specifications, from which programmers prepare detailed flow charts, programs, and tests. The employee coordinates closely with programmers to endure proper implementation of program and systems specifications. He or she analyzes the problem and determines what information is relevant to its resolution. The Computer Systems Analyst confers with functional components to determine application requirements and recommend system alternative solutions.

(7) COMPUTER PROGRAMMER

The Computer Programmer analyzes systems requirements and design specifications. The employee develops block diagrams and logic flow charts. He or she translates detailed design into computer programs. Computer Programmers test, debug, and refine the computer program to produce the required product. He or she prepares required documentation including both program and user level documentation. The Computer Programmer enhances program(s) to reduce operating time or improve efficiency.

(8) ADP TECHNICAL SPECIALIST

The ADP Technical Specialist provides highly technical and specialized guidance regarding solutions to complex information processing problems. He or she must be knowledgeable in state-of-the-art software/hardware solutions involving micro-, and mainframe computers, specialized software, data base management systems, data communications facilities, protocols, and interactive graphics. The ADP Technical Specialist performs analyses and studies, testing and acceptance phases. He or she reviews computer system in terms of machine capabilities, and man and machine time. The ADP Technical Specialist prepares reports and gives presentations to upper management. Contract tasks may require enhancements of teleprocessing utility/software programs.

(9) DATA COMMUNICATIONS SPECIALIST

The Data Communications Specialist participates in systems analyses and feasibility studies concerning data communications and communications networks. He or she plans, coordinates, and participates in design, acquisition, and implementation of data communications systems. Analyzes proposed and existing ADP applications, particularly in the area of federal procurement, in terms of data communications requirements and costs. Prepares studies and gives presentations on updated data communications concepts. Prepares, or participates in preparing, functional specifications for acquiring commercially-available data communications facilities. Consults with user management to assure proper problem identification and that the solution meets requirements.

(10) INSTRUCTOR/TRAINING SPECIALIST

Instructors/Training Specialists are to provide training to DOI employees in the operation of the software. Instructors shall be knowledgeable of the acquisition system delivered under this contract. Instructors shall possess the necessary skills to effectively communicate this knowledge to others. The audience to receive this instruction will be diverse requiring Instructors to be resourceful in this presentation. Instructors shall possess in-depth knowledge technical knowledge concerning IDEAS and shall be capable of addressing all pertinent questions, circumstances, and situations which will arise in the classroom. The Instructor shall be knowledgeable of the Department's and Bureaus' acquisition policies and procedures.

(11) QUALITY ASSURANCE

ADDITIONAL INFORMATION WILL BE PROVIDED AT THE TIME OF RFP RELEASE.

C386 DOCUMENTATION

Documentation is detailed information which describes the product software and is directed toward meeting the needs of (1) managers who will supervise procurement operations using IDEAS; (2) system analysts who may review Bureau maintenance or enhancement requests; (3) computer staff; and, (4) end users who process information, enter data or retrieve system information within the DOI environment.

(1) The Contractor shall deliver documentation to support system users and administrators. User documentation shall include comprehensive coverage of system usage and operation, and its hardware, software, and communications components. It shall include, but not necessarily be limited to, user manuals, operation manuals, job aids, and other documentation required to supplement training. Format, content, and required number of copies of the documentation shall be delivered to the COR for review and approval in accordance with the delivery schedule set forth in Section F981.

(2) The Contractor shall prepare and deliver documentation in accordance with the following requirements:

(a) Documentation shall be delivered in a format and size in accordance with the Contractor's standard commercial practice (i.e., 6 1/4 by 8 ½ inch, etc.). Documentation shall be clear and legible; insertion in a 3-ring loose leaf binder is preferred. The Contractor shall deliver one (1) each single-sided, camera-ready original 8 ½ inch by 11 inch (reproduction "master") as part of the documentation package.

(b) The Contractor shall deliver updated versions or change pages as changes occur to all documents prepared and delivered in the performance of this contract. These update will be delivered to the COR, at the address set forth in Section F980. The Contractor shall deliver changed documents in the same quantities as the original submittal within ten (10) work days after the changes have been approved by the COR.

(c) In addition to the reproduction master and updated versions and change pages identified in paragraphs (a) and (b) above, the Contractor shall prepare and deliver one (1) copy of all documents on compact disc (CD). Such media shall utilize Microsoft® Word. The Contractor shall deliver concurrently to the Contracting Officer, a copy of the letter transmitting the documentation to the COR.

(3) All documentation delivered shall be the latest version, updated to reflect software changes and all operational effects.

(4) All documentation delivered under this contract shall be detailed, well organized and presented, and shall contain features that ensure ease of sue as reference and training materials.

C387 <u>REQUIRED OPTIONS</u>

C387 (A) <u>SOFTWARE COPIES</u>

(1) The Government has unlimited rights to the software delivered. The Government may duplicate or order additional copies of the software from the Contractor [i.e., additional copies beyond the basic two (2) copies in Section C385 (B)]. These additional copies will be ordered through the issuance of delivery orders in accordance with Section H.

(2) All basic, functional and technical requirements set forth in this contract shall apply to subsequent acquisitions of later versions of this software. Those deliverables associated with each subsequent acquisition shall be subject to inspection and acceptance by the Government.

(3) Requirements associated with optional acquisitions include:

(a) The Contractor shall be responsible for up-to-date versions of all deliverables (including installation, documentation, and training) as defined within the scope of this contract.

(b) Software copies shall be compatible with essentially similar hardware environments (i.e., similar to the one associated with this contract). Some minor modifications may, however, be necessary in order to conform to specific installation conventions.

C387 (B) SUPPLEMENTAL TRAINING

(1) The Government may require the Contractor to provide additional training in support of subsequent DOI system implementations. Supplemental training is similar in scope to Contractor provided training set forth in Section C385 (D) but is expanded to include additional Bureau implementation sites.

(2) Course content and documentation requirements shall be similar in nature for all versions, but the Government may require the contractor to customize the training to meet specific needs of individual Bureaus. The number of trainees, formal implementation of training classes, and training sites will be determined by the Government at a later date. However, in no case will the class size exceed the maximum class size defined in the Contractor's final Training Plan.

C388 OPTIONAL FEATURES

C388 (A) ELECTRONIC SIGNATURE

The Government seeks a capability that would provide for electronic signature and its verification. Those authorized to sign/approve requisitions, solicitations, contract awards, and modifications could affect the equivalent of a signature electronically within the IDEAS system. The system would identify each authorized signatory in the system. A security component would preclude the use of each electronic signature by other than its authorized user.

(1) Requisition and pre-award requirements – This feature would be used by individuals authorized to approve requisitions and to certify that funds are available. The Contracting Officer could "sign" his synopses to the CBD and provide an electronic signature authorizing the issuance of solicitations.

(2) Award and Contract Administration – The Contracting Officer could use this feature to electronically execute contracts, modifications and delivery/task orders.

C388 (B) ELECTRONIC ARCHIVAL

The Government seeks the capability to store/archive documents (e.g., contracts and supporting file documents) in an electronic medium for the purpose of economical storage.

C388 (C) FEDERAL ASSISTANCE

Bureau procurement offices that award and administer both contracts and Federal assistance may elect as an optional feature to process both within the IDEAS system. Federal assistance, as defined by the Federal Grant and Cooperative Agreement Act, 41 United States Code 502, consists of grants and cooperative agreements whose primary purpose is to stimulate and support a public purpose such as research or education.

(1) Federal Assistance Requisition Generation/Tracking feature:

(a) The main objective of this feature is to permit procurement offices that handle both procurements and Federal assistance to receive and process requisitions and perform status tracking for both types of transactions under the same IDEAS system.

(b) The features shall provide the capability to allow the generation and processing of requisitions for Federal assistance in the same manner as requisitions for procurements.

(c) The feature shall permit status tracking and reporting capabilities (both ad hoc and standard) as identified in the requisitioning and contracts functional requirements. The feature shall provide the capability to differentiate between requisitions for assistance and requisitions for procurements. This feature shall allow for the generation of reports that combine information on both. An example would be generation of a "Buyer Workload Report" identifying active requisitions assigned to a buyer for both procurements and Federal assistance.

(2) Federal Assistance Award Data System (FAADS) Reporting feature:

(a) The system shall permit the generation and printing of the Federal assistance award document cover sheet in a format meeting, at a minimum, the informational requirements of DM Part 505, 2.10. The system shall incorporate applicable data from the requisition. At a minimum, the system shall allow Bureaus to customize these award cover sheets in order to meet Bureau-unique requirements.

(b) The system shall permit on-screen entry of data in order to generate and print a DI-1961 form (see Attachment J, Section J). Currently, hard copies of the DI-1961 are submitted to the DOI because the Department does not possess the capability for electronic receipt of FAADS data. In the event that this capability becomes operational in the future, the Government may request that the system accommodate the electronic transmission of FAADS data to the DOI.

C388 (D) ACQUISITION PLANNING

The system shall have the capability to generate, edit, consolidate, print and transmit for approval an Advance Procurement Plan (APP) document in accordance with Part 404 DM 2.3.

Sample 17

Environmental Study of Vetiver Grass

Type of Work: Environmental Services

Objective: To assess the potential of using vetiver grass (Vetiveria zizanoioides) to slow soil losses in tropical nations.

SOW Type: Functional

Comments:

- These work statements for studies were developed by the National Academy of Science for internal use.
- The work statements are more functional in nature, rather than performance-based, because they don't describe in detail how the studies and reports should be developed.
- The work statement descriptions are fairly succinct, but could use a little more detail and clarity in certain areas. For example, one description states that "The panel's task is to assess the state of knowledge, the promise, and the limitations of vetiver use." There is no further

explanation as to what is meant by "the state of knowledge" and "the promise." It may be beneficial to clarify these further.

- If these statements were used outside of the National Academy of Science, they would require an estimated level of effort.

Code Designator for Group Described: ______________

Office of International Affairs	______________
Major Unit	Committee
Board on Science and Technology for International Development	Panel on Vetiver
DIVISION, OFFICE, OR BOARD	SUB-UNIT

Staff Officer: ______________

STATEMENT OF TASK

(Make clear what is expected of the group described and by whom the project is sponsored. Limit to not more than this page.)

The U.S. Agency for International Development (USAID), the World Bank, and the USDA Soil Conservation Service have requested the Board on Science and Technology for International Development (BOSTID) to assess the potential of vetiver grass (Vetiveria zizanoioides) as a possible way to slow soil losses in tropical nations. Planted in lines along the contours of hill slopes, vetiver quickly forms narrow but very dense hedges. Its stiff foliage reportedly blocks the passage of soil and debris while slowing runoff, giving rainfall a better chance of soaking in. It has been reported that hedges of this persistent and supposedly non-weedy grass have restrained erodible soils for decades in Fiji, India, and some Caribbean nations.

The panel's task is to assess the state of knowledge, the promise, and limitations of vetiver use. The study will evaluate the ecological advantageous and potential risks in using this erosion control measure, which might eventually be applied across vast areas of the tropics. A panel of agricultural and environmental scientists will meet in Louisiana, where vetiver-grass hedges are said to be working well. There it will visit stands of this grass, review information gathered by staff, and draft its report.

This project is part of BOSTID's ongoing assessment of underexploited natural resources. The product will be an easily comprehensible text written for decision makers, researchers, agronomists, and the economic development community at large.

______________	______________
(Date of Statement)	(Date of Previous Statement) (if applicable)

Work Statement

(To be included in the "Organization and Members" Directory)

Committee Code ___________________
(Committee Membership Records
Office Use Only)

Code Designator for Group Described: _________________

Office of International Affairs	______________________________
Major Unit	Committee
Board on Science and Technology for International Development DIVISION, OFFICE, OR BOARD	Panel on Vetiver SUB-UNIT
Staff Officer:	______________________________

WORK STATEMENT

(Make clear what is expected of the group described – not to exceed 10 lines)

The panel's task is to assess the state of knowledge, the promise, and the limitations of vetiver use. The study will evaluate the ecological advantages and potential risks in using this erosion control measure, which might eventually be applied across vast areas of the tropics. A panel of agricultural and environmental scientists will meet in Louisiana, where vetiver-grass hedges are said to be working well. There it will visit stands of this grass, review information gathered by staff, and draft its report.

Include in "O&M"? ____ Yes X No

Index Selection ____________________________________ (Limited to 45 characters per selection)

Index Selection ____________________________________

______________________________	______________________________
(Date of Statement)	(Date of Previous Statement) (if applicable)

Approved by:

______________________________ ______________________________

Executive Director, Major Unit

Code Designator for Group Described: ______________

Office of International Affairs	______________
Major Unit	Committee
Board on Science and Technology for International Development	Panel on Neem
DIVISION, OFFICE, OR BOARD	SUB-UNIT

Staff Officer: ______________

TASK STATEMENT

(Make clear what is expected of the group described and by whom the project is sponsored. Limit to not more than this page.)

The neem tree offers great potential for agricultural, industrial, and commercial exploitation, and is potentially one of the most valuable of all arid-zone trees. It shows promise for pest control, reforestation, and improving human health. Safe and effective pesticides can be produced from seeds at the village level with simple technology. The leaves can be used as mulch and as fodder, and the seed pulp as fertilizer. In addition, a highly biologically active fraction has been isolated that shows strong antiviral and antimicrobial activity as well as blood-sugar lowering and perhaps contraceptive properties. Neem can grow in arid and nutrient-deficient soils and is a fast-growing source of fuel-wood.

Research teams all over the world are excited over the properties of this once obscure plant. A BOSTID panel will produce an illustrated report laying out the promise and potential problems associated with the broader use of this remarkable resource. This study is funded by the Office of the Science Advisor of the Agency for International Development.

Staff and program costs for this study are provided by the U.S. Agency for International Development, Grant No. DAN-5538-G-SS-1023-00.

______________	______________
(Date of Statement)	(Date of Previous Statement) (if applicable)

WORK STATEMENT

(To be included in the "Organization and Member" Directory)

Committee Code ___________________
(Committee Membership Records Office Use Only)

Office of International Affairs Major Unit	______________________ Committee
Board on Science and Technology for International Development DIVISION, OFFICE, OR BOARD	Review Panel on Neem SUB-UNIT
Staff Officer:	______________________

WORK STATEMENT

(Make clear what is expected of the group described – not to exceed 10 lines)

The neem tree (Azadirachta indica) shows promise for agricultural, industrial, and commercial exploitation, and is potentially one of the most valuable of all arid-zone trees. It shows promise for pest control, reforestation, and improving human health. Safe and effective pesticides can be produced from seeds at the village level with simple technology. A BOSTID panel will produce an illustrated report laying out the promise and potential problems associated with the broader use of the neem tree (Azadirachta indica). This study is funded by the Office of the Science Advisor of the Agency for International Development. The result will be a report available in January XXXX.

Include in "O&M"? ____ Yes X No

Index Selection ______________________________ (Limited to 45 characters per selection)

Index Selection ______________________________

______________________ (Date of Statement)	______________________ (Date of Previous Statement) (if applicable)

Approved by:

______________________ Executive Director, Major Unit	______________________

Sample 18

Renovation of a Fire Station

Type of Work:	Design and Construction Services
Objective:	To partially demolish an existing fire station and renovate the administrative and sleeping areas on the current site. Install a new wash rack for the building and a new fire sprinkler system throughout the facility. Evaluate, upgrade, or replace the existing electrical and mechanical systems. Route the existing apparatus floor drains to an existing oil water separator and install a standing seam metal roof over the renovated facility.
SOW Type:	Design
Comments:	▶ Good description of the general scope of services. ▶ Detailed description of the design policy and criteria, particularly the applicable standards that the renovation must follow and adhere to. ▶ Detailed description of the architect-engineer services.

- Clear identification of milestones to be accomplished through the final design submittal.
- The term "etc." is used multiple times throughout the document. The use of this term creates uncertainty about and hedges the requirements.

STATEMENT OF WORK
FOR
ADAL Fire Station
HOMESTEAD ARS FL

1.0 STATEMENT OF WORK:

1.1 GENERAL DESCRIPTION: The Architect-Engineer (A-E) shall furnish all services, materials, supplies, equipment, investigations, studies, project supervision, and travel as required in connection with this Statement of Work (SOW), and all furnished and referenced design instructions.

1.1.1 ORGANIZATION: This SOW is organized as follows:

Paragraph	Topic
1.0	Statement of Work
2.0	Design Policy and Criteria
3.0	Cost and Scope Limitations
4.0	Drawing and Specification Standards
5.0	Contract Schedule
6.0	Architect-Engineer Services
7.0	Initiation of Work
8.0	Government Review
9.0	Special Conditions
10.0	Submittals

1.1.2 Project Specifics:

INSTALLATION	PROJECT NO.	PROJECT DESCRIPTION	SCOPE	CONST COST LIMITATION (CCL)
Homestead ARS	KYJM999022	ADAL Fire Station	10,000 SF Alter 6,500 SF Add	$2,400,000

1.2 PROJECT CONSTRUCTION REQUIREMENTS: The existing Fire Station will be partially demolished as part of this project and the administrative and sleeping areas will be renovated on its current site. One new apparatus stall to include a wash rack will be added to the northeast end of the building. A new addition will be constructed in the back courtyard of the facility so that administrative and living areas can be rearranged and sized to meet current Air Force standards. A new fire sprinkler system will be installed throughout the facility. Existing electrical and mechanical systems must be evaluated and upgraded or replaced as needed. Existing apparatus floor drains must be routed to an existing oil/water separator. Standing seam metal roof will be installed to cover the renovated facility.

1.3 GENERAL SCOPE OF SERVICES:

1.3.1 INTENT: It is the Government's intent to advertise in accordance with Federal Acquisition Regulations (FAR) and Air Force Supplements to the FAR (AFFAR) for a contractor to construct the project to be designed under this Statement of Work. In order for the Government to take advantage of the latest state-of-the-art developments in construction, it is our intent that the construction documents utilize Construction Specifications Institute (CSI) type specification system format in sixteen divisions recognized as standard in the construction industry. This SOW identifies the services required to prepare the above mentioned construction documents. The required services of this contract are more specifically described below.

1.3.2 *Special emphasis is being placed on environmentally sensitive materials, recycling, and sustainable design and construction principles in this project. This emphasis is added to comply with various executive directives meant to help alleviate the drain of natural resources and reduce the negative impact to the environment some aspects of the construction industry have caused. This emphasis will also provide valuable experience with environmentally responsible design and construction which will be shared with other Air Force and Department of Defense organizations.*

1.3.3 The work shall include a Comprehensive Interior Design (CID) package to include furnishings, structural finishes, art work and other related items, along with the necessary sample submittals, budgets, and design analysis. Submittals shall be as described in Interior Design Presentation Format, Nov 96.

1.3.4 In order to accomplish this intent, the A-E shall provide 100% drawings and specifications, complete cost estimate and supporting design analysis based on the requirements set forth in this scope of work. It is intended this level of detail will allow the construction contract bidder to submit a complete bid, covering the complete scope of work. Any floor plans and elevations provided by the Government to the A-E are intended as guidance and not to be interpreted as the only solution.

2.0 DESIGN POLICY AND CRITERIA:

2.1 DESIGN POLICY: The Air Force will furnish basic design criteria to the A-E from which he can develop and produce the construction documents and CID package as described below. Suggestions that will improve the operational functions, enhance appearance, and prove to be more economical and advantageous shall be made at the appropriate time.

2.2 DESIGN INSTRUCTIONS: The design shall incorporate the requirements as discussed in the pre-proposal and site visit conferences, the Design Charrette, and requirements of the publications and Government Furnished Information listed below. Upon request from the Contracting Officer, all Government-Furnished materials shall be returned to HQ AFCEE within 30 days.

2.3 PROJECT CRITERIA: The project design shall conform to the following criteria:

2.3.1 APPLICABLE STANDARDS:

a. National Electric Code, NFPA No. 70.

b. National Electric Safety Code (ANSI C2).

c. Uniform Building Code (ICBO).

d. Uniform Plumbing Code (ICBO).

e. Uniform Mechanical Code (ICBO).

f. Mechanical Systems - ASHRAE and SMACNA Standards.

g. National Fire Protection Association (NFPA 101) Life Safety Code.

h. ANSI B31.8 (1968) and B31.8b (1969) Gas Transmission and Distribution Piping Systems.

i. Air Force Fire Station Design Guide

j. Air Force Environmentally Responsible Facilities Guide

k. “A Guide to Buying Recycled, The Air Force Affirmative Procurement Guide”

l. DoD Directive 6050.9 Ozone Depleting Chemicals.

m. ETL 94-4, Energy Usage Criteria for Facilities in the Military

Construction Program (MCP)

n. Uniform Federal Accessibility Standards (USAF)

o. Americans with Disability Act Accessibility Guidelines (ADAAG)

p. FAR 52.236-22 DESIGN WITHIN FUNDING LIMITATION (APR 1984)

q. FAR 52.236-23 RESPONSIBILITY OF THE ARCHITECT-ENGINEER CONTRACTOR (APR 1984)

r. FAR 52.236-25 REQUIREMENTS FOR REGISTRATION OF DESIGNERS (APR 1984)

s. FAR 52.236-24 WORK OVERSIGHT IN ARCHITECT-ENGINEER CONTRACTS (APR 1984)

t. South Florida Building Code, 1994 (as supplemented)

2.3.2 GOVERNMENT FURNISHED INFORMATION AND MATERIALS: The following information and materials will be furnished to the A-E by the government for the execution of the project work:

a. Project Location Plan.

b. Utility Maps of the project site (electrical, sewer, water, and gas) as available for use as reference.

c. Conceptual Design Drawings.

d. Standard reproducible Mylar cover sheet and second sheet with preprinted title block.

e. DD Form 1391.

f. Project Management Plan (PMP).

g. Base Guidelines.

h. Environmental Assessment.

i. Statement of Sustainability Goals.

3.0 COST AND SCOPE LIMITATIONS:

3.1 GENERAL: The intent of this A-E Services Contract is to design completely functional and operational facilities within the identified scope and cost limitations. The Government will provide all existing construction drawings and specifications available for the existing facility. ***The A-E shall develop drawings and specifications in accordance with the emphasis on environmentally sensitive materials, recycling, and sustainable design and construction principles cited in paragraph 1.3.2. The A-E shall incorporate these principles into the specifications at the 50% submittal and clearly indicate these inclusions using bold-italicized lettering. A narrative shall also be provided in the design analysis which clearly identifies these areas of the specifications. This narrative shall be supported with manufacturer's catalogue sheets as indicated in paragraph 6.9.3.*** The A-E will consider all design options and criteria reductions that may be necessary in those instances where possible cost overruns may be experienced. This information will be included in the design analysis.

3.2 CONSTRUCTION COST ESTIMATES:

3.2.1 The construction cost limitation is listed in paragraph. 1.1.2, above. The construction cost includes construction, demolition and renovation of the building and necessary supporting facilities, to include contractor lay down areas, roads, drives, landscaping, recreation areas, parking, and all utilities. The A-E is responsible for a design which provides completely functional and operational facilities within the construction cost limitation and scope constraints for this project. If at any time the Architect-Engineer determines that the estimated construction cost or scope of the project exceeds, or is likely to exceed, the construction contract limitation or scope set forth in this Statement of Work, the Architect-Engineer shall report this fact in writing to the Contracting Officer and submit a cost estimate and recommendations for reducing the project construction cost and/or scope to within established limits. Any proposed deviation from criteria must be approved prior to implementation. The cost of the CID is not included in the construction cost limitations; however, the required estimates are to be included in the design of this facility.

3.2.2 Construction Cost Estimates shall be furnished with each design submittal and just prior to issuance of the IFB and supporting documents, if the final submittal estimate is older than six (6) months. The estimate shall include a summary sheet and back-up sheets as follows:

a. SUMMARY SHEET

Authorized Scope.
Designed Scope.
Authorized Construction Cost $________
Designed Construction Cost $________
Percentage Over/Under Auth. Cost ____
Building (to 5' line) $________
Site Work $________
Demolition $________
Contractor's Design Costs $________
Overhead and Profit $________
TOTAL ESTIMATED CONSTRUCTION CONTRACT COST $________

b. BACKUP SHEETS

(1) Primary item cost breakdown sheets shall be provided to serve as backup to the submitted estimate. This breakdown shall show as many construction item quantities and costs as possible at each stage of design. Items such as foundations and footings may be included by lineal feet, exterior walls by square footage, plumbing by fixture, etc. When aggregate items such as these are used, insure a description is included in the cost. Contractor labor, mark-up, taxes, overhead and profit may be included in the unit prices if a general note is added indicating percentage amounts that are included.

(2) Support items include all work outside the five foot line of the building and must be estimated on a quantity contract price. Basic lump sum costing is not acceptable when quantities can be readily calculated.

(3) ***If unusual design features or conditions are included in the project which materially affect the cost, attach a separate sheet to the backup material with sufficient explanation and cost information to sup-***

port them. This is a very important part of the analysis for including recycled content items from the EPA Comprehensive Procurement Guideline (CPG) into the project design and specifications.

3.3 CONFIDENTIALITY: Quantity surveys and cost estimates shall remain the sole property of the Government, and shall not be made available to others for any purpose. The sale of takeoffs of quantities and costs to prospective bidders or estimators is prohibited. The A-E shall be aware of and take such precautionary measure as necessary to maintain the confidential nature of all estimates prepared under this contract. Subcontracting of estimating services is governed by the General Provisions of this contract.

4.0 DRAWING AND SPECIFICATION STANDARDS:

4.1 CONTRACT DRAWINGS: Drawings shall be prepared on AutoCAD release 14.0 or compatible format. All drawings will utilize the Tri-Service Spatial Data Standards (TSSDS) Version 1.8, for compliance with the installation standards. Four copies of all drawing files shall be provided on CD-ROM with the 100% final submittal. (One set shall be delivered to 482 SPTG/CES and three sets shall be delivered to HQ AFCEE, as per Section 4.3.) All contract drawings shall be well prepared, complete, and accomplished in accordance with the best professional practice to show clearly and concisely the type and extent of work to be performed. The drawings shall be drawn to appropriate scales and dimensioned completely and accurately. Extensive explanatory notes on the drawings should be held to a minimum or placed in the specifications. Dimensions shall be shown in standard metric units with equivalent English units in parentheses. Standard building material indications and symbols for architectural items and for mechanical and electrical equipment shall be used to the greatest extent possible. Drawings shall be delivered in hard copy, standard black line quality paper, at review stages in the number listed in paragraph 10.0, SUBMITTALS. All sets of review drawings and corrected final drawings for HQ AFRC and HQ AFCEE shall be one-half size. The remaining sets of review drawings and corrected final drawings shall be full size. Corrected final drawing submittal shall include one set of full size drawings on 5 mil, reproducible/erasable Mylar sheets delivered to 482 SPTG/CES. The Mylar sheets shall be dated using the 100% final submission date. The Mylar drawing requirements are in addition to the CAD files described above and the number of copies listed in paragraph 10.0, SUBMITTALS. Full size drawings shall be approximately 28" X 42" with the Headquarters Air Force Reserve Command title block.

4.2 SPECIFICATIONS: Specifications shall be delivered in hard copy, bound on 8-1/2" x 11" paper (minimum 20% recovered content, 20% post consumer content), double sided copied at the various stages in the number listed in paragraph 10.0, SUBMITTALS. In addition to the final submittal sets, one set of original, unbound final specifications in hard copy shall be delivered to 482 SPTG/CES. The unbound final specifications shall be single sided copied and completely free of the A-E's names, address, and phone number. The cover sheet for this specification shall be dated using the 100% final submission date. Four copies of specification files on CD-ROM shall also be provided with the 100% final submittal. (One set shall be delivered to 482 SPTG/CES and three sets shall be delivered to HQ AFCEE, as per Section 4.3.) Refer to 482 SPTG/CES standards for additional guidance for written portions of the construction documents. Specifications, including all technical and special conditions, shall be based on CSI format and shall be prepared by the A-E to meet government standards for competitive bidding for all work. An index and marked-up specifications may be submitted with the Preliminary Submittal. The 100% final specifications shall be descriptive enough to permit full and free competition among bidders. References will be made to Federal Specifications, ASTM, ANSI, and other trade standards when applicable to establish a uniform standard. All such references must be dated with the latest revisions annotated. All standards and specifications used in the text will be listed in the specification section's opening reference paragraph. In general, the A-E should avoid the use of "proprietary type" specs. When necessary to use a manufacturer's name to describe a type of product, at least three manufacturers shall be named, if possible, and shall include the words "or approved equal." All materials, components, and equipment shall be specified for approval by the Contracting

Officer. All items designated for submittal and test shall be sufficiently described to provide the government a basis for review and approval or disapproval. "Contracting Officer" shall be used in the specs rather than references to "owner" and "Architect Engineer." The specific recycled-content percentage requirements shall be clearly stated in each specification section that calls out the use of an EPA CPG item.

4.3 MISCELLANEOUS SUBMITTAL DATA: Final submittals shall be provided in hard copies, and CD-ROM copies. The CD-ROM copies will be sent to AFCEE and to Homestead ARS. All other recipients will receive hard copies. The drawings on the CD-ROM will be in the AutoCad 14 (.dwg) format, as well as, raster image output (.cal) for electronic bid solicitation. An index file of drawings shall be created using SourceView software (.svd). All specifications shall be in the Microsoft Word (.doc) format, as well as, the Adobe Acrobat Exchange (.pdf) format. Provide CD-ROMs which will facilitate 1) uploading the raster and .pdf files to the Internet for electronic bid solicitation, 2) issuing a stand-alone CD-ROM organizing the drawings, specifications, contract documents, amendments, and other documents as required for bidding through Contract Viewer software, and 3) archiving all files, documents and products associated with the project on a single CD-ROM.

5.0 CONTRACT SCHEDULE:

5.1 DELIVERY SCHEDULE: The work, design, other related data and services required in accordance with the "Basic" contract and any "Option" indicated below shall be accomplished to produce the project documents within the limitation of cost and project scope stated above. The schedule for delivery of documents to the Contracting Officer is in calendar days. Calendar days for each requirement extends from the date of the Notice to Proceed (NTP) or approval of the previous milestone, except as otherwise noted. See paragraph 10.0, SUBMITTALS, for submittal quantities. Percentages below apply to the construction document package.

ITEM	MILESTONE	BASIC CONTRACT	SUBMITTAL DELIVERY SCHEDULE	REVIEW PERIOD	CONFERENCE LOCATION
1.	Design Charrette (10%) Development of approved preliminary floor plans, elevations, site work, cost estimate.	X	*10-14* Days After Notice to Proceed	N/A	HOMESTEAD ARS
2.	Charrette Report Submittal (50%) Compilation of charrette results.	X	*7* Days After Completion of Charrette	14 Days	Not Required
3.	Preliminary Design Submittal (50%) Further development of floor plans, elevations, site work, specifications, cost estimate, design analysis.	X	*40* Days After Completion of Charrette Report Review	21 Days	HOMESTEAD ARS
4.	Final Unchecked Design Submittal (90%) Finalized floor plans, elevations, site work, specifications, cost estimate, design analysis.	X	*35* Days After 50% Submittal Review Conference	21 Days	HOMESTEAD ARS
5.	Corrected Final Design Submittal (100%) Floor plans, elevations, site work, specifications, cost estimate, and design analysis, all corrected per all review comments.	X	*14* Days After 90% Submittal Review Conference	N/A	Not Required

6.0 ARCHITECT-ENGINEER SERVICES:

6.1 SITE DESIGN DATA: The A-E shall perform field reconnaissance, surveys, and site investigations, including travel, and work required to obtain engineering information and design data for the accomplishment of the contract documents of the project in accordance with requirements of this Statement of Work (SOW).

6.2 FIELD MEASUREMENTS: The A-E shall be required to make his own field investigations to verify dimensions and other information shown on government furnished reference drawings.

6.3 SCHEDULES / SAMPLES: Interior and exterior finish and color schedules, door, window, and light fixture schedules shall be included. Sample material chips for each finish shall be included in the design analysis, organized and displayed on a sample board, as well as manufacturer's catalogue sheets for windows, doors, and light fixtures. CID submittals shall be as described in Interior Design Presentation Format, Nov 96. *Additionally samples of specific items, whether classified as finishes or not, selected for recycled content shall be provided on a similar sample board.*

6.4 TOPOGRAPHIC SURVEY, DRAINAGE STUDY, SUBSURFACE INVESTIGATION: The A-E shall produce a topographic survey of the existing construction site. This survey will be included in the construction contract documents. The survey will be used by the A-E to study the site drainage study and produce grading plans to include in the contract documents. The end product will be a grading plan which creates a positive drainage for the new construction site. The A-E will also provide an analysis of the subsurface conditions that exist on the site and provide soil boring logs and a narrative describing the existing conditions and recommending design solutions for the foundations and slabs of the new construction. The logs and narrative shall be included in construction contract documents.

6.5 PROVISIONS FOR ACCESSIBILITY: New construction and alterations to existing facilities are to be designed and constructed to meet the requirements of the Americans with Disabilities Act Architectural Guidelines (ADAAG), and the Uniform Accessibility Standards (UFAS), with the most stringent standards applied in the event of conflicts.

6.6 IRRIGATION, LANDSCAPING, RECREATION AREA, AND GRADING PLANS: Recreation area, grading, and landscape plans, including associated irrigation systems, shall be developed by registered professionals. These plans shall be based upon 482 SPTG/CES standards and other criteria documents indicated above, as appropriate. The "landscaping" design will consist of complete design and layouts with plant selections based on orientation and configuration.

6.7 TASK 1, DESIGN CHARRETTE: The Government will provide all available existing construction drawings and specifications for the existing fire station facility. The A-E shall conduct a Design Charrette at Homestead ARS with the purpose of developing a preliminary floor plan, elevations, site and utility layout, and cost estimates for approval by the various Government user groups. The Charrette shall be attended by various disciplines of the A-E firm to identify and address all areas involved in the project. Cost estimating capabilities must also provide a clear status of cost control throughout the Charrette. The Charrette is anticipated to last no more than one week and will require daily progress presentations to the Base leadership, HQ AFRC, and HQ AFCEE personnel as well as a final presentation. The A-E shall submit a Design Charrette Report within 7 calendar days of completing the charrette. The report shall consist of a compilation of the products produced during the charrette as well as all applicable supporting narrative material, minutes of meetings, and documentation of the sustainable development goals and objectives established for the project.

6.7.1 ASBESTOS TESTING: The A-E shall perform all necessary testing to identify asbestos abatement needed during the construction contract. The A-E shall include the testing of 10 samples of the project facility under this Task.

6.7.2 LEAD BASED PAINT TESTING: The A-E shall perform all necessary testing to identify lead based paint abatement needed during the construction contract. The A-E shall include the testing of 20 samples of the project facility under this Task.

6.9 TASK 2, PRELIMINARY DESIGN SUBMITTAL (50%): Architect-Engineer shall submit preliminary construction contract documents. This submittal shall be reviewed by the Government and review comments provided to the A-E.

6.9.1 FORMAT: The A-E will be responsible for the development of input for Section B, Bid Schedule. The A-E shall provide a proposed project design/construction time schedule and a complete listing of material and equipment submittals required to be approved by the Government prior to construction. The minimum content and format of the A-E's products is as follows:

PART 1. CONTRACT

a. Section B-Bid Schedule

b. Submittal Listing

PART 2. DATA AND CRITERIA

a. Project Specifications

PART 3. DRAWINGS

a. List of Drawings, Related Data, Legends & Abbreviations

b. Existing Conditions Topographic Survey

c. Existing and New Site & Utilities Drawings, Including Preliminary Dimensions

d. New Grading Plans

e. New Landscaping Plans

f. Demolition Plans

g. Floor Plans, Including Finish, Color, Window, and Door Schedules

h. Exterior Elevations & Interior Elevations (as needed)

i. Cross-Sections Through Building

j. Wall Sections

k. Roof Plan

l. Structural Plans (Foundation & Framing)

m. Mechanical & Plumbing Floor Plans

n. Electrical Plans (Power & Lighting)

6.9.2 ENERGY AND ENVIRONMENTALLY CONSCIOUS DESIGN: Energy design shall comply with energy efficiency requirements listed in ETL 94-4. ***Environmentally responsible design considerations are discussed in the Air Force Environmentally Responsible Facilities Guide. To the maximum extent possible and practicable, the design shall incorporate recycled content materials as mandated by EPA's Comprehensive Procurement Guide (CPG) and ETL 94-7. Non-availability of materials or technologies, lack of competition, failure to meet performance standards, and unreasonable price are all valid reasons for exclusion of CPG items. Note that in addition to fulfilling the CPG requirements, designers should explore other construction alternatives in the Environmentally Responsible Facilities Guide, as well as other aspects of "green" design and construction currently practiced in industry yet not mandated by EPA or the Air Force. The ultimate goal is to increase sustainability in construction, yet common sense must be applied to decisions made in this area.***

6.9.3 DESIGN ANALYSIS: The A-E shall develop a Design Analysis to document the development of the design by discipline. The Design Analysis shall also contain results of required testing and studies, cost estimates, construction schedule, and energy efficiency compliance calculations. *Additionally specific items selected for recycled content from the EPA Comprehensive Procurement Guideline shall be highlighted. In addition to desired design features and qualities, obtain manufacturer's information describing percentage of recycled content, as well as the material recycled. These submittals, together with specific cost data analysis will be used to document compliance with the project's environmentally responsible design goals.*

6.10 TASK 3, DESIGN COMPLETION & BIDDING

6.10.1 FINAL DESIGN SUBMITTAL (90%): The final design submittal will be a development of the preliminary design to a 100% design package level, including integration of the Government review comments resulting from previous reviews along with a refined cost estimate and anticipated construction schedule. The specifications shall include the various construction options identified for inclusion by the Government during the course of the design. These construction options shall identify material upgrades for certain items within the project. The upgrades may be purchased under the construction project should funds be available. This submittal shall be reviewed by the Government and review comments provided to the A-E.

6.10.2 CORRECTED FINAL DESIGN SUBMITTAL (100%): The completed (100%) design will include the final (90%) design documents with all previous review comments incorporated.

6.10.3 ARCHITECTURAL RENDERING: The A-E shall provide and deliver a professionally-framed, color rendering of the project. The color rendering will be 18" x 24" minimum overall. A brief description or work sketch shall be provided in advance describing the type of view to be taken, i.e., birds-eye view, eye-level view, etc. In addition to the original rendering, the AE will provide two full-size (18" x 24"minimum) color photographic prints. These are all to be provided with the submission of the corrected final design documents.

6.10.4 ADDITIONAL MEETINGS AND STUDIES: The A-E shall be required to attend a design process analysis meeting at Homestead ARS for the purpose of general discussions of the design relative to sustainability. This additional meeting is not associated with any of the project development stages or review conferences described above, and shall last approximately eight hours. Two individuals are anticipated for the meeting. ***The purpose of the design process analysis meeting is to assess the Government's efforts to implement the sustainable design and construction requirements into the project and review any lessons learned from the overall effort. The meeting will be conducted as a round table discussion session. The A-E will provide a written analysis of the environmental goals of this project and the design's success in meeting these goals. The A-E shall also provide a summary of tools examined and processes used to research and implement these goals and their results. Cost comparisons and estimates of material weights and volumes shall be provided as back-up information. Additionally the A-E shall provide a summary of the actual man-hours expended by the***

A-E Design Team to implement these requirements. The AE will also be responsible for compiling all of this information into a sustainable development case study for the project that can be posted on the AFCEE Sustainable Development web site.

6.10.5 RESPONSIBILITIES DURING BID PERIOD: The A-E shall be responsible for answering Bidders questions to the construction documents and Requests for Information during the bidding period. This may take the form of narratives, drawings, specifications, and/or sketches. The A-E will also be required to attend a Pre-Construction Conference at Homestead ARS with the project team and the selected construction contractor, for the purpose of reviewing the sustainable goals and objectives applicable during construction.

7.0 INITIATION OF WORK: The A-E may not proceed or initiate any work or any succeeding Task, as defined in this SOW, prior to receipt of original notice to proceed, receipt of approval of the preceding Task, or receipt of a contract modification initiating an option. Any work done without being directed to do so by the Contracting Officer shall be at the A-E's own risk.

8.0 GOVERNMENT REVIEW: The Contracting Officer or his authorized representative may furnish the Architect-Engineer review comments on the data submitted. The Government's review is intended to be limited to functional aspects, with limited technical review of a general cursory nature only. Any review by the Government of technical items shall not be construed to relieve the A-E of responsibility for technically correct and complete documents in compliance with applicable codes, industry standards, and the intent of this SOW. Review comments for compliance with Federal Acquisition Regulations (FAR) will also be provided by the Contracting Officer. The Architect-Engineer shall comply with the review comments in the development of data for the next submittal. If any review comment requires clarification and/or amplification to assure compliance, the Architect-Engineer shall notify the Contracting Officer or his authorized representative in writing. After each review, the A-E will be furnished one set of comments to be annotated and returned to the Government. Comments annotated by the A-E with a "D" - do not concur, "E" - exception, or "X" - delete, shall have an explanatory note added to justify the noncompliance with the comment. The A-E shall furnish these annotated comments to the Government no later than 7 calendar days after receiving the comments. Review periods listed under paragraph 5.0 are in calendar days and are the minimum time required and may be extended. Review conferences shall be scheduled after receipt of submittals.

9.0 SPECIAL CONDITIONS:

9.1 PERFORMANCE OF WORK:

9.1.1 MANPOWER: The A-E shall furnish sufficient technical, supervisory, and administrative personnel at all times to ensure prosecution of the work in accordance with the delivery schedule.

9.1.2 QUALITY CONTROL: Professional level skills and management practices are required in the performance of this contract. Accordingly, the A-E shall establish an effective quality control program to assure that the end product meets professional standards and complies with the contract requirements.

9.2 PROJECT MANAGERS:

9.2.1 A-E PROJECT MANAGERS: The A-E shall appoint a project manager to serve as the single point-of-contact and liaison between the A-E and the Contracting Offices or his representative for all work under the contract. Upon receipt of the NTP, the A-E shall immediately furnish for approval, the name of the designated individual to the Contracting Officer, in writing. The project manager will be responsible for the complete coordination of all work developed under the contract. All work will be accomplished with adequate internal controls and review procedures which will eliminate conflicts, errors, and omissions, and ensure the technical accuracy if all designs, drawings, and specifications.

9.2.2 GOVERNMENT PROJECT MANAGERS: The Government Technical Representative for this project is The Air Force Center For Environmental Excellence/DC, 8004 Arnold Drive, Brooks Air Force Base, Texas 78235-5361. The Government Functional Representative for this contract is 482nd Civil Engineering Squadron/CEC, 29050 Coral Sea Boulevard, Box 68, Homestead

ARS, Florida 33039-1299.

9.2.3 QUESTIONS: Any questions regarding the work under this contract should be directed in writing by the designated A-E Project Manager to the Contracting Officer.

9.3 CONFERENCES AND CONFIRMATION NOTICES:

9.3.1 A-E PARTICIPATION: The A-E or his representative(s) will be required to attend and participate in all design review conferences pertinent to the work under the basic contract or any options incorporated into the contract.

9.3.2 CONFIRMATION NOTICES: The A-E shall provide a record of all conferences, site visits, meetings, discussions, verbal directions, telephone conversations, etc., participated in by the A-E or his representatives on matters relative to the contract and the work. These records, entitled "CONFIRMATION NOTICES," shall be numbered sequentially and shall fully identify participating personnel, date and time of day, subject discussed, and any conclusions reached. The A-E shall forward to the Contracting Officer or his authorized representative, each agency listed in paragraph 10.0, and each organization represented at the particular event, a clearly legible copy of each confirmation notice within 7 calendar days. Record of Review Conferences may reference "attached annotated review comments."

9.4 INSPECTIONS: The A-E shall visit and inspect/investigate the site as necessary and required during preparation and accomplishments of the elements of this Statement of Work. All work and data developed under this contract shall be related to current site conditions and to other proposed work within the specified project area. The A-E shall take a discretionary number of 5" X 7" color print pictures or arrange for the taking of such pictures of the site and/or structures in connection with the project as necessary to portray the initial conditions affecting the design. One copy of all pictures taken shall be furnished the Contracting Officer or his authorized representative at the time of the first design review of the project. The A-E shall notify the

Contracting Officer of any items encountered/discussed in accordance with the requirement for Confirmation Notices. Additional work shall be accomplished only at the direction of the Contracting Officer. All travel, photographic materials, and expenses incurred by the A-E and/or his representative(s), including consultants for such design visits, inspections, and investigations, are included in the basic price of this contract.

9.5 TRAVEL: If the A-E and/or his representative(s) are required to travel to locations not specifically covered in the basic bid price of the contract, the Government will reimburse the A-E for transportation, including commercial aircraft where necessary, and allow for such travel, not to exceed the then current delivery rates for Government employees, including per diem, mileage, etc., in lieu of all other expenses. Transportation by automobile on such required travel shall be likewise reimbursed. Travel time and mileage will be determined in accordance with Joint Travel Regulations. All travel shall be either authorized or approved in writing by the Contracting Officer prior to the travel occurring.

10.0 SUBMITTALS: A dated submittal letter shall be provided with each submittal to the Contracting Officer with distribution to the agencies listed below. This letter shall indicate to whom and the number of copies delivered. Submittals shall be delivered via two day delivery service. One set is considered to contain specifications, attachments, drawings, design analysis, and cost estimate. Additional items listed in the paragraphs above are not included in this table. As stated in Paragraph 4.1, all sets of review drawings and corrected final drawings for HQ AFRC and HQ AFCEE shall be one-half size. The remaining sets of review drawings and corrected final drawings shall be full size.

NUMBER OF SUBMITTAL SETS

AGENCY	DESIGN CHARRETTE REPORT	50% PRELIMINARY DESIGN SUBMITTAL	90% FINAL DESIGN SUBMITTAL	100% FINAL DESIGN SUBMITTAL
HQ AFCEE/DCD 8004 ARNOLD DR BROOKS AFB TX 78235-5361	6	6	6	6
HQAFRC/CEC 155 2nd STREET ROBINS AFB GA 31098-1635	1	1	1	1
482 SPTG/CES 29050 CORAL SEA BLVD., BOX 68 HOMESTEAD ARS FL 33039-1299	12	12	12	12

Appendixes

Appendix I

Department of Defense Handbook for Preparation of Statement of Work (SOW)

* Department of Defense, *Department of Defense Handbook for Preparation of Statement of Work (SOW)*, MIL-HDBK-245D, 3 April 1996. Online at http://www.dla.mil/DSS/dss-a/download/DoD%20SOW%20Handbook.pdf (accessed January 2008).

NOT MEASUREMENT SENSITIVE

MIL-HDBK-245D
3 APRIL 1996
SUPERSEDING
MIL-HDBK-245C
10 SEP 1991

DEPARTMENT OF DEFENSE

HANDBOOK FOR PREPARATION OF STATEMENT OF WORK (SOW)

This handbook is for guidance only. Do not cite this document as a requirement.

AMSC N/A **AREA MISC**

DISTRIBUTION STATEMENT A. Approved for public release; distribution is unlimited.

MIL-HDBK-245D

FOREWORD

1. This handbook is approved for use by all Departments and Agencies of the Department of Defense.

2. This handbook is for guidance only and cannot be cited as a requirement in any DoD contract. Contractors may, at their option, utilize this document for guidance in preparing responses to Government requests for proposals.

3. This handbook provides guidance to enable personnel to create a completed contract Statement Of Work (SOW) applicable to any material acquisition life-cycle phase. It also covers the SOW preparation for non-personal services contracts.

4. Modern weapon systems have traditionally contained many more specifications and greater detailed SOWs than those of the past. Contrast the Army Signal Corps SOW for the Wright Brothers' heavier-than-air flying machine in 1908 to the Air Force SOW for the Advanced Tactical Fighter in 1986. Requirements in the 1908 SOW (e.g., be easily taken apart for transport in Army wagons and be capable of being reassembled for operation in an hour, carry 350 pounds for 125 miles, and maintain 40 miles per hours in still air) and other contract conditions were specified on one page. The requirements section in the 1986 SOW for the Air Force Advanced Tactical Fighter is 85 pages long with 300 paragraphs of requirements. Today's SOWs are much more complex requiring greater attention to detail.

5. The handbook is organized so that the SOW writer after reviewing Section 3, General Description, can proceed to that portion of Section 4, Detailed Requirements, that pertains to the type of SOW required. Each portion of Section 4 has detailed instructions on the specific requirements for each type of SOW tailored to specific needs. The specific instructions provide techniques for defining task elements, and a method for organizing these elements into a comprehensive SOW. Sample outlines and significant DO's and DONT's are provided.

6. The tendency of SOW writers is to include requirements which belong in other parts of a government contract. Contract requirements should be specified in Sections A - M and should not be restated in other parts of the contract. Quantitative technical requirements should be specified in the specification and not be restated in other parts of the contract. Work requirements should be specified in the SOW, and all data requirements for delivery, format, and content should be in the Contract Data Requirements List (CDRL) in conjunction with the appropriate Data Item Description (DID) respectively, with none of the requirements restated in other parts of the contract. Redundancy invites conflict.

7. This handbook provides guidance, following DoD direction, that will enable SOW writers to rely on commercial contracting practices. The new SOW will specify what tasks need to be accomplished but leave "how to" accomplish those tasks up to the contractor.

MIL-HDBK-245D

8. Beneficial comments (recommendations, additions, deletions) and any pertinent data which may be of use in improving this document should be addressed to: Commander, Space and Naval Warfare Systems Command, Attn.: SPAWAR 05L1, 2451 Crystal Drive, Arlington, VA 22245-5200 by using the Standardization Document Improvement Proposal (DoD Form 1426) appearing at the end of this Handbook.

MIL-HDBK-245D

CONTENTS

MIL-HDBK-245D

APPENDICES

FIGURES

MIL-HDBK-245D

1 SCOPE

1.1 Background. This handbook applies to the preparation of Statements of Work (SOWs) for projects and programs that have deliverables and/or services performed. It is written to implement the acquisition policies established in DoDD 5000.1. It covers the preparation of SOWs which correlate to the acquisition life cycle phases identified in Department of Defense (DoD) Acquisition Instructions such as DoDI 5000.2. This handbook is for SOWs in DoD solicitations and contracts and covers work requirements, in conjunction with applicable performance/design requirements contained in specifications, but also data deliverables contained in Contract Data Requirements Lists (CDRLs). The Federal Acquisition Regulations (FAR) and Defense Federal Acquisition Regulation Supplements (DFARS) discuss the essentiality of the SOW for sound contracting. An offeror submits a proposal based on his perception of the Government's needs as defined in the RFP. Precisely stated requirements will enable the offeror and the Government to negotiate a fair price for the deliverables and/or services to be provided. This handbook has been developed as a framework to assist the responsible manager in providing a consistent, orderly, and complete description of work required.

1.2 Importance of SOW. The majority of government contracts include a SOW which forms the basis for successful performance by the contractor and effective administration of the contract by the government. A well-written SOW enhances the opportunity for all potential offerors to compete equally for Government contracts and serves as the standard for determining if the contractor meets the stated performance requirements.

1.3 Introduction of Statement of Objectives (SOO). This document introduces a new concept called the SOO which shifts the responsibility for preparing the SOW from the government to the solicitation respondents. Following recent DoD direction to lower Government costs by encouraging innovative contract options and flexible design solutions, the SOO captures the top level objectives of a solicitation and allows the offerors complete freedom in the structure and definition of SOW tasks as they apply to the proposed approach. However, the requirement, content and purpose of the SOW in the contract remain unchanged. The SOO concept is explained in detail in Section 5.

MIL-HDBK-245D

2 APPLICABLE DOCUMENTS

2.1 General. The documents listed below are not necessarily all of the documents referenced herein, but are the ones that are needed in order to fully understand the information provided by this handbook.

2.2 Government documents.

2.2.1 Specifications, standards, and handbooks. The following specifications, standards, and handbooks form a part of this document to the extent specified herein. Unless otherwise specified, the issues of these documents are those listed in the latest issue of the Department of Defense Index of Specifications and Standards (DoDISS) and supplement thereto.

STANDARDS

DEPARTMENT OF DEFENSE

MIL-STD-881	Work Breakdown Structures for Defense Material Items
MIL-STD-961	Department of Defense Standard Practice for Defense Specifications

HANDBOOKS

DEPARTMENT OF DEFENSE

MIL-HDBK-248	Acquisition Streamlining

2.3 Other Government Documents, Drawings and Publications. The following Government documents, drawings, and publications form a part of this handbook to the extent specified herein:

REGULATION

FEDERAL ACQUISITION REGULATION

FAR 52.215-33	Order of Precedence

DEFENSE FEDERAL ACQUISITION REGULATION SUPPLEMENTS

DFARS 211	Describing Agency Needs
DFARS 212	Acquisition of Commercial Items - General
DFARS 227.71	Rights in Technical Data

DFARS 237.104	Personal Services Contracts
DFARS 252.211-7000	Acquisition Streamlining

MANUALS

DEPARTMENT OF DEFENSE

DoD 5010.12-L	Acquisition Management System and Data Requirements Control List (AMSDL)
DoD 5010.12-M	Procedures for the Acquisition and Management of Technical Data

DIRECTIVES

DEPARTMENT OF DEFENSE

DoDD 5000.1	Defense Acquisition
DoDI 5000.2	Defense Acquisition Management Policies and Procedures

FORMS

DEPARTMENT OF DEFENSE

DD Form 1423	Contract Data Requirements List (CDRL)
DD Form 1664	Data Item Description (DID)

(Unless otherwise indicated, copies of the above specifications, standards, handbooks, or publications are available from the Standardization Document Order Desk, 700 Robbins Avenue, Building 4D, Philadelphia, PA 19111-5094. Any documents required by manufacturers in connection with specific acquisition functions should be obtained from the contracting activity or as directed by the contracting officer.)

MIL-HDBK-245D

3 GENERAL DESCRIPTION

3.1 Purpose. The SOW should specify in clear, understandable terms the work to be done in developing or producing the goods to be delivered or services to be performed by a contractor. Preparation of an effective SOW requires both an understanding of the goods or services that are needed to satisfy a particular requirement and an ability to define what is required in specific, performance-based, quantitative terms. A SOW prepared in explicit terms will enable offerors to clearly understand the government's needs. This facilitates the preparation of responsive proposals and delivery of the required goods or services. A well-written SOW also aids the Government in conduct of the source selection and contract administration after award. A Data Requirements Review Board (DRRB) may review each SOW to ensure compliance with the policy, guidance and procedures contained in this handbook (see DoD 5010.12-M for requirements for conducting the DRRB). The SOW is aligned with the acquisition milestones and phases discussed in detail in Section 4.

3.2 Relationship between Statement Of Work and Specification. The SOW defines (either directly or by reference to other documents) all work (non-specification) performance requirements for contractor effort. Qualitative and quantitative design and performance requirements are contained in specifications developed according to MIL-STD-961. Such specifications are typically referenced in the SOW, but the specific qualitative or quantitative technical requirements should not be spelled out in the SOW. For example, the referenced specification may cite reliability and maintainability requirements in terms of quantifiable mean-time-between failures (MTBF) and mean-time-to-repair (MTTR); the SOW should task the contractor to establish, implement and control a reliability and maintainability program.

3.3 Relationship Between the SOW and Contract. The SOW should be compatible with these provisions:

Requirements that are mandated by law, established DoD policy or necessary for effective management of its acquisition, operation, or support.

At the outset of development, system-level requirements should be specified in terms of mission-performance, operational effectiveness, and operational suitability.

During all acquisition phases, solicitations and contracts, the SOW should state management requirements in terms of results needed rather than "how to manage" procedures for achieving those results.

DFAR 252.211-7000, Acquisition Streamlining, is required in all solicitations and contracts for systems acquisition programs. This enables a contractor to effectively evaluate and recommend the tailored application of management systems and specifications and standards for use in the appropriate phase of the program life cycle.

3.4 SOW and Contractor Performance. After contractor selection and contract award, the contract SOW becomes a standard for measuring contractor performance. Consequently, the SOW writer must consider the contractual and legal implications of the SOW during its preparation. As the contracted effort progresses, the government and the contractor will refer to the SOW to determine their respective rights and obligations. In this respect, the SOW defines the contract and is subject to the interpretations of contract law. The SOW must clearly define the work to be performed, since the language detailing the contractor's effort may be pertinent to legal questions concerning the scope of work. In a dispute concerning performance, rights, or obligations, clearly defined requirements will enhance the legal enforceability of a SOW, which has a high level of precedence in the solicitation document and contract as stated in FAR 52.215-33.

3.5 Relationship of Contract Sections. The government Request for Proposal (RFP) or solicitation defines the government's requirements and constitutes the cornerstone of the program, as it ultimately shapes the resultant contract. Therefore, the SOW must be consistent with all sections of the RFP. The SOW preparer should work closely with the overall RFP drafter and all contract section authors to achieve consistency. If acceptance and inspection of supplies or services is required to satisfy the contract, RFP Section E should address the acceptance criteria. Data deliverables are identified in Contract Data Requirements List (CDRL) exhibits to the contract. Section F (Deliveries or Performance) requires delivery of data listed in these exhibits. Clauses required by law, regulation, or any other clauses that may apply to a resulting contract are cited in Section I (Contract Clauses). Section J is a listing of all exhibits and attachments to the contract. Sections K, L, and M apply only to RFP's. They are contained at the end so that when the contract is awarded, they can be removed. Section K includes provisions that require representations, certifications, or the submission of other information by offerors. Section L includes provisions and other information or instructions to guide bidders/offerors in preparing their offers or bids in a manner that is responsive to the government's RFP. Section M identifies the factors that will be considered in awarding the contract. It contains the evaluation criteria listed in order of importance and other factors for award. The SOW and Work Breakdown Structure (WBS) are utilized in preparing the corresponding CDRL, Section L, Section M, and other parts of the RFP/contract. The relationship of RFP/contract sections to the SOW is illustrated on Figure 1. Figure 1 is provided for general guidance and shows that the SOW and SOO may, at the preference of the procuring activity, be placed in one of several different locations in the solicitation. Because of the complex interrelationships among RFP/contract documents, use of a cross-reference matrix may be helpful (see Figure 2).

MIL-HDBK-245D

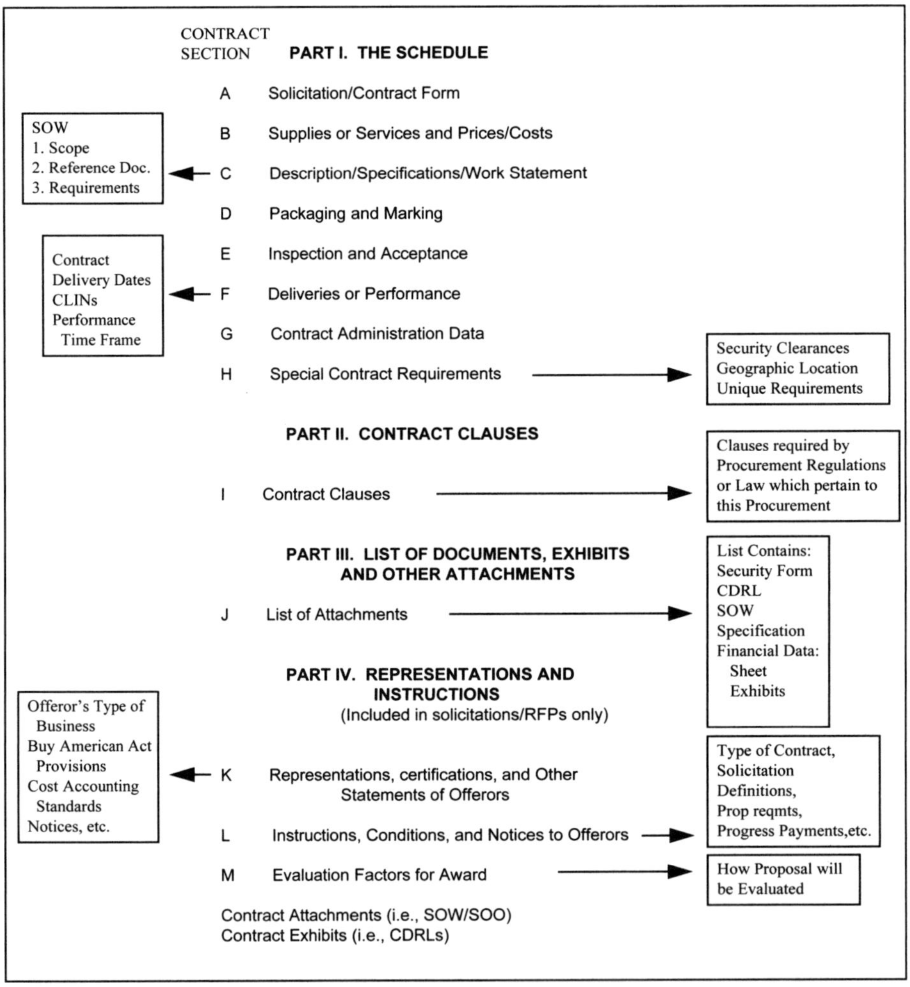

FIGURE 1. Relationship of Government solicitation/contract sections to SOW/SOO.

The following matrix is intended to reduce internal RFP inconsistencies and aid in proposal preparation. It is provided as a reference tool for information only. In the event of conflict between this matrix and any other section of the RFP, the other section shall take precedence.

WORK DESCR	WBS ELEM	SOW PARA	CLIN	CDRL	INSTR TO OFFERORS (SEC L)	EVAL FACTORS (SEC M)	PROP LOC
Design B	2.2	3.2.2	0001	N/A	3.B.1	Tech 1.A	V1-p.64
Build A	2.3	3.2.3	0002	A001	3.B.2	Tech 1.B	V1-p.75

FIGURE 2. Cross reference matrix.

3.6 Standard Format. The standard format for the SOW is as follows (subject to variations specified in Section 4 for specific types of SOWs):

SOW Section	Title
1	SCOPE
2	APPLICABLE DOCUMENTS
3	REQUIREMENTS

Deviations from the standard format may be made by the writer when necessary to accommodate overriding program needs.

3.6.1 SOW Section 1 - Scope. This Section includes a brief statement of what the SOW should cover. The scope paragraph defines the breadth and limitations of the work to be done. In some cases, the use of an introduction, background, or both, is preferred. Separate indentures under this Section are used in SOWs to accommodate complex acquisitions requiring lengthy background information. Background information should be limited to only that information needed to acquaint the proposer with the basic acquisition requirement. The items listed below should not be included in the "Scope" Section.

a. Directions to the contractor to perform work tasks.
b. Specification of data requirements.
c. Description of deliverable products.

MIL-HDBK-245D

3.6.2 SOW Section 2 - Applicable Documents. Military handbooks, government instructions, service regulations, technical orders, and policy letters, as a type, are not written in language suitable for contract application. In the event requirements of these documents must be included in a SOW, excerpts only should be used and should be made into either a clear task statement or a clear reference statement for guidance only, and not for contract compliance. Any documents called out in Section 2 of the SOW should have the specific version referenced, i.e. by date or by revision letter.

The SOW writer should refer to DFARS 252.211-7000 with respect to referenced documents and begin with a zero base situation. The requirement for any specification and standard should be justified before being placed in Section 2 of the SOW. Therefore, Section 2 should not be prepared until the draft of the requirements Section, Section 3, is complete. Sections 2 and 3 are reciprocal. Documents invoked by specific reference in Section 3 of the SOW must be identified and listed in Section 2. When invoked in Section 3 of the SOW, the application should be tailored to invoke only those minimum requirements from the document which are absolutely necessary for program success as described in MIL-HDBK-248. The applicability of each document listed in Section 2 of the SOW should be specified in Section 3 and identify only that portion needed to perform the work. Improper document referencing (e.g., blanket imposition) was often a major cost driver since total compliance with a document listed in Section 2 of the SOW was implied unless Section 3 specified otherwise.

3.6.3 SOW Section 3 - Requirements. Specific work tasks are called for in SOW Section 3 (see Appendix D). These tasks, developed to satisfy program needs, are essentially the contractor work requirements. Although the Source Selection Evaluation Board (SSEB) is responsible for the examination of SOW requirements in order to eliminate nonessential requirements, such examinations may be accomplished by the functional technical groups during development of the SOW. A well-written SOW has the following attributes:

a. Specifies requirements clearly to permit the government and offerors to estimate the probable cost and the offeror to determine the levels of expertise, manpower, and other resources needed to accomplish the task.

b. States the specific duties of the contractor in such a way that the contractor knows what is required and can complete all tasks to the satisfaction of the contract administration office.

c. Written so specifically that there is no question of whether the contractor is obligated to perform specific tasks.

d. References only the absolute minimum applicable specifications and standards needed. Selectively invokes documents only to the extent required to satisfy the existing requirements. (The tailoring of reference document requirements should result in a reduction to the overall costs otherwise incurred if all requirements stated in a document are invoked).

e. Separates general information from direction so that background information and suggested procedures are clearly distinguishable from contractor responsibilities.

f. Avoids directing how tasks are to be performed and states only what results are required.

3.6.4 SOW Do's and Don'ts.

a. Do's:

- Select a competent team with an experienced team leader.
- Exclude "how to" requirements since the offeror should be tasked to provide the deliverables under the contract in the most cost effective manner.
- Use the program Work Breakdown Structure (WBS), as discussed in paragraph 3.8.1 in this handbook to outline the required work effort.
- Set SOW objectives in support of the Acquisition Plan (AP), if applicable.
- Explicitly define the tailored limitations of all standards and specifications cited.
- Exclude design control or hardware performance parameters because these requirements should be covered in a specification.
- Educate personnel with respect to acquisition streamlining. (DFARS 211.002-70 Contract Clause).
- Give priority to commercial items over specification items when the former satisfies military requirements.
- Give priority to commercial practices as a means of acquisition (DFARS 212 Acquisition of Commercial Items - General).

b. Don'ts:

- Order, describe, or discuss Contract Data Requirements List (CDRL) data.
- Invoke, cite, or discuss a Data Item Description (DID). Although the text of the SOW should not include the data format and content preparation instructions and/or data delivery requirements, a data item description number listed on the CDRL may be cross-referenced in the SOW.
- Specify technical proposal criteria or evaluation factors.

MIL-HDBK-245D

- Establish a delivery schedule. (May include significant milestones for clarity.)

- Specify design control parameters or the performance of hardware because these items should be covered in a specification.

- Impose on the contractor a Government format when a contractor format is acceptable.

- Overspecify. Specify only what is required and let the contractor establish the best method to fulfill the requirement.

- Invoke in-house management instructions.

- Use the SOW to establish or amend a specification.

- Invoke handbooks, service regulations, technical orders, or any other document not specifically written according to DoD standards. (Non-government documents excluded.)

3.6.5 Title Page and Table of Contents. All SOWs should have a title page or cover that shows the SOW title, preparation date, procurement request number or contract number, revision number, date, and identity of the preparing organization (see Figure 3). A table of contents should be used when the SOW exceeds five pages (see Figure 4).

3.6.6 Paragraph Numbering and Identification. Each paragraph and subparagraph should be numbered consecutively within each SOW Section using a period to separate the number representing each sublevel. Paragraph numbering should be limited to the third sublevel, if possible, as shown in the following example for SOW Section 3:

Requirement	3
1st Sublevel	3.1
2nd Sublevel	3.1.1
3rd Sublevel	3.1.1.1

Paragraph breakdowns should be kept to that level necessary to clearly define required contractor tasks. Only one task should be provided in a numbered paragraph or sub paragraph to facilitate costing, referencing and tailoring of tasks. Each paragraph and sub-paragraph should be titled.

MIL-HDBK-245D

13 NOV 1995

STATEMENT OF WORK

FOR

RAPID DEPLOYABLE COMMUNICATIONS SYSTEM

Prepared by

SPACE AND NAVAL WARFARE SYSTEMS COMMAND

FIGURE 3. Sample Title Page.

MIL-HDBK-245D

CONTENTS

FIGURE 4. Sample Table of Contents.

MIL-HDBK-245D

3.6.7 Language Style. SOW requirements should be written in language understandable to all potential program participants. Requirements should be stated explicitly in a topical, logical, chronological, or similarly structured order, avoiding words which allow for multiple interpretations. Use technical language sparingly with simple wording predominating in concise sentences. Use "shall" whenever a provision is mandatory. “Will” expresses a declaration of purpose or intent; for example, "The Government will review all recommendations and provide direction within thirty calendar days". Use active rather than passive voice; for example, "The contractor shall establish a program", not "A program shall be established by the contractor.”

Spell out acronyms and abbreviations the first time and put the abbreviated version in parentheses after the spelled-out phrases. This will define them for each subsequent use. Acronyms and abbreviations may be defined in a glossary. Many of the common acronyms used are found in Appendix A.

Use verbs that identify work and performance task requirements (See Appendix B) and answer the explicit question: "What are the work requirements?" When selecting the appropriate work word which properly expresses the degree of contractor involvement, the SOW writer must explicitly define the total nature of the work requirement.

Avoid using “Any,” “Either,” “And/Or,” as these words imply that the contractor can make a choice which may not support the intent of the SOW. Do not use pronouns. Repeat the noun to avoid any misinterpretation. Terminology should be consistent throughout the SOW. When referring to a specific item, use the same phrase or word, particularly when referring to technical terms and items. Where words can be spelled in several different ways, employ the most common spelling. Make every effort to avoid ambiguity. A list of ambiguous phrases is provided in Appendix C.

3.7 Data Management. As the contractor performs and completes the SOW tasks, data may be developed. Submissions of this data are generally expensive. Proper tailoring and scheduling of data submission items requires particular attention by the SOW preparers. Data costs can be minimized by selectively eliminating unnecessary reports and requiring appropriately phased submissions. A review of anticipated data requirements should therefore include definition of a time line defined for data submission. The contractor's format may be the acceptable form for submission of data products. The SOW preparer should make every effort to ensure that the CDRLs and DIDs reflect the anticipated need for data and to ascertain whether the specific data required will in fact be generated and available prior to the proposed delivery date stated on the proposed CDRL.

3.7.1 Use of Contract Data Requirements List (CDRL) Data. The ordering and delivery of data which the Government requires are specified and scheduled through the use of the Contract Data Requirements List (CDRL), DD Form 1423, in conjunction with the appropriate Data Item Description (DID), DD Form 1664. The CDRL is used to order the data required and tailor the

DID. The DID's use is to describe the data's format and content requirements. The SOW task(s) that will produce data requirements should be referenced in Block 5 of the CDRL. The SOW author should exercise considerable care and attention to the data delivery implications of the SOW. While data may be inherently generated by a work task, recording and delivering the data in a specific format are cost drivers that must be considered when preparing the SOW and CDRLs. The CDRL should specify that the contractor's format is acceptable, wherever possible.

3.7.2 Data Item Description (DID). After the need for recording and delivery of data resulting from a work task has been determined, appropriate DIDs should be selected from DoD 5010.12-L, Acquisition Management System and Data Requirements Control List (AMSDL). If certain elements of data are not needed, the DID should be tailored downward noting deletions in CDRL Block 16. When the contractor format for a data product will meet the Government's needs, it should be specified in block 16 of the CDRL if the DID does not already state contractor format is acceptable. The CDRL should only require data specifically generated in a SOW work task. The SOW, and not the DID, must task the contractor to perform work. At the end of each SOW task paragraph, the DIDs that are associated with the effort described in the task may be identified in parentheses.

To understand the relationship of a SOW to the CDRL and DID (see Figure 5), consider the example where the SOW establishes a requirement that, "the contractor shall establish, implement and control a Configuration Management (CM) program". The associated CDRL would order a CM data item and identify due date, distribution and other such parameters while the DID would provide the format and content requirements for that particular CM item, with non-essential references tailored out of the DID.

3.8 SOW Development. Section 4 of this handbook describes how the SOW content may change depending on which acquisition phase it supports. The following paragraphs will describe a general planning and development approach that is applicable to all SOWs regardless of which acquisition phase is to be supported.

3.8.1 Work Breakdown Structure (WBS). A WBS should be used in developing the SOW. MIL-STD-881 may be used for guidance. A WBS provides the framework for a disciplined approach of structuring and defining the total project or program. It is a product-oriented family tree composed of equipment, services, and other items which make up the project or program, and provides the basis for progress reporting, performance and engineering evaluations, and financial data reporting. When preparing the SOW a complete application of a WBS may not be necessary in all programs, however, the underlying philosophy and structured approach can and should be applied. The Contract Line Item Number (CLIN) and the SOW should be constructed to correlate with the WBS. Use of a WBS during SOW development facilitates a logical arrangement of the SOW elements and provides a convenient check-list to trace all necessary elements of the program and ensure that they are addressed in the SOW. The WBS will evolve into greater detail as the system definition and acquisition phases advance. For each phase, the WBS must be in sufficient detail to cover all the required work in that phase, as well as to produce the technical

MIL-HDBK-245D

information needed for the next phase. The WBS may be tailored to the minimum level requi to manage program risk.

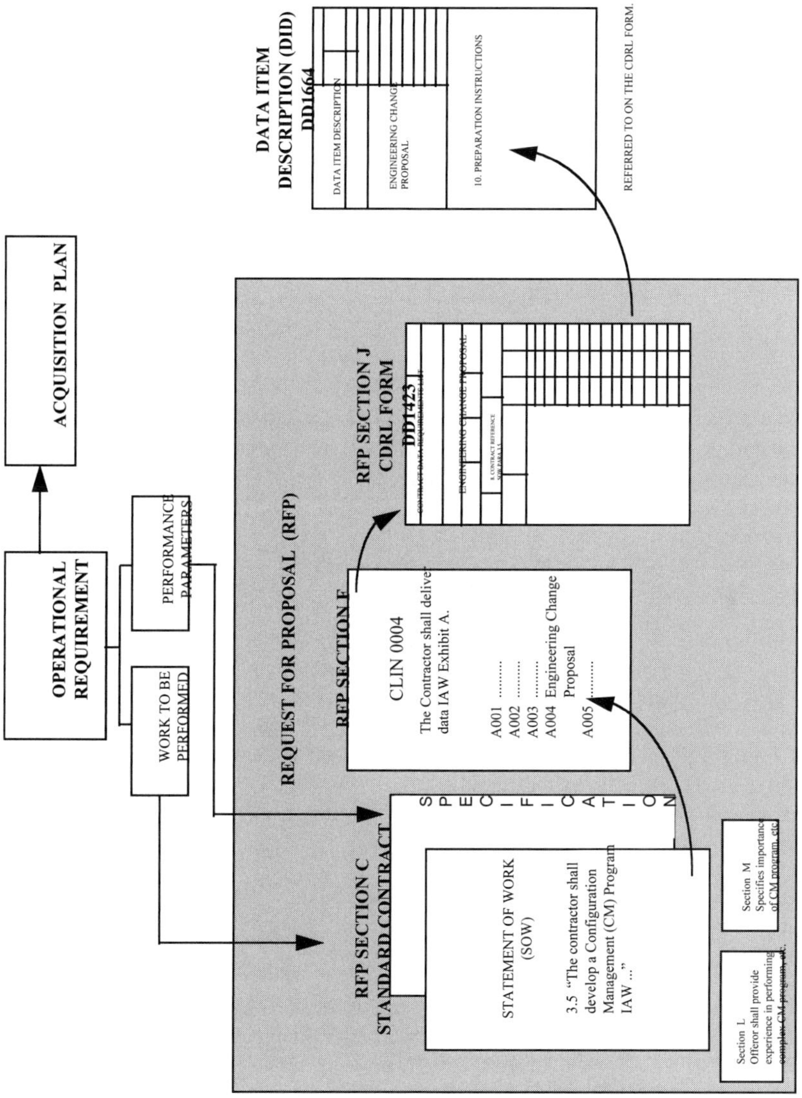

FIGURE 5. SPEC-SOW-CDRL-DID Relationship.

MIL-HDBK-245D

3.8.2 Development Approach. A systematic process is essential for SOW development. Select a competent team (expert in managerial, technical and contractual fields) with a team leader who is experienced in systems acquisition and SOW development. The SOW preparer and all contract section authors must first understand all program requirements to be supported. Following the systematic process shown on figure 6, the team should:

a. Ensure that only those tasks which add value to the product, whether a management system or technical requirement, are included in the SOW. (See DFAR 211.002 policy.)

b. Conduct market research to determine whether commercial items or nondevelopmental items are available to meet program requirements.

c. Review the requirements documents which authorize the program and define its basic objectives.

d. Review the various DoD/Services/Joint Services requirements documents for program management, acquisition and control impact.

e. Prepare a bibliography citing the specific portions of all applicable governing instructions, directives, specifications, and standards with which the program must comply. Keep these requirements to the absolute minimum and do not include citings that direct "how" work is to be performed.

f. Categorize the work described by the program WBS into that which will be done in-house and that which needs to be contracted.

g. Compile all work that needs to be contracted into an Acquisition Plan (if applicable) which will identify the various RFPs/contracts required, type of contract, the time-phasing, estimated cost, method of contractor selection/award, and period of performance among other things. For each RFP/contract so identified, a SOW must be prepared covering all of the WBS work elements included in that RFP/contract.

h. Identify all organizations and persons who will participate in preparing the SOW, and determine the participants' areas of responsibility.

i. Prepare the SOW following the guidelines of this handbook. For each WBS work element, identify tasks that define the scope of the work effort to satisfy the minimal needs of the program and identify required data deliverables.

j. Ensure that the specifications are consistent with the SOW. Ensure technical performance requirements are properly contained in the system specification and not in the SOW.

MIL-HDBK-245D

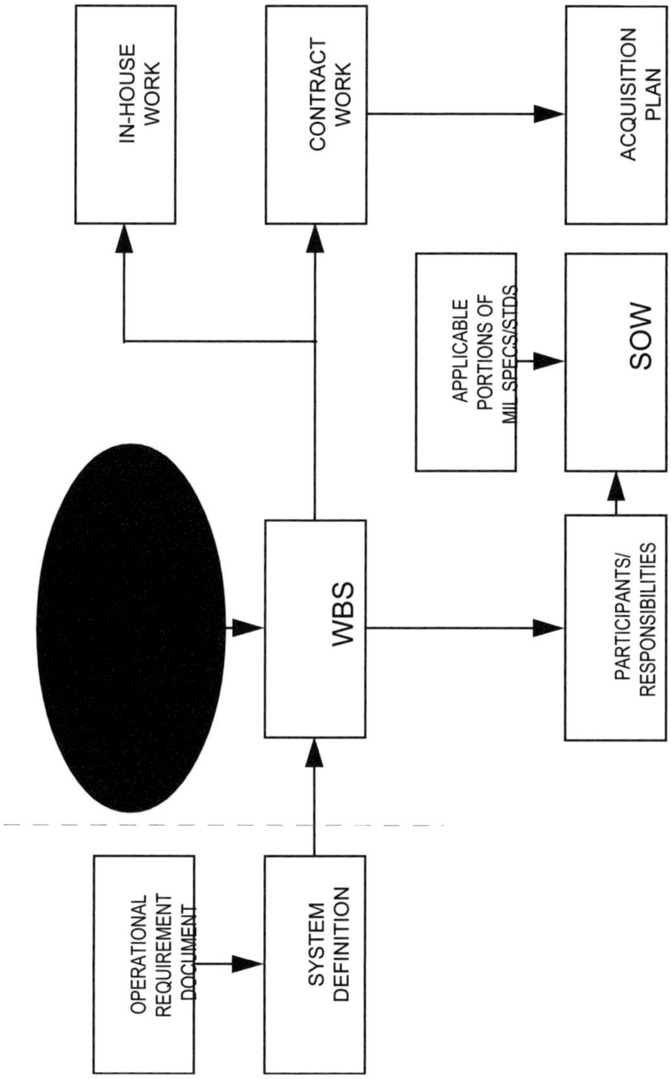

FIGURE 6. Systematic approach to SOW preparation

MIL-HDBK-245D

k. Utilize the SOW and WBS in preparing the corresponding CDRL, Section L Instructions to Offerors, Section M Evaluation Factors for Award, and other parts of the RFP/contract following DFARS.

3.8.3 Non-Complex SOW Development. It is essential to establish a SOW outline for non-complex acquisitions which do not lend themselves to utilization of a WBS.

a. Define end items (line items) to be acquired, such as hardware, software, engineering analysis, software validation or simulation, etc.

b. Establish the requirements which apply to each end item and, as a minimum, develop a bibliography as described in 3.8.2.e above.

c. Determine what services or data will be needed to support each end item after delivery to the Government.

d. Identify all participants (see 3.8.2.h)

e. Prepare the SOW following the guidelines of this handbook.

MIL-HDBK-245D

4 DETAIL REQUIREMENTS

4.1 SOW Phasing and Results. All programs, including highly classified programs, should accomplish certain core activities. These activities must be tailored to satisfy an identified need using common sense and sound business practices. The acquisition process is structured in logical phases separated by major decision points called milestones. Each milestone is an opportunity for a review to determine if the program should continue. The decision to enter the next phase or not is based on results obtained in the acquisition phase preceding that milestone. SOW requirements are tailored to support the acquisition of information, hardware, software, technical data and the logistic support required during any particular life cycle phase.

4.1.1 Determining Mission Needs and Identifying Deficiencies. All acquisition programs are based on identified, documented, and validated mission needs. Mission needs result from assessments of current and projected capability requirements. Mission needs may establish a new operational capability, improve an existing capability, or exploit an opportunity to reduce costs or enhance performance. If the potential solution results in a new program, an appropriate level review should be held to document its validity and joint potential, and confirm that the requirements have been met or considered.

4.1.1.1 Elements of Information. Where preliminary studies involving systems analyses, preliminary cost effectiveness, or trade-off studies are to be contracted, there are certain distinctive elements of information to be included in the SOW. These can be included in either the introduction or background descriptions of the Scope in Section 1.

These areas are as follows:

a. *Statement of the problem(s).* A brief description and background of the problem(s) to be solved, and a succinct discussion of the need giving rise to this requirement.

b. *System description.* A short functional description of the overall system. If practicable, a pictorial representation that will quickly orient the reader to the desired system and the proposed use should be considered for inclusion in this Section of the SOW.

c. *Major milestones. A* graphic display of major program milestones should be included in the background information.

4.1.1.2 Requirements. The Section 3 paragraphs will establish what the contractor shall do, and may properly contain discussions of the following requirements and conditions:

a. *Component and subsystem relationships. A* functional flow diagram, explaining what is visualized as possible or practical at this time and showing the system and each associated subsystem (or major component).

b. *Alternative courses of development.* A summation of the alternatives for development as they are visualized at this time, pointing out the possible differences in operational effectiveness in terms of performance, reliability, maintainability and operability. The SOW should clearly indicate the basis of comparison, e.g., previous experience or extrapolations.

c. *Phasing.* Where the studies to be accomplished are divisible into time phases or into other separable areas of work. The SOW should spell out these requirements.

MIL-HDBK-245D

4.1.2 Phase O: Concept Exploration - Examining Alternative Concepts to Meet Deficiencies. Phase objective is to define and evaluate alternative system design concepts which fulfill mission needs and program objectives. During this phase, technological advances, concept feasibility, schedules and costs are evaluated by the program manager in order to identify a viable solution to a military requirement. Because of the evolving nature of the desired product, the SOW used during this phase must be limited to an expression of the mission need objectives and goals. The precision with which operational goals or technical objectives can be defined during this phase will impact the Government's and the contractor's ability to estimate cost and risk. In the majority of early stage research programs, including preliminary explorations and studies, the work to be performed cannot be described precisely. When preliminary exploration and studies have indicated a high probability that the development is feasible a more definitive SOW can be drawn. Based on program needs, the contractor in this phase may develop a Type A system or system/segment specification for use by the Government in the solicitation for the next phase.

4.1.2.1 Detailed Requirements. The Concept Exploration Phase SOW instructs the contractor to assess the merits of the concepts and define the most promising concepts in broad terms of objectives for cost, schedule, performance and overall acquisition strategy. Initial measures of effectiveness and performance are also identified in this phase.

4.1.3 Phase I: Program Definition and Risk Reduction. During this Phase, the program becomes defined as one or more concepts, designs, and/or technologies are investigated. Early development models, demonstrations, and operational assessments are conducted as required to reduce risks prior entering the program's next phase. Cost, schedule and performance trade-offs are conducted. Key activities include: strategy review, identification of program specific accomplishments for the next phase, initial manpower estimates, and the identification of potential environmental impacts.

4.1.3.1 Detailed Requirements. The Program Definition phase SOW should contain enough detail to enable the successful bidders to translate program requirements into an effective development program. It should delineate specific tasks for evolving the system requirements into system type specifications or system segment specifications.

4.1.4 Phase II: Engineering and Manufacturing Development - Detailed Design, Integration Testing, and Establishing a Manufacturing Capability. The objectives of this phase are: to translate the selected design into a stable, producible, supportable, and cost effective design; to validate the manufacturing or production process; and to demonstrate system capabilities through testing.

4.1.4.1 Detailed Requirements. The Engineering and Manufacturing Development phase SOW efforts include verification that adequate resources have been programmed to support production, deployment, and logistics support of the operational system; verification of the system's software design, coding, integration and tests.

4.1.5 Phase III: Production, Deployment, and Operational Support. In the Production, Deployment, and Operational Support Phase, the system developed in the previous phases is produced and installed and any support required for operational use is provided. All tasks which were deferred until the Production Phase are addressed and action is initiated for their completion. These include efforts deferred in support areas such as, supply support (provisioning), technical publications and training. Systems engineering management will ensure on a continuing basis that the design is feasible and sound. Additionally, they will initiate, evaluate and integrate engineering changes throughout the Production Phase to provide the capability for continued support after the system is deployed. The evaluation of system Engineering Change Proposals (ECPs) and value engineering changes, and the preparation for turnover of system operation to the using service are important tasks to be accomplished during this phase. The need for continued system effectiveness and product assurance work as well as CM work will be based on the impact of engineering changes. Operation and Maintenance manuals, and supply support documents, are updated during this Phase and the finished system is tested and approved for DoD use.

4.1.5.1 Product Specifications. The product specification is the primary procurement control document used during the production phase to determine the product baseline, control design, and establish system performance. The content of the specifications is limited to requirements intended to control design and establish performance requirement of the purchased product. The SOW should not conflict with the product specification. Typical SOW requirements which should be tailored to the minimal Production Phase needs are: ILS, CM, technical manuals and publications, training, quality program requirements, calibration and instrumentation, reliability, maintainability, human factors, safety, Planned Maintenance Subsystem (PMS) and other contractor provided services needed in conjunction with the production buy. Many of these areas have already been addressed during the development phases and should now be well defined and documented. Some SOW tasks are no longer required, while others require continued effort or the introduction of new tasks compatible with the Production Phase.

4.1.6 Examples. Figure 7 provides a standard SOW format, and Appendix D illustrates an example of SOWs for both products and services. The example SOWs are intentionally incomplete in the interest of brevity.

4.2 Services (Non-personal). The product of a non-personal services SOW (Appendix D2) is the result of some work task being performed. The requirements that establish the work must be defined in terms of work words and not product words. The need for non-personal services may occur at any time. If the work to be performed is painting a building, the task

MIL-HDBK-245D

STATEMENT OF WORK FORMAT

1 Scope. Include a statement about what this SOW covers. Some background information may be helpful to clarify the needs of the procurement.
1.1 Background. Do not discuss work tasks in Section 1.

2 Applicable Documents. All documents invoked in the requirements section of the SOW must be listed in this section by document number and title. These documents may include Standards, Specifications and other reference documents needed to identify and clarify the work task or deliverable product. However, DoD and Departmental Instructions are provided to control in-house work effort and should not be used in the SOW to control contractor effort. Also, any document listed in this section must be invoked and selectively tailored to meet minimal needs of the planned procurement in the requirements section. The exact version of any document cited in the SOW should be specified in this section.
2.1 Department of Defense specifications.
2.2 Department of Defense standards.
2.3 Other Government documents.
2.4 Industry documents.

3 Requirements. The arrangement of technical tasks and subtasks within the Requirements section will be dictated by program requirements. If a WBS is being used in the program, tasks should be arranged in accordance with that WBS. It may be helpful to have a general task to orient the planning and use of the subsequent subtasks. The following outline is a generalization. Care should be exercised to scope the program tasks to meet only the minimal needs for the phase SOW or requirements.
3.1 General.
3.2 Detail tasks.
3.2.1 System engineering.

a. Technical studies - including life cycle costs.

b. System effectiveness planning, for example, reliability, maintainability, and human factors.

FIGURE 7. SOW format.

must define what is to be painted and to what standards. The product of such a contract is obviously a building painted and completed by a certain time. If the SOW is prepared properly, contractor monitoring can be kept to a minimum as long as the task is completed on time and within cost. This would be a proper non-personal services contract. The Government is then left with the requirement to inspect the product and either accept or reject it based on the contractor's conformance to the prescribed work requirement. The wide variety of non-personal services requirements cause this type of contract to take on many forms. However, in all applications, two factors are important to ensure that the services purchased are indeed non-personal. These factors are: (a) the SOW must establish explicitly what work is to be done and require the delivery of a product or result other than periodic progress reports and (b) the contractor's employees must not be supervised or controlled by the Government during the execution of the work and production of the product or result. In this regard, the SOW must be explicit, inclusive and comprehensive in prescribing the work requirements. For a more complete discussion of a personal versus a non-personal services contract, refer to DFARS 237.104.

4.2.1 Product Definition. As the product or service becomes more involved and technical in nature, defining in adequate detail what is needed to enable a contractor to produce the product independently becomes more difficult. If the job is an analysis, the task must say precisely what is to be analyzed and the criteria for performing the analysis, including any particular elements to be considered. If some conclusion is to be drawn as a result of the analysis, be precise about what the DoD needs to obtain as a result of this analytic work. If it is important how or in what sequence the analysis is to be conducted, spell it out. Specify explicit needs, leaving nothing to the contractor's imagination.

4.2.2 Terminology. A frequent problem encountered in defining the tasks in an SOW is the use of non-specific words and phrases such as: “any”, “assist”, “as required”, “as applicable/as necessary” and “as directed”. Do not use any of these words. The following rationale for precluding their use is provided:

a. *Any.* "Any" is an ambiguous word. Writers may intend it to denote "plurality" and readers may interpret it to denote "oneness”. Also, when "any" is used to describe the selection of items from a list, it's the reader who does the selecting, not the writer. Which items, and how many the reader selects are beyond the control of the writer.

b. *Assist.* “Assist” connotes personal services. It infers working side-by-side, being subject to supervision. The word is totally undefined in terms of identifying the work and its range and depth. Spell out explicitly what the contractor must do.

c. *As required.* The result of this approach is an undefined work condition. It has no expressed limitations. It places the Government in a position of not expressing its minimal needs. It could lead to a debatable condition concerning the contractor's compliance with the contract or order. The SOW must be declarative as to its minimal needs.

d. *As applicable/As necessary.* If the Government does not know what is necessary or applicable, it must not leave to the contractor the responsibility for determining the minimal needs of the contract. The SOW should forthrightly state the requirements so that the contractor can comply with the requirement using his best efforts and expertise to accomplish the tasks.

e. As *directed.* This condition, as a part of a work task in a SOW, connotes a personal services situation in which the contractor is placed under direct supervision. "When directed" may be used in conjunction with a task order contract to indicate that specific tasks may be initiated at various times during the period of contracted performance.

f. *Including but not limited to.* This term is generally inserted when the drafter is unsure of requirement or criteria. However, it creates an unspecific requirement which creates ambiguity. Only list known requirements.

g. *Etc.* This word also introduces potentially more unidentified ambiguous requirements.

4.2.3 Word Usage. Another area of concern in establishing the SOW for non-personal services is the overuse of the words and phrases "support" and "engineering and technical services".

a. Support is an ambiguous term. Specify the specific type of support needed.

b. The terms "engineering and technical services" encompass a broad area of expertise. The SOW must state the minimal needs, even if it means broadening the work limitations to cover anticipated work tasks. For clarification, the SOW may include some examples of typical work to be done.

c. Perhaps one of the most vexing problems in contracting is the problem of loopholes. Contractors and inspectors go by the letter of the contract SOW. In one instance, an engineer intended to have a damaged roof edge repaired and repainted. He wrote "match existing," but did not specify "repaint." The contractors who did the work matched the existing metal flashing strip but refused to paint the new flashing. The inspector could only agree with the contractor, since the engineer had not adequately described what was intended. The writer and reviewers at all levels of review have a responsibility to ensure that loopholes do not exist in the final SOW.

MIL-HDBK-245D

5 STATEMENT OF OBJECTIVES (SOO) METHOD

5.1 SOO Introduction. The SOO is a Government prepared document incorporated into the RFP that states the overall solicitation objectives. It can be used in those solicitations where the intent is to provide the maximum flexibility to each offeror to propose an innovative development approach. Offerors use the RFP, product performance requirements, and SOO as a basis for preparing their proposals including a SOW and CDRL. Note: The SOO is not retained as a contract compliance item.

5.1.1 SOO Purpose. The program SOO should provide the basic, top level objectives of the acquisition and is provided in the RFP in lieu of a Government written SOW. This approach provides potential offerors the flexibility to develop cost effective solutions and the opportunity to propose innovative alternatives meeting the stated objectives. It also presents the Government with an opportunity to assess the offeror's understanding of all aspects of the effort to be performed, by eliminating the 'how to' instructions to accomplish the required effort normally contained in the SOW the Government provides to prospective offerors.

5.2 SOO Content " . The Government may include a SOO as part of the RFP, listed in Section J, attached at the end of the RFP, or referenced in Section L and/or M, defining the top level program objectives. Alternatively, the SOO may be placed in Section L of the RFP (e.g., as an annex). Figure 8 provides a notional SOO format. It is developed to be compatible with the mission need statement (MNS); operational requirements document (ORD), technical requirements from the system requirements document (SRD)/systems specification; and the draft work breakdown structure (WBS)/dictionary. The SOO should address product oriented goals rather than performance requirements. SOOs are normally in the 2-4 page range. The SOO is not a one for one replacement of the SOW. Sections L and M should logically follow with instructions to the offerors asking for proposal information supporting the objectives and evaluation criteria that clearly identify how the offerors' responses will be evaluated. Each portion of the RFP must support one another. The key is to keep the SOO clear and concise and to provide potential offerors with enough information and detail to structure a sound program, designed to be executable and satisfy government objectives. The SOO is used, along with other information and instructions in the RFP, by offerors, to develop the contract work breakdown structure, statement of work, and other documents supporting and defining the offerors proposed effort. SOO content depends both on the type of program and on the program phase. It is possible that a 'mature' program, such as one which has been fielded for some time, could require slightly more detail in the SOO to properly integrate with other, ongoing parts of the program. The SOO is replaced at contract award in the contract by the proposed SOW.

MIL-HDBK-245D

1.0 Program Objectives

(a) multi-phased program
(b) one program, multi-contractor
(c) one phase contract

2.0 Contract Objectives (WBS 00000)

(a) Objectives in paragraph 2.0 are traceable to Level 0 WBS
(b) For multi-phase programs, describe objectives for each phase in a format similar to an indentured list (clearly indicate which phases are part of the anticipated contract and any phases that will involve separate contracts).

Note: The SOO should not address each WBS element, but each WBS element should be traceable to something in the SOO. For example, a SOO may instruct the bidder to address his engineering approach. That is not a particular WBS element, but several WBS elements might be created to breakout the engineering tasks. Generally, a broad and sweeping objective statement will trace to more WBS elements than would be the case for a very narrowly focused objective statement.

FIGURE 8. Notional Statement of objectives (SOO) format.

5.3 SOO Development Approach. A systematic process is essential for SOO development. The following steps are an integral part of that process:

a. Conduct market research to determine whether commercial items or nondevelopmental items are available to meet program requirements.

b. Review the requirement documents which authorize the program and define its basic objectives. Complete a risk assessment and expound the basic objectives of the program to incorporate the major technical and programmatic risks.

c. Review the various DoD/services/joint services requirements documents for program management, acquisition and control impact.

d. Prepare a bibliography citing the specific portions of all applicable governing instructions, directives, specifications and standards with which the program must comply. Keep these requirements to the absolute minimum.

MIL-HDBK-245D

e. Categorize the work described by the program WBS into that which will be done in-house and the objectives of that work which needs to be contracted.

f. For each RFP/contract defined, prepare a SOO from the objectives identified.

5.4 SOO-RFP Relationships.

a. Section L: Section L of the RFP must include instructions to the offeror that require using the SOO to construct and submit a SOW and CDRL. An example of such wording follows:

"The Statement of Objectives (SOO), included as (cite location of SOO in the RFP), provides the Government's overall objectives for this solicitation. Offerors shall use the SOO, together with other applicable portions of this RFP, as the basis for preparing their proposal, including the CWBS, SOW and CDRL. The offeror shall ensure all aspects of the SOO are addressed. The SOW should specify in clear, understandable terms the work to be done in developing or producing the goods to be delivered or services to be performed by the contractor. Preparation of an effective SOW requires both an understanding of the goods or services that are needed to satisfy a particular requirement and an ability to define what is required in specific, performance based, quantitative terms. The offerors understanding of both required goods/services, and work effort required to accomplish should be fully demonstrated in the offeror's proposed CWBS, SOW, and CDRL. For complex interrelationships among RFP/contract documents, use of a cross-reference matrix may be helpful (see figure 2 in Section 3 of this handbook).

The offeror shall use his proposed SOW to prepare a CDRL including appropriately tailored data item description references. The requirements listed below (if any) are known minimum Government data requirements. The offeror may include additional data requirements. All data requirements shall be traceable to specific tasks defined in the SOW. Each specific data requirement shall be selected from DoD 5010.12-L and specified on DD Form 1423.

(1) (cite minimum data requirements here if any)
(2) . . .
(3) . . ."

(End of Section L example wording.)

b. Section M: Evaluation Factors for Award should include sufficient criteria to:

(1) Evaluate the offeror's ability to successfully achieve the SOO objectives,
(2) Ensure a sound approach is proposed, and
(3) Verify that all requirements can be met.

MIL-HDBK-245D

The Government's intention to evaluate the proposed SOW should be stressed in both Section L and Section M. The offeror's proposed CWBS, SOW, and CDRL's will be evaluated as critical elements in assessing the offerors understanding of both required goods/services, and work effort required to accomplish them.

MIL-HDBK-245D

6 NOTES

6.1 Subject term (key word) listing.

Acquisition Plan (AP)
Contract Data Requirements List (CDRL)
Contract Line Item Number (CLIN)
Commercial off-the-shelf (COTS)
Data Item Description (DID)
Non-Developmental Item (NDI)
Operational Requirement Document (ORD)
Request for Proposal (RFP)
Statement of Objectives (SOO)
Statement of Work (SOW)
Work Breakdown Structure (WBS)
Work Breakdown Structure, Contract (CWBS)

6.2 Changes from previous issue. Marginal notations are not used in this revision to identify changes with respect to the previous issue due to the extent of the changes.

MIL-HDBK-245D

APPENDIX A
ACRONYMS

ADM	Advanced Development Model
AMSDL	Acquisition Management Systems and Data Requirements Control List
AP	Acquisition Plan
ASP	Acquisition Strategy Panel
CDRL	Contract Data Requirements List
CLIN	Contract Line Item Number
CM	Configuration Management
COTS	Commercial off-the-shelf
CWBS	Contract Work Breakdown Structure
D&V	Demonstration and Validation
DAB	Defense Acquisition Board
DFARS	Defense Federal Acquisition Regulation Supplement
DID	Data Item Description
DoD	Department of Defense
ECP	Engineering Change Proposal
EDM	Engineering Development Model
EMC	Electromagnetic Compatibility
FAR	Federal Acquisition Regulation
FMS	Foreign Military Sales
ILS	Integrated Logistics Support
IPS	Integrated Program Summary
LSA	Logistic Support Analysis
LSAR	Logistics Support Analysis Records
MILDEP	Military Department
MNS	Mission Needs Statement
MTBF	Mean-Time-Between-Failure
MTTR	Mean-Time-To-Repair
NDI	Non-Developmental Item
ORD	Operational Requirement Document
PMS	Planned Maintenance Subsystem
R&D	Research and Development
RDT&E	Research, Development, Test, and Evaluation
RFP	Request for Proposal
SOO	Statement of Objectives
SOW	Statement of Work
SPEC	Specification
SRD	System Requirements Document
STD	Standard
T&E	Test and Evaluation
WBS	Work Breakdown Structure

MIL-HDBK-245D

APPENDIX B
WORK WORDS/PRODUCT WORDS

B.1 Select the key word that properly expresses the degree of contractor involvement. Specify what is to be done and the total nature of the work requirement. The word list provided in this Appendix is not complete but is provided to stimulate the thinking of the SOW writer by pointing out the critical differences in the meaning of work words versus the product words identified in connection with deliverable data.

B.2 Work words. When selecting the key work word that properly expresses contractor's involvement, the SOW writer must define explicitly the total nature of the work requirement in terms of what is to be done. In some cases, the "why" or the application of the results of the performed work may be stated if it clarifies the requirement. The following sample list contains words which have the inherent value of work. This list is offered as a reminder of the various shades of meaning conveyed by choice of words.

analyze (solve by analysis)
annotate (provide with comments)
ascertain (find out with certainty)
attend (be present at)
audit (officially examine)
build (make by putting together)
calculate (find out by computation)
consider (think about, to decide)
construct (put together; build)
control (direct; regulate)
contribute (give along with others)
compare (find out likeness or differences)
create (cause to be; make)
determine (resolve; settle; decide)
differentiate (make a distinction between)
develop (bring into being or activity)
define (make clear; settle the limits)
design (perform an original act)
evolve (develop gradually, work out)
examine (look at closely; test quality of)
explore(examine for discovery)
extract (take out; deduce, select)
erect (put together; set upright)
establish (set up; settle; prove beyond dispute)
estimate (approximate an opinion of)
evaluate (find or fix the value of)
fabricate (build; manufacture, invent)
form (give shape to; establish)

MIL-HDBK-245D

APPENDIX B

formulate	(to put together add express)
generate	(produce, cause to be)
identify	(to show or to find)
implement	(to carry out, put into practice)
install	(place; put into position)
inspect	(examine carefully or officially)
institute	(set up; establish, begin)
interpret	(explain the meaning of)
inquire	(ask, make a search of)
integrate	(to add parts to make whole)
investigate	(search into; examine closely)
judge	(decide; form an estimate of)
make	(cause to come into being)
maintain	(to keep in an existing state, to continue in, carry on)
manufacture	(fabricate from raw materials)
modify	(to change, alter)
monitor	(to watch or observe)
notice	(comment upon, review)
observe	(inspect, watch)
originate	(initiate, to give rise to)
organize	(integrate, arrange in a coherent unit)
perform	(do, carry out, accomplish)
plan	(devise a scheme for doing, making, arranging activities to achieve objectives)
probe	(investigate thoroughly)
produce	(give birth or rise to)
pursue	(seek, obtain or accomplish)
reason	(think, influence another's actions)
resolve	(reduce by analysis, clear up)
record	(set down in writing or act of electronic reproduction of communications)
recommend	(advise, attract favor of)
review	(inspection, examination or evaluation)
revise	(to correct, improve)
study	(careful examination or analysis)
seek	(try to discover; make an attempt)
search	(examine to find something)
scan	(look through hastily, examine intently)
screen	(to separate, present, or shield)
solve	(find an answer)
test	(evaluate, examine)
trace	(to copy or find by searching)
track	(observe or plot the path of)
update	(modernize, make current)

MIL-HDBK-245D

APPENDIX B

B.3 PRODUCT WORD LIST. Although Non-personal Services contracts may not result in data as a deliverable product, a large portion do. This list of product words is provided to assist in identifying those products.

agenda
audio visual aids
books
cards
certificates
charts
decks
disc-magnetic
documentation
drafts
drawings
drums-magnetic
equipment
files
findings
forms
guides
graphics
handbooks
illustrations
lists
ledgers
logs
manuals
manuscript
materials
minutes
outlines
proposals
pamphlets
plans
procedures
publications
recommendations
records
recordings
reproducible
reports
requests
sheets
specifications
standards
systems
tapes
transparencies

MIL-HDBK-245D

APPENDIX C

PHRASES HAVING MULTIPLE MEANINGS

C.1 This list of phrases having multiple meanings is provided as an example of those to be avoided.

To the satisfaction of the contracting officer,

As determined by the contracting officer,

In accordance with instructions of the contracting officer,

As directed by the contracting officer,

In the opinion of the contracting officer,

In the judgment of the contracting officer,

Unless otherwise directed by the contracting officer,

To furnish if requested by the contracting officer,

All reasonable requests of the contracting officer shall be compiled with,

Photographs shall be taken when and where directed by the contracting officer.

In strict accordance with,

In accordance with best commercial practice,

In accordance with best modern standard practice,

In accordance with the best engineering practice,

Workmanship shall be of the highest quality,

Workmanship shall be of the highest grade,

Accurate workmanship,

Securely mounted,

Installed in a neat and workmanlike manner,

MIL-HDBK-245D

APPENDIX C

Skillfully fitted,

Properly connected,

Properly assembled,

Good working order,

Good materials,

In accordance with applicable published specifications,

Products of a recognized reputable manufacturer,

Tests will be made unless waived,

Materials shall be of the highest grade, free from defects or imperfections, and of grades approved by the contracting officer.

Kinks and bends may be cause for rejection,

Carefully performed,

Neatly finished,

Metal parts shall be cleaned before painting,

Suitably housed,

Smooth surfaces,

Pleasing lines,

Of an approved type,

Of standard type,

Any phrases referring to "The Government inspector".

MIL-HDBK-245D

APPENDIX D - STATEMENT OF WORK EXAMPLES

APPENDIX D1: EXAMPLE SOW FOR PRODUCTS

APPENDIX D2: EXAMPLE SOW FOR SERVICES

MIL-HDBK-245D

APPENDIX D1

EXAMPLE SOW FOR PRODUCTS

1 SCOPE. This Statement of Work (SOW) defines the effort required for the design, engineering development, fabrication, and test of an Advanced Development Model (ADM) of the _______________ System for the Program Definition and Risk Reduction Phase. It includes the associated program management, human engineering, and logistic support planning requirements.

1.1 Background. The ______ program has been initiated to design, develop, produce, and deploy an _______improved system that will fulfill the______ requirements as specified in Operational Requirement No.______. The _____ System will replace the XYZ System, and will significantly improve _____ capabilities. The ______ System specification for the ADM was developed during the Concept Exploration Phase conducted over the past two years. Upon successful testing and acceptance of the ADM developed during this Program Definition and Risk Reduction Phase, it is intended to obtain Department of Defense approval to competitively procure Engineering Development Models (EDMs) using performance specifications and program plans developed under this SOW.

2 APPLICABLE DOCUMENTS. The following documents are applicable to this Statement of Work and attached appendices to the extent specified herein.

2.1 Department of Defense Specifications.
(List documents as appropriate.)

2.2 Department of Defense Standards
(List documents as appropriate.)

2.3 Availability of DoD Documents. Unless otherwise indicated, copies of specifications, standards and handbooks listed above are available from the Standardization Document Order Desk, 700 Robbins Ave, Bldg 4D, Philadelphia PA 19111-5094

2.4 Non-Government standards and other publications.
(List documents as appropriate.)

2.5 Availability of Non-Government standards and other publications. Application for copies should be addressed to the (name and address of the source).

3 REQUIREMENTS.

3.1 General. The work required by this contract shall be performed in accordance with _______ System Specification (#) and this Statement of Work (SOW).

MIL-HDBK-245D

APPENDIX D1

The contractor shall design, develop, fabricate, and test an Advanced Development Model as listed in Section C of this contract to meet the performance criteria specified by ______ System Specification (#) and in accordance with the detailed requirements in paragraph 3.2.1 below.

The contractor shall provide program management, human engineering management, and logistic support planning in accordance with the detail requirements of 3.2.2 below.

3.2 Detail Tasks.

3.2.1 Design, Engineering, Fabrication and Test.

3.2.1.1 Design and Engineering. The contractor shall design and develop an ADM of the _____ System to meet the specification and criteria of ______ System Specification (#) utilizing engineering trade-offs between performance, reliability, maintainability, supportability, producibility, and life cycle costs. The ______ System design shall include the equipment performance and physical characteristics, subsystem component location, materials, the software program design elements of a top-down design, basic module description, and interface design.

3.2.1.2 Design Analysis. The contractor shall conduct a detail design analysis of the selected design. Detailed physical and performance design characteristics shall be specifically identified including the engineering decision process for using one methodology over another. Design documentation shall include discussion of alternatives and the ramifications thereof, risk assessments, and trade-offs made.

3.2.1.3 Preliminary Design Review (PDR) and Design Formalization. The contractor shall conduct a Preliminary Design Review. Informal design reviews may be held at times agreed to by the Government and the Contractor.

As a result of the design analysis conducted in paragraph 3.2.1.2 and the PDR in 3.2.1.3, the contractor shall finalize and formalize the design for fabrication. Written procuring activity approval of the design is required before the contractor is authorized to proceed with ADM fabrication.

3.2.1.4 Fabrication. The contractor shall correct and document any design characteristics that are found to inhibit or make fabrication unnecessarily costly but that do not otherwise alter performance or system effectiveness characteristics.3.2.1.5 Test and Evaluation. The contractor shall conduct and evaluate the results of environmental and performance tests on the ADMs to demonstrate full compliance of all equipment and software with _____ System Specification (#). The tests shall be conducted in accordance with the developmental test plan developed by the contractor and approved by the Government. The tests may be conducted at the contractor's facilities or at an independent laboratory or commercial testing facility.

MIL-HDBK-245D

APPENDIX D1

3.2.1.6 Critical Design Review (CDR). The contractor shall conduct a Critical Design Review. At the CDR, the contractor shall formally report the results of the developmental tests, address design changes made during the fabrication process, and recommend design changes as a result of the developmental tests including trade-off impacts. The contractor shall incorporate all design changes approved during the CDR.

3.2.2 Program Planning

3.2.2.1 Program Management. The contractor shall establish and maintain management operations that shall include the following areas:

(a) Program Planning and Control
(b) Subcontractor Control
(c) Financial Management
(d) Data Management
(e) Management and Accountability for Government Furnished Equipment, Material or Information.
(f) Risk Management

The contractor shall develop and implement a Management Program that clearly defines how the ________ Program Definition and Risk Reduction Project will be managed and controlled. A task matrix keyed to the Work Breakdown Structure (WBS) shall be developed in sufficient detail to identify Contractor and subcontractor responsibilities. The Contractor shall develop and implement a management program that clearly defines how the _______ Program Definition and Risk Reduction Project will be managed and controlled.

The contractor shall establish and implement a program management office function to manage all technical performance, including reliability, maintainability, ILS, cost, schedule, and data delivery requirements of the contract.

3.2.2.2 Human Engineering Program. The contractor shall develop and implement a Human Engineering Program (HEP) to ensure that appropriate studies are performed and that human engineering criteria are applied to subsystem hardware and computer software design.

3.2.2.3 Logistic Support Planning. The contractor shall implement an ILS program to ensure that supportability design criteria and characteristics are considered and incorporated into the design consistent with the trade-off studies and that meet the operational availability requirements of _______ System Specification (_#_). The ILS program shall use a Logistic Support Analysis (LSA) as the principal analytic effort within the design process.

MIL-HDBK-245D

APPENDIX D2

EXAMPLE SOW FOR SERVICES

1 SCOPE. This SOW covers systems engineering, technical and management support services to the _______ Program Office This support encompasses engineering analysis and recommendations for technical logistical and life cycle support for _______ system.

2 APPLICABLE DOCUMENTS.

3 REQUIREMENTS.

3.1 Production Support.

3.1.1 Conduct independent review of __________ production programs to identify requirements consistent with directives governing the acquisition of system and equipment.

3.1.2 Using acquisition plans, existing hardware contracts and inherent lead-time items, construct schedules for inclusion in documentation for weapon system and equipment acquisitions.

3.1.3 Based on production program schedules as well as weapon system configurations, formulate technical documentation for these programs itemizing all supplies, data and services to be obtained.

3.1.4 Provide impact statements when deviations or changes occur and alternative recommendations when required to maintain individual program production integrity.

3.1.5 Identify, compile, and utilize available information, update and input data for manual or automated production scheduling information systems, prepare government production reports germane to maintaining weapons system production status and inventory.

3.1.6 Prepare production documentation for input into the applicable Management Information System (MIS).

3.1.7 Prepare recommendation for identifying project data to be entered into existing Automatic Data Processing (ADP) programs. When data system deficiencies are discovered, provide recommendations for solutions.

3.2 Foreign Military Sales (FMS) Support.

3.2.1 Compare actual deliveries with contract schedules for Military Departments (MILDEP) and FMS.

MIL-HDBK-245D

APPENDIX D2

3.2.2 Track components and deliverable end items, and compile monthly acceptance reports and quarterly production reports. Consolidate delivery schedules by fiscal year, weapons, components, support equipment and manufacturer.

3.2.3 Compare schedule with industrial capacities and weapon station buildup capabilities and identify shortcomings and problem areas in meeting these requirements.

3.2.4 Correlate consignment instructions, acceptance reports and production/weapon build-up capabilities.

3.2.5 Maintain and track material inspection receiving reports status reports of system components and support equipment.

3.3 MILDEP Support.

3.3.1 Identify unique MILDEP requirements for the system, its components and associated equipment, based on MILDEP production planning and production support requirements.

3.3.2 Compare current MILDEP acquisition plans and project directive with MILDEP delivery and performance requirements to identify firm and provisioned requirements by component and associated support equipment.

3.3.3 Determine the compatibility of requirements, military specifications and engineering documentation with MILDEP standard and specifications.

3.3.4 Provide recommendations to incorporate MILDEP stated requirements into the overall program schedules. Correlate and maintain the status of MILDEP monthly status reports thereof.

MIL-HDBK-245D

APPENDIX E

EXAMPLE SOO

E.1 Refer to Figure 8 in the body of this document for a general example. For specific examples of SOOs, contact Air Force Custodian - Code 10 (see DoD Standardization Directory (SD-1), which has all Preparing Activity codes, addresses, and telephone numbers).

MIL-HDBK-245D

Custodians:
Army - CR
Navy - EC
Air Force - 10

Review activities:
Army - AT
Navy - SH, AS, MC
Air Force - 11, 13

User Activities:
Army - SC
Navy - YD

Preparing activity:
Navy - EC
(Project Number MISC-0214)

STANDARDIZATION DOCUMENT IMPROVEMENT PROPOSAL

INSTRUCTIONS

1. The preparing activity must complete blocks 1, 2, 3, and 8. In block 1, both the document number and revision letter should be given.
2. The submitter of this form must complete blocks 4, 5, 6, and 7.
3. The preparing activity must provide a reply within 30 days from receipt of the form.

NOTE: This form may not be used to request copies of documents, nor to request waivers, or clarification of requirements on current contracts. Comments submitted on this form do not constitute or imply authorization to waive any portion of the referenced document(s) or to amend contractual requirements.

I RECOMMEND A CHANGE:	1. DOCUMENT NUMBER MIL-HDBK-245D	2. DOCUMENT DATE (*YYMMDD*) 960403

3. DOCUMENT TITLE
PREPARATION OF STATEMENT OF WORK (SOW)

4. NATURE OF CHANGE (*Identify paragraph number and include proposed rewrite, if possible. Attach extra sheets as needed.*)

5. REASON FOR RECOMMENDATION

6. SUBMITTER

a. NAME (*Last, First Middle Initial*)	b. ORGANIZATION	
c. ADDRESS (*Include Zip Code*)	d. TELEPHONE (*Include Area Code*) (1) Commercial (2) AUTOVON (*if applicable*)	7. DATE SUBMITTED (*YYMMDD*)

8. PREPARING ACTIVITY

a. NAME COMMANDER, SPACE AND NAVAL WARFARE SYSTEMS COMMAND (SPAWAR 05L1)	b. TELEPHONE ((Include Area Code) (1) Commercial) (703) 602-7234 (2) AUTOVON 332-7234
c. ADDRESS (Include Zip Code) 2451 CRYSTAL DRIVE ARLINGTON, VA 22245-5200	IF YOU DO NOT RECEIVE A REPLY WITHIN 45 DAYS, CONTACT: Defense Quality and Standardization Office 5203 Leesburg Pike, Suite 1403, Falls Church, VA 22041-3466 Telephone (703) 756-2340 AUTOVON 289-2340

DD Form 1426, OCT 89 Previous editions are obsolete. 198/290

Appendix II

NASA Guidance for Writing Work Statements

* National Aeronautics and Space Administration, *NASA Guidance for Writing Statements of Work*, NPG 5600.2B, December 1997. Online at http://www.hq.nasa.gov/office/procurement/newreq1.htm (accessed January 2008).

NATIONAL AERONAUTICS AND SPACE ADMINISTRATION
NPG 5600.2B
DECEMBER 1997

STATEMENT OF WORK (SOW)

* * *

GUIDANCE FOR WRITING WORK STATEMENTS

Preface

The objective of this guide is to provide guidance and assistance to our technical and program customers when it is necessary to develop a statement of work for a procurement.

This document provides guidance, instructions and references for the preparation of statements of work for NASA acquisitions. Although it provides coverage for statements of work in general, it emphasizes the use of Performance (Based) Work Statements (PWS). It is the NASA policy that all contracts will be considered for PWS and focus on outcomes or results and not methods of performance or processes. Acquisition reform is striving to reduce Government risk by using performance-based specifications and standards, which make the contractor responsible for providing the product requested, assuming the risk for meeting performance requirements, and seeking innovations to efficiently and effectively achieve performance objectives. Contractors will be given more latitude for determining methods of performance, with more responsibility for performance quality. The use of PWS should lead to more cost-effective acquisitions and better value.

Chapter 4, Section 403 provides the NASA Procurement internet address (URL) for Performance Based Contracting. It contains policy documents, guidance, training modules and statement of work templates to help in preparing PWSs.

This handbook replaces the Statements of Work Handbook, NHB 5600.2A.

/Original Signed/
Deidre A. Lee
Associate Administrator for Procurement

CONTENTS

[The page numbers shown in this Internet document track to the distributed paper copy only.]

CHAPTER 1
REQUIREMENTS DOCUMENTS

101 GENERAL

NASA expends approximately 90% of it annual budget each year through the acquisition process. In order to acquire goods, services, research, products and other items through this process, our needs must be described to contractors, suppliers and vendors. This description is called a specification, needs statement or statement of work. The Federal Acquisition Regulation (FAR) (Part 11) prescribes policies and procedures for describing agency needs. It has established an order of priority that requirement documents, such as statements of work, should be "performance-oriented". The next type of needs document is a "detailed design-oriented" document. Lastly, the FAR lists government standards and specifications as the least preferred type of needs document.

Developing a needs or requirements document can be a very complex and challenging task. Statements of work are the most challenging of the requirements documents. Normally a statement of work is employed when the simpler needs requirements documents cannot be used and it must describe in sufficient detail what must be accomplished. The statement of work must be done properly and with high quality. Contracting for timely, high quality products or services is wholly dependent on the statement of work or requirements document. If the needs are not well described it is highly likely that a contractor will have difficulty producing what NASA needs to support its mission.

As a result, this guidance is being issued to assist technical and program personnel in writing the most difficult requirements document, the statement of work.

102 ALTERNATIVES TO A STATEMENT OF WORK

Once a requirement of need has been identified, it is possible that a requirements document or statement of work may not be necessary. There are a number of Governmentwide and Agency initiatives that may save time and effort by using existing other contracts or a streamlined acquisition method.

For small dollar acquisitions credit cards can now be used across the Federal Government. Should a requirement fit into the credit card program, a very short and succinct statement may be all that is needed. Federal Supply Schedules have been expanded to include many services that NASA uses. Two other NASA initiatives may also be considered before embarking on a formal statement of work. First, is the Consolidated Contracting Initiative (CCI). This program involves sharing of contract resources across the agency and the government. Products and services that are used by more than one NASA Center are acquired under one contract at one Center. Any Center can order off of the contract for their mission needs. Many other Federal agencies have contracts that are available to NASA which are also included in this system.

Second is the mid-range procurement initiative. This is a very streamlined method of procurement for acquisition between \$1 million and \$5 million. It requires less documentation and much less time.

Acquiring commercial items is another method of procurement that eliminated the need for a formal statement of work. The principle employed here is that the Government acquires supplies and services from the commercial sector the way they sell to each other. A statement of need is developed which explains to industry what needs to be accomplished, the type of product or service to be acquired, the performance requirements and/or the essential physical characteristics. It is also the preferred manner in which to conduct an acquisition. Should your requirement appear to meet this commercial items method it offers shorter procurement lead time and other advantages.

To find out more about these streamlined approaches and whether any would satisfy your need, contact your Center procurement office.

103 STATEMENTS OF WORK

Statements of work are the most essential documents in any Federal solicitation or contract. They are read and interpreted by government and industry personnel with diverse backgrounds such as engineers, scientists, accountants, lawyers, contract specialists and other business fields. Therefore, the statements of work must be written so that technical and non-technical readers can understand them during the solicitation, award and administration phases of the acquisition cycle. An initial investment of time and effort to write a clear and high quality statement of work will:

a. enable offerors to clearly understand the requirements and needs of NASA;

b. allow offerors to more accurately cost or price their proposal and submit higher quality technical proposals;

c. provide a baseline for the development of other parts of the solicitation, particularly the evaluation criteria, technical proposal instructions and independent cost estimate;

d. minimize the need for change orders which can increase the cost or price and delay completion;

e. allow both the Government and contractor to assess performance ; and

f. reduce claims and disputes under the contract.

104 KINDS OF STATEMENTS OF WORK (SOW)

There are three major types of statements of work (SOW) and they are:

a. Design/detailed specification;

b. Level of effort; and

c. Performance oriented (based).

Although there are other types and variations of each, this guide will work within these three categories.

Design/detail statements of work tell the contractor how to do the work. It may include precise measurements, tolerances, materials, quality control requirements, and other government requirements that control the processes of the contractor. There are wide variances in application of this type of SOW. It is as varied as the requirements that are acquired under them. The point is that the government, to a large degree, requires the contractor to follow the government's way of performing the task or making a product. This causes the risk of performance to be borne by the government. For instance, if the contractor builds and/or performs a task and follows the government's SOW exactly, and the product or service is faulty, who is to blame? Absent malfeasance or shoddy workmanship it is the government's process that the contractor was implementing so the contractor cannot be faulted. Although this type of SOW is primarily used for manufacturing or construction, other work efforts are described in this rigid format.

Level-of-effort SOWs can be written for almost any type of service unless it is an inherent government function. The real deliverable under this type of contract is an hour of work. They are normally associated with task order and delivery order contracts. Services or products are acquired via individual orders issued by the Contracting Office. The SOWs are usually very broad and describe the general nature, scope or complexity of the services or products to be procured over a given period of time. It is important in writing these SOWs to assure all work items are sufficiently covered. Task orders or delivery orders can only be issued in those areas specifically covered in the SOW. All activities outside of the SOW must be acquired through a separate procurement action.

Performance-based statements of work are the preferred method of stating needs. A performance based statement of work structures all aspects of an acquisition around the purpose of the work to be performed and does not dictate how the work is to be accomplished. It is written to ensure that contractors are given the freedom to determine how to meet the Government's performance objectives and provides for payment only when the results meet or exceed these objectives. It maximizes contractor control of work processes and allows for innovation in approaching various work requirements. Performance based SOWs emphasize performance that can be contractually defined so that the results of the contractor's effort can be measured in terms of technical and quality achievement, schedule progress, or cost performance. The goal of PBC is to:

a. Save money by reducing contract costs from elimination of unnecessary effort, through innovation by the contractor, and also by reducing Government surveillance.

b. Enable NASA to shift its emphasis from processes to outputs.

c. Hold contractors accountable for the end results. Ensure that contractors are given the freedom to determine how to meet NASA's performance objectives.

105 NASA POLICY

All new NASA contracts for services, hardware, and research and development will be considered for suitability for PBC and focus on required outcomes or results, not methods of performance or processes (NFS 1815.406-2). Justification is required for the use of other than PBC methods when acquiring services.

CHAPTER 2
STATEMENT OF WORK CONSIDERATIONS

201 ADVANCE PLANNING

Attention to the early stages of program and procurement planning is critical to achieving a successful acquisition. Identify and contact your Center Contracting Officer or representative. Inform them of what you are planning and ask for any suggestions. Keep them informed as you progress. There may be items such as, reporting requirements, market research, appropriateness of contract type, and the incorporation of effective incentive provisions that relate to your SOW that the contracting office can help you with. The amount of planning will be proportional to the complexity of the contemplated procurement. Program and Project Offices must determine what work will be performed by civil servants and by contractors. The SOW should be structured so that it is conducive to efficient performance. Contractors and civil servants must be given complete and severable pieces of work for which they are accountable. It is much easier to write a SOW around the required output if a complete task is turned over to the contractor.

201.1 Market Research

Agencies are required by Part 10 of the Federal Acquisition Regulation (FAR) to ensure that legitimate needs are identified and trade-offs evaluated to acquire items that meet those needs. Market research can include the Project Officer's knowledge of the marketplace, information gleaned from prior acquisitions, or from a formal sources sought synopsis published either in the Commerce Business Daily (CBD) or over the NASA Acquisition Internet Service (NAIS). **Research must determine if commercial or nondevelopmental items are available to meet NASA's needs.** FAR Parts 11 and 12 require NASA to buy a commercial product or service if feasible. If a commercial item is not available, the requirement must be reviewed to see if it can be revised to encompass commercial items.

201.2 Early Communication with Industry

Work with the contracting office to determine whether to release draft SOW and solicitation documents. This pre-release is recommended and has the following advantages:

(1) permits early industry review and comment on complex specifications or Statements of Work,
(2) promotes competition,
(3) encourages informal resolution of procurement problems,
(4) improves industry's understanding of NASA's requirements and evaluation criteria, and
(5) encourages proposers to replace Government standards with non-Government standards as recommended by Office of Management and Budget (OMB) Circular A-119.

NASA normally requires a draft solicitation to be issued permitting early identification and resolution of industry's questions, concerns, and recommendations. Conferences with prospective offerors can also be held to clarify or explain requirements or to address industry questions or recommendations on how to state those requirements. These may be Pre-solicitation Conferences (held before release of the solicitation) or Pre-proposal Conferences (held after release of the solicitation but before proposals are due).

202 PREPARATION GUIDANCE

This section provides suggestions for developing and writing statements of work. The suggestions are organized by topic.

202.1 General

a. The SOW will be read and interpreted by a variety of people from diverse disciplines, such as attorneys, acquisition personnel, cost estimators, accountants, technical specialists, engineers, etc. It is imperative that the words be understood not only by the writer of the SOW, but by the readers.

b. The SOW/specification, as an integral part of a contract, is subject to contract law. A fundamental legal principle is that because the Government is the drafter, any ambiguity usually is construed against the Government by the courts; that is, when two reasonable interpretations are possible, the court will adopt the interpretation espoused by the non-drafting party. The interpreter must look to what the contract actually says, not what the Government meant to say or would like to have said. Drafters of SOWs are often tempted to write vague language because they think it gives them the flexibility to loosely interpret the SOW at a later date. However, the drafter (Government) would lose in a contract dispute based on an ambiguity in the SOW. Further, ambiguous work statements result in protests, unsatisfactory contractor performance, delays, claims, disputes, and increased contract costs. Conversely, a high-quality document leads to a greater likelihood of successful contractor performance. When drafting a SOW, strive for clarity above all else.

c. Simple words, phrases, and sentences are used for clarity. Well-understood words and phrases improve the PWS by minimizing ambiguities. Be concise, precise, and consistent. Careful and exact descriptions will avoid misunderstandings before and during the life of a contract. Keep sentences short and to the point.

d. Choice of Verbs.

(1) Use **Active verbs**. Examples include: analyze, audit, calculate, create, design, develop, erect, evaluate, explore, interpret, investigate, observe,

organize, perform, and produce (work words). For instance, the PWS could require the contractor to "conduct the experiment and produce a report describing and analyzing (or interpreting) the results." (2) Avoid **Passive verbs** that can lead to vague statements. For example, the phrase "the contractor shall perform," is preferred in lieu of "it shall be performed" because the latter does not definitively state which party shall perform. Avoid "should" or "may" because they leave the decision for action up to the contractor. Use "shall" when describing a provision binding on the contractor. Use "will" to indicate actions by the Government.

e. To reduce the possibility of misinterpretation, terminology must be consistent. The same words and phrases must be used when describing the same requirement. It is confusing if a hole is referred to as an "orifice" and later called an "aperture".

f. When contracting for services, NASA must ensure that any final Agency action reflects the informed, independent judgment of NASA officials. Contractors must not be allowed to perform inherently Governmental functions as defined in OFPP Policy Letter 92-1, Inherently Governmental Functions. These functions include those activities that require either the exercise of discretion in applying Government authority or the making of value judgments in forming decisions for the Government.

g. Avoid redundancy. Redundancy can reduce clarity, thereby increasing the possibility for ambiguity and contradiction. If amplification, modification, or exceptions are required, make specific reference to the applicable portions and describe the change.

h. Vague/inexact words and generalizations are open to so many interpretations that they become meaningless. Phrases such as "securely mounted", "properly assembled", and "carefully performed" are examples of unenforceable language. Avoid catch-all and open-ended phrases, such as "is common practice in the industry," "as directed," or "subject to approval."

i. Note that common industry or in-house terminology is not always as universally defined as might be assumed. Technical terms must be specifically defined since judges settling disputes lean toward the "ordinary and usual" meaning and usually interpret the meaning against the drafter. If the writer is unable to define the term, potential offerors will have the same difficulty.

j. Avoid using "any," "either," or "and/or" unless NASA wants to give the contractor a choice in what must be done. Also, avoid the use of "etc.," because the reader doesn't have any idea of the items that could be missing.

k. Include definitions that provide a common basis for understanding between the contractor and NASA. Ensure each "term of art" has only one universally understood meaning; otherwise define it.

l. Use abbreviations or acronyms only after spelling them out the first time they are referenced. When there are many, it is advisable to provide an appendix.

m. Any document referenced in the solicitation must be either furnished with the solicitation or available at a location identified in the solicitation. The date or version of each document must also be specified, not listed as "version in effect on date of award."

n. Do not duplicate material in the SOW that the CO will include in other parts of the contract. Consult the CO for guidance during the early stages of SOW preparation.

o. As part of the initial proposal, offerors can (1) be required to submit detailed plans for compliance with Safety and Health Requirements, Quality System and Assurance Requirements, and similar items, or (2) allowed to submit summary plans accompanied by a statement to provide more detailed plans if selected. A preference must be stated in the PR package.

p. The Project Manager should indicate, if appropriate, desired design output, verification, and how design changes will be managed. The inspection portion shall address inspection and testing requirements (if appropriate, reference ISO element 4.10). It may be helpful to have the contractor develop a quality plan or documented procedure that will be used to inspect and test the product or identify non-conforming items. If appropriate, reference ISO elements 4.4 (Design) and 4.9 (Process Control).

q. In all cases, statements of work must:

(1) be definitive enough to protect the Government's interests;
(2) serve as a basis for contractor response, evaluation of proposals, and source selection; and
(3) provide a meaningful measure of performance so both the Government and the contractor will know when the work is satisfactorily completed (see Appendix D).

202.2 Deliverables

a. This section contains information on what the contractor is to provide NASA and when it is required. Identify only those outputs that are essential and a part of the performance requirement's summary. Express the outputs in concise, easily understood, measurable terms.

b. Clearly state which party will perform each task by delineating a division of responsibilities between NASA, the contractor, and others.

(1) If review is to be provided by NASA, a time limit must be set within which review/comment must be provided. Each time the contractor suspends activity to wait for NASA's response, time and money are expended. To avoid a breach of contract by the Government, the contract should state "*the contractor shall presume "no comment" and proceed if comment is not provided within* ________________________" (a specified period). (2) Clauses or statements that make contractor performance dependent on NASA must be avoided. A contract shall clearly state the intended effect of interim reviews to avoid releasing the contractor from subsequent liability. For example, if the contractor's overall obligation is to design and build an item that meets a final specification but NASA's review of the design is required before proceeding, such review should not be considered as an approval. Courts have generally held that an approval transfers responsibility to the approving party. Beware of the contractor giving accountability back to the Government while they are being paid to be accountable. A contractor may readily agree or even request NASA's review and approval of their plans and procedures. Do not do it! Make contractors accountable.

c. Provide a realistic delivery schedule for contract performance and completion. Schedules that are unnecessarily short or difficult to attain tend to restrict competition and result in higher contract prices. Provide sufficient information for the contractor to establish its own milestones against which its progress can be measured. Be sure this section is consistent with the rest of the solicitation.

202.3 Data Requirements

a. Minimize the data requirements. Buy only the data needed by NASA to make a decision and/or comply with a higher level requirement. Reduce costs by requesting data that will normally be created in performance of the contract. Avoid contractor proprietary information management or technical data systems that hinder Government oversight or create a sole source problem in follow-on procurements. Don't request reports that NASA can generate on its own from contractor data.

b. The PR Initiator must prepare a list of all data to be delivered under the contract, including the time and frequency of delivery. This includes information on the status of the contractor effort, information needed to support, manage, and operate the system, and using contractor formats or those common to the contractor's customers, if feasible.

c. In major system acquisitions, all data requirements must be specified in a separate line item listed in a section of the solicitation other than the PWS.

202.4 Government Property

a. FAR Subpart 45.3 requires that contractors provide all facilities required for performance of Government contracts unless the contracting situation falls within one of the stated exceptions in FAR 45.302. Facilities in this context refers to real property (i.e., land, buildings, and other structures) and plant equipment (i.e., general purpose equipment, test equipment, furniture, computers, vehicles, and similar items). The same rule applies to furnishing material, except the Government may do so to achieve significant economy or standardization, or when in the Government's interest.

b. Providing equipment to contractors on-site must be done sparingly since the contractor will be dependent upon the Government for care and maintenance. This dependence may hinder the ability of contractors to be fully accountable.

c. When furnishing property to contractors appears necessary, care must be taken to assure that regulatory authority exists and that appropriate documentation is prepared justifying an exception to general policy. Following this determination, the identification of each item, time of delivery, and condition (if feasible) of the Government property must be itemized.

203 PROTECTING THE INTEGRITY OF THE PROCESS

The Government acquisition process must be conducted in a manner above reproach, with complete impartiality and with no preferential treatment. NASA personnel associated with the acquisition process have a responsibility to protect its integrity and must abide by the following:

(1) All potential offerors must be given equal access to information on competitive acquisitions. Generally draft Requests for Proposals (RFPs),

pre-solicitation/ pre-proposal conferences, and/or one-on-one discussions between NASA technical personnel and potential offerors improve the acquisition process. However, any information that could give an offeror a competitive advantage must be made available to all potential offerors. (2) In the interval between release of a competitive solicitation and contract award, all communication with prospective contractors relating to the acquisition must be through the Contracting Officer. (3) Proprietary and source selection sensitive information must be protected from unauthorized disclosure. Violations of the procurement integrity provisions in Section 27 of the Office of Federal Procurement Policy Act and FAR 3.104 may lead to civil and criminal penalties for improper disclosure of information relating to a procurement. (4) Specifications and SOWs must not be unnecessarily restrictive to avoid unfairly excluding one vendor or increasing prospects for award to another. (5) Contractors that prepare NASA SOWs are generally prohibited from proposing on that same requirement. This is an organizational conflict of interest.

204 KEY PARTICIPANTS

The organization needing contractor support is required to provide the SOW or Specification; however, writing these documents must always be a team effort. The Project Manager and the Contracting Officer will build a team that includes personnel who are experts in the technical disciplines, financial management, fabrication, test, logistics, configuration management, operations, safety, reliability, maintainability, and quality assurance. Contractor personnel or consultants cannot be members of this team without written justification by the appropriate Head of the Center and prior written consent from the Headquarters Office of Procurement.

204.1 Project Manager

The requesting organization will assign an individual who is familiar with the technical requirements of the procurement to be responsible for writing the SOW. This person will define and articulate the contract requirements and is also responsible for planning, program control functions, developing program objectives, delivery requirements, scheduling, estimating, budgeting, specific project plans, surveillance plan development, and participating in the source selection.

204.2 Contracting Officer (CO)

Contracting Officers are responsible for ensuring performance of the contract, and safeguarding the interest of the U.S. in its contractual relationships. The CO does not decide NASA's need, but rather assists the project manager in preparation of a SOW/specification that clearly states NASA's needs in conformance with the regulations. A CO is the only member of the team that has authority to obligate the Government (FAR 2.101).

204.3 Contracting Officer's Technical Representative (COTR)

The technical Program Office will nominate as COTR an employee with the technical expertise necessary to administer the contract. This person must have received the mandatory COTR training, and is often the Project Manager who initiated the Procurement Request (PR). At contract award, the CO will issue a letter of delegation that specifies the limits of the COTR's authority. This appointment enables the COTR to assist the CO with the technical aspects of the contract. See NFS 1842.270.

204.4 Quality Representative (QR)

The QR provides the quality assurance requirements, and assists in developing performance standards and project surveillance plans. The QR is also responsible for evaluating contractor performance in accordance with the pre-established Surveillance Plan described in ¤604.

CHAPTER 3
REQUIREMENTS ANALYSIS

301 GETTING STARTED

Requirements analysis determines what NASA's needs are, and what kinds of services and outputs are to be provided by a contractor. A systematic process for SOW development begins with an analysis of what work is to be performed and breaks down the work into components. It ends with a clear description of performance output requirements.

302 WORK BREAKDOWN STRUCTURES (WBS)

a. The WBS is a top-level overview that provides the basis for monitoring a program or project by subdividing the work into successively smaller increments until a manageable element is reached. It develops a program-team consensus on what the customer wants. Together with a make/

buy determination, it can be a useful tool in deciding what elements are performed by civil servants and by contractors. A good WBS assures that significant tasks are not overlooked. b. Although the WBS can be a valuable tool, it is not necessary for all procurements. When used, the WBS must avoid stifling innovative ideas. Rigid control of every detail is neither necessary nor desirable. It must not be so explicit that there is no room for creative thinking or individual empowerment, yet it must be sufficiently defined and all work elements identified to permit inspection and acceptance. c. NASA Systems Engineering Handbook sets forth policies and processes for preparation of the WBS.

303 GATHERING HISTORICAL DATA

a. After identification by means of the WBS of services or products that are required, resource data are gathered for both in-house and contractor efforts. This involves collecting and analyzing historical data (indicating what, when, how much, etc. relative to prior work performed) to describe the job, establish how often the service or output is needed, and ensure that we don't pay for something that has already been done. Then define objectives or goals that differentiate the programs. Finally, establish a historical background of prior successes/failures throughout this program. b. Data required is available from NASA's Lessons-Learned System, from other databases or records (such as sampling or on-the-job observation), or from other agencies that have acquired similar services. Also, where applicable, review past safety violations, OSHA judgments, EPA violations or citations, and employee lost-time accident rates.

303.1 Benchmarking

The purpose of benchmarking is to improve the workings of your own organization by taking advantage of another organization's Lessons Learned and to avoid mistakes made in the past. In the early steps of planning, communicate with other organizations to gain insight on similar requirements. Then follow the four basic steps to benchmarking: preparation, observation, comparison, and action.

(1) Preparation means identifying contracts similar to the one you are trying to write, but do not limit the search to Government contracts. Networking at procurement offices can often lead to other connections. Be prepared with specific questions concerning expected deliverables, services, etc., and what measures they use in determining success. (2) The second and most important step is observation. Write down all facts that are useful. Find out what the organization has learned, both good

and bad. Observe how successful its approach has been. You could also request a copy of their SOW to use as a template. (3) The third phase is comparison. Look at the information gained and ask, "what useful and relevant information did I get?" Make a matrix of what is needed and what you got to assist in understanding how to apply the information received. (4) The final phase is action. Now apply what was learned by drafting the SOW. Continue working with procurement, your technical staff, and other managers so problem areas and missing details can be identified. You may want to have one of the benchmarking organizations help you, but be careful since you may be in a procurement-sensitive phase.

303.2 Output Data

One of the most important and difficult tasks of the team is to find how often output services will be furnished during contract performance. Historical information must be modified by incorporating anticipated changes. In Performance-Based Contracting this information may be made available to the contractor for information purposes only.

WORKLOAD

SERVICE	HISTORICAL WORKLOAD	KNOWN (ANTICIPATED) CHANGE	ESTIMATED WORKLOAD
Launches	7 per year	± 1	6 to 8 per year
Payloads	2 Major, 3 Minor per Flight	-1 to 1	1 Major, 2 to 4 Minor per Flight

303.3 Physical Resources Data

Another challenging task is to gather data on facilities, materials, and equipment required to support the work to be performed. As a general rule, contractors are required to provide all resources for work they will be doing. However, in the rare exceptions where equipment is furnished, writers of the SOW will use the resources data to develop their list of Government-furnished property.

FACILITY: ENGINE PROCESSING

FACILITY	DESCRIPTION	SQ. FT.	LOCATION
Building #223	Engine Processing facility. A single story type building used to shelter Flight Hardware and workers during turnaround activities.	25,000	KSC

MATERIALS: ENGINE REPAIR

NAME	STOCK N0.	DESCRIPTION	QTY.	LOCATION	ESTIMATED YEARLY USE
Hydrogen	100357	Used for engine propellant	20 tons per flight	Bldg 223	150 Tons

EQUIPMENT: ENGINE REPAIR

NAME	STOCK NO.	DESCRIPTION	LOCATION	QTY.
Engine Stand	101135	Holds engine for turnaround activity	Vehicle Overhaul Facility, Bldg #233	1

303.4 Personnel Resources Data

Gather data on the numbers and types of personnel that may be needed to perform each service output. This will be useful in evaluating a proposal's cost realism and in developing the Government estimate. It is the responsibility of the contractor to manage its own staffing plan. This gives the contractor latitude to manage its own work force and choose its own methods for work accomplishment. The contract should not normally specify staffing levels or use "key personnel" clauses.

303.5 Quality Systems Data

Data on the contractor's ability to meet contract requirements must be in accordance with ISO 9000; including quality system and QA requirements.

304 PROJECT WORK BREAKDOWN STRUCTURES (PWBS)

a. The WBS will be further developed from the program level downward to a project-by-project basis by means of the PWBS. A PWBS is prepared when project definition permits and will be refined and changed as design concepts change to reflect new system and subsystem approaches. Until a project is completed, the PWBS is a flexible working tool.

(1) It includes all effort required to achieve an end objective. It encompasses total project content by relating the elements of work to each other and to the end product. A PWBS, which describes inputs, covers both in-house and contractor efforts.

(2) It is developed by displaying and defining the total effort to be performed in identifiable and measurable elements. A PWBS element can represent varying aggregations of individual jobs or tasks, each of which is planned, approved, and managed at an appropriate level. No task should be overlooked.

(3) It provides the framework for project planning and control and also for making decisions conducive to effective use of contractor support.

(4) It provides means for integrating and assessing technical, schedule, and cost performance.

(5) It provides a framework for performance measurement.

(6) It provides all applicable quality systems and quality assurance requirements, as well as definition of the type and extent of control to be exercised on subcontracts.

(7) All element descriptions are concise and easy to understand.

b. A PWBS must also be compatible with the coding structure defined in NASA Financial Management Manual FMM 9100. c. Following a PWBS breakdown, the section of the PWBS identifying contracting efforts is extended by using a contract WBS (CWBS).

305 CONTRACT WORK BREAKDOWN STRUCTURES (CWBS).

a. For non-routine, more complex requirements, a CWBS is created. A CWBS is a hierarchical diagram for a specific contract. It identifies the requirements to be satisfied, **leaving the contractor free to determine how to achieve the desired result**. b. A CWBS is prepared prior to writing the SOW and serves as an "outline" for the technical requirements contained in the SOW. A good CWBS makes a SOW easier to write, facilitates preparation of contractor proposals, helps in preparation of the in-house estimate, and assists with evaluation and source selection activities.

(1) The first step is to provide a systematic approach to facilitate project management by breaking the effort into easily managed units of work that have an identifiable output and a similar technical or managerial nature. Divide the overall requirement into major phases or tasks that represent a logical, and usually chronological, division of the work effort.

(2) For the second step, the major tasks required to achieve the end objectives are identified.

(3) Then, in the third and final step, each task is broken down further into sub-phases; normally to no more than three levels of detail. **Remember, each level identified by the Government in the SOW will limit the innovation and creativity allowed to the contractor on that level.** In addition, avoid developing the PWBS to a level so low that it will be in conflict with industry's normal management practices.

(4) When complete, the CWBS will break down each component, when the primary end item is hardware, as follows:

	Levels
1. Contract, Space Shuttle System	I
1.1 Propulsion System	II
1.1.1 Fan	III
1.1.2 Compressor	
1.1.3 Turbine	
1.2 Guidance	
1.3 Life Support System	
1.4 Project Management	
1.4.1 Performance Reports	

Note: Changes to the CWBS recommended by the contractor should be examined. In the above chart, a choice was made by NASA to go down to three levels. Remember, this limits the contractor in proposing any innovative methods in lieu of what is required in those three levels.

305.1 Extension of the CWBS by Contractors

a. In the RFP, contractors will be instructed to include in their proposals an extension of the CWBS to a level compatible with their management systems, e.g., earned value reporting.

b. The proposals normally include:

(1) **A Configuration Item** that is an aggregation of hardware/computer programs or any of its discrete portions, which satisfies an end-use function and is designated by NASA for configuration management. They may vary widely in complexity, size, and type. During development and manufacture of the initial (prototype) production configuration, they are those specification items whose functions and performance parameters must be defined and controlled to achieve the overall end-use function and performance. An item required for logistic support and designated for separate procurement is a configuration item.

(2) **High Risk Items** that involve technological, manufacturing or other state-of-the-art advances or considerations. They are critical in achieving program objectives, reliability, maintainability, safety, quality assurance or other such factors. They are designated by program/project management as requiring special attention.

(3) **Major Subcontracts and Inter-divisional Work** that are identified at the appropriate level on the extended CWBS. If they are large or complex enough, they are broken down to the same extent as if the tasks were a prime contract.

(4) **Cost Accounts** that are clear definitions of work to be performed and are distinct from other cost accounts. They have measurable beginning and end points.

c. Whenever NASA Form 533 (NASA Contractor Financial Management Reporting) is required, the 533 reporting categories must correlate with the CWBS (see NHB 9501.2, NASA Contractor Financial Management Reporting) as well as with the contractor's accounting system. In addition, each CWBS shall be designed to facilitate accounting for costs in accordance with the Agency-wide Coding Structure found in the NASA Financial Management Manual FMM 9100.

d. The extended CWBS will help in evaluating the contractor's understanding of the work to be done and of cost realism.

305.2 Contractual Use of the CWBS

a. The CWBS may be changed during negotiations to meet the needs of NASA and/or the contractor. In routine efforts, it becomes the basis, in conjunction with the SOW, against which the contractor performs the effort. In non-routine efforts, the CWBS should be a flexible guide developed by and for the use of the contractor, but the acceptance of the product should be against the performance standards.

b. Upon award, the levels of the CWBS that become part of the contract are what have been agreed upon by both parties; this is usually the top three levels. At that point, the CWBS cannot be changed except by modification of that contract.

306 GOVERNMENT COST ESTIMATE

a. Preparation of an estimate of costs to perform the effort is a responsibility of the Project Manager, with support from other technical experts and budget personnel. Estimated costs for each service output, based on available data, include details of assumptions made in preparing the estimate. These costs are also used in evaluating proposals and determining positive and negative performance incentives. The level of documentation required is dependent on the complexity and dollar value of the procurement. For major acquisitions, an independent cost estimate is often required.

b. NASA has decided to integrate full cost accounting, budgeting and management changes and practices to optimize the anticipated cost effective mission benefits of its full cost initiative. Full cost accounting is required by Federal legislation and related guidance. Full cost budgeting and management are indicated in Federal legislation and related guidance but are not specifically required. The strength and benefits of NASA's full cost practices are optimized by the integration and synergy of changes in each area. Full cost accounting by itself, over time, would likely lead to gradual budget and management improvements. However, concurrent changes to full cost practices in the accounting, budgeting and management areas can be expected to ensure that NASA optimizes improvements in each area immediately.

c. NASA must also consider commercial costs of performing similar work in the private sector. d. In-house cost estimates (labor hours, material costs, software requirements, etc.) developed by the cost estimating specialists must be reviewed by SOW contributors. Such reviews will permit early trade-off consideration on the desirability of requirements that are not directly related to essential technical objectives. These estimates will also be used to assist evaluators in determining if proposal costs are realistic.

CHAPTER 4
PERFORMANCE (BASED) WORK STATEMENTS (PWS)

401 GENERAL

Performance-Based Contracting means structuring all aspects of an acquisition around the purpose of the work to be performed - not to dictate how the work is to be accomplished. It is designed to ensure that contractors be given the freedom to determine how to meet the Government's performance objectives, the appropriate performance levels are achieved, and that payment is only made for results that meet these levels. It maximizes contractor control of work processes and allows for innovation in approaching various work requirements. Remember, when contractors are not told "how" to do the job, their ingenuity may surprise you.

PBC emphasizes performance that can be contractually defined so that the results of the contractor's effort can be measured in terms of technical and quality achievement, schedule progress, or cost performance. The significant steps in the PBC process include:

(1) emphasizing contract performance requirements that can be measured by a meaningful performance evaluation;

(2) selecting contractors that provide "best value" with proven past performance;

(3) providing positive incentives for good performance;

(4) determining contract type and incentives in accordance with a fair assessment and assignment of performance risk;

(5) performing contract surveillance and administration for insight only into essential areas of contractor performance; and

(6) being mindful of the need for conservation of Government resources.

The goal of PBC is to:

(1) Save money by reducing contract costs by eliminating unnecessary effort and through innovation by the contractor, and also by reducing Government surveillance.

(2) Enable NASA to shift its emphasis from processes to outputs.

(3) Hold contractors accountable for the end results.

(4) Ensure that contractors are given the freedom to determine how to meet NASA's performance objectives.

c. The following decision tree must be used by those who draft requirement documents.

PBC Roadmap

<table>
<tr><td>Can the Government assign performance responsibility to the contractor, and can performance be validated against a performance standard?</td><td>Yes —></td><td>Write a performance-based contract</td></tr>
<tr><td colspan="3">If No—</td></tr>
<tr><td>Can discrete portions of the effort be assigned to the contractor for performance responsibility, and can performance against those portions be validated against performance standards?</td><td>Yes —></td><td>Specify performance standards in the contract.</td></tr>
<tr><td colspan="3">If No—</td></tr>
<tr><td colspan="3">Specify critical processes in the contract or contract-referenced documents.</td></tr>
</table>

To be considered PBC, a PWS must include meaningful measurable performance standards and the quality level the NASA expects the contractor to provide. There are two categories of PBC-type contracts: contracts of a routine nature and contracts of a non-routine nature.

401.1 Routine Services

a. In contracting for services of a routine nature, whether high or low "tech" (e.g., computer service, guard service, or janitorial), it is essential to avoid under-specifying NASA's requirements. Work inadvertently omitted may later be construed to be outside the requirements of the contract and could require a contract change and increased costs. Even worse, omissions outside the scope of the contract could require a significant effort from NASA; a new competition or a Justification for Other Than Full and Open Competition (JOFOC). b. The PWS for routine services is usually written to require **output** (see Appendix D, ¤102). In the absence of a performance-based standard, NASA may not be able to ensure that the contractor completes the work at an acceptable level. In that event, NASA may be obligated to accept whatever product or service the contractor provides or make changes in the work requirements and pay more to acquire what is actually needed. c. There is usually a significant amount of data available for routine services plus a competitive marketplace with several suppliers; consequently, a firm-fixed price contract with deduction schedules (which are applied when performance is inadequate) is commonly used.

401.2 Non-Routine Requirements

When acquiring supplies, engineering, or unique non-routine services (including studies, analyses, or R&D efforts), performance-based specifications must **avoid over-specifying** NASA's requirements. Accordingly, the PWS for non-routine work is usually written to require an **outcome** (see Appendix D, ¤102). The policy limits the involvement of Government employees and provides contractors maximum flexibility in meeting NASA's need. If that need is succinctly defined, the contractor should be entrusted to fulfill that need.

402 GUIDELINES FOR WRITING A PWS

a. The contract will be a completion form (something is accomplished) as opposed to a term/level-of-effort form. b. To the maximum extent practicable (FAR Part 11.002), state the requirements in terms of:

(1) Functions to be performed;

(2) Performance required; or

> The PWS must include performance requirements and verification requirements that are measurable or quantifiable.

c. Without specifying how to perform the work, the PWS must clearly indicate the expected outcomes or outputs from the contractor such that contractor performance can be measured against the performance standards in the PWS. The definitions of standard performance, maximum positive and negative performance incentives, and the units of measurement will be established in the solicitation. They will vary from contract to contract and are subject to discussion during source selection.

d. To aid in continuity and to avoid confusion, the PWS format must conform to the numerical coding of the related task elements of the CWBS (see ¤305c). The coded task descriptions clearly define each deliverable end item, product, and task.

402.1 Hardware or End Item Deliverables

The PWS/specification describes, at the highest practicable level, what the end product must do (performance) and any critical constraints (e.g., size, weight). It eliminates process-oriented (how to) requirements and includes only minimally essential reporting requirements. The contract requirements and incentives are clearly communicated. Actual demonstrated performance of the end item is normally one of the measures -- in some cases the only measure.

402.2 Performance Based Specification

a. A major effect of acquisition reform is that the number of performance statements should be increased and the number of detailed, design-solution statements should be decreased. A performance specification, which shall be used to the greatest extent practicable, describes the work broadly by form, fit, and function instead of using detailed drawings, specifications, and standards. Offerors are free to meet the requirements in any way they can. This increases NASA's access to commercial, state-of-the-art technology. Requirements are expressed in terms of minimum acceptable performance standards (Appendix E) and place maximum responsibility for performance on the contractor. Additional information, such as standards, may be referenced as information to providers to improve understanding, but should be clearly distinquished/separated from requirements.

b. A performance specification also requires results, with criteria for verifying compliance without stating methods for achieving the required results. By not specifying an approach in manufacturing, design, or quality assurance to be used by the contractor, it permits a wide variety of contractor methods; thereby potentially increasing the number of contractors who can satisfy the requirement. Contractors can use their creative and innovative skills to the maximum.

c. Nevertheless, PBC emphasis does not preclude highly descriptive specifications, which (if expressed in performance terms) accurately and inclusively describe what we want done or delivered. d. In writing performance-based specifications, avoid the following:

(1) Performance specified at the subsystem or component level when it could be more appropriately specified at a higher level; e.g., the reliability of the system or vehicle should be specified instead of specific components with the system.

(2) Requirements that are not measurable or verifiable.

(3) Statements that constrain the solution to a single solution; e.g., "shall be fabricated from composite material."

(4) Orphan requirements; i.e., requirement statements that are not traceable to a specific performance or verification requirement statement in the specification.

(5) Requirement statements that are not appropriate for an effort in this phase of development or production.

(6) Specifications relying solely on directives to define performance, not the mission requirements.

(7) Citing standards and processes when performance standards can be developed.

(8) Citing of mandatory standards without justification.

(9) Requirements that are vague (e.g., "in accordance with commercial practices" in lieu of citing a commercial standard).

(10) Language in the specification that belongs in the PWS.

e. Listed below are key elements to be considered in preparing specifications and the related technical requirements.

(1) Description of supplies, or data that identifies the requirement. When appropriate, describe requirements broadly by form, fit, and function.

(2) Quantity (and unit).

(3) Packaging and marking requirements.

(4) Inspection, acceptance, and quality assurance. The concern for quality must be expressed by providing standards which result in proposals that offer credible responses concerning the ability to perform quality work; e.g., if the surface must not contain imperfections exceeding .01 inch, specifically state this as the assessment of quality.

(5) Place of delivery, performance and delivery dates, period of performance, and f.o.b. point. Efforts shall be made to give prospective contractors adequate time to produce the item or to provide the required service.

(6) Other information as necessary.

402.3 Major Systems Contracts

a. Contracts for definition and development of Major Systems have short, concise outcome PWSs that do not necessarily go into great detail. There is usually a specification/contract deliverable requirements list associated with these contracts, which may contain specific requirements for the product(s). The PWS must, however, state all requirements necessary to complete each task element of the WBS and be complete enough to allow the contractor to generate all information necessary to design, prototype, test, and verify.

b. A good approach for the acquisition of major systems is to acquire the effort in phases, with each phase having a limited but clear objective (see NFS Sub Part 1834.005-1). This approach also is a safeguard against committing scarce resources to an effort prematurely.

c. For study and preliminary definition contracts, the PWS must allow the contractor wide latitude for creativity, innovation and research. Describe efforts necessary to supplement existing information and bring present knowledge to a point where further detailed study for the most promising systems can be made.

402.4 Support Services

The PWS generally describe all of the services to be performed and includes explicit, measurable performance standards, surveillance procedures, and incentives. It includes only minimally essential reporting requirements, but the contractor will be held accountable for failure to meet those minimum requirements. The outline will be similar to the following:

1. Introduction

2. Scope of Work

3. Management Administration

4. Description of Services

4.1 Performance Standards

4.2 Performance Requirements Summary

5. Contract Deliverables

6. Minimally Essential Reporting Requirements

7. Appendices

8. Special Terms and Conditions

In preparing a PWS or a task assignment consider the following:

a. The PWS clearly describes the specific requirements the contractor is required to meet in performance of the contract. Specify the minimum required level of performance and quality, failing which, the objective of the contract or task will not be met.

b. Over-defining the contractor's responsibilities in terms of methods or procedures must be avoided since the Government is purchasing a result/service or some requirement which includes not only the contractor's labor, but also its expertise in the services to be provided and the management of those services. Place the responsibility for success on the contractor, not the Government.

c. On the other hand, provide enough information to define clearly and precisely the magnitude and complexity of the outcome/output desired. This will slightly restrict the contractor in managing their work force, but will help ensure all bidders clearly visualize the extent of effort required. d. In addition to the desired outputs or outcomes:

(1) specify the schedules of accomplishment and/or time limitations in which all services must be completed,

(2) provide a list of mandatory operating and safety procedures that the contractor must follow, and

(3) provide historical data on previous contracts or work by in-house personnel. This needs to be done carefully to avoid specifying staffing levels, etc.

e. In those cases where the Government can provide only a broad description, use of a task order contract shall be considered. Individual task orders can be written that clearly define each deliverable end item or product and include performance standards and incentives. All essential tasks must be included.

402.5 Research and Development (R&D) Contracts

a. Unlike contracts for supplies and services, most R&D contracts are directed toward specified objectives and knowledge where the work or methods cannot be precisely described in advance. It is difficult to judge the probabilities of ultimate success or required effort for technical approaches. R&D PWSs can be difficult to write if the contract's objectives are not defined sufficiently, yet they must be flexible enough to allow contractors freedom to exercise innovation and creativity. The most important performance-based element is to clearly define the requirements and/or the schedule such that the performance of the contractor is measurable. Following is a sample outline:

1. Introduction
2. Scope of Work
3. Description of Tasks to Be Performed/outputs desired
4. Schedule
5. Reporting Requirements
6. Attachments, Appendices and Exhibits

b. Typically for R&D, the contractor has a cost-type contract, therefore, has no cost risk. However, if the contractor receives a small fee for performing "best efforts," the substantive portion of any fee must be tied to successful performance - an objective measurement is preferred, however, at times a subjective determination could be meaningful and acceptable.

402.6 Basic Research

a. In basic research results cannot be determined in advance and often no deliverable is required except for a final report. In that case, the performance standards may be focused on timeliness, organization and thoroughness of the report, comprehensive bibliography, etc. These performance standards shall be used to "gate" contractor eligibility for fee, if any. b. When the principle purpose of the research is for the direct benefit or use of NASA, a contract shall be used. When not a direct benefit or use to NASA, the proper procurement vehicle is usually a grant or cooperative agreement.

403 PBC INTERNET REFERENCES, GUIDANCE AND TRAINING

The NASA Procurement home page has information, policies and guidance on PBC and contracting. It also has PBC templates from The U.S. Navy and the Department of Energy for use in preparing PBC statements of work. A tutorial is also available at this site.

CHAPTER 5
OTHER CONSIDERATIONS

501 SINGLE PROCESS INITIATIVE (SPI)

The purpose of the Single Process Initiative is to eliminate duplicative, highly tailored or customer unique requirements from NASA , DoD and other agency contracts and adopt instead a single process proposed by the contractor unless these requirements are essential to ensure mission safety and reliability. The thrust of this initiative is to enable contractors to propose single processes that meet the needs of multiple Government customers. Thus, eliminate duplicative and expensive contractor systems that are similar, and are required to satisfy various Government customers. SPI is expected to improve process efficiencies, improve product quality, reduce the contractors' operating costs, and ultimately reduce Government procurement costs. If, however, proprietary processes are selected over recognized consensus standards, the Government's competitive options may be limited.

Whenever possible, remove highly tailored or customer-unique requirements from contracts and adopt instead the single process principle. SPI would eliminate many unique systems and processes that are imposed by each of the contractor's many customers. For example, if a contractor is allowed to use a single soldering standard for all work at its facility instead of a unique standard for every customer, costs to every affected customer would be reduced while increasing the contractor's responsibility and accountability for quality.

PBC and the SPI are closely interrelated acquisition initiatives that affect how contract requirement documents are drafted. Ideally, all requirement documents would be completely performance-based. However, in some cases, that may not be practicable for some, or even all of the work. NASA may not want to relinquish performance responsibility and risk to the contractor, or the attainability of the desired performance may be in doubt. It may be necessary to describe the requirement in terms of processes to be followed, not in terms of required outcomes. Where processes must be specified, OMB Circular A-119 requires the use of existing voluntary consensus standards in preference to Government processes, unless impractical. It is preferable that processes be based on voluntary consensus standards to minimize reduction of the Government's competitive systems by being tied to a proprietary option.

502 STANDARDS AND DIRECTIVES

All potentially relevant directives must be screened to determine which will be used, if any. When only a part of a directive applies, excerpt (by reference) only the required parts of the directive into the contractual document.

The number of directives must be held to a minimum. Negative effects from excessive or inappropriate application of directives include: confusion or errors in performing work; undermining NASA's ability to enforce performance; increases in the cost of performance; unwarranted dictation of how work is to be performed; and discouraging or foreclosing contractor use of innovative or cost-effective performance methods. Remember, if NASA specifies "how to perform", it assumes the responsibility for the outcome.

OMB Circular A-119 requires the use of voluntary consensus standards in preference to Government standards unless their use is impractical or inconsistent with law.

503 THE METRIC SYSTEM

As part of an effort to maintain the competitiveness of the U.S. in international trade, the Metrics Conversion Act of 1975, as amended, requires Federal agencies to use the metric system of measurement in procurements, grants, and other business-related activities, except when impractical. NASA Management Instruction 8010.2 entitled, *"Use of the Metric System of Measurement in NASA Programs,"* specifically requires that all new projects use the metric system unless a waiver is obtained. Hybrid approaches, where metric units are used for new design elements and inch-pound units are used for existing designs, are acceptable but should be documented. PR initiators are responsible for determining the extent to which the metric system is used for their requirements and providing for waivers.

504 VALUE ENGINEERING (VE)

Value engineering is a program that rewards contractors for suggesting innovative ways to conduct work at a lower life-cycle cost without impairing essential functions. During the course of contract performance, contractors may submit Value Engineering Change Proposals (VECP). NASA evaluates each proposal and the estimated savings, and if a change is accepted, the contractor will share in any savings realized. See FAR Part 48.

Vague and unclear SOWs make VE assessments extremely difficult. Overstated requirements can provide opportunities to a contractor to be rewarded for eliminating requirements that should never have been included. On the other hand, failure to clearly state requirements makes it impossible to subsequently determine if the VECP covered work that was expected to be performed under the contract or is, in fact, innovative and worthy of award.

505 SHARED SAVINGS

This program provides an incentive for contractors to propose and implement, with NASA approval, significant cost reduction initiatives. NASA will benefit as the more efficient business practices that are implemented lead to reduced costs on current and follow-on contracts. In return, contractors are entitled to share in cost savings subject to limits established in a contract. See NFS subpart 1843.7101.

APPENDIX A
DOCUMENT REVIEW CHECKLIST

The following Checklist should be reviewed prior to forwarding the PWS/ specification for approval. It is a guide only, and items should be added or deleted to tailor it to the specific document.

1. Can I give the contractor full management responsibility and hold them accountable for the end results? Can I perform a meaningful evaluation of performance? Does my draft PWS reflect this strategy?

2. Is the PWS sufficiently detailed to permit both the Government and the contractor to estimate costs, to tabulate labor and other resources required to accomplish each task element? Will the contractors be able to prepare a sound technical and cost proposal?

3. Are standards clear that make it possible for all parties to measure performance?

4. Is the PWS/specification too restrictive? Does it tell contractors how to run their business?

5. Are proper quantities and delivery dates indicated for each deliverable?

6. When necessary to reference other documents, is the proper reference document described and cited? Is the entire document pertinent to the task or should only portions be referenced? Is it cross-referenced to the applicable SOW task element?

7. Have all requirements for data been specified separately in a Data Requirements section? Have all extraneous data requirements been eliminated? Are requirements specified adequately to obtain sufficient data to permit competition for anticipated follow-on procurements?

8. Have appropriate Government and industry standards been researched and referenced in the PWS, as necessary? Have requirements to use Government standards been limited to those where it is impractical to use non-Government standards? Have options been provided for proposers to recommend suitable replacement of Government standards with non-Government Standards?

9. Are all safety, reliability, quality assurance, and security requirements defined for the total life of the contract?

10. Has extraneous material been eliminated?

11. Has the document been checked for format and grammar? Are subheadings compatible with the subject matter of the heading? Is the text compatible with the title? Is a multi-decimal or alpha-numeric numbering system used in the PWS that can be cross-referenced to the CWBS?

12. Are all terms used consistently throughout, and adequately defined, including "industry-wide" terms?

13. Does the PWS cover the requirements imposed on the contractor's quality system to ensure that products conform to requirements?

14. Does the PWS cover any design or process control requirements required by NASA?

15. Does the PWS cover any specific Government requirements for inspection and testing?

16. Does the PWS provide for corrective/preventive action by the contractor in the event the product delivered is non-conforming to the specified product?

APPENDIX B
DEFINITIONS

CONTRACT. A bilateral agreement between two or more parties, enforceable by law, that obligates the seller to furnish something, and obligates the buyer to pay for it.

COOPERATIVE AGREEMENT. A legal instrument to reflect a relationship between the Government and a recipient to transfer a thing of value (money) to the recipient to accomplish a public purpose of support or stimulation authorized by Federal Statute.

COST-PLUS-AWARD-FEE CONTRACT (CPAF). A cost-reimbursement contract that provides for a fee consisting of an award amount, based upon a judgmental evaluation by the Government, sufficient to provide motivation for excellence in contract performance.

COST-PLUS-INCENTIVE-FEE CONTRACT (CPIF). A cost-reimbursement contract that provides for the initially negotiated fee to be adjusted later by a formula based on the relationship of total allowable costs to total target costs. The contract may include technical performance incentives when it is highly probable that the required development of a program is feasible and the Government has established its performance objectives.

COST-REIMBURSEMENT CONTRACT. A type of contract that provides for payment of allowable incurred costs, to the extent prescribed in the contract. These contracts establish an estimate of total costs for the purpose of obligating funds and establishing a ceiling that the contractor may not exceed without approval of the CO.

FEDERAL ACQUISITION REGULATION (FAR). The Federal regulation that implements procurement-related statutes and governs Government procurement.

FIXED-PRICE CONTRACT. A contract where the contractor agrees to deliver supplies or services at the times specified for an agreed upon price that cannot be changed unless the Government modifies the contract.

GOVERNMENT-FURNISHED PROPERTY (GFP). Property in the possession of, or directly acquired by, the Government and subsequently made available to the contractor.

GRANT. A legal instrument to transfer a thing of value (money) to the recipient to accomplish a public purpose of support or stimulation authorized by Federal statute.

MAJOR SYSTEM ACQUISITION. Those programs that are directed at and critical to fulfilling a NASA mission, entail the allocation of relatively large resources, and warrant special management attention.

NASA FAR SUPPLEMENT (NFS). NASA's supplement to the FAR, which together with the FAR governs NASA procurements.

NEGOTIATIONS. Written or oral discussions usually conducted with the selected offeror(s) to settle cost and other terms, which will be incorporated into the resultant contract.

NONDEVELOPMENTAL ITEM. Any previously developed item used by the Federal Government, state or local government, or a foreign government that the U.S. has a mutual defense cooperation agreement with.

OBJECTIVE PERFORMANCE MEASURE. Based on the attributes of physical objects that can be measured or counted.

OFFER. A response to a solicitation that, if accepted, would bind the offeror to perform the resultant contract. Responses to invitations for bids (sealed bidding) are offers called "bids" or "sealed bids." Responses to requests for proposals (negotiation) are offers called "proposals."

OUTCOME MEASURE. An assessment of the results of a program activity compared to its intended purpose (objective).

OUTPUT MEASURE. The tabulation, calculation, or recording of activity or effort and can be expressed in a quantitative or qualitative manner.

PERFORMANCE-BASED CONTRACTING. Structuring all aspects of an acquisition around the purpose of the work to be performed as opposed to either the manner by which the work is to be performed or broad and imprecise statements of work.

PERSONAL SERVICES CONTRACT. A contract that, by its express terms or as administered, makes the contractor personnel appear, in effect, Government employees (see FAR 37.104).

PROPOSAL. A response by a prospective contractor to a Request for Proposals issued by the CO in negotiated acquisitions. It is an offer (including technical performance, as well as cost or price terms) that can be accepted by the Government to create a binding contract, either following negotiations or when certain conditions are satisfied. The term "bid" is used in sealed bid procurements.

PROPOSAL EVALUATION FACTORS. Factors against which proposals are evaluated. The RFP must explain these factors and their order of importance.

PURCHASE OR PROCUREMENT REQUEST (PR). The document prepared by the requiring activity which (1) describes the supplies or services to be acquired, (2) certifies the availability of funds, and (3) includes other information and approvals necessary for the CO to initiate an acquisition action.

REASONABLE COST. A cost which in its nature and amount does not exceed that which would be incurred by a prudent person in the conduct of competitive business. If challenged, the burden of proof for determining cost reasonableness rests with the contractor.

REQUEST FOR PROPOSALS (RFP). The Government's invitation (solicitation) to prospective offerors to submit proposals based on the terms and conditions set forth in a RFP.

SERVICES. The performance of identifiable tasks rather than the delivery of an end item of supply. Services also include tasks that are delivered under a contract where the primary purpose of the contract is to provide supplies.

SOLE SOURCE CONTRACT. A contract awarded as a result of a solicitation that was provided to only one offeror or as a result of an unsolicited proposal.

SOLICITATION. A formal invitation by the Government to prospective offerors to submit offers to satisfy a Government need. It describes the requirements in sufficient detail to allow prospective offerors to determine their ability to meet that need and to submit a meaningful offer. It also includes the terms, conditions, and instructions under which offers may be submitted and resultant contracts will be awarded.

SOURCE EVALUATION BOARD (SEB) PROCEDURES. Formal procedures established for the solicitation, evaluation and negotiation for major negotiated procurements. SEB procedures are conducted in accordance with the NASA Source Evaluation Board Handbook set forth in NFS 18-70.

STATEMENT OF WORK (SOW). A tasking document that specifies effort to be performed by a contractor.

SURVEILLANCE: The continual monitoring and verification of status of an entity and analysis of records to ensure specified requirements are being met. Surveillance activities may be delegated to other disinterested parties on behalf of the customer. It may be 100%, statistically-based sampling, qualitative sampling, or the result of discussion with individuals who have first hand knowledge. It also may include the monitoring of contractor supplied metrics, available contractor data, sampling, or surveys.

TECHNICAL EVALUATION. The measurement of a technical proposal against the technical requirements and the rating factors stated in the solicitation. Cost may be considered as an indicator of understanding of technical requirements.

TECHNICAL STANDARD. A common and repeated use of rules, conditions, guidelines or characteristics for products or related processes and production methods. It includes the definition of terms, classification of components, delineation of procedures, specification of dimensions, materials, performance, designs, or operations. It includes measurement of quality and quantity as well as a description of fit and measurements.

UNSOLICITED PROPOSAL. A unique and innovative proposal that is made to the Government by a prospective contractor without prior formal or informal solicitation from a procuring activity.

VOLUNTARY CONSENSUS STANDARDS. Standards developed or used by voluntary consensus standards bodies, both domestic and international, which are made available in a manner which includes provisions requiring that owners of relevant intellectual property have agreed to make that intellectual property available on a non-discriminatory, royalty-free or reasonable royalty basis to all interested parties.

WORK BREAKDOWN STRUCTURE (WBS). A product-oriented, hierarchical division tree of deliverable items and associated services that relates the elements of work to each other and to the end item.

APPENDIX C
ACRONYM LIST

CO	Contracting Officer
COTR	Contracting Officer's Technical Representative
CWBS	Contract Work Breakdown Structure
DoD	Department of Defense
FAR	Federal Acquisition Regulation
FMM	Financial Management Manual
JOFOC	Justification for Other than Full and Open Competition
NASA	National Aeronautics and Space Administration
NFS	NASA FAR Supplement
NHB	NASA Handbook
NPD	NASA Policy Directive
OFPP	Office of Federal Procurement Policy (a branch of OMB)
OMB	Office of Management and Budget
PBC	Performance-Based Contracting
PR	Purchase or Procurement Request
PWBS	Project Work Breakdown Structure
PWS	Performance Work Statement
QR	Quality Representative
RFP	Requests for Proposals
R&D	Research and Development
SOW	Statement of Work
SPI	Single Process Initiative
VE	Value Engineering
WBS	Work Breakdown Schedule

APPENDIX D
PBC PERFORMANCE STANDARDS AND INCENTIVES

CHAPTER 1
PERFORMANCE STANDARDS

101 INTRODUCTION

a. A PBC must contain performance standards — the criteria for determining whether the work requirements are met. A performance standard must be assigned to essential or critical (but not incidental) tasks or products.

b. A baseline is established from which continuous improvement will be sought over the life of the contract, and is composed of three elements:

(1) *Outcome or Output.* The desired result, or necessary effort, being acquired.

(2) *Performance Standard.* The measurement threshold or limit that establishes that point at which successful performance has been accomplished.

(3) *Surveillance.* The monitoring and verification of performance.

102 OUTCOME OR OUTPUT

a. An **outcome** measure is an assessment of the results of a program activity compared to its intended purpose. An outcome-based contract is often ideal for non-routine efforts.

b. An **output** measure is the tabulation, calculation, or recording of activity or effort and can be expressed in a quantitative or qualitative manner. For routine efforts an output contract may be more desirable.

c. Describe the outcome/output but do not give specific procedures or instructions on how to produce them unless absolutely necessary. When NASA specifies a procedure (how to do it), NASA assumes responsibility for ensuring that the design or procedure will end with the desired result. However, if NASA specifies the outcome/output performance and its quality standard, the contractor must then use its best judgment in determining how to achieve that level of performance. A key tenet of PBC is that the contractor will be assigned the responsibility to meet the Government's requirements together with the flexibility to decide how it will meet those needs. NASA then evaluates the contractor's performance against the standard. In many cases, the final arrangement can be a hybrid contract with a limited number of critical specifications being imposed on the contractor.

103 PERFORMANCE STANDARDS

a. Explicit, measurable performance standards must be included in the PWS or specification for a contract to be considered performance based. Under PBC, NASA expresses its willingness to accept the contractor solution as long as it meets performance requirements.

b. A Performance Standard states requirements in terms of required results, with criteria for verifying compliance but without stating the methods for achieving required results. It defines the requirements for the item and/or services, the environment in which it must operate, and interface and interchangeability characteristics. Performance standards must be:

(1) Meaningful. An objective measurement is preferred, however, at times a subjective determination could be meaningful and acceptable.

(2) Understandable, and clearly communicated to the contractor.

(3) Realistically achievable.

(4) True indicators of outcome or output.

(5) Reflective of actual NASA needs.

c. Typical standards are rates (e.g., cost per pound to orbit), limits (e.g., not more than and not less than), and criteria (e.g., fit and other forms of external interface standards, power, weight, volume, life, accuracy).

d. Identification of systemic performance standards is recommended. The more critical the result is to objective accomplishment, the more appropriate it is to develop a performance standard to evaluate that result. The level of detail must correspond to that expectation. Performance standards need not be identified explicitly if the requirement is so clearly stated that a standard for performance has been unmistakably established in the PWS or specification.

e. Always consider the cost. Applying performance standards appropriately should actually reduce overall costs as performance deficiencies are identified and improvements to these processes are made. Nevertheless, performance standards must be very selective and at the appropriate level. Do not spend money for performance standards you do not really need. Ask the questions:

(1) Is this level of detail necessary?

(2) What performance can be measured by querying the contractor's data system?

(3) What is the risk of not having this level of performance?

f. "Best value" is a combination of competitive pricing and improved performance. Offerors should be encouraged to propose improvements above the minimum requirements and to propose lower cost alternatives that meet the performance criteria.

g. Standards should be published and well recognized. OMB Circular A-119 requires preference for national, international, or industry-wide standards. Standards developed by NASA with industry input may be used if technically suitable voluntary consensus standards are not available. This may be done through public meetings, public comment, or a Solicitation for Information per FAR 15.405.

103.1 Progress/Performance Measurement

a. Results can be measured by both progress and performance. Both are critical to effective management.

(1) **Progress** measurement identifies what you did, not necessarily how well you did it. The most typical example is milestone completion. For managing progress, either maintain or achieve a specific and definable performance level and/or requirement.

(2) **Performance** measurement identifies achievement of outcome or output in terms of quality, quantity, timeliness, and cost productivity.

b. Performance is measured by comparing the performance level against the range identified in the performance standards.. The standards must require performance reflecting NASA's minimum (or minimum and maximum) needs, failing which the objective of the contract will not be met. Standards cannot be level-of-effort or procedures. This approach has an inherent advantage because it allows far greater contractor flexibility in how to satisfy these performance requirements.

c. The **Performance Goal** is a target level of performance expressed as a tangible, measurable objective, against which actual achievement can be compared. A performance goal may be expressed as an absolute or as a range of acceptable performance (usually expressed in percentages); for example:

For launches, the goal shall be 100%.

97% (3% of all tests completed on time, with a Minimum Acceptable Performance of 94% of the tests completed on time.

d. Such a measurement process could include multiple data points over time, be as quantitatively measurable as possible, and provide early identification of potential problems with the process, product, or service allowing management intervention. It often facilitates continuous improvement.

103.2 Performance Requirements Summary (PRS)

If there are a number of tasks and deliverables, summarize them in a PRS. List the contract and work requirements considered to be most critical to satisfactory contract performance, such as tasks, deliverables, and quality levels. Provide the minimum performance standard for each.

PRS NON-ROUTINE REQUIREMENT AEROSPACE SYSTEMS

TASKS	MINIMUM PERFORMANCE STANDARD	GOAL
1. Optimize the computational time and memory usage efficiency of developed deterministic or non-deterministic dynamics and control analysis.		
2. Develop simulation and computer programs that implement improvements for validation.	10% Improvement	25% Improvement
3. Perform simulations with one defined test case to demonstrate the accuracy and efficiency of the optimized algorithms.		

104 PROJECT SURVEILLANCE PLAN (PSP)

a. NASA shall, to the maximum extent practicable, assign contractors full responsibility for quality performance and shall avoid cumbersome and intrusive process-oriented inspection and oversight programs to assess that performance (OFPP Policy Letter 91-2). This must be done for each major PWS task with formal, measurable performance standards. Government established performance quality levels must be achieved, and the contractor rewarded only for services that meet or exceed those levels.

b. The contractor's quality plan shall be part of the contract. It shall describe how the contractor will assure quality. NASA's surveillance plan shall not be made part of the contract, but a copy will be provided to the contractor.

It shall balance oversight and insight methods of surveillance and may be modified as necessary.

c. Before NASA can process a contractor's invoice for payment, NASA has the responsibility of determining whether or not the contractor has performed to the standards of the contract. PSPs provide a systematic approach to evaluate the contractor's performance. PSPs set forth Government responsibilities in determining whether contractor performance is acceptable.

104.1 Insight Method

a. **Insight** refers to the process of gathering a minimum set of product or process data that provides adequate visibility into the integrity of the product or process. The data may be acquired from contractor records, usually in a non-intrusive parallel method.

b. **Oversight** is an intrusive process of gathering contractor product or process data through on-site in-series involvement in the process (e.g., we don't do the welding, rather surveillance of the process). Oversight entails very detailed monitoring of the process itself. Oversight is an in-line involvement in an activity, principally through inspection with review and approval authority implicit to the degree necessary to assure that a process or product's key characteristics are stable and in control.

c. One of the initiatives of OFPP letter 91-2 is that the Government refrain from obtrusive in-process surveillance. PBC is based on the premise that the contractor has the ability to execute the job without considerable Government oversight. Because of this premise, NASA surveillance programs would not require oversight to be as intense or as frequent once the product quality is considered to be acceptable. In most cases, NASA will conduct insight (rather than oversight) surveillance to assure the Agency has received what it requested at the time it was requested. A project-specific surveillance plan defines how NASA will accomplish "insight."

d. The PSP is created by NASA initially as a draft document in concert with the project PWS/RFP. It will describe very explicitly the project manager's overall strategy to execute a surveillance program. It reduces project risk by focusing insight activities on contract performance areas with the greatest potential to disrupt or prevent successful completion of the program. The plan shall then be revised to reflect contractor response to the RFP and the final negotiated agreement. As the program evolves, it continues to be a dynamic, living, and changeable document. At the beginning of work, a fully formed NASA PSP must be in place that identifies strategy, activities, metrics, and control limits.

e. Contractors are responsible for providing quality control, and these plans insure that a proper level of performance is maintained. It is important to select a contractor with a proven record of quality performance.

104.2 Hybrid Approach

a. A hybrid surveillance approach may be instituted at a contractor's facility when a high level of confidence does not exist relative to the contractor's ability to identify, manage, and control programmatic risks. This may occur when new technology is acquired or unproven processes are employed by a contractor. In this situation, intense oversight is conducted until sufficient data exist that demonstrate the contractor has all critical processes under control. The oversight activities usually impose mandatory Government inspection points in-series with the contractor's manufacturing processes. Only after the contractor's demonstration of risk mitigation capabilities will NASA consider transitioning to insight activities that rely predominantly on internal contractor data. Insight activities generally are conducted in parallel to contractor processes and do not impose control functions over the processes. The transition period between oversight to insight activities is hybrid and accomplished incrementally, depending on contractor performance.

b. The PSP is further described in NHB 7120.5, *Management of Major System Programs and Projects*.

CHAPTER 2
PBC PERFORMANCE INCENTIVES

201 GOALS AND OBJECTIVES

> A contractor who only meets the minimum performance standards merits only a minimum fee.

a. Performance-based contracting must assure that NASA obtains the products, services, and cost savings that it wants by providing tangible incentives that motivate the contractor to achieve levels of performance that exceed the minimum and have benefit to the Government. As NASA moves into this environment, the basic business premise requires that the contract results in a mutual value for both partners. Many contractors will not necessarily move into this higher risk performance-based business realm unless they can anticipate a reward. Incentives must make it worthwhile to the contractor to find ways to improve performance.

b. Incentives are tools to improve the probability of better performance when the tasks are complex, critical, or have a history of performance or cost-overrun problems. A contract may include technical performance incentives when performance beyond the minimum is desirable, potentially achievable, and withstands the test of cost-benefit analysis.

c. The earning of incentives shall be based on a meaningful rating of the contractor's performance; normally, an objective measurement is preferred, however, some circumstances would allow for a subjective assessment. Where meaningful objectively measurable outcome criteria exist, combine cost incentives (CPIF and FPIF) and performance incentive provisions in preference to cost-plus-award-fee (CPAF).

d. For service-type contracts, reduction schedules may be used where appropriate.

e. A performance incentive shall be included in all cost-reimbursable contracts where the primary deliverable is hardware and where total estimated cost and fee is greater than $25 million unless it is determined that the nature of the acquisition (e.g., commercial off-the-shelf computers) would not effectively lend itself to performance incentives. NFS Part 1816.402. The criteria listed in ¤202b must be used to establish the right incentives.

202 INCENTIVE CRITERIA

a. Incentive criteria must be focused on program/project objectives. Contractor input shall be obtained through the draft RFP process.

b. The contractor's performance in meeting major program objectives will be measured utilizing explicit, predefined criteria, such as the following:

(1) Incentives must be relevant to performance. Follow-up must be accomplished to ensure that desired results are achieved; i.e., establish measures to determine the extent to which performance is actually achieved.

(2) The criteria for incentives must center on the areas of value to NASA and those of high risk **that are within the control of the contractor**. Do not provide the contractor an incentive for work that is the responsibility of NASA personnel.

(3) Reasonable and attainable targets must be established, which are clearly communicated to the contractor.

(4) The Government must benefit significantly from performance above the minimum.

(5) The cost of the incentives must be less than or equal to the added value of the enhanced performance.

(6) They must be consistent with contract requirements and other program documents.

(7) They must be measurable and the measurement systems must be reliable.

(8) The contractor should not earn a big incentive for a small, easily reached achievement.

c. NFS Subpart 1816.402-270(b) describes the use of NASA technical performance incentives, as follows:

"When a performance incentive is used, it shall be structured to be both positive and negative based on hardware performance after delivery and acceptance. In doing so, the contract shall establish a standard level of performance based on the salient mission performance requirement. This standard performance level is normally the contract's minimum performance requirement. No incentive amount is earned at the standard performance level. Discrete units of measurement based on the same performance parameter shall be identified for performance both above and below the standard. Specific incentive amounts shall be associated with each performance level from maximum beneficial performance (maximum positive incentive) to minimal beneficial performance or total failure (maximum negative incentive). The relationship between any given incentive, both positive and negative, and its associated unit of measurement must reflect the value to the Government of that level of hardware performance. Contractors are not to be rewarded for above-standard performance levels that are of no benefit to the Government."

/END/

Owner: Ken Sateriale Last updated on 12/29/1997

Appendix III

Advertisement, Contract, and Specification for a Heavier-than-Air Flying Machine

Signal Corps Specification, No. 486

ADVERTISEMENT AND SPECIFICATION FOR A HEAVIER-THAN-AIR FLYING MACHINE

To the Public:

Sealed proposals, in duplicate, will be received at this office until 18 o'clock on February 1, 1908, on behalf of the Board of Ordnance and Fortification for furnishing the Signal Corps with a heavier-than-air flying machine. All proposals received will be turned over to the Board of Ordnance and Fortification at its first meeting after February 1 for its official action.

Persons wishing to submit proposals under this specification can obtain the necessary forms and envelopes by application to the Chief Signal Officer, United States Army. War Department, Washington, D.C. The United States reserves the right to reject any and all proposals.

Unless the bidders are also the manufacturers of the flying machine they must state the name and place of the maker.

Preliminary. – This specification covers the covers the construction of a flying machine supported entirely by the dynamic reaction of the atmosphere and having no gas bag.

Acceptance. – The flying machine will be accepted only after a successful trial flight, during which it will comply with all requirements of this specification. No payments on account will be made until after the trial flight and acceptance.

Inspection. – The Government reserves the right to inspect any and all processes of manufacture.

GENERAL REQUIREMENTS

The general dimensions of the flying machine will be determined by the manufacturer, subject to the following conditions:

1. Bidders must submit with their proposals the following:

    a. Drawings to scale showing the general dimensions and shape of the flying machine which they propose to build under this specification.
    b. Statement of the speed for which it is designed.
    c. Statement of the total surface area of the supporting planes.
    d. Statement of the total weight.
    e. Description of the engine which will be used for motive power.
    f. The material of which the frame, planes, and propellers will be constructed. Plans received will not be shown to other bidders.

2. It is desirable that the flying machine should be designed so that it may be quickly and easily assembled and taken apart and packed for transportation in Army wagons. It should be capable of being assembled and put in operating condition in about one hour.

3. The flying machine must be designed to carry two persons having a combined weight of about 350 pounds, also sufficient fuel for a flight of 125 miles.

4. The flying machine should be designed to have a speed of at least forty miles per hour in still air, but bidders must submit quotations in their proposals for cost depending upon the speed attained during the trial flight, according to the following scale:

    40 miles per hour, 100 percent.
    39 miles per hour, 90 percent.
    38 miles per hour, 80 percent.
    37 miles per hour, 70 percent.
    36 miles per hour, 60 percent.
    Less than 36 miles per hour rejected.
    41 miles per hour, 110 percent.
    42 miles per hour, 120 percent.
    43 miles per hour, 130 percent.
    44 miles per hour, 140 percent.

5. The speed accomplished during the trial flight will be determined by taking an average of the time over a measured course of more than five miles, against and with the wind. The time will be taken by a flying state, passing the starting point at full speed at both ends of the course. This test subject to such additional details as the Chief Signal Officer of the Army may prescribe at the time.

6. Before Acceptance a trial endurance flight will be required of at least one hour during which time the flying machine must remain continuously in the air without landing. It shall return to the starting point and land without any damage that would prevent it immediately starting upon another flight. During this trial flight of one hour it must be steered in all directions without difficulty and at all times under perfect control and equilibrium.

7. Three trials will be allowed for speed as provided for in paragraphs 4 and 6, three trials for endurance as provided for in paragraph 8, and both tests must be completed within a period of thirty days from a date of delivery. The expense of the tests to be borne by the manufacturer. The place of delivery to the Government and trial flights will be at Fort Myer, Virginia.

8. It should be so designed as to ascend in any country which may be encountered in field services. The starting device must be simple and transportable. It should also land in a field without requiring a specially prepared spot and without damaging its structure.

9. It should be provided with some device to permit a safe descent in case of an accident to the propelling machinery.

10. It should be sufficiently simple in its construction and operation to permit an intelligent man to become proficient in its use within a reasonable length of time.

11. Bidders must furnish evidence that the Government of the United States has the lawful right to use all patented devices or appurtenances which may be a part of the flying machine, and that the manufacturers of the flying machine are authorized to convey the same to the Government. This refers to the unrestricted right to use the flying machine sold to the Government, but does not contemplate the exclusive purchase of patent rights for duplicating the flying machine.

12. Bidders will be required to furnish with their proposal a certified check amounting to ten percent of the price stated for the 40-mile speed. Upon making the award for this flying machine those certified checks will be returned to the bidders, and the successful bidder will be required to furnish a bond, according to Army Regulations, of the amount equal to the price stated for the 40-mile speed.

13. The price quoted in proposals must be understood to include the instruction of two men in the handling and operation of this flying machine. No extra charge for this service will be allowed.

14. Bidders must state the time which will be required for delivery after receipt of order.

JAMES ALLEN,
Brigadier General, Chief Signal Officer of the Army

Signal Officer,

Washington, D.C., December 20, 1907

Contract and Specification for a Heavier-than-Air Flying Machine Wright Brothers, February 28, 1908

Form 10
Signal Corps, United States Army

The Articles of Agreement entered into this tenth day of February, nineteen hundred and eight, between Chas. B. Wallace, Captain, Signal Corps, United States Army, of the first part, and Wilbur and Orville Wright, trading as Wright Brothers, of 1127 West Third Street, Dayton, in the county of Montgomery, State of Ohio of the second part, Witnesseth that in conformity with copy of the advertisement, specifications, and proposal hereunto attached, and which, in so far as they relate to this contact, form a part of it, the said Chas. B. Wallace, Captain, Signal Corps, United States Army, for and in behalf of the United States of America, and the said Wright Brothers (hereinafter designated as the contractor) do covenant and agree, to and with each other, as follows, vis:

Article I. That the said contractor shall manufacture for and deliver to the United States of America,

One (1) heavier-than-air flying machine, in accordance with Signal Corps Specification No. 486, dated December 23, 1907.

Article II. That the deliveries of the supplies and materials herein contracted for shall be made in the manner, numbers, or quantities, and for each number or quantity, on or before the date specified therefore, as follows, vis:

The complete delivery shall be made on or before Auguest 28, 1908.

Article III. All supplies and materials furnished and work done under this contract shall, before being accepted, be subject to a rigid inspection by an inspector appointed on the part of the Government, and such as do not conform to the specifications set forth in this contract shall be rejected. The decision of the Chief Signal Officer, United States Army, as to quality and quantity shall be final.

Article IV. That for and in consideration of the faithful performance of the stipulations of this contract, the contractor shall be paid at the office of the Chief Signal Officer of the Army, at Washington, D.C., for all supplies and materials delivered in conformity with the requirements of this contract, on or before the dates above specified (Article II, supra) and accepted, the following prices, vis:

> One (1) heavier-than-air flying machine at a total cost of twenty-five thousand (25,000) dollars,

to be paid as soon as practicable after the acceptance of the same, in funds furnished by the United States for the purpose, reserving ____ percent from each payment until final settlement, on completion of the contract or otherwise.

Article V. It is further agreed that for all supplies and materials which shall not be delivered in conformity with the requirements of this contract on or before the dates prescribed therefore in Article II, above, but which shall be subsequently delivered and accepted, the prices shall be as follows:

Article VI. That in case of the failure of the said contactor to perform the stipulations of this contract within the time and in the manner specified above, Articles I to III, inclusive, the said party of the first part may, instead of waiting further for deliveries under the provisions of the preceding article, supply the deficiency by purchase in open market or otherwise, at such place as may be selected (the articles so procured to be the kind herein specified, as near as practicable); and the said contractor shall be charged with the increased cost of the supplies and materials so purchased over what they would have cost if delivered by the contractor on the date they were received under such open-market purchase.

Article VII. It is further agreed by and between the parties hereto that until final inspection and acceptance of, and payment for, all of the supplies and materials and work herein provided for, no prior inspection, payment, or act is to be construed as a waiver of the right of the party of the first part to reject any defective articles or supplies or to require the fulfillment of any of the terms of the contract.

Article VIII. The contractor further agrees to hold and save the United States harmless from and against all and every demand, or demands, of any nature or kind for, or on account of, the use of any patented invention, article, or process included in the materials hereby agreed to be furnished and work to be done under this contract.

Article IX. Neither this contract nor any interest herein shall be transferred to any other party or parties, and in the case of such transfer the United States may refuse to carry out this contract by said contractor are reserved to the United States.

Article X. No Member of or Delegate to Congress, nor any person belonging to, or employed in, the military service of the United States, is or shall be admitted to any share or part of this contract, or to any benefit which may arise therefrom.*

Article XI. That it is expressly agreed and understood that this contract shall be noneffective until an appropriation adequate to its fulfillment is made by Congress and is available.

Article XII. That this contract shall be subject to approval of the Chief Signal Officer, United States Army.

IN WITNESS WHEREOF the parties aforesaid have hereunto placed their hands the date first hereinbefore written.

WITNESSES:

______________________________ as to

____
Captain, Signal Corps, U.S. Army

______________________________ as to

______________________________ as to

____

______________________________ as to

APPROVED: February 28, 1909

Brigadier General,
Chief Signal Officer of the Army

* Here add to any contract made with an incorporated company for its general benefit the following words, vis: "But this stipulation, so far as it relates to Members or Delegates to Congress, is not to be construed to extend to this contract." Section 8730, Revised Edition.

Appendix IV

Excerpt from the Competition in Contracting Act

* Competition in Contracting Act, U.S. Public Law 98-369, July 18, 1984. Implemented in 10 U.S.C. 2305, "Contracts: Planning, Solicitation, Evaluation, and Award Procedures." Online at http://www4.law.cornell.edu/uscode/10/2305 .html (accessed January 2008).

Sec. 2305. (a)(1)(A) In preparing for the procurement of property or services, the head of an agency shall –

(i) specify the agency's needs and solicit bids or proposals in a manner designed to achieve full and open competition for the procurement;

(ii) use advance procurement planning and market research; and

(iii) develop specifications in such manner as is necessary to obtain full and open competition with due regard to the nature of the property or services to be acquired.

(B) Each solicitation under this chapter shall include specifications which –

(i) are consistent with the provisions of this chapter, permit full and open competition; and

(ii) include restrictive provision or conditions only to the extent necessary to satisfy the needs of the agency or as authorized by law.

(C) For the purposes of subparagraphs (A) and (B), the type of specification included in a solicitation shall depend on the nature of the needs of the agency and the market available to satisfy such needs. Subject to such needs, specifications may be stated in terms of –

(i) function, so that a variety of products or services may qualify;

(ii) performance, including specifications of the range of acceptable characteristics or of the minimum acceptable standards; or

(iii) design requirements.

(2) In addition to the specifications described in paragraph (1), a solicitation for sealed bids or competitive proposals (other than for small purchases) shall at a minimum include –

(A) a statement of –

(i) all significant factors (and significant subfactors) which the head of the agency reasonably expects to consider in evaluating sealed bids (including price) or competitive proposals (including cost or price, cost- or price-related factors, and noncost- or nonprice-related factors); and

(ii) the relative importance assigned to each of those factors (or subfactors); and

(B)(i) in the case of sealed bids –

(I) a statement that sealed bids will be evaluated without discussions with the bidders; and

(II) the time and place for the opening of the sealed bids; or

(ii) in the case of competitive proposals –

(I) a statement that the proposals are intended to be evaluated with, and award made after, discussions with the offerors, or a statement that the proposals are intended to be evaluated, and award made, without discussions with the offerors (other than discussions conducted for the purpose of minor clarification), unless discussions are determined to be necessary; and

(II) the time and place for submissions of proposals.

(3) In prescribing evaluation factors to be included in each solicitation for competitive proposals, the head of an agency shall clearly establish the relative importance assigned to the evaluation factors and subfactors, including the quality of the product or services to be provided (including technical capability, management capability, and prior experience of the offeror).